Kazakhstan: Snow Leopard at the Crossroads

This volume examines the experience of Kazakhstan's transition over the past 30 years, explaining the political and economic performance of the country since the collapse of the USSR, through the country's institutions, policy choices, and external environment.

In an exploration of more than 1,000 years of institutional development, the chapters analyse and assess the development of political arrangements and governance, and economic institutions, from pre-Russian colonization through to the Soviet experiment, and then take a magnifying glass to developments in a post-Soviet, independent Kazakhstan. Using a broad range of sources and data across disciplines, this book is the first to explicitly survey Kazakhstan's transition as a function of its history, its people, and its institutions. Breaking new ground in institutional economics, it provides readers with a comprehensive examination of the history and development of Kazakhstan, and points to where it may be heading in the 21st century.

The subject matter is accessible to a broad academic audience: to scholars in political science, economics, and the history of Central Asia and Russia, as well as to those with an interest in general transition economics.

Christopher A. Hartwell is Professor of International Business Policy, ZHAW School of Management and Law, and Professor of International Management, Kozminski University.

Europa Emerging Economies

The Europa Emerging Economies series from Routledge, edited by Robert E. Looney, examines a wide range of contemporary economic, political, developmental and social issues as they affect emerging economies throughout the world. Complementing the *Europa Regional Surveys of the World* series and the *Handbook of Emerging Economies*, which was also edited by Professor Looney, the volumes in the *Europa Emerging Economies* series will be a valuable resource for academics, students, researchers, policy-makers, professionals, and anyone with an interest in issues regarding emerging economies in the wider context of current world affairs.

There will be individual volumes in the series which provide in-depth country studies, and others which examine issues and concepts; all are written or edited by specialists in their field. Volumes in the series are not constrained by any particular template, but may explore economic, political, governance, international relations, defence, or other issues in order to increase the understanding of emerging economies and their importance to the world economy.

Robert E. Looney is a Distinguished Professor at the Naval Postgraduate School, Monterey, California, who specializes in issues relating to economic development in the Middle East, East Asia, South Asia and Latin America. He has published over 20 books and 250 journal articles, and has worked widely as a consultant to national governments and international agencies.

Pakistan at Seventy
A handbook on developments in economics, politics and society
Edited by Shahid Javed Burki with Iftekhar Ahmed Chowdhury and Asad Ejaz Butt

Mauritius: A Successful Small Island Developing State
Edited by Boopen Seetanah, Raja Vinesh Sannasee and Robin Nunkoo

Development and Stabilization in Small Open Economies
Theories and Evidence from Caribbean Experience
DeLisle Worrell

Kazakhstan: Snow Leopard at the Crossroads
Christopher A. Hartwell

For further information, see https://www.routledge.com/Europa-Perspectives-Emerging-Economies/book-series/EPEE.

Kazakhstan: Snow Leopard at the Crossroads

Christopher A. Hartwell

Routledge
Taylor & Francis Group
LONDON AND NEW YORK

Designed cover image: Creative Commons image

First published 2023
by Routledge
4 Park Square, Milton Park, Abingdon, Oxon OX14 4RN

and by Routledge
605 Third Avenue, New York, NY 10158

Routledge is an imprint of the Taylor & Francis Group, an informa business

British Library Cataloguing in Publication Data
A catalogue record for this book is available from the British Library

ISBN: 978-1-032-08009-3 (hbk)
ISBN: 978-1-032-08013-0 (pbk)
ISBN: 978-1-003-21250-8 (ebk)

DOI: 10.4324/9781003212508

Typeset in Times New Roman
by Taylor & Francis Books

This book is dedicated to those who stand in the defence of liberty and economic freedom.

Contents

Illustrations

Figures

Tables

Foreword

This book, my third sole-authored endeavour, came about specifically from a request from the editor of this series, Robert E. Looney, but in reality it had been brewing for some time before that (although it took Robert and Cathy Hartley at Routledge to extract the proto-book in a timely manner!). I started my career working at the Harvard Institute for International Development (HIID) after receiving my master's in public policy at Harvard's Kennedy School in the mid-1990s, when transition was still a hot topic and when we could clearly see divergence in outcomes due to different approaches and policies. While living in Germany and working as an intern for the Ministry for Economics in 1996 in between the first and second years of my master's, I had my first exposure to Central and Eastern Europe and their struggles with post-communism, including a memorable trip to Russia (where I was almost arrested by a drunk police office brandishing an AK-47 for, get this, street singing). This whetted my appetite and made me want to go further afield, and during my time at HIID I was exposed to many different projects (mainly in Ukraine) and they served to fuel my interest in transition more broadly.

It wasn't until around 2000, however, when I moved to Washington, DC, that Kazakhstan and the rest of Central Asia truly began to appear on my radar. While working for a private equity firm dedicated to emerging markets, and alongside the former Finance Minister of Pakistan, I became fascinated by this region which was at the crossroads of China and Russia: who actually were "the Stans" and why had transition seemingly passed them by? Why was some development evident despite autocracy, and why had others lapsed into civil war? What was the Russian influence and how long would it last? As our firm was looking to move into more substantive technical consulting, I hit upon an idea that we would bid for a multifaceted USAID project in Kazakhstan, making use of our own expertise in the region writ large but also bringing our private sector acumen. With that, I booked a flight to Almaty (which I mistakenly called Alma-Ata, as it was once known) and, despite us losing the USAID bid egregiously (none of us in the office had ever written one before), I spent two weeks in Kazakhstan to understand its context and to see where the business opportunities might be.

Without boring you with the tales of the trip, I was hooked. Kazakhstan was indeed the Wild West: everything seemed possible; transition was indeed underway after the Russian crisis of 1998; and Almaty was a gem of a city. With the help of new friends, I gradually absorbed more about the country, its past, and its uncertain future. Over the coming years, I returned to Kazakhstan many times: first in the year after the 11 September attacks, when Central Asia suddenly became crucial to US foreign policy and the Taliban was toppled in Afghanistan (sadly no longer the case), then in later years as an adviser on Eurasian integration, as a researcher working on a project for the National Bank of Kazakhstan, as a participant and panel member at the Astana Economic Forum, as a keynote speaker at a workshop organized by KIMEP University, and as a consultant for the Soros Foundation in the country. Throughout it all, I continued to be entranced by the country and saw it as a place which was informed by the recent past – above all its Soviet subjugation – but which also was attempting to unearth its more distant history to create a narrative for the present. It had promise, it had potential, it had an exotic quality to those of us from far away, and it had a proud and interesting people.

This book digs deeper into that history to show that not all the institutional influence of centuries past is contrived or dressed up for marketing purposes. In taking this approach, this book builds on my previous manuscripts but also my journal articles and ongoing research on institutions, their persistent effects, and how institutional change comes about. But above all, it remains a uniquely Kazakh story, further underscoring the importance of context, path dependence, and culture on institutional evolution.

All books are difficult to write, but this one was more difficult than my previous ones. During the writing of this book, the COVID-19 pandemic raged, I underwent an international move with my family, took up a new position in a new country, and adjusted to life as the father of a child in school rather than a mobility-limited toddler. Given these challenges, many, many people must be thanked for their help during the years in Kazakhstan and elsewhere for directly and indirectly making this book a reality. In the first instance, Julie Kussidi, whom I serendipitously met in a bar for expats in Almaty, has been a source of help and friendship for over two decades, and I give thanks to her for being my Sherpa on Kazakhstan! Similarly, Balzhan Suzhikova, formerly of the excellent KIMEP faculty and now blissfully in retirement, has also been steadfast and true over two decades – one of my fondest memories is bringing her son Vince Carter Nike shoes in 2002, and the realization that her son must be in his thirties now is quite depressing! So many other people from Kazakhstan have helped me over the years to navigate the country and its economy, including Christopher Ansley, Anton Artemyev, Gaukhar Akylbekova, Jonathan Cahn (who was a fantastic guide during my first trip), Marek Dąbrowski, Erlan Dosymbekov, Boris Evseev (a good friend), Roger Holland, Aset Irgaliyev, Kasymkhan Kapparov, Kairat Kelimbetov, Laurent Lavigne, Pauline Mercado, Natalya Kozlenkova, Gerald

Pech, Krzysztof Rybinski, Dina Sharipova, Fiorenzo Sperotto, Venkat Subramanian, Jan Tomczyk, and William T. Wilson (sadly missed). Special thanks go to Nargis Kassenova, with whom I worked on a project for the Soros Foundation in Kazakhstan and with whom I have kept in touch, and who brought me back to Harvard for the first time in 25 years as a visiting scholar at the Davis Center for Eurasian Studies – a trip which gave me some blessed quiet to work on this book and was directly responsible for the completion of Chapter 4. Sincere thanks are also due to Donna Cadarelli and the Swissnex Mobility Scheme, which allowed me to travel from Zurich to Cambridge for this quality writing time, reintroducing me to the place where I got my master's (I believe I have now hit the quota for the number of times that one is supposed to mention Harvard).

Apologies to anyone who I have overlooked, as it has been a long time since that first trip and the many that followed, but I assure you that your help and guidance were warmly appreciated.

Additionally, I have already mentioned the efforts of Robert Looney at the Naval Postgraduate School in Monterey, California, and Cathy Hartley at Routledge, both of whom have been instrumental in bringing together my thoughts and analyses on Kazakhstan into a coherent and usable academic form. Any errors remain my own, although if the mere existence of this book offends you then, yes, Robert and Cathy do share some of the blame.

Special thanks must go to all the wrong-headed people on the internet (thanks, Twitter!) who somehow know it all and enjoin others to "read a book." Well, if you are reading these words, you have obviously listened to them and thus I am in their debt for driving you in my direction. In a similar spirit of gratitude, I would like to thank all the people whom I have encountered in my life who taught me how to be an effective manager and researcher, simply by showing me all the wrong ways to do it – thus ensuring that I would know what to avoid. EB, AR, and SH, you are thanked for providing such clear signposts.

As with my previous books, the music I listened to while writing greatly influenced my mood and my productivity. Les Claypool gets another mention here (even though I never heard back from him after sending him my last book), mainly for his stellar work in reinterpreting Pink Floyd and, of course, for creating his own genre of weirdness. Daisy Martey also gets high praise, as her voice could soothe even the most savage of beasts. I feel she is severely underrated in all her incarnations (mainly with Noonday Underground but also her one album with Morcheeba), and she created a wonderful background for my writing. Thelonious Monk, Charlie Parker and Charles Mingus also assisted in pushing through Chapters 5 and 6. And, since I am a metalhead at heart, a big thank you also goes to the back catalogue (and the new album that was released during the writing this book) of Helloween, German power metal masters extraordinaire. Bruce Dickinson, Steve Harris, Nicko McBrain, Janick Gers, Dave Murray, and Adrian Smith also get a mention for helping me through the parts which might have been "a matter of life and death." Last but not least, from the ska world, Reel Big Fish, the Allstonians, and the Mighty Mighty Bosstones also had a large role to play, just as they did in the mid-1990s. To any other artists I have missed out, an apology and sincere thanks. I'd like to think they know who they are.

Finally, I also must thank the most important person in my life, Kristen Wysocki Hartwell, for saying "I do" in 2007 and then living up to our vows every single day since. And then I need to thank her again for bringing the other most important person in the household, Magnus Hartwell, into our lives in 2015. Without this wonderful family, to paraphrase Nietzsche, life would be an irritation. And this book would not be a reality.

1 Introduction

Nur-Sultan was, at the time of the beginning of the writing of this book, the name of the capital of the landlocked Central Asian country of Kazakhstan. Although its name remains a source of contention as of the completion of this book, what is not in dispute is just how incredibly cold it is in winter. In fact, this description is woefully inadequate in capturing just how cold it actually is. Known at various times during history as Tselinograd ("virgin lands" in Russian) and, most recently (and perhaps again), as Astana (literally "capital city" in Kazakh), the moniker that fits best is "Aqmola," or "white tomb" (also in Kazakh); despite being much further south than better-known Russian villages such as Oymyakon (the coldest permanently inhabited settlement on Earth), Nur-Sultan has a continental climate with an average temperature of –20 degrees Celsius in the winter but often gets much colder. Being located on flat, unhindered land for miles around, it is buffeted by winds which make one's face feel frozen after being outside for just a few minutes. During particularly harsh winters, locals will often advise visitors to "enjoy the weather" when it warms up to a balmy −25 degrees, and −40 degree temperatures are not unheard of, nor are they rare.

Despite its harsh climate, Nur-Sultan, since the mid-2000s, has been transformed into a wannabe Central Asian Dubai on the steppe, flouting the country's oil wealth and becoming the undisputed seat of power in the region. Such a transformation could not have been foreseen even in the aftermath of the decision to relocate the capital of independent Kazakhstan in December 1997; always the poor stepsister to cosmopolitan Almaty (formerly Alma-Ata) in the south which has snowy mountain backdrops and a small-town feel, the city formerly known as Astana was still a sleepy steppe town even by 2001. Indeed, the main road into town was dotted with buildings with new bright pink siding covering Soviet-era concrete, leading to a popular joke that the housing units had the "face of [leader] Nazarbayev and the ass of the *akim* [mayor]." But over the next 20 years, with the assistance of world-renowned architects driven by the impetus to make Astana the centrepiece of Kazakh identity and culture (Köppen 2013), the original village has expanded to encompass a "sheaf of glass and steel skyscrapers" (Laszczkowski 2016:1).

DOI: 10.4324/9781003212508-1

The tale of Nur-Sultan and its emergence from the Kazakh steppe is an apt metaphor for the emergence of the country of Kazakhstan itself in the post-Soviet era, less a "land of contrasts" in the armchair Eurasia-watcher's standard cliché and more a country being pulled in several directions at once by various impulses, some reinforcing but many of which are contradictory. One of the most obvious of these, directly related to Nur-Sultan, was the emphasis on creating a modern urban centre in a country which remains one of the least densely populated in the world. According to the World Bank, its population density in 2018 (the most recent year for which data are available) was a mere seven people per square kilometre, a number which is probably being driven higher simply because of the density of its cultural capital Almaty (approximately 2,300 people per square kilometre in 2018). Despite a sweeping land mass – geographically, Kazakhstan is the ninth largest country in the world, equivalent to all the countries of Western Europe combined – its population of 19.2 million (a mid-2020 estimate from the US Central Intelligence Agency) tends to be located in thin bands scattered across the interior of the country rather than clustered in cities (Figure 1.1). A nomadic people by heritage, it is highly unlikely that one might find a large agglomeration of groups on the windswept steppe; however, disruptions caused by the transition led to an influx of rural Kazakhs into the cities (Yessenova 2005), meaning that Nur-Sultan may be an accurate representation of a new Kazakh identity.

Indeed, the Nur-Sultan project goes beyond merely building a capital city, but also helps to underscore how difficult the broader project of building the *nation* of Kazakhstan has been (Truspekova et al. 2019). Of course, for those who exist outside of academia (and happy are those people), Kazakhstan lives on in popular imagination either as a country of nomads similar to the Mongols or (to the chagrin of the Kazakhs) in popular culture through the ludicrous antics of Sacha Baron Cohen's "Borat." Contrary to these characterizations, however, since it emerged from the ruins of the Soviet Union as an independent country for the first time (notwithstanding the four days in December 1991 when, as the last republic to declare its independence, the Soviet Union consisted solely of Kazakhstan), the country's leadership has persistently sought to forge a common and modern identity for the country (Spehr and Kassenova 2012). For three decades, Kazakh politicians and the people themselves have been assembling some very disparate parts for this identity, including some taken from the distant past (including a focus on language, see Dave 1996 and Fierman 1998), some taken from recent (Soviet) history (Burkhanov and Sharipova 2014), and some hastily assembled from the menu of options offered by Western aid and technical assistance agencies. As mentioned above, the amalgamation of these building blocks has not been easy and has resulted at times in bewildering policies, disunity, and over-reliance on external, top-down change rather than organic, bottom-up evolution.

This is perhaps most visible in the economic performance of the country over the past 30 years, as Kazakhstan has made impressive economic gains while at the same time suffering massive missteps. In common with other post-Soviet countries, Kazakhstan underwent a traumatic economic contraction at the beginning of its transition, one in line with the Russian Federation in scope and duration but more severe than its (admittedly less transitioned) neighbour, Uzbekistan (Figure 1.2). And like other former Soviet Union countries, especially those in Central Asia, Kazakhstan was a laggard in implementing reforms, only increasing the pace of its liberalization in 1994, meaning that by 1996 the private sector accounted for a mere 40 per cent of gross domestic product (GDP) (Auty 1999). Despite this slow start out of the gate, Kazakhstan recorded impressive growth in the early 2000s in the wake of the Russian financial crisis as well as in the wake of the global financial crisis post-2009, more than tripling its GDP per capita by 2019 from its nadir in 1995. At the same time, Kazakhstan has developed its natural resources intensely, a reality which has been both a blessing and a curse for the economy but which cannot be ignored in driving the evolution of Kazakhstan's economic structure (Kalyuzhnova and Patterson 2016). Much like its iterative process of forging an identity, the economy has bounded into the future as a modernizing entity but has retained traces of its planned legacy, suffering from the overhang of the Soviet industrial mentality during its attempts to reorient towards a modern service economy. This reality has had serious ramifications for the development of key economic institutions such as property rights, the judiciary, central banking, and international trade, as the move towards creating indigenous institutions has been based on the blueprints of others but with an attempt to craft them in a "Kazakh" way.

This schizophrenia in institutional development has not been limited to culture or economics, as the country's evolution has been inextricable from its political development. While the country has broken free of its binding Soviet era political ties, the country has been bounded by its geographic position between Russia and the People's Republic of China, constraining its

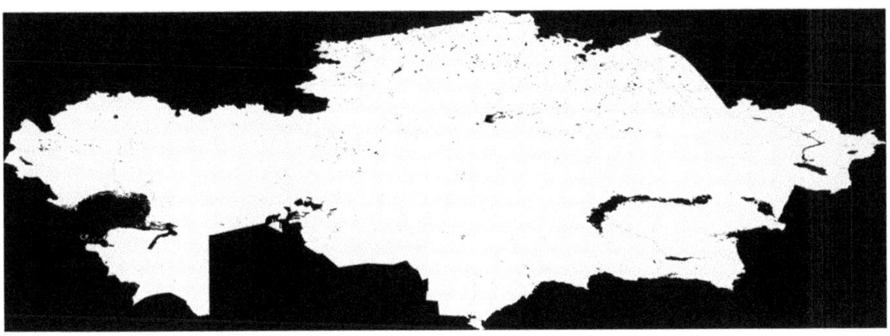

Figure 1.1 Spatial Distribution of Population in Kazakhstan, 2020
Note: Census/projection-disaggregated gridded population datasets for 189 countries in 2020 using Built-Settlement Growth Model outputs. WorldPop; licensed under a Creative Commons Attribution 4.0 International License. Larger dots indicate greater density of population.
Source: WorldPop and CIESIN (2022).

policy choices somewhat and making the Sino-Russian rivalry a key factor in external relations. Perhaps not surprisingly, due to its large Russian ethnic minority and historical experience of colonization by Moscow, Kazakhstan's leaders have preferred to stay close to Russia, literally since the moment the Soviet Union fell apart, seeking to reintegrate regionally with its overbearing neighbour to the north. The rise of China and the influx of Chinese migrants, however, have made Kazakhstan more in tune with its own economic and political imperatives, and this has contributed to an independent streak in terms of its dealing with Russia and within the main regional integration body, the Eurasian Economic Union (EAEU).

Perhaps more important than its external relations has been the relative stagnation of Kazakhstan's domestic political institutions, a key determinant of economic institutional development. As shown in the collection of indicators from the Polity IV database in Figure 1.3, the country emerged from the Soviet era as fairly autocratic and became more autocratic early on in its transition; at the same time, executive constraints have been fairly low (improving since 2005 but still not as good as pre-1995) and the regulation of political participation is exactly where it was at independence (the most common value for Kazakhstan is classified as "sectarian" competition, whereby competing identity groups use power to shut out others). Both Kazakhstan's political development and that of the city of Nur-Sultan has been driven by the city's namesake, Nursultan Nazarbayev, the last Soviet leader of the Kazakh Soviet Socialist Republic, the first President of independent Kazakhstan until his surprise resignation in 2019, and a man

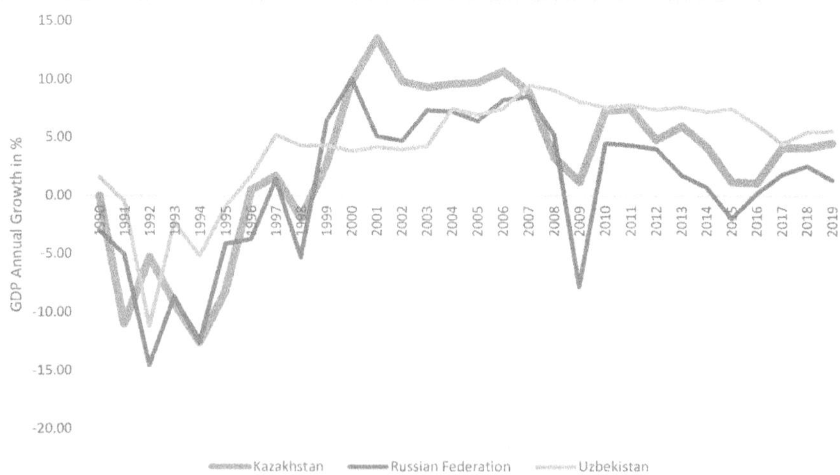

Figure 1.2 GDP Growth in Kazakhstan, Russia, and Uzbekistan, 1990–2019
Source: World Bank World Data Indicators, https://hub.worldpop.org/geodata/summary?id=46955.

bestowed with the title of "Father of the Nation" (*Elbasy*), at least until January 2022.

Nazarbayev's impact on the country's political institutions will be felt for a long time because, despite serving as perhaps the most benign dictator in a region known for harsh repression, he remained a dictator, nonetheless, tolerating little dissent (Axyonova 2013), keeping power via the veneer of democracy (Levitsky and Way 2002; Ó Beacháin and Kevlihan 2015), and acting in ways directly counter to international human rights norms (Lillis 2018). The manner in which he ruled also helped to shape political institutions, as, according to Isaacs (2010), informal political coalitions were key in consolidating the country's authoritarianism in the early 1990s, providing a buffer against uncertainty; at the same time, Skalamera Groce (2020) notes that Nazarbayev was able to survive in office for 29 years by constructing a series of patron-client ties which rendered politicians and businessmen dependent upon the office of the presidency. Nazarbayev's continued involvement in the country's political functioning, even after passing the torch to Kassym-Jokart Tokayev in March 2019 (a move which was confirmed in a snap election in June of that year), means that it remains to be seen if Kazakhstan can begin a process of political evolution to go along with its economic one – or, if such an evolution does not occur, if there is the real

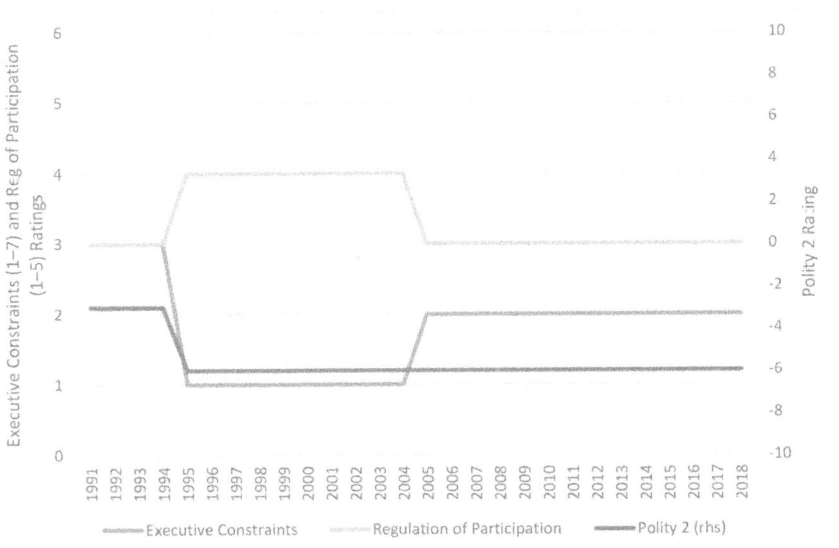

Figure 1.3 Polity IV Ratings of Kazakhstan's Political Institutions, Then and Now

Note: The Polity 2 variable is coded from –10 to 10, with numbers below 0 more autocratic and above 0 more democratic. Executive constraints are coded from 1 to 7, with higher numbers signifying more constraints. Finally, regulation of participation is coded from 1 to 5, with higher numbers related to higher regulation of political participation.

Source: Polity IV Database, www.systemicpeace.org/polityproject.html.

possibility that political stagnation will hold the economy back. The worst-case scenario may also be in play, that any political transition which is mishandled could lead to instability and threaten Kazakhstan's economic gains.

The Elusive Snow Leopard: A Plan to Track It

Given these disparate impulses, uneven development, and the rollercoaster ride and instability of transition, the purpose of this book is to examine Kazakhstan as an economic entity and to understand precisely how it reached its current position. While there is much scholarship (especially in Russian) on Kazakhstan, mainly related to security issues, cultural identity, urban/regional studies, and natural resource abundance, there is little sense of a narrative regarding its economic development which brings together these separate threads. This is perhaps not surprising given that it is a daunting task for any country to combine so many currents, but especially for a relatively new one located remotely from researchers and with many fundamental components simultaneously in flux.

In order to achieve the ambitious goal of understanding Kazakhstan's economic development, it is perhaps helpful to examine the parallel development of one of Kazakhstan's national symbols, an elusive and vulnerable creature found in the Tian Shan mountains in the south and east of the country – the snow leopard. Befitting its importance as a longstanding part of Kazakh mythology (Fishler 2019), Almaty, Kazakhstan's first city and the one most proximate to the hunting grounds of the leopard, has adopted the snow leopard as its permanent symbol; at the same time, the city's zoo has kept at least one of the creatures since independence, building on a breeding programme that was instigated during the late Soviet years (Braden 1994). In line with attempts to make Astana a new symbol of Kazakhstan while at the same time maintaining a connection to Kazakhstan's heritage, the snow leopard featured prominently on the city's official seal (White 2018).[1] The rare creature also appeared on the back of the 10,000 tenge banknote which was issued in 1993, forever associating the snow leopard with the largest denomination of the first issuance of an independent currency in the country's history.

Much like the country which put the animal on its currency, the snow leopard has seen its fortunes wax and wane since Kazakhstan became independent. A predator by nature, the snow leopard's habitat has shrunk (Mahmood et al. 2019) due to poaching and human encroachment (Holt et al. 2018), and there are now probably only approximately 150 left in Kazakhstan, with the last rigorous census (Zhirjakov 1990) conducted over 30 years ago recording approximately 20 snow leopards in the mountains surrounding Almaty. In fact, the collapse of the Soviet economy and state capacity meant that poaching became a much more lucrative enterprise, a problem which afflicted not only Kazakhstan but also Kyrgyzstan in particular, thereby causing the number of the magnificent beasts to dwindle yet further (McCarthy and Chapron 2003).

Hearteningly, the recovery of Kazakhstan's economy has also resulted in greater emphasis being placed on the conservation and protection of the snow leopard (Jackson et al. 2010), and, while more needs to be done to ensure the survival of the species across its entire habitat, the population decline has been arrested: perhaps incredibly, following the imposition of a lockdown in May 2020 to curb the spread of the COVID-19 pandemic, at least three snow leopards were spotted on camera roaming areas close to the city usually frequented by hikers (see Auyezov 2020). And in line with the broader literature correlating economic development with better environmental outcomes (e.g. Grossman and Krueger 1995 or Panayotou 2016), we should expect to see a richer Kazakhstan lead to better protection of the snow leopard as consumers and participants in the economy demand more "green" solutions.

While the health of the snow leopard has tracked the overall health of Kazakhstan, there is another critical similarity between the snow leopard and the development of economic outcomes in the country. As noted above, one of the most prominent attributes of the snow leopard is its rarity, meaning that its existence often needs to be traced not through direct contact nor via photography (although cameras have captured images of the creature in the wild), but through the evidence of its existence such as fresh tracks. In many ways, economic development also needs to be traced in the same way, as we see the results of economic success (GDP growth, increases in investment, falling poverty), but we rarely are able to catch development as it is occurring across disparate units uncoordinated across time and space. Thus, for economic development, like the snow leopard, we often have to observe the habitat and ecosystem for clues as to its overall health.

In an economy, the habitat in which economic activity occurs has been accurately described as "the stuff of socio-economic reality" (Hodgson 2001:302), referring to a country's institutions. Institutions are usually simply defined in the terminology of the Nobel Laureate Douglass North as "the rules of the game" (North 1990), but they are of course much more than that when it comes to the functioning of a country's economy. As I wrote in 2013, "Institutions are a set of rules, constraints, and behavioral guidelines, enforced by either formal or informal means external to the individual, which are designed or arise to shape the behavior of individual actors" (Hartwell 2013:17), a definition which encompasses most of the functions and the shapes of various types of institutions. Importantly, by delineating institutions according to their function (political, economic, social) and their mode of expression (formal or informal), we can encompass the many strands of "socio-economic reality" which underlie a country, including its cultural norms, its governance, the behaviour of its many citizens, and its set of constraints and options as regards external and internal actors. Put another way, institutions are endogenous creatures which are formed due to the basic tenets or rules that the people making up a delineated geographic space (most often the country, but also at much smaller levels) have devised according to and constrained by national and personal identity (Hartwell 2021) and are simultaneously acted on and are being acted upon by those same people. Institutions are the expression of rules by the people who comprise them but, despite their semi-permanent nature (i.e. what distinguishes an institution from a policy or merely an organization), they can change if the underlying currents sustaining them also change.

The reality of the endogeneity of institutions, and the fact that they influence and are influenced at the same time, means that we often have to look deep into history to understand the genesis of certain institutions. This does not mean that history is destiny, however, as external shocks and shifting cultural tenets can overwhelm institutions and make them seem anachronistic (and even force them to cease their operations). I have argued elsewhere (Hartwell 2018) that policies also have an effect on institutional functioning, as poor policies can shift expectations and undermine a country's entire institutional set, allowing for institutional collapse and evolution in unforeseen ways. But these instances of either evolution or revolution tend to be the exception rather the rule, with institutional change being far too slow to perceive. Indeed, institutions display a large amount of inertia (Kingston and Caballero 2009), finding it easier to do things "the way they've always been done," rather than necessarily adapting to the world around them. Given this reality, how institutions were originally conceived or put into place is important to understanding their current functioning. At the same time, some institutions have stood the test of time not because they need to adapt and change, but because they adhere to simple and universal tenets which are easily understood: property rights, for example, have endured in some form or another because the rationale of "this is mine, this is yours" is a basic human impulse from our earliest ages. The simplicity of the rule leads to a resilience which means that the core institution is also fairly resistant to change.

In any event, understanding institutions is fundamental to understanding the functioning of an economy simply because institutions are *the mediators of incentives in a society*. If institutions are truly the rules of the game, then institutions determine who can be the winners and losers, what it takes to become one (or the other), and how the score of the game is tallied. For example, if cultural norms state that some pre-determined level of wealth is "excessive," then it is likely that a society would have the necessary economic and political institutions to enforce this norm, perhaps via excessive taxation and redistribution; in this manner, incentives will be mediated as well, as perhaps the top income brackets are no longer the goal for individuals and income mobility is restricted, an effect which has follow-on consequences for economic activity within a country. Similarly, a country which admires successful people may place a premium on business freedom or property rights, giving leeway to the entrepreneur and structuring incentives so that risk-taking is rewarded. In both cases, the institutional structure of a country, driven by economic calculations, utility, and culture, determine the pay-off matrix for various avenues of economic activity. In this sense, the importance of institutions cannot be understated.

Given the centrality of institutions to economic life, this book thus attempts to understand the experience of economic and political transition in Kazakhstan over the past 30 years through an institutional lens: in particular, I will attempt to explain the political and economic performance of the country as a function of its institutions, in addition to its policy choices and, crucially, its external environment. Such an approach is not always easy to undertake, as, like the snow leopard, institutions are often only rated by what they leave behind rather than being observed in practice. However, a holistic look at a country's institutional matrix, one which focuses on both formal institutions (rules, government, laws, regulations) and informal practices (social arrangements, culture, identity, customs), can still provide a full picture of the overall ecosystem for growth. As noted above, this approach builds on my previous works, which have both taken a rigorous and comprehensive look at institutional change in transition economies writ large (Hartwell 2013) and set up a methodology for analysing the political and economic institutional workings in transition (Hartwell 2016). In fact, this current book will follow my earlier research comparing the transition experience of Poland and Ukraine, applying the same taxonomy to trace the development of institutions in Kazakhstan and understand the effect that these institutions have had on the country's economic evolution.

This approach is meant to focus on four overarching themes related to the institutional facets of Kazakhstan's transition.

What were the initial conditions of institutions in Kazakhstan at the beginning of transition, and how did the forces of history influence these institutions?

When one looks back at the early literature from the 1990s on transition, it is apparent that there is a focus on explaining then-current conditions by the recent past, with prominent papers such as those by Fischer et al. (1996), Krueger and Ciolko (1998), and especially de Melo et al. (2001, but circulating in some form since 1994) contrasting the legacies of the former Soviet Union and Central and Eastern European countries. These early papers attributed divergence in transition to the experience of Soviet rule, with countries that were once actually part of the Soviet Union facing more distortions, greater obstacles, and a poorer performance than those which were independent during the communist era.

While this evidence has been validated in recent years, it is also crucial to note that the initial conditions as they applied in 1989 or 1991 also fell away rapidly as a determinant of economic outcomes (Di Tommasso et al. 2007), especially as late reformers either finally undertook reforms (Ukraine is a key example here) or found themselves in a natural resource bonanza (Azerbaijan and our subject of examination, Kazakhstan, fall into this camp). Additionally, for many countries of the former Soviet Union, the issue was indeed

Soviet central planning but also pre-existing distortions; that is, for many countries, the Soviet experiment was unwillingly grafted onto an institutional organism which then quickly shed its trappings but reintegrated some of its distortions. Building on these transition paths and the reality that the recent past may not hold as much importance as the cumulative weight of history, the first portion of the book will focus on the initial conditions prevailing in Kazakhstan and how the Soviet era itself was shaped by Kazakhstan's history. This research line will not only clarify the different institutions that are of most interest for us, but also examine closely the pre-communist era (in particular during the Russian Empire) and especially the policies pursued during the Soviet era, and how they may have influenced institutional development. The end result of this inquiry will be to demonstrate Kazakhstan's "path dependence" in its institutional evolution, as historical and governance factors might have led to very different economics outcomes if they had changed; however, we shall also demonstrate sources of continuity in Kazakhstan's history, meaning that initial conditions were not an irrevocable destiny. The sum of this examination will be to offer clues as to where and how institutions evolved in the following three decades.

How did political institutions evolve – or not – in Kazakhstan during the transition?

The political development of post-Soviet countries – or, more accurately, their lack of development – and in particular the political machinations in Central Asia, have been the interest of many a political scientist (see in particular Matveeva 1999, Collins 2002, and Dagiev 2013), especially when one considers the remarkable continuity in leadership over three decades. From the point of view of economic development, political institutions also assume paramount importance, as they both set and periodically alter the rules of the game when it comes to the economy, influencing profoundly how economic institutions evolve (Acemoglu et al. 2005). Thus, this book's first foray into the transition era in Kazakhstan will focus on the development of the country's political institutions and how these have fed into economic development, policymaking, and institutions. As with any good institutional examination, we will not just focus on the most obvious of the formal political institutions, i.e. the presidency, we will also draw on extant scholarship and the historical analysis of the first portion of the book to understand local political development, informal clan and network politics, and the interplay of informal and formal political institutions in affecting economic life. This examination will also be coloured by the upheavals that occurred in Kazakhstan in January 2022, and how they represent another milestone in Kazakhstan's political development.

In order to explore these various facets of the political ecosystem in Kazakhstan, Chapter 5 will focus on different aspects of Kazakhstan's political institutional development, including:

- *the evolution of democratic processes and elections*: despite its move towards autocracy, Kazakhstan continues to hold regular elections, although they are regularly derided as neither free nor fair (Kendall-Taylor 2012; Schatz and Maltseva 2012; Schedler 2015). How has the democratic process and its associated political institutions proceeded in the post-Soviet era, and where has there been either progress or setbacks?
- *the constitutional process and legal overhang from the Soviet Union:* as with many post-Soviet states, the legalistic traditions of communism (Bodnar and Schmidt 2012; Muratovna and Serikbayevna 2020) and the overwhelming emphasis on rules and standards have unfortunately persisted in Kazakhstan. At the same time that the Soviet legal history placed an emphasis on written strictures (including in the constitution), the practice of law was derived from power rather than judicial institutions and/or popular legitimacy. We will examine how Kazakhstan's current constitution came to be created and the role it – and the judicial and legal sector – have played in the development of the country's economy;
- *an examination of executive constraints in both theory and practice*: as an autocratic state (and as shown in Figure 1.3), the leader of Kazakhstan has acted in ways which are unchecked by other branches of government. However, this does not mean that the executive is entirely unconstrained, as informal norms and other institutions may present speed bumps on the way towards realizing the leader's will. We will examine the importance of executive constraints to economic development, and how they have played a role in shaping the economic path of Kazakhstan during the transition; and finally
- *how has the political system in Kazakhstan been affected by international actors?* As a state bordering two powerful and expansionist neighbours, Kazakhstan has, throughout its history, been subjected to the whims of the empires it adjoins. Russia has, above all, been the neighbour of most concern, absorbing Kazakhstan into its empire in the 18th and 19th centuries and acting as the driving force in both the Soviet Union and in the EAEU. At the same time, one cannot ignore the colossus of China located to Kazakhstan's east, an economic powerhouse which was home to 18 per cent of the global population in 2019 and which has begun to exert an influence on the country via its Belt and Road Initiative (Kassenova 2017). Kazakhstan's political life and its economic policies in particular have been shaped by its geography and its geographic location, and we will endeavour to understand how the linkage from neighbourhood to political institutions to economic outcomes has operated.

As noted above and, comporting with the tenets of new institutional economics (see Williamson 2009 and Casson et al. 2010 in particular), emphasis will be made throughout the book, especially with reference to political institutions, on the difference between formal and informal institutions and how they can influence economic outcomes. In the context of Kazakhstan, this will entail a focus on the divergence between the formal and legalistic approach to political institutions, one which relies on legislation and written codes, but which represents *potential* political institutions, to that of the *actual* (or *realized*) political institutions within Kazakhstan, focused on the practice and the power relationships among various actors and branches. This is done precisely to avoid the trap of considering institutions solely in terms of their formal orderings, which may appear to follow international best practices and/or be optimal, but which in reality operate very differently. Indeed, one of the lessons of international development is that the true functioning of political institutions may be so informal as to defy placement on an organizational chart: as Casanegra de Jantscher (1990) famously remarked in the context of taxation, administration *is* policy, a maxim which has been extended to note that personnel is policy, too.[2] Understanding this reality is key for understanding how Kazakhstan's institutions have come to be and why they have evolved the way they have – and, in a novel twist, how informality has come to be formalized (Sharipova 2018).

How did economic institutions evolve in Kazakhstan?

Political institutions, especially at the formal level, are often the easiest national-level institutions to spot, and in the case of Kazakhstan, have kept political scientists busy with their examinations of "state-building" and "capacity" and "imagery" and "national identity." However, and more importantly for our purposes, economic institutions should have a much more direct influence on economic outcomes, given that they are designed or arise expressly to influence economic actions, actors, and incentives (Hartwell 2013). Put another way, while political institutions may have a second order effect on economics, they are not explicitly built for economic outcomes but are concerned with the distribution of political power; on the other hand, economic institutions have a first-order goal of influencing economic activity, creating incentive structures and rules surrounding economic life. If we are to look at the overall functioning of an economy, thus, we must drill down to the ecosystem of economic institutions to understand how trade is ordered, how culture translates into commerce, and how the rules of the game are structured. As a final point regarding political versus economic institutions, from the point of view of an economist, while political orderings may directly influence economic ones, this does not mean that economic institutions are wholly dependent upon political ones. In fact, economic institutions can have a significant influence on the path of political evolution as well, even if that is also second order (Hartwell 2018).

Recognizing this fact, and with our emphasis more broadly on Kazakhstan's economic path over the past 30 years, this book will delve deeply into the various economic institutions that encompass a market economy and how they have evolved in Kazakhstan. In line with the extant literature, both theoretical (Demsetz 1964; Alchian 1965; De Soto 2002) and empirical (Goldsmith 1995; Claessens and Laeven 2003; Besley and Ghatak 2010; Hartwell 2013), which focuses on the importance of property rights, we will home in on this key meta-institution as *primus inter pares* for economic outcomes. Property rights occupy a special place in the pantheon of economic institutions not only because of their follow-on effects for finance and investment, but also because the economic system of communism – which Kazakhstan adhered to for 70 years – was predicated precisely on destroying these economic relations. Thus, understanding how Kazakhstan has experienced both informal and formal property rights, and what remains to be done, will be a huge step in understanding current economic conditions. Along these lines, additional economic institutions such as the freedom to trade and the financial sector, in addition to supporting institutions such as the judiciary (and corruption), will be examined to determine their role in Kazakhstan's transition and to see where opportunities were seized – and missed.

As with political institutions, the tale of the nation of Kazakhstan cannot be told in isolation from its broader neighbourhood, and thus our examination of economic institutions through Kazakh history will also attempt to understand the role of modern Russia, the Russian Empire, and the Soviet Union in influencing these institutional changes. Given that the chain of causality for most institutional changes is long, one often does not take into account the way in which power politics or one's neighbourhood can affect the microeconomic orderings of institutions; in Kazakhstan's case, however (as in most of the former Soviet Union), the outsize influence of Russia and especially its conquering of Kazakhstan had a direct and immediate effect on the institutions that the country adopted in the economic sphere. This long shadow has continued into Kazakhstan's transition, as the creation of the EAEU and the continued trade links between Russia and Kazakhstan have undoubtedly shaped the path which Kazakhstan followed. Through this examination, we will also attempt to see if Kazakhstan can effectively break away from the Russian model of development (or, indeed, if it already has) in terms of economic institutions, and, if not, what can be done going forward.

What can be done today to make Kazakhstan's transition complete – and successful?

It is this last point, on what can be done going forward, which is both the key issue of the book (derived from the historical analysis) and also the point which will seem the most dated in five, 10, 20 years hence. Given the reality that institutions, like the snow leopard in the mountains, are path-dependent and complex, it is difficult to predict where the human interactions currently occurring in Kazakhstan will lead the country over the coming decades. Indeed, institutional complexity is one of the key points of the book, in that institutions are highly dependent upon initial conditions and external stimuli, but they also can be jostled off the path, be hijacked by self-interested actors, bump into more powerful institutions, or form a barrier to change which then translates to slower economic development. But, despite the complexity of institutions, they continue to exist, they continue to influence economic outcomes, and they continue to exert an influence over human action and behaviour.

With this caveat in mind, the ultimate goal of this work is to derive a rough blueprint for successful institutional reforms for Kazakhstan, to help it understand what it did right and what it did wrong in the transition, and how it can yet become a fully market-oriented economy for the benefit of its citizens. In this sense, I am already giving away the ending, as Kazakhstan has indeed made great strides from its humble beginnings as a modern society as an outpost of the Russian Empire (as shown in Figure 1.2), but there is so much more to do in order to create a "Dubai on the steppe." The difficulty in constructing lasting institutions, much like the pink siding-clad houses of Astana of the early 2000s, is that the building or the skeletal framework is not enough; they cannot be mere facades, Potemkin villages, but must have substance, strong foundations, and be filled with legitimacy, resilience, and trust. And for an institution to be effective – and there are many different criteria by which an institution can be "effective"[3] – it must not only live up to its own provenance, but in modern economic parlance it must also help to facilitate market transactions. As noted in my earlier work (Hartwell 2013), the whole point of economic transition was *eventually* to increase consumption and effective investment and lower poverty, but the *immediate* objective was to replace the institutions which facilitated a centralized, planned economy with those which facilitated a free market economy. This means more than merely the trappings of a market economy (laws and organizational forms), but the entrenchment of institutions which aid commerce, encourage freedom and responsibility, and devolve power to the individual and away from the state. Kazakhstan's transition and its track record of institutional change will thus necessarily be judged by this criterion above all.

To return to our opening panorama of the country's capital city, it is yet to be seen if the impressive edifices of Nur-Sultan are a demonstration of Kazakhstan's institutional progress, as measured against this criterion. Of course, they show the increased wealth and power that has come with Kazakhstan's economic emergence, but it will be the purpose of this book to discover if their tinted windows are hiding hollow interiors or if they merely shielding the necessary processes of evolution from the exterior. Over the coming chapters, as we explore the history of Kazakhstan's institutions and the changes in its political and economic institutional matrix, it is hoped that we will come closer to understanding the answer to this question – and if the current reality of institutions in Kazakhstan, facade or substance, is the destiny for the future of the country going forward. Although the snow leopard cannot change his spots, he can change his path, and our goal will be to ascertain how much of an adjustment the country must make to create a sustainable and effective institutional ecosystem.

Notes

1 Interestingly, the snow leopard is no longer on the seal of the renamed Nur-Sultan.

2 The phrase "personnel is policy" has been attributed to Scot Faulkner, the Director of Personnel for Ronald Reagan's 1980 presidential campaign in the US, and the title of an op-ed he wrote in 2016 for the *Washington Examiner* newspaper, available at www.washingtonexaminer.com/personnel-is-policy.

3 In fact, one of the dividing lines between the "old institutional economics" (OIE) of economists such as Veblen and Commons and the "new institutional economics" of North and Williamson was the OIE insistence that effective institutions were those that fulfilled their own mandate, not that they contributed to societal or economic efficiency. As noted in the text, this viewpoint is especially egregious when considering the process of transition.

References

Acemoglu, D., Johnson, S., and Robinson, J. A. (2005). Institutions as the fundamental cause of long-run growth. In P. Aghion and S. N. Durlauf (Eds.), *Handbook of Economic Growth: Volume 1A* (pp. 385–472).North Holland: Elsevier.

Alchian, A. A. (1965). Some economics of property rights. *Il politico*, 30(4), 816–829.

Auty, R. M. (1999). *The IMF Model and Resource-Abundant Transition Economies: Kazakhstan and Uzbekistan* (No. 295495). Helsinki: United Nations University, World Institute for Development Economic Research.

Auyezov, O. (2020). Rare snow leopards spotted near Kazakh city amid lockdown. *Reuters*, 25 May. www.reuters.com/article/us-health-coronavirus-kazakhstan-wildlif-idUSKBN23110K.

Axyonova, V. (2013). When security threatens human rights: Reviewing the case of Central Asia. *Security and Human Rights*, 24(2), 159–168.

Besley, T., and Ghatak, M. (2010). Property rights and economic development. In D. Rodrik and M. Rosenzweig (Eds.), *Handbook of Development Economics* (Vol. 5; pp. 4525–4595). North Holland: Elsevier.

Bodnar, A., and Schmidt, E. K. (2012). Rule of law and judicial independence in Eastern Europe, the South Caucasus, and Central Asia. In *OSCE Yearbook 2011* (pp. 289–303). Baden-Baden: Nomos.

Braden, K. (1994). The snow leopard in independent Kazakhstan. *Snow Line*, 12(1), 6–7.

Burkhanov, A., and Sharipova, D. (2014). Kazakhstan's civic-national identity. In M. Y. Omelicheva (Ed.), *Nationalism and Identity Construction in Central Asia: Dimensions, Dynamics, and Directions* (pp. 21–39). New York: Lexington Books.

Casanegra de Jantscher, M. (1990). Administering the VAT. In M. Gillis, C. S. Shoup and G. Sicat (Eds.), *Value-Added Taxation in Developing Countries* (pp. 171–179). Washington, DC: World Bank.

Casson, M. C., Della Giusta, M., and Kambhampati, U. S. (2010). Formal and informal institutions and development. *World Development*, 38(2), 137–141.

Claessens, S., and Laeven, L. (2003). Financial development, property rights, and growth. *The Journal of Finance*, 58(6), 2401–2436.

Collins, K. (2002). Clans, pacts, and politics in Central Asia. *Journal of Democracy*, 13(3), 137–152.

Dagiev, D. (2013). *Regime Transition in Central Asia: Stateness, Nationalism and Political Change in Tajikistan and Uzbekistan*. London: Routledge.

Dave, B. (1996). National revival in Kazakhstan: Language shift and identity change. *Post-Soviet Affairs*, 12(1), 51–72.

De Melo, M., Denizer, C., Gelb, A., and Tenev, S. (2001). Circumstance and choice: The role of initial conditions and policies in transition economies. *World Bank Economic Review*, 15(1), 1–1.

De Soto, H. (2002). Law and property outside the West: A few new ideas about fighting poverty. *Forum for Development Studies*, 29(2), 349–361.

Demsetz, H. (1964). The exchange and enforcement of property rights. *The Journal of Law and Economics*, 7, 11–26.

Di Tommaso, M. L., Raiser, M., and Weeks, M. (2007). Home grown or imported? Initial conditions, external anchors and the determinants of institutional reform in the transition economies. *The Economic Journal*, 117(520), 858–881.

Fierman, W. (1998). Language and identity in Kazakhstan: Formulations in policy documents 1987–1997. *Communist and Post-Communist Studies*, 31(2), 171–186.

Fischer, S., Sahay, R., and Végh, C. A. (1996). Economies in transition: The beginnings of growth. *The American Economic Review*, 86(2), 229–233.

Fishler, A. (2019). Philosophical heritage of the Turkic peoples: Sacred animals in the life of Turkic world, in Kazakhstan and Kyrgyzstan. *Journal of Philosophy, Culture and Political Science*, 66(4), 131–135.

Goldsmith, A. A. (1995). Democracy, property rights and economic growth. *The Journal of Development Studies*, 32(2), 157–174.

Grossman, G. M., and Krueger, A. B. (1995). Economic growth and the environment. *The Quarterly Journal of Economics*, 110(2), 353–377.

Hartwell, C. A. (2013). *Institutional Barriers in the Transition to Market: Explaining Performance and Divergence in Transition Economies*. Basingstoke: Palgrave Macmillan.

Hartwell, C. A. (2016). *Two Roads Diverge: The Transition Experience of Poland and Ukraine*. Cambridge: Cambridge University Press.

Hartwell, C. A. (2018). The "Hierarchy of Institutions" reconsidered: Monetary policy and its effect on the rule of law in interwar Poland. *Explorations in Economic History*, 68, 37–70.

Hartwell, C. A. (2021). Identity and the evolution of institutions: Evidence from partition and interwar Poland. *Forum for Social Economics*, 50(1), 61–82.

Hodgson, G. (2001). *How Economics Forgot History: The Problem of Historical Specificity in Social Science*. London: Routledge.

Holt, C. D. S., Nevin, O. T., Smith, D., and Convery, I. (2018). Environmental niche overlap between snow leopard and four prey species in Kazakhstan. *Ecological Informatics*, 48, 97–103.

Isaacs, R. (2010). Informal politics and the uncertain context of transition: Revisiting early-stage non-democratic development in Kazakhstan. *Democratization*, 17(1), 1–25.

Jackson, R. M., Mishra, C., McCarthy, T. M., and Ale, S. B. (2010). Snow leopards: Conflict and conservation. In D. W. Macdonald and A. J. Loveridge (Eds.), *The Biology and Conservation of Wild Felids* (pp. 417–430). Oxford: Oxford University Press.

Kalyuzhnova, Y., and Patterson, K. (2016). Kazakhstan: Long-term economic growth and the role of the oil sector. *Comparative Economic Studies*, 58(1), 93–118.

Kassenova, N. (2017). China's Silk Road and Kazakhstan's Bright Path: Linking dreams of prosperity. *Asia Policy*, 24(1), 110–116.

Kendall-Taylor, A. (2012). Purchasing power: Oil, elections and regime durability in Azerbaijan and Kazakhstan. *Europe-Asia Studies*, 64(4), 737–760.

Kingston, C., and Caballero, G. (2009). Comparing theories of institutional change. *Journal of Institutional Economics*, 5(2), 151–180.

Köppen, B. (2013). The production of a new Eurasian capital on the Kazakh steppe: Architecture, urban design, and identity in Astana. *Nationalities Papers*, 41(4), 590–605.

Krueger, G., and Ciolko, M. (1998). A note on initial conditions and liberalization during transition. *Journal of Comparative Economics*, 26(4), 718–734.

Laszczkowski, M. (2016). *"City of the Future": Built Space, Modernity and Urban Change in Astana* (Vol. 14). New York: Berghahn Books.

Levitsky, S., and Way, L. A. (2002). Elections without democracy: The rise of competitive authoritarianism. *Journal of Democracy*, 13(2), 51–65.

Lillis, J. (2018). *Dark Shadows: Inside the Secret World of Kazakhstan*. New York: I. B. Tauris.

Mahmood, T., Younas, A., Akrim, F., Andleeb, S., Hamid, A., and Nadeem, M. S. (2019). Range contraction of snow leopard (Panthera uncia). *PLOS one*, 14(8), e0218460.

Matveeva, A. (1999). Democratization, legitimacy and political change in Central Asia. *International Affairs*, 75(1), 23–44.

McCarthy, T. M., and Chapron, G. (2003). *Snow Leopard Survival Strategy*. Seattle, WA: International Snow Leopard Trust and Snow Leopard Network. www.catsg.org/fileadmin/filesharing/3.Conservation_Center/3.4._Strategies___Action_Plans/Snow_leopard/McCarthy_et_al_2003_Snow_leopard_survival_strategy.pdf.

Muratovna, B. A., and Serikbayevna, S. S. (2020). Legal culture of Soviet Kazakhstan. *Journal of Environmental Treatment Techniques*, 8(1), 319–322.

North, D. C. (1990). *Institutions, Institutional Change and Economic Performance*. Cambridge: Cambridge University Press.

Ó Beacháin, D., and Kevlihan, R. (2015). Imagined democracy? Nation-building and elections in Central Asia. *Nationalities Papers*, 43(3), 495–513.

Panayotou, T. (2016). Economic growth and the environment. In N. Haenn, R. Wilk and A. Harnish (Eds.), *The Environment in Anthropology: A Reader in Ecology, Culture, and Sustainable Living* (pp. 140–148). New York: New York University Press.

Schatz, E., and Maltseva, E. (2012). Kazakhstan's authoritarian "persuasion." *Post-Soviet Affairs*, 28(1), 45–65.

Schedler, A. (2015). Electoral authoritarianism. In R. A. Scott and S. M. Kosslyn (Eds.), *Emerging Trends in the Social and Behavioral Sciences: An Interdisciplinary, Searchable, and Linkable Resource* (pp. 1–16). Wiley Online.

Sharipova, D. (2018). *State-building in Kazakhstan: Continuity and Transformation of Informal Institutions*. New York: Lexington Books.

Skalamera Groce, M. (2020). Political transition on the Great Steppe: The case of Kazakhstan. *Survival*, 62(1), 157–168.

Spehr, S., and Kassenova, N. (2012). Kazakhstan: Constructing identity in a post-Soviet society. *Asian Ethnicity*, 13(2), 135–151.

Truspekova, K. K., Galimzhanova, A. S., and Glaudinova, M. B. (2019). National identity and architecture of Nur-Sultan. *Humanities & Social Sciences Reviews*, 7 (5), 374–386.

White, K. D. (2018). The snow leopard and cultural landscape in contemporary Kazakhstan. *Society & Animals*, 28(1), 58–80.

Williamson, C. R. (2009). Informal institutions rule: Institutional arrangements and economic performance. *Public Choice*, 139(3), 371–387.

WorldPop and Center for International Earth Science Information Network (CIESIN) (2022). *Global High Resolution Population Denominators Project – Funded by the Bill and Melinda Gates Foundation (OPP1134076)*. https://dx.doi.org/10.5258/SOTON/WP00675.

Yessenova, S. (2005). "Routes and roots" of Kazakh identity: Urban migration in postsocialist Kazakhstan. *The Russian Review*, 64(4), 661–679.

Zhirjakov, V.A. (1990). On the ecology of snow leopard in the Zailisky-Alatau (Northern Tien Shan). *International Pedigree Book of Snow Leopards* (Vol. 6, pp. 25–30). Helsinki: Helsinki Zoo.

2 A Brief Institutional History of Kazakhstan

From Antiquity to 1917

Situated squarely in the heart of Central Asia, bordered by the Russian Federation, the People's Republic of China, the Kyrgyz Republic, Uzbekistan, and Turkmenistan, Kazakhstan is situated at the crossroads of Europe, East Asia, and South Asia but remains very distant (geographically and culturally) from all of these locales. Indeed, Kazakhstan embodies the idea of *Central* Asia, drawing on Turkic, Mongol, and Russian culture to create a very specific identity befitting its central location (Crowe 1998), one which then translates into specific administrative and institutional forms (Perlman and Gleason 2007). But while literally thousands of pages have been written on this first issue, i.e. the forging of Kazakh identity and a coherent culture (distinct from its influencers on all sides), the purpose of this book is predicated on the second issue, namely the development of institutions at the national level, and how they have been influenced by and in turn have influenced economic development. This chapter sets the stage for the institutional analysis later in the book by providing a brief history of Kazakhstan and how the current institutional matrix of the country came to be during its formative years. As a brief history, it will have to focus on the broader currents contributing to institutional change, and is not meant to be comprehensive; however, the turning points which it does highlight will show how the institutional paths leading to the present day were set.

Of course, we are immediately disadvantaged in tracing the institutional history of Kazakhstan by the reality that the country now known as Kazakhstan has only existed for 30 years (as of this writing). From its conquest by the Mongols in the 1200s to its incorporation into the Russian Empire in the 18th century and then into the Soviet Union, Kazakhstan has seemingly always been more than influenced by others; indeed, for long stretches of its history it has actually been under the dominion of others (Aldashev and Guirkinger 2017). Thus, to take a long, historical view of the development of the country, we must take care to analyse the institutions of *others*, that is, not Kazakhstan itself but the empires and countries that the current land mass of Kazakhstan was subjected to. As already noted, this means delving back into the culture and identity issues which others have explored at length, but not with an interest in understanding how a

DOI: 10.4324/9781003212508-2

"Kazakh" identity was forged or even what disparate parts it is comprised of. Rather, it is to understand how the exposure to foreign institutional systems, and especially their imposition on Kazakhs on their own territory, shaped future institutional paths.

This turn towards understanding the institutions of colonizers also confronts us with a large literature, similar to that on identity, on the idea of "transplanting" institutions. Much of this research has been done in development economics and political science and focuses on how external institutions often fail to be transplanted from one country to another because of differing cultural contexts (Roland 2004), different economic conditions (Guinnane 1994), or even simply lack of capacity or infrastructure to handle the requirements of an institution (Alshorbagy 2012). On the other hand, occupation and subjugation – especially in an environment which lacks specific institutions or institutional innovations – can be successful in transplanting institutions simply by virtue of controlling the entire institutional environment and forcing acceptance thereof. This does not mean that every instance of colonization will successfully implant institutions, as Russia was to find during its occupation of Poland in the 19th century (Hartwell 2016). However, colonization can result in successful institutional transplantation when it creates institutions where they did not actually exist (De Jong et al. 2002). In the economic literature, there is a burgeoning research stream on the persistence of such institutions even after colonization has ended, with papers such as those by Grosfeld et al. (2013), Grosfeld and Zhuravskaya (2015), or Becker et al. (2016) showing how occupation under various empires has resulted in specific patterns of economic activity, ideologies, or political behaviours which persist to this day. Thus, understanding the past, and even the long distant past, is crucial for understanding the institutional basis of Kazakhstan in the present day, given its particular history of domination and colonization by others.

Finally, and crucially, before we begin our brief tour of Kazakhstan's institutional history, the importance of Mongol and Russian occupation is not the only factor in the development of Kazakhstan's indigenous institutions. Indeed, it would be folly to attribute all of Kazakhstan's current institutional matrix to the actions of outsiders, as such an approach not only robs Kazakhs of any agency, it simply is not accurate. The Kazakh Khanate, flourishing mainly in the 16th and 17th centuries but in reality stretching over 400 years, was also a fundamental step on the path towards developing Kazakh national institutions (as we will see). Similar to countries such as Ukraine, which was shaped by the Crimean Khanate (Hartwell 2016), this semi-monarchical governance was to have important ramifications for the development of Kazakhstan's identity and politics, and even today remains a link to an earlier time of independence. While we cannot claim that any institutional memory has persisted from the long-ago era of the Khanate, the same forces which gave birth to its structures are still at play in present-day Nur-Sultan and Almaty. This reality does perhaps take us full circle back to the idea of identity and culture, but it also shows that culture itself is endogenous, malleable, and subjected to institutional influence, especially when it interacts with prevailing economic activities.

Tribes, Mongols, and Golden Hordes

Unlike the collapse of the Soviet Union, which provides us with a clearly and legally defined definition of the start of the modern nation of Kazakhstan, tracing the origins of a pre-modern "Kazakhstan" is more difficult, and is a task best left to historians, anthropologists, and archaeologists. Ayupova (1998) notes that the first appearance of what could be considered a Kazakh "state" occurred in the seventh century, with the formation of the West Turkic Khaganate, an independent entity which split from the Turkic Khaganate of Mongolia in the late sixth century. The Khaganate, a confederation of ten separate tribal groupings known as *On Oq* or the "ten arrows" (Golden 2011), stretched over an area encompassing all of the modern-day Central Asian republics and much of southern Siberia (Abazov 2008 calls this region their heartland), but also pushed west during its conquests, reaching Transcaucasia (and modern-day Georgia and Armenia). As Ayupova (1998:49) notes,

> The West Turkish Kaganate [*sic*] left a long-lasting imprint in the area including Semireche and the whole of modern central and western Kazakhstan. Most of the Turkish people continued tribal organization and a nomadic way of life, but in Semireche, even at this point, a settled way of life reigned … Thus, it is not surprising that it was in Semireche that centers of a state system appeared, such as public power and territorial organization and management.

While the governance system of the overall Turkic Khaganate was focused on the Khan, a despot with unlimited power, the workings of the independent Western Turkic Khaganate were somewhat less absolutist, mainly by happenstance rather than by design: according to Kundakbayeva (2021), the tribal nobility of the Western Khaganate was riven by strife and inter-court politics, meaning that merchants were able to exercise power as a balancing force in the political life of the Khaganate. The locus of this commercial power was Bukhara (Burton 1997), but Sogdian traders located in southern Kazakhstan, modern-day Kyrgyzstan, and throughout Uzbekistan and Tajikistan had a firm command of commerce traversing the Silk Road (Normatov 2020). Ayupova (1998:50) also notes that these various power poles resulted in "complex and stratified societies consisting of aristocrats, urban traders, oasis farmers, pastoral nomads, and a professional warrior class sufficiently skilled to prevent the Arab armies from crossing the Syr-Darya River until 739 A.D." However, as is so often the case with empire, the Western Khanagate engaged in a serious of pointless wars of conquest which brought no real benefit to its rulers (Abazov 2008), leaving it weakened and totally subjugated under the Tang Dynasty in the late seventh century (Lewis 2012).

The ensuing three centuries saw a succession of Khanates come and go across the land which now makes up modern-day Kazakhstan, with much intrigue occurring to the east (in the Uyghur Khaganate just across the Tian Shan mountains, which also oversaw the break-up of the Turgesh Khaganate, one of the many successors of the Western Turkic Khaganate) and with the added challenge of Arab incursions into the region as emissaries of Islam (Abazov 2008). Indeed, the entire region of Transoxiana (the former Western Turkestan) was to experience a bewildering yet small-scale shifting of tribal alliances and unions, as from the 800s through the early 11th century, Kazakh territory transformed from the so-called Kangar Union (referring to the Kengeres or Pecheneg tribes) to the Kimek Khaganate after the Oghuz Turks seceded from the Union and waged war with the Kimeks on the Kangars (Kovalev and Mako 2016).

Zimonyi (2018) notes that the Kimek Khaganate is one of the earliest examples of a "Kazakh" state, with Kumekov (2013) stressing the importance of the Khaganate in the formation of Kazakh identity; this view contrasts with that of Omarov (2006), who instead focuses on the western Khazar state (encompassing modern Atyrau and Aktau) as the first Kazakh state, even though its gaze was decidedly different (and far removed) from the more eastern successors of the Turkic Khaganate. At the same time, Ayupova (1998) asserts that the Karakhanid Khaganate that ruled from the tenth to the 13th centuries is properly thought of as the early Kazakh proto-state, mainly because – despite its lands being to the south of the Kimek Khaganate and existing roughly in parallel – it encompassed tribes which fit the "traditional' view of Kazakhs, namely steppe-dwelling nomadic peoples.

The debate over the "proper" precursor state may continue to rage (and to be coloured by the current political situation), but the reality for our purposes is that such a debate does not matter much for understanding the institutional evolution of the region, as each Khaganate had very similar institutional structures, both political and economic. The political organization of the Khaganate, noted as the "highest" form of political institutions by Kovalev and Mako (2016), was ultimately centralized in the Khan, with the administration of territory being done via his staff and supplemented by viceroys and embassies in outer regions of the empire to keep an eye on the periphery; at the same time, "this administrative system [was] superimposed on a complex hierarchy built on the combination of political, ethnical, social and other principles" (Vasyutin 2019:94). These undercurrents, combined with the lack of a permanent ruling class (i.e. a bureaucracy), meant that the centralization of politics was not always complete. Indeed, when such an administrative apparatus failed in the case of nomadic peoples (Kradin 2002) or – in another context – among mountain or other tribes on the periphery (Scott 2009), Khans retreated inward to their inner circle, dispensed rents to maintain their status, and outsourced politics to traditional clan or tribal relationships and only demanded tribute in return (Vasyutin 2019). In this sense, the vagaries of attempting to rule over large territories with highly mobile populations led to minimalist state-building and the preservation of privilege above all else.

As noted above in the context of the Western Turkic Khaganate, these later nomadic empires such as the Kimek, Khazar, or Karakhanid Khaganates also had another power source to contend with, namely the merchant class. Being situated on various branches of the Silk Road and, working as intermediaries for traders travelling either to east or west, the merchants were able to create separate power poles via craft production and trade. In the Khazar Khaganate, for example, "Unlike those nomads who were dependent upon the food, goods, and luxury items coming from sedentary neighbors, the khaganate was remarkably self-sufficient" (Noonan 2007:209). Thus the political institutional form of the Khaganate could survive but it was highly dependent upon the revenues generated by merchants (Polek 2013). Similar effects were to be found in the Kimek Khaganate, where control of and participation in caravan routes (especially those related to the fur trade) resulted in revenue and stability for the political masters (Kovalev and Mako 2016), but the creation of rents also caused political elites to overreach in later years as they became addicted to the revenue (see Barisitz 2017 on this problem in the Oghuz Khaganate). Moreover, commerce resulted in a boon familiar to any student of growth economics, namely a "technology shock," as breeding of better pack animals and improved organizational forms of caravans (Abazov 2008) helped to increase trade and, by extension, wealth.

In a twist that we will see recurring throughout the history of Central Asia more broadly and Kazakhstan in particular, the merchant class in the khaganates of Central Asia also were able to influence somewhat the political process for their own benefit. While nowhere near as influential as the oligarchs or businessmen of the modern post-Soviet period in Russia or Ukraine, and lacking any sort of democratic process to facilitate entrance to political institutions, merchants were able to utilize the crucial nature of their service (especially in relation to revenues of the state) to funnel what we would now call "public works projects" in their own direction. In particular, merchants and their trade were instrumental in convincing Khans to maintain and expand the network of toll roads constructed by both the Chinese and Arabic invaders (Barisitz 2017), thereby facilitating easier commerce and, not coincidentally, control over the routes followed by traders (i.e. allowing for points where tolls and taxes could be collected). At the same time, the importance of trade to the khaganates meant that "public" funding was also spent – perhaps more importantly – on fortresses and other military infrastructure for the protection of commerce (Diyarbekirli 1992), ensuring that traders would continue to traverse a certain khaganate rather than take another branch of the Silk Road. Much as with modern investment climate reforms, such competition for revenues led to a "race to the top" and "the steppe states did all they could to protect the caravans" (Asadov 2000:180).

This of course did not mean that modern market mechanisms were allowed to flourish, and many of the institutional prerequisites for a market economy were sorely lacking. As Barisitz (2017:87) notes in respect to the Karakhanid Khaganate, "All lands were declared to be the leader's property. The state was divided into many small units with unstable borders. These administrative units—appanages—were distributed among members of the ruling clan and high-ranking representatives of the nomadic nobility." Throughout the period of the Khaganate's existence, public control of prices for staple products such as meat persisted, and the emergence of Ibrahim Tamgach Khan in the 11th century led to a centralization of money creation (see Davidovich 1998); prior to Ibrahim, rulers of the appanages were often allowed to coin their own money (Barisitz 2017), fostering a substantial competition in money as well as trade. The centralization of coinage may have created standardization (Davidovich 1998 claims that this standardization was beneficial for commerce overall), but the extension of currency reforms across the Khaganate led to uneven effects (not unsurprising for a common currency across many different economic units). Tempted as all rulers are by the need for cheap money, debasement of the unified currencies occurred throughout Ibrahim's rule, causing inflation across the Khaganate (Baipakov et al. 1997); it was especially serious in modern-day southern Kazakhstan (Barisitz 2017). However, despite these deleterious issues, which could have and probably did stifle commerce, Ibrahim Tamgach Khan was also known for supporting commercial endeavours, for showing "respect for property, trade, and currency circulation" (Davidovich 1998:135), and in particular for ensuring the security of commerce by "uprooting" thieves and bandits.

Unfortunately for both political and economic institutions throughout the region, the Karakhanid Khaganate dissipated in the early 13th century under the pressure of external conquest (in particular the Persian Khwarazmian Dynasty across the southern portions of Kazakhstan) and was subjected to the defining event of the Middle Ages, the Mongol conquest of Central Asia. Starting with the conquering of Kara (Qara) Khitai, the Chinese Khaganate which covered most of modern-day Xinjiang up to the Tian Shan mountains, in 1216, Genghis Khan expanded his reach into Central Asia over the coming years. The defining event precipitating the invasion came from the Seljuk Empire, which covered much of present-day south-western Kazakhstan; as Hiro (2009:19) notes, "the Seljuks became power-drunk and overconfident" and "aroused [Genghis Khan's] wrath in 1218 when they executed his emissary and decapitated 450 tradesmen for continuing to trade with the Mongols. Within two years, Genghis Khan would march into Bukhara and avenge the killing of his envoy with a massacre of 30,000 people." As part of this conquest, Genghis defeated the Khwarazmian Dynasty and Samarkand, moving small garrisons into the steppes north of the Aral Sea (Abazov 2008) and capturing cities such as Otrar, claimed by modern Kazakh ethnologists as a uniquely "Kazakh" state (Diener 2002).

The effect of the Mongol conquest cannot be understated in terms of its effect on future policies in the proto-state of Kazakhstan (and into the post-Soviet era; see Olcott 2010), but for our purposes, the conquering of Kazakhstan by the Mongols also presaged changes in the institutional evolutionary paths of the region. The most immediate effects which the Mongol conquest brought were an assault on and the destruction of many of the economic underpinnings of the nomadic and pastoral life that the tribes of modern-day Kazakhstan pursued. As Abazov (2008:50) notes, the negative supply shock of invasion decimated the economic institutions of Central Asia:

> The region lost a significant proportion of its population, especially educated and skilled professionals. Estimates of human losses vary between two and four million people out of a total population of between 10 and 16 million. The entire economy of the region was destroyed, as well as local, regional and international trade with prosperous neighbors in the south and west. Many cities and areas took from 30 to 50 years to recover; some never recovered at all.

This massive negative shock was truly exogenous and a one-time occurrence, however, and the Mongols appear to have chanced upon an early "solution" to the institutional transplantation problem, one that would be familiar to any student of Second World War reconstruction (Jacoby 2007): it is easiest to transplant institutions where none existed before and the territory is *tabula rasa*, but since countries are never blank slates, it is only after destruction (and occupation) that new institutional paths may be laid down.[1] After the razing of much of what had been built previously, the Mongols were to embark on a path of institutional expansion via conquest and subjugation which was to occur for another century or more. In fact, after the death of Genghis Khan in 1227, his sons pushed westward past the Volga and into the Caucasus, Bulgaria, Poland, and Hungary, wreaking destruction wherever they conquered but also seeding the territory with new institutional mechanisms.

Moreover, the scale of destruction of existing institutions was uneven. Unlike regions in China and Afghanistan which refused to submit voluntarily to the Mongol armies – and thus faced certain annihilation and/or replacement – the peoples of the Kazakh steppe were quick to accept the reality on the ground and retained some degree of autonomy and, importantly, their leadership structures (Barisitz 2017). This did not mean that their governance structures survived intact, however, and early settlements (*auls*) along the Silk Road were dispersed and, more importantly, tribal distinctions were vitiated in favour of more formalized territorial administration (Kupbaeva et al. 2018). Moreover, the trend towards standardization which began in early khaganates also was maintained by the Mongols in the form of the *yassa* (*yāsā*), a set of acts and legal documents forming a body of law binding on the Mongol people and all nomadic people whom they subjugated (Morgan 1986); notably, this did not apply to the sedentary vassals of Russia, China, or Persia (Riasanovsky 1948).

The *yassa* was concerned mainly with criminal justice and the organization of a rudimentary legal system centred on the Khan that dispensed the death penalty regularly (Morgan 1986); however, it also had economic ramifications. According to Barisitz (2017:100), "As trade was important to the Mongols, Genghis Khan promoted the free and unencumbered circulation of merchandise throughout his empire and, as far as possible, beyond. He and Ögöday [his third son] relaunched transcontinental Eurasian long-distance [Silk Road] trade." As part of this emphasis on commerce, the *yassa* contained instruction on the use of common lands by neighbourhood groupings (Mearns 1993), as well as defining measurements and standardization for counting livestock (Tyukhteneva 2017). Concurrently, the Mongol Empire after Genghis's death also instituted a large-scale postal and messenger system (*yam*), important for delivering edicts from the Khan to the conquered lands but also used as a means to help merchants in dealing with the far-flung portions of the empire (Morgan 2007). As Bira (1998:263) notes, the *yam* "system of communication greatly favored commercial travel," as the empire subsidized commercial trade via preferential access to the horse relay system of the *yam* (Barfield 2001), while "the caravan trade was generally protected and encouraged' (Bira 1998:263). As economists were to start to advocate 500 years later, the dismantling of trade barriers and in particular the removal of borders and customs posts led to lower prices and increased volumes of trade (Masselos 2010).[2]

As this conquest continued, however, the difficulty of ruling such a massive land mass – combined with infighting among Genghis's sons and grandsons – led to a fracturing of the Empire and the political institutional structure also began to crack. The westernmost portion of the Mongol conquests acted as a de facto Khaganate under the name of "the Golden Horde," covering the steppe lands of modern-day Kazakhstan as the easternmost part of the horde. Much as with the overall Mongol Empire, the Golden Horde was quite concerned with protecting trade and, as Schamiloglu (2018:21) notes, "the Golden Horde combined both the function of state security for international commerce and the function of sponsorship of marketplaces under a single state apparatus." The diversity of the Golden Horde's landscape meant that there was a diversity of production within the Khaganate, with the nomadic lifestyle of its easternmost regions being supplemented by extensive agricultural abilities further west, especially in what is today southern Russia and eastern Ukraine in the Black Earth Region (Nedashkovskii 2009). At the same time, additional institutional innovations began to blossom, including the organization of business structures similar to a modern corporation, with requirements for separate books of accounts and the recording of transactions and revenues (Kiliç 2018). Additionally, the Golden Horde had another institutional innovation to offer the Kazakh steppe, namely the involvement of women in the political and commercial realm of the empire. Most famous of them all was Taydula, the wife of Öz Beg Khan, who used her position to both advocate for Christian communities and to involve herself in commercial endeavours and policies (Kovács 2020). Supplemented by a sound money policy, and in particular the minting of standardized silver coins, the Golden Horde was to preside over a revitalization of trade and a more prosperous economy for both the nomads and the more sedentary denizens (Akhmedov 1998). Perhaps most importantly, the Golden Horde was also able to establish key trading relationships within Europe, particularly with Genoese merchants, and a booming trade in both craft production and metals developed throughout the 1300s (Jackson 2005).

The time of the Golden Horde also coincided with the formal adoption of Islam across the region, spearheaded by the same Öz Beg Khan in the early 14th century (who was converted by the mystical Baba Tükles; see DeWeese 1994), but this shift immediately affected only the arid regions of western Kazakhstan (modern-day Atyrau and Aktau on the Caspian Sea and inland as far as the town of Sygnak). This obviously was not the region's first interaction with Islam, as the Arabic incursions between the eighth and tenth centuries introduced the idea of Islam and most of the sedentary populations of southern Central Asia (especially in modern-day Uzbekistan) were converted, but the nomadic peoples of the Kazakh steppe were less affected (Yemelianova 2014). Indeed, pre-Islamic beliefs of the Kazakh steppe people persisted throughout the turn of the millennium, with the spread of Islam occurring mainly among elites and only slowly moving through the different strata of society (Kaynar and Sakhitzhanova 2016). But the adoption of Islam as the "state religion" under Öz Beg Khan accelerated the adoption of Islam by nomads on Kazakh lands, even as the Golden Horde pushed deeper into Russian and subjugated lands of Muscovy, however, as Omelicheva (2011) correctly notes, the stubborn nomads refused to be bound by the hierarchical structure of Islam and instead utilized the idea of being a "Muslim" to refer to membership of a like-minded community rather than strict adherence to Islamic law. In any event, the ties to Islam had been forged and the influence of Islam on local institutions was to grow in the coming centuries (Yemelianova 2014).

The Golden Horde's dominance over the Kazakh lands was to come to an end due to two specific events, with the first and most important being the ascendance of Timur bin Taraghay Barlas (better known as Timur the Lame or "Tamerlane" in the West) in the late 14th century. From 1391 to 1395, Timur's armies continued their push through Central Asia, building on successes in the Fergana Valley, northern Persia, and Afghanistan, and defeated the leader of the Golden Horde, Tokhtamysh, during two separate major military encounters (Abazov 2008). Tokhtamysh had himself been successful at military expansion and in uniting the separate factions of the horde, conquering Azerbaijan and overcoming resistance in Muscovy, but his attempted conquest of Bukhara led to irreconcilable differences with Timur and, eventually, the eastern portion of the horde falling under Timur's suzerainty. As Hiro (2009) notes, the rule of Timur helped to stamp the regions of Transoxiana with a decidedly Turkic character, nearly eradicating the last vestiges of Persian culture which had existed, while also establishing Samarqand as a major city and centre of the empire.

From an economic and institutional standpoint, however, the ferocity of Timur's conquests had a massively disruptive effect on trade routes, destroying cities along the Silk Road routes (Gilomen 2014), and leading to higher prices in the region due to shortages, all at a time when price inflation was becoming a problem globally (Fleet 1999). Moreover, as Barisitz (2017) notes, the gilded success of Samarqand was accomplished mainly by plunder and expropriation, with heavy tributes levied on subjugated peoples and physical relocation of tradespeople (including via slavery; see Levi 2002) to Samarqand to serve Timur's purposes. Even when there were moves towards the introduction of beneficial economic institutions – including the most beneficial of all, the right to own property – the structure of the rights conferred meant that they were merely "a form of servile landholding under the aegis of the state, in its capacity as the supreme proprietor of the lands conveyed" (Ashrafyan 1998:340).

The cumulative economic effect of the revenge-laden rampage in the Kazakh steppe lands (and elsewhere) was to shift important trading routes south towards lands of relative peace, leading to a substantial decline in trade and, subsequently, standards of living along the "northern" route of the Silk Road (Barisitz 2017). Kauz (2009) went so far as to note that the massive shock of Timur's conquests, resulting in millions of deaths and the decimation of the extensive human capital which had accumulated in the region, was to end Central Asia as a world economic power indefinitely. Indeed, as Norel (2009) was to boldly assert, the Mongol and Timurid conquests were to shift the balance of global economic power away from Central Asia to the Italian city-states of Genoa and Venice, with the Silk Road trade enabling the emergence of capitalism in the West, albeit that the destruction in the East was preventing these same benefits from accruing. Thus, despite the strides made institutionally in the Turkic Khaganates and then in the Turkic lands under Mongol rule, the dawn of the 15th century and the conquests of Timur meant that the heart of the empire was privileged to the exclusion of elsewhere, with the resulting "brain drain" and institutional destruction hitting the heart of the Kazakh steppe (Abazov 2008).

The Uzbek and, ultimately, Kazakh Khanate

The sudden death of Timur in 1405 following an ill-advised winter military campaign meant that, in the first instance, the uneasy succession process was to begin again, with all the strife and conflict it entailed; second, it also meant that outside competitors were quick to seize on the power vacuum, and in this case, it meant the quick rise of the Uzbek Khanate over the lands of modern-day Kazakhstan. The Uzbek Khanate did not last as long as other ruling arrangements in the Kazakh steppe,[3] but it swiftly consolidated its power over the steppe lands, benefiting from seizing richer towns first to fund its conquests (Barisitz 2017). From 1428 to roughly the mid-15th century, the Uzbek Khanate drew on both its nomadic routes and its sedentary peoples but retained the Timurid style of governance (even though it clashed with the actual Timurid successors to the south), meaning an emphasis on predation rather than proto-legalism and almost constant infighting among leaders (Trepavlov 2018). Elsewhere in former lands of the Golden Horde, economic institutions were being built: Ulugh Beg in Samarqand, for example, was both instrumental in the ascendance of Uzbek Khan Abu'l Khayr and also in creating monetary reforms and stability for commerce to flourish, emphasizing trade with India and infrastructure above all else (Mukminova 1998). However, in the lands of Abu'l Khayr, the desire for expansion meant that warfare continued unabated, disrupting commerce as the Khanate underwent a long-term plan for expansion (Kim 2009). These plans meant that, while reforms focused on governance and the economy were to follow in the years of the 16th century (Kilic-Schubel 2004), the 15th century remained a time for conquest rather than creation.

Facing this maelstrom of military activity, and on the heels of setbacks experienced by Abu'l Khayr against the Oirat Mongols to the east of the Khanate, a nomadic rebellion against the ruling Uzbek Khanate was led by Zhanibek and Kirai (sons of Barak Khan from the White Horde) across the steppe (Olcott 1995). The tension between nomads and sedentary people had existed seemingly since the beginning of time, and the term "Kazakh" was first applied to those tribal Uzbeks of the steppe who broke free of the Abu'l Khayr regime and formed their own confederation: as noted by Barisitz (2017:147), the term itself meant "fugitives, freebooters, roamers" in Turkic. This confederation, known as the Kazakh Khanate, consolidated itself in south-eastern Kazakhstan during the 1450s and 1460s, but brought large numbers of migrants from the Uzbek Khanate, nomads who were dissatisfied with the Uzbek rule and looking to become part of a new political organization (Dzhunusova 2004). In short order, the Khanate expanded along the Syr Darya river valley in southern and south-western Kazakhstan, aggrandizing territory in order to support their animals (searching for pastureland; see Olcott 1995) and especially clashing with its former allies in the fragmented Uzbek state, namely the Khanates of Khiva and Kokand (Zardykhan 2002).

At the same time, it formed a capital city in Turkestan and oversaw the transition to a "viable economic system, self-regulating and self-sufficient" (Olcott 1995:9). In fact, the Kazakh Khanate, in addition to being the ethnogenesis of the "Kazakh" people, also put in place many of the governance structures that the mainly nomadic people of the steppe were to follow for the next 300 years. As Zardykhan (2002) notes, the Khanate was a unified political entity but achieving the "unification" of some other Khanates was a tall order for the leaders of this proto-state, as "the ambition of Kazakh khans almost always exceeded their ability to unify the tribes under their nominal control, given the great authority wielded by local and regional subordinates" (Lazzerini 2016:1). Although it has been generally accepted that the actual founding of the Khanate occurred between 1465 and 1472 (Kazakh President Nursultan Nazarbayev proclaimed in 2014 that the year 2015 would be the 550th anniversary of Kazakhstan, thus settling on 1465 as the founding date), Berdyguzhin (2016) notes that it was not until 1511, with the ascendance of Zhanibek Khan's son Kasym (Khassym, Kassym, or Qasym are other transliterations in use), that the Khanate began to come into its own as a distinct political entity.

The Khanate reached its zenith during this period and well into the 16th century, as the foundations which Kasym laid began to resemble a modern state, replete with a legal code and foreign policy.[4] With regard to a legal code, although the governance structure in the Khanate was based on traditional nomadic tents of seniority, clan, and primogeniture – and the relationships between the Khan and local leaders were fluid, depending upon status and context (Erofeeva 2004) – the confederation of Turkic, Hun, and Mongol tribes existed as a political union (Olcott 1995), meaning bonds on the basis of hierarchy and rules rather than kinship. The first code of laws (*Zhargy*) in the Kazakh lands were introduced by Kasym in 1520, known variously as either "the Golden Path," "the Bright Path," or (perhaps more accurately) "the Treacherous Path"; as a first attempt at codification of the law of the steppe, the "path" focused on property rights, a criminal code, and other articles on religious observation, military law, and civil ceremonies and public obligations (Ryszhanova and Complak 2018). Based on a set of ideas known as "military democracy" (Margulan 1975), the code of laws did not deviate substantially from customary law at the time, especially with regard to the administration of common use lands and military obligations (Barisitz 2017), with the power of the Khan deriving from their military skill. However, its foray into formalizing what had heretofore been "customary" was a key step forward into creating a political state which had some facets of representative democracy as currently understood. As Dzhunusova (2004:15–16) notes,

> The enthronement of a khan was traditionally accompanied by the ancient ceremony of raising him on a large piece of white felt, which symbolized the purity of his intentions and of the origins and wealth of his clan … The ritual of raising the elected khan on the white felt as a symbol of his authority, in the presence of the people and with their express approval, was testimony to the Kazakhs' political rights, proof that their political culture could not be reduced to patron-client relations but included elements of democracy.

This did not mean that the title of Khan was akin to that of President or Prime Minister in modern parlance, however, as the power conferred by the title of Khan was not vested in the institutionalized office or position but instead rested within the particular person, meaning that shifting fortunes could leave a particular leader out in the cold rather quickly (Dzhunusova 2004). Yet, Ayupova (1998:51), being perhaps even more direct in tracing the antecedents of the modern Kazakh state to the Khanate, argued that "from the very beginning of its own Kazakh Khanate, the idea of freedom and independence became the national idea of the Kazakh people," an assertion that is not wholly incompatible with the ability to turn out a politician if they incurred the wrath of their subjects.

And yet, despite this early manifestation of democracy, the creation of a modern administrative apparatus was still centuries away, as the first codification of legislation co-existed with a strict and sometimes confusing social hierarchy. All Kazakh subjects were classified into one of two social categories, either White Bone (*aksuyek*) or Black Bone (*kara-suyek*), "differing not so much in economic as in political and legal attributes" (Dzhunusova 2004:14). The White Bone were the elite of the social strata, divided into two separate aristocratic groups, the *tore* (descendants of Genghis Khan) and the *khoja*, who were religious leaders (Kassymova et al. 2012), enjoying several privileges not accorded to others, including the right of tribute (Bikenov et al. 2016) and exemption from punishment (Dzhunusova 2004), and were the only class which could ever hope to ascend to the position of Khan (Erofeeva 2004). However, much as in English class structures, members of the Black Bone were paradoxically freer to pursue their own interests and less bound by rigid conventions associated with aristocracy, leading to a wide variety of members of the class but with plenty of opportunities for upward mobility (Olcott 1995). Indeed, as the Khanate progressed into the 17th century, many merchants from the Black Bone were to amass influence and to have a say in the political direction of the state (Bodger 1980).

Another crucial aspect of Kazakh social relations during this time was the embrace of Islam, as "the development of economic and cultural relations between the Kazakhs and the sedentary Central Asian populations in the 16th–17th centuries … promoted the intensive dissemination and reinforcement of Islam" (Dzhunusova 2004:20). While Islam, as noted above, had been present throughout the Kazakh steppe since the 1300s, the nomadic lifestyle of the progenitors of the Kazakhs had been ill-suited to the Islamic lifestyle (although various Islamic tenets had made their way into customary law in the Khanate). The expansion of the Khanate, its formalized social tenets, and its move towards more sedentary endeavours in particular made Islam more accessible, however, as merchants became instrumental in the spread of Islam throughout the Khanate and religious leaders were elevated to the status of White Bone elites (Baipakov and Kumekov 2003). But even with the renaissance in Islamic ideas across the Kazakh steppe, old habits die hard, and the spread of Islam among the Kazakhs was circumscribed to the elite; as Olcott (1995) notes (and Baipakov and Kumekov 2003 echo), the average Kazakh of the Black Horde had little use for or knowledge of the tenets of Islam, and its renaissance tended to be confined to more sedentary populations than nomads and pastoral herders. For the man on the steppe, traditional forms of worship such as animism and/or ancestor veneration came first, with perhaps bits and pieces of Islam assimilated but never dominating.

This demarcation between White/Black Bone and the demarcation between Islamicized elites and animist nomads made societal and political relationships even more complicated by the sheer fact that they were replicated three times over in the Kazakh Khanate from the mid-16th century onward. The size of the Khanate meant that the confederation was soon separated into three separate hordes (*zhuze*) based on geography: the *Uly zhuz* (Greater Horde), based in Semirechiye and south-western portions of the Kazakh steppe; the *Kishy zhuz* (Lesser Horde), which was based to the north-west; and the *Orta zhuz* (Middle Horde), which was wedged between the other hordes (Esenova 2002; Diener 2002). The standing of an individual within the Kazakh Khanate was thus predicated not only on their socio-economic status but also their geographic location, and, in many ways, membership of a particular *zhuz* was (and still is) more important than the White/Black Bone demarcation. As Diener (2002) notes, the recent attempts by the government of the country of Kazakhstan to project back national continuity over the Kazakh steppe lands misses the point that any geographic grouping of nomads was just as likely to be absorbed by another confederation; thus, what made these groupings truly cohesive in terms of manners, customs, social interactions, and institutions, was their geographic positioning, i.e. their belonging to a specific horde.

Moreover, important for our discussion later in the book, the hordes remained fairly autonomous economically from one another, keeping to their own geographic area with regard to grazing and pasturing (Barisitz 2017). As Nichols (1997:1252) accurately assessed, the hordes were "virtually sovereign Khanates of their own." This is not to say that the economic life on the Kazakh steppe was stagnant nor does it imply that there were hard-and-fast boundaries among hordes which could have interrupted commerce. Indeed, the ties of ethnicity may have helped to overcome the pervasive lack of trust inherent in any economic transaction across the steppe (albeit on a smaller scale due to the cleavages among hordes and social classes). Ayupova (1998:51–52) describes the economy of the Khanate, noting that it was "based on nomadic cattle breeding and farming … [and] the region supplied neighboring China, the Central Asia Khanates, and Russia with products of animal husbandry such as cattle, skins, wool and fat in exchange for wheat, textiles, tools, and arms." While much of the early trade from the Khanate, emerging in the early to mid-15th century, was focused on acquiring goods from more sedentary neighbours (Zhappasov and Botash 2017) – sometimes by force (Rossabi 2014) – the Kazakh Khanate also witnessed the development of its own small urban centres (Sygnak and Desht-i Qipchaq primarily, but with Otrar also prominent) and especially the cultivation of settled and semi-settled agriculture (Dzhunusova 2004). Moreover, informal organizations began to arise among the settled populations to support trades and crafts, above all the formation of guilds to set standards and offer advancement for craftsmen (Baipakov and Kumekov 2003), an activity which eventually was prized by nomads as well (and who offered protection to guilds in return for goods; see Khazanov 2019).

The underpinning of this expansion into different forms of economic activity was a "quasi-feudal land ownership" structure, allowing local rulers to collect taxes from sedentary populations. While this system may have "point[ed] to a relatively high degree of nomadic-sedentary economic integration in the framework of the Kazakh Khanate" (Barisitz 2017:160), it also showed the lingering tensions between the nomadic Kazakhs and those who took up farming and/or remained in one place. In fact, this "integration" was very rarely of mutual benefit, as nomadic Kazakhs tended to regard sedentary farmers as "the enemy" due to their aggrandizement of pasture lands. To the nomads, wealth was linked to the size of a nomad's herd rather than to any permanent plot of land, and thus land had no intrinsic worth (Olcott 1995). This approach towards property, in addition to the nomadic dependence on natural resources in a sometimes unforgiving climate, set up the Khanate for a clash of interests between the nomads who required free roam pasture land, who lived off the land, and who struggled due to the elements (Baipakov and Kumekov 2003), and the sedentary farmers who also lived off the land but laid claim to a particular area and were able (in theory) to exclude others from utilizing these resources. The fact that nomads were the highest caste in the Khanate's complex social hierarchy meant that property rights, as it were, could be violated at any time and burdens (such as taxation or tribute) levied on the sedentary population (as noted in Barisitz 2017).

This state of affairs meant that even if formal legal structures were amassed, deriving from customary law, they tended to be related to issues that nomads felt were particularly important rather than to broader rules of the game. Dzhunusova (2004:20) supports this interpretation, stating that "customary law arose under the impact of the nomadic style of life. It expressed and preserved the values and ideals of nomadic culture and supported and served nomadic society." A key example of this development of law among the Kazakh people was the *Zhety Zhargi* (Seven Laws) of Tauke Khan, who ruled at the end of the 17th century during a time when the Kazakh Khanate was besieged by the Dzungar Khanate (see below) and was shrinking rapidly in influence and territory. The Seven Laws were highly influenced by Islamic *Shari'a* law and dealt mainly with the application of the death penalty for various crimes, including murder, theft, and treason (all transgressions which could threaten the unity of a tribal unit, but which also had broader applicability); indeed, five of the seven laws have capital punishment as their basis (Ruskulovna 2019). However, the last two laws deal specifically with disputes of interest to nomads: first, the case of conflict among individuals resulting in injury to a person's eyes; and second, the case of restitution for stealing a horse. These oddly specific laws, coupled with the surrounding customary rules regarding witnesses and the relative roles of men and women (Saira et al. 2015), had little value for urban dwellers and remained fairly narrowly circumscribed with regard to economic activity.

Despite this complex interaction of informal social and geographically determined economic institutional orderings within the Khanate, the 16th and 17th centuries did in fact witness the development of a cohesive and independent political unit on the territory of modern-day Kazakhstan which had been lacking in previous years. Dzhunusova (2004:16) commented that "periods of Kazakh unity occurred sporadically … because the khans of the other hordes acknowledged the military superiority of these individuals and were willing to defer to their authority," meaning that in many ways the proto-state of the Kazakh Khanate was a precursor of the modern nation of Kazakhstan. At the same time, the Kazakh Khanate also birthed the idea of a distinct ethnicity apart from Uzbeks for the steppe nomads, a construct which was to prove useful for both formal political institutions and, as noted above, economic ones. However, the power relations within the Khanate, including its reliance on client-patron relationships (Erofeeva 2004), and above all the nomadic spirit which refused to submit to any ruler for too long meant that the Kazakh Khanate could be no more than a transitional institutional structure from the traditional form of governance to the rapidly ascending modern nation-state. Moreover, as with so many empires in the region beforehand, the Khanate was beset with conflict, both internal and – much more detrimental for the integrity of the political union – external.

The main conflicts during the years of the Khanate came first and foremost from the south, and its rivalry with the Uzbek Khanates, but in time also from the Moghuls and, most devastatingly, the Dzungar Khanate, with alliances shifting rapidly and fluidly throughout the late 16th and the entire 17th centuries. Like Kondratiev waves, the Khanate appeared to wax and wane during this period, going through times of consolidation and decline and then emerging to expand, dependent upon the prevailing Khan at the time. During the 16th century, the Khanate reached its zenith and faced only sporadic resistance to its territorial expansion, but the 17th century was to bring a more existential threat from the unified Mongols (Oirat or Kalmuks/Kalmyks) from Xinjiang, the Dzungars, which resulted in a series of defeats and retreats across the Khanate (Baipakov and Kumekov 2003). By the time of the reign of Tauke Khan (1680–1718), the Dzungars had conquered all of southern Kazakhstan, razing cities such as Sairam to the ground, controlling trade routes, and choking off any external assistance or even economic activity (Olcott 1995). The fragmentation of the Khanate into three distinct hordes had made concerted resistance to the invaders difficult, and the success of the Dzungars resulted in even more fragmentation; it was not until the first half of the 18th century that the hordes were able to successfully unite once more to rebel against the Dzungars, but the success of the rebellion from 1726 to 1730 was fleeting and the Dzungars began to push back in 1731. The forced migration (the Kazakhs called it the "Great Retreat') to the west increasingly brought the Kazakhs closer to another expansionist power from its north, namely the Russian Empire, trapping the Kazakhs between two empires with designs on their ancestral homelands (Kim 2009).[5] It is here, with the Kazakh Khanate in a perilous state, that the fateful influence of Russia on the steppe begins, and where the history of the Kazakhs also takes a new path.

The Russian Empire Enters the Steppe

The Russian Empire has been the most important influence in Kazakh history over the past 300 years, and it is during the early 18th century that the story of Kazakhstan truly begins to take shape in Western historiography (mainly because the interaction with the expanding Russian Empire led to a proliferation of sources on the conditions of the Kazakh people at that time). Indeed, as nomadic peoples, the Kazakhs relied on customs and oral tradition, whether this was with regard to their laws (and the customary law or *adat* which formed the basis of the more codified laws of Kasym or Tauke) or their shaping of an ethnic and national narrative. By contrast, the Russians had a semi-modern state (notwithstanding their economic backwardness vis-à-vis the rest of Europe and their absolutist monarchy) and were well acquainted with modern innovations such as the printing press in order to record and disseminate information (Marker 2014). Moreover, as with the Russian Empire of the 21st century, the empire of the 16th through to the 20th centuries was very concerned with its own image and how this could enable voluntary cooperation and/or occupation, and thus the conquest of its periphery (not only in Central Asia but in the Caucasus and the Far East) needed to be recorded for posterity (LeDonne 2004).

Beyond these contrasts, the Russian Empire and the Kazakh Khanate had actually a long history of contact prior to the 18th century, even before the Duchy of Muscovy became a proper "empire" (dated usually to when Peter the Great was named Emperor in the late 17th century; see Noda 2016). Most prominently, the Siberian Khanate, another successor to the Golden Horde, was founded just to the north of the Kazakh steppe in the 15th century, approximately at the same time that the Kazakh Khanate was being consolidated, and the Turkic Khanate acted as a buffer between Muscovy to the north and the Kazakhs (as well as the Kipchaks) to the south. However, the recurrent attacks on Muscovy from the east – originating mainly from the Kazan Khanate, which marched on Moscow in 1439 – created an impetus for Russia to push its own borders outwards, and Russia spent over 100 years in conflict with Kazan before eventually overrunning the city's defences in 1552 (Pelenski 1967, 1974). With the conquering of Kazan, the Russian frontier and Russian fur traders in particular began to range further east, coming into contact with the Siberian Khanate and precipitating a number of skirmishes over the course of three decades (Lincoln 2007), which Russia used as a pretext for further expansion: as LeDonne (2004:32) notes,

"Russia's expansion across Siberia had little in common with its advance into the other two theaters. Distances were enormous, resistance was insignificant, local societies were loosely organized, and there was no danger of meeting the armed opposition of a powerful state." These facts meant that the Siberian Khanate was subjugated much more quickly as a result of a Russian expedition in 1582 (although resistance continued until 1598 and the precise extent of Siberian forces was underestimated; see Lincoln 2007), with the city of Tobolsk founded in 1590 as the centre of Russia's power in Siberia (Ostrowski 2016).

The establishment of a permanent settlement in Siberia by the Russians perhaps made it inevitable that there would be friction with the Kazakhs, which now bordered directly on the Russian Empire, but the immediate effect of Russia's expansion was détente, as Russian aims lay further east rather than to the south (LeDonne 2004). In the previous 50 years, there had been some trade contacts between the Russians and the Kazakh hordes, but the first attempt at formal contact came about as Muscovy sought allies against the Siberian Khanate and sent a mission (unsuccessfully, as the envoy was killed en route) to enlist the Kazakhs (Olcott 1995). For much of the 17th century, however, the demarcation line between the Kazakhs and the Russian Empire was mainly peaceful, with Russian fortifications built and migration to frontier lands "pushing up" against the Kazakhs but with no overt conflict (Shalgimbekov et al. 2020).

It was not until events on the steppe, independent of decisions taken in Moscow, helped to create an opening for the Russians, an opening which – when combined with Russian interests that were waning elsewhere – gave a push to formal expansion into the steppe. In particular, the continued onslaught of the Dzungars and other enemies throughout the 17th century meant that the beleaguered Kazakhs were in search of allies. As early as the 1580s, missions from the Khanate to Russia seeking arms and military support had been undertaken, but with little success (Olcott 1995); by the 1680s, Tauke Khan had sent emissaries to Moscow for assistance against the Dzungars, which again proved unsuccessful but the overtures and subsequent successes of the Kazakhs on their own meant that the foundation was laid for future Russo-Kazakh alliances (LeDonne 2004). These future "alliances," however, were, like other alliances entered into by the Russian Empire, extremely one-sided and generally resulted in total subjugation of local institutions and politics to rule from Moscow. This was, unfortunately for the Kazakhs, to be the case, as the Dzungar invasion continued into the early 18th century (as noted above), putting the Kazakh hordes into an increasingly precarious position.

At the same time that the Kazakh hordes were disintegrating after decades of conflict, within the Russian Empire strategic imperatives were also changing. In 1722, Peter the Great outlined a new strategy for Russia in Central Asia, noting that "although the Kyrgyz-Kaisak [*sic*] horde is a steppe and frivolous people, only to all Asian countries and lands this horde is a key and a gate; and for that reason, this horde needs to be under Russian protection, so that only through them in all countries the commons can have and to the Russian side useful measures" (quoted from the memoirs of diplomat Alexey Tekelev in Tasmagambetov 2005:219). Even before this explicit mention of Russian designs on the region, the expansion of Kazakh-Russian trade – and, much more importantly, the position of the Kazakh Khanate with relation to India and Persia – had led to Russia's growing interest in pacifying the steppe in the late 17th century, with a concomitant emphasis on increasing their influence to secure these vital trade routes (Olcott 1995). After quashing a rebellion from the Bashkirs, the Russians sought to construct a line of fortified settlements as a forward projection of power, in rapid succession moving in ethnic Russians and Cossacks to new settlements such as Omsk and Semipalatinsk (Abazov 2008).

With the Kazakh steppe noted as a key for the developing future Russian policy towards the south, it was no surprise that the next plea from help from the Kazakh hordes to Russia in fighting the Dzungars was looked upon quite favourably. In 1726, facing repeated attacks, a summit of Kazakh tribal leaders and Khans across the hordes (*kurultai*) was convened, at which it was decided that emissaries would be sent to St Petersburg to ask for Russian assistance; however, taking it upon himself to represent all the hordes as a unified whole (which, by that point, they most certainly were not), Abulkhair, the Khan of the Lesser Horde, altered the instructions of the ambassadors to ask for more than an alliance and actually for the Junior and Middle Hordes to become protectorates of the Russian Empire (Bodger 1980; Kadyrbekov and Veselov 2019). Although such a course was not approved by his own advisers and nobles, Abulkhair's terms were more than generous to the Russians, promising loyal service, payment, and repatriation of hostages in exchange for Russian protection, a bargain which was eagerly approved by Empress Anna, and which included additional obligations regarding the safety of Russian merchants (Kendirbay 2020).

Although Abulkhair was pleased with this turn of events and pledged an oath to the Russian Empire, "to the Kazakh leaders, these oaths were purely formal, implying a loose, voluntary form of patronage which could be unilaterally abrogated when convenient" (Bodger 1980:40).[6] Abulkhair himself was not always the most loyal subject, as, despite his overtures to the Russians, he also attempted to make a separate peace with the Dzungars and sided with the Bashkirs against Russia in 1738 (and even attacked the fortification of Orenburg; see Olcott 1995). The continued predations of the Dzungars, however, meant that the Kazakhs were in no position to play rivals off one another, and in short order the "protection" of the Russian Empire was extended not only for the Lesser Horde but to the Middle Horde and parts of the Greater Horde, as these Khans requested Russian intervention against a new Dzungar invasion (Baipakov and Kumekov 2003).

While Russia's incursion into the Kazakh Khanate can be seen as opportunistic, and definitely returned far less than Abulkhair and other leaders believed would be attained, there was some hope on the Kazakh side that Russia would remain at arm's length, and early moves after the Empress accepted the Kazakh application seemed to support such a belief: Olcott (1995) notes that the Empress Anna took her time (and it was hotly debated in St Petersburg) before the Kazakh application for Russian suzerainty was granted, did not immediately demand tribute from her new subjects (as she was counselled it would cost more to collect than it was worth), and maintained a minimum of contact with the Kazakhs (and, importantly, Russian maps from the era showed that there was actually a dividing line between the Khanate and Russian territory; see Afinogenov 2019). Indeed, after a century of decline, it appeared that appealing to the Russians, the predominant military power in the region, was a savvy move, as otherwise the fragmented Khanate was destined to be not long for this world (Bodger 1980 disputes this argument, noting that the Dzungar threat was perhaps overstated and definitely underplayed in the contemporary notes of Abulkhair and other Kazakh leaders).

However, even though the remoteness of the Kazakh Khanate (and the Greater Horde in particular) meant that immediate absorption into Russia was not feasible for the empire (Barisitz 2017), there was also no immediate *need* to absorb the Kazakh lands, as other avenues were already moving in that direction:

> From the middle of the eighteenth century onwards, Russia began to build lines of defense in Kazakhstan, along the rivers Yaik, Irtysh and Ishim. The defense works afforded great scope for the Russians to colonize Kazakhstan. They acquired the best and most fertile land, with the result that the area of grazing land was reduced and traditional migrations were disrupted.
>
> (Baipakov and Kumekov 2003:100)

Additionally, the Dzungars continued to pick apart the Khanate even while under nominal protection from the Russians (Barisitz 2017), who saw little advantage to actually utilizing their military power in favour of an unreliable ally that continued to attack Russian traders and settlements (Kendirbay 2020). This strategy, of pleading insufficient manpower while their erstwhile allies were once again suffering an onslaught, meant that not only would there be little resistance when Russia did choose to move in but that the Kazakhs would remain dependent upon the expanding defensive fortifications of the Russians when the situation became very grave. Given this longer-term strategy for eventually pushing south, it can be argued that "strategic imperial interests took clear precedence over economic ones" (although the economics of trade with India and Persia were undoubtedly a factor) and that "Russian imperialism [in the Kazakh Khanate] was as selfish, predatory, and exploitative as any[where else]" (Kazemzadeh 1974:195).

The shift towards the Kazakh lands becoming part of Russia proper accelerated in the second half of the 18th century after the Dzungars were decimated from their rear by the Chinese (Rossabi 2014) and the Kazakh hordes once again swore fealty to the Russian Tsar (Barisitz 2017). The death of Abulkhair following internal strife between his supporters and Sultan Barak of the Middle Horde further fragmented the Kazakhs, and the Russians pushed for his successor in the Lesser Horde, Nur Ali, as it was believed that he would be more pliant to Russian interests (Olcott 1995). The Russian presence was becoming much more pronounced in addition to working through a vassal, however: as noted above by Baipakov and Kumekov (2003), the Russians had already begun to enclose pastureland for themselves, awarding it to Cossack settlers and removing approximately 80,000 square kilometres from the Kazakhs by 1743 (LeDonne 2004). Shortly thereafter, in 1756, a decree (*ukase*) was also issued which prohibited the Kazakhs from grazing in the lands between the Ural and Volga Rivers (Bodger 1991), a reality which forced leaders of the Lesser and Middle Hordes to come to terms with the Chinese conquerors of the Dzungars in the hope of acquiring new pastureland to the east (Ablai, the Khan of the Middle Horde, actually swore his fealty to the Qing emperor precisely for this reason; see Olcott 1995). Concurrently, the Pugachev Rebellion in lands adjacent to the Lesser Horde gave the Kazakhs the ability to participate in armed actions against the Russians well beyond the cessation of hostilities in Russia proper, as well as to take advantage of Russian difficulties and reclaim pastureland in the "inner lands" between the Volga and the Urals (Bodger 1993). However, as Olcott (1995) shows brilliantly, any successes against the Russians were quickly reversed and instead led to continued strife within the Lesser Horde, perhaps demolishing any semblance of Kazakh unity for good.

The Clash of Institutions

These setbacks for the Kazakhs, as noted above, hastened their incorporation into the empire and the extinguishing of the institutional matrix which belonged to an independent Kazakh territory. Indeed, the Russian Empire was an entirely different creature in terms of its political and economic institutions, and thus the extension of its rule and absorption of the Kazakh Khanate was bound to have a profound effect on the economic development of the Kazakh steppe. While the realities of Kazakh life in the 18th century are far less covered than previous centuries (Bodger 1991), the subsequent moves of the Russian Empire at the beginning of the 1800s and, in particular, their institutional efforts, illuminate the challenges which confronted the institutions of the now-former Kazakh Khanate.

Based, as empires are, on large urban agglomerations which can be taxed, supported by forward outposts at its frontiers, and revolving around a code of laws which in reality were dictated by the whims of the sovereign, the sedentary-yet-expansionist Russian Empire was precisely the opposite of the nomadic, custom-bound Kazakh Khanate. Indeed, the political organization of the Kazakh Khanate fell into place along the same customary lines that it had for hundreds of years (Martin 2001), but with the added twist of the Kazakhs having some semblance of decentralized authority across three hordes. As Khodarkovsky (2002:13) notes, "the authority of a khan was severely circumscribed by the members of the nobility, who preserved their influence and a power base"; later in the same book, he also calls our attention to the fact that, "In the eighteenth century, successive Russian officials who were charged with implementing government policies toward the Kazakhs reported, in continual bemusement, how little power the Kazakh khans had over their people" (Khodarkovsky (2002:31). This fragmentation from ruler to nobility led to an early version of checks and balances within the Khanate (Bodger 1980) – although not enough to stop Abulkhair Khan from giving away the store – and can be thought of as an analogue to 16th-century Poland, where the *szlachta* (Polish nobility) had a considerable say in electing and constraining the King via the principle of unanimous voting (Hartwell 2016). Simultaneously, while the Kazakh Khanate was seemingly always at war, and indeed did engage in its own territorial aggrandizement, the exigencies of nomadic life meant that a permanent empire was never the ultimate intent, merely the acquisition of more pastureland according to customary law (Martin 2001) and (if necessary) the subjugation of sedentary peoples to fill the economic holes that pastoralism could not. To put it in modern crude terms, the Kazakh people truly were in search of *Lebensraum* rather than a *Reich.*

By contrast, Tsarist Russia was a monolithic state with all authority encapsulated in the person of the Tsar, and its body of legislation reflected the sovereign's wishes rather than the consent of the governed (Zhivov 2002:256 called the pretence of legality in Tsarist Russia a "cultural fiction"). This radically different political system, brooking no opposition or other poles of power (much less veto players), was immediately in conflict with the Kazakh Khanate and its various strata of leadership (in addition to its fragmentation across three hordes). To deal with the clash of political institutions, the Russians attempted two distinct strategies during the 18th and 19th centuries: the first approach was, as noted above, a more hands-off policy during the first half of the 18th century, translating practically into a form of support for strong rulers in the Khanate to keep the peace (this was the strategy behind the Russian support of Khan Nur Ali, as noted in Olcott 1995). This approach, in addition to outsourcing the policing of Kazakh raiders to the Kazakhs themselves, had the additional benefit of minimizing the active involvement of Russia as it chased objectives elsewhere.

However, the inability of Abulkhair (mainly) and then Nur Ali (still substantially) to halt Kazakh attacks on Russian merchants, outposts, or supply lines – as well as their demonstrated independence in attempting to secure more favourable allies elsewhere in the region – meant that a different approach was required (Erofeeva 2004). In what was to become a recurring theme related to Russian involvement abroad, the Tsar changed direction in the second half of the 18th century and attempted to quell the issues on the periphery by ensuring instead that the local leadership remained weak and disorganized. As Beisembayeva (2021:10) correctly notes, "Tsarism pursued a far-reaching policy, putting forward the weak and removing strong rulers," thus removing any potential rivals or charismatic leaders on the steppe who might have ideas about challenging the empire. Rather than working through proxies, the Tsar would pacify the Kazakhs by making them Russian citizens, achieving "direct domination of the traditional rulers of the steppe" (Erofeeva 2004:68). The first push in this more robust approach was taken in 1786 under an *ukase* from the Tsarina Catherine II (also known as Catherine the Great), which asserted that Nur Ali had lost the confidence of the horde (Olcott 1995) and directed the Governor-General of Orenburg, Osip A. Iglestrom, to hold Nur Ali on Russian territory "until the steppe is pacified" (letter from Catherine II to Iglestrom, reproduced in Malikov 2019:49) and to strip him of his title of Khan. The new Khan would be selected by the Russians and paid a sizeable stipend but would be forced to live in Orenburg, where it would be easier to oversee their activities and exert pressure on them (Allworth 1994). The ultimate goal, in language that was striking for an internal letter from the Tsar, was to avoid "rais[ing] suspicion among the Kirghizes [*sic*] that We desire to suppress their self-administration" (Malikov 2019:49).[7]

As part of the transition of power, also included in this *ukase* was a far-reaching plan for reforming both the social and political institutions of the Kazakhs. With regard to social reforms, Catherine and especially Iglestrom advocated for the building of mosques and religious schools on the territory of the Lesser Horde, using a strategy of incorporating Islamic leadership into the structure of government as a way to co-opt opposition (Fisher 1968); as Olcott (1995:47) notes, the Tsarina also "hoped that Islam would serve as a civilizing force for the wild and unpredictable Kazakhs." Bringing in Muslim clergy from Tatar lands, i.e. loyal subjects of the Russian Crown, this state-sponsored variant of Islam was thus both a way to instil leaders who were on board with the colonization project and, as a bonus, a way to undercut the Kazakh religious nobles, the *khoja*, from expanding their influence (Yemelianova 2014). Crews (2014:130) put it best when he observed that "Islam became a pillar of a conservative imperial order," an attempt to inculcate loyalty to the Russian Empire through the guise of religious observance.

Beyond the issue of the Kazakhs' mortal souls, and more in line with the pure administrative challenge of supplanting the Khan on the Lesser Horde's lands, Catherine II also envisioned setting up a series of frontier courts to adjudicate disputes with both Russian and Kazakh representation (Khodarkovsky 2002). However, the peril of executive weakness also soon reared its head here, as nearly every administrative reform attempted by the Russians (spearheaded by Inglestrom) in the 1780s and 1790s met with concerted opposition across the various factions still active in Kazakh leadership, and the office of the Khan was restored on the death of Nur Ali in exile in 1790 (Olcott 1995). But despite these short-term setbacks in imposing a coherent administrative apparatus on the unruly Kazakhs, time was on the empire's side (Khodarkovsky 2002), as the death of Nur Ali left no heir apparent, and the Kazakh tribes appeared incapable of settling their differences among one another, creating more strife and even more openings for Russian influence (Olcott 1995).

Moreover, the attempts to create an adequate infrastructure for controlling the Khanate provided valuable information on what would and would not work (Shaukenov 2013) and, especially, what was necessary to reign among the nomads as part of a broader reorganization of Russia's internal space (Mattingly 1955). Indeed, as economic institutions were so instrumental in determining the political organization of the nomadic Kazakhs, with their disdain of artificial borders (Shaukenov 2013), the key steps needed to tame the Kazakhs would be to transform their economic activity. Part of this was accomplished through the commerce and trade which nomads looked down upon, as Kazakhs "made their existence impossible without Russian manufactures" (Muhammad Salikh Babadzhanov, quoted in Malikov 2019:54). This has been echoed by Shaukenov (2013:289), who notes that "the situation of the nomad, who was constrained by ancestral ties and whose authoritative status was in a nomadic space, was now substantially dependent on economic capital except for his cultural, social and symbolic assets (e.g., prestige, reputation and name)." By closing off the route of raids on sedentary populations (although by no means ending them altogether), the Russians forced the nomads into a reliance on the goods which nomadism was poor at procuring, as well as allowing them to acquire a taste for things that nomadism would never produce, such as tea (Muhammad Salikh Babadzhanov, quoted in Malikov 2019:54, decried the fact that "almost half of the Horde's population drinks tea").

Alongside this reorientation towards the luxuries of the sedentary, and perhaps more importantly, the Russians also began a long-running tradition of instituting policies which forced the Kazakhs to stay put rather than to roam. According to Ohayon (2009:21),

> Sedentarization during tsarism was not limited to the territorial oppression of the nomads. In the first phase it was accompanied by a process of cultivation, resulting in a partial easing of nomadic mobility, but also by profound political transformations associated with the establishment of the system of colonial rule.

Olcott (1981:15) notes that

> during the first thirty years of colonial rule, the sedentarization of the Kazakh nomads was seen as desirable but was not a priority of the Russian government. Although the nomadic economy was considered to be wasteful, there was really no additional demand for the steppe land.

This reality led to limited first attempts to pen the Kazakhs into a narrowly circumscribed geographic area, namely the aforementioned banning of grazing in the "inner lands": however, Nur Ali and several others ignored this rule and the prohibition led to much strife and a prolonged rebellion against Russian rule from 1783 to approximately 1797 (Barisitz 2017). As a further attempt to coral the Kazakhs into a more manageable territory, as well as to defuse the land issue, in 1801 the Russians created their own "Inner (Bukei) Horde," a conglomeration of 7,500 Kazakh families under the leadership of Nur Ali's son Sultan Bukei with permission to settle on the inner lands between the Volga and Ural rivers in exchange for a tax paid to the Russian authorities (Olcott 1995). As Allworth (1994) notes, the proximity of tsarist fortifications and military strength would make the Inner Horde easier to oversee, while it was hoped that the siphoning off of families would weaken the Lesser Horde and make it easier to incorporate it when the time was right. This approach also allowed for the resettling of Kazakhs during times of stress, such as the famine of 1808, when 20,000 Kazakhs were relocated to Bashkir land to the north (Beisembayeva 2021).

These moves towards physically reining in the nomadic Kazakhs were to be repeated and amplified over the course of the next 100 years (see below), but the concurrent tactic of formally incorporating the Khanate into the Russian Empire administratively also had recurrent failures in the first two decades of the 19th century; unable to bear the opposition that outright absorption would cause, the Russians relied on proxies and in 1806 created a council of advisers to aid the Khan in governing the Lesser Horde (Olcott 1995). However, the effort in creating a body of legislation to govern the steppe people was always an ultimate goal of the Russian Empire, "aimed at the consolidation and expansion of tsarist autocracy in Kazakhstan and gradual[ly] transforming it into the outlying district of the Russian Empire" (Otepova 2014:96). Such an eventuality could only occur if conditions on the ground favoured the enforcement of restrictive legislation (Shaukenov 2013), and the cessation of hostilities in Europe after the defeat of Napoleon in 1815 was precisely the window which allowed Russia to alter the status quo in the Kazakh Khanate (Beisembayeva 2021).

In the first instance, the reorganization of Russia's own bureaucratic apparatus came quickly on the heels of the victory over France and, in 1819, an "Asia Department" was created by the Ministry of Foreign Affairs to deal with the affairs of the Kazakhs and other Central Asian peoples (Raskin 2004). However, in a much more telling move, by 1821, the responsibility for the Middle Horde was transferred out of the ministry and to the West Siberian Omsk oblast (Khodarkovsky 2002), perhaps in recognition of the fact that the Kazakh steppe would soon no longer be "foreign." These moves set the stage for the elimination of the Lesser Horde itself and the abolishment of the title of Khan in 1822 (followed by the abolishment of the Khan in the Middle Horde in 1824 and in the Inner Horde in 1845; see Allworth 1994). The basis for these moves was the creation of the *Ustav o Sibirskikh*

Kirgizakh (Regulation of the Siberian Kirghiz) of 1822 under Mikhail Speranskii (Governor-General of Siberia), a comprehensive set of laws which attempted to introduce Russian legal norms to the Kazakhs; more importantly, their ultimate purpose to serve "the strategic interest of the Russian Empire … determined a course for the adaptation and reorganization of society and the political subordination of the population of this vast territory" (Dzhunusova 2004:23). To that end, the laws replacing the Lesser and Middle Hordes with a series of administrative units (*okrugy*), a new "organizational pattern [which] resembled the Russian peasant system, appealing to a Russian administrator's native sensibilities" (Sabol 2003:237). Simultaneously, in line with the longstanding policy of Russia in the region, the laws also sought to outsource some of the administration of justice to tribal elders and provided for an elaborate description of the criminal law process on the steppe.

However, the regulations left no doubt that the Russians were in charge. For example, the new legal code transformed many customs of the Kazakhs into crimes, most of all the practice of *barimta.* A perfect example of a legal mechanism which arose to support nomadic culture specifically, *barimta* referred to the practice of driving away a nomad's livestock by an aggrieved party who felt that the livestock owner had committed an offence, holding the livestock for themselves until an agreement had been reached (which often resulted in some of the livestock being transferred to the aggrieved party as payment; see Martin 2001). Although this practice was understood by the Russians as robbery, it was perceived by the Kazakhs as an integral part of their own customary laws and as an act of reprisal; as Martin (1997:250) accurately states, "to the Russians, the cultural significance of *barimta* had no legal weight; to the Kazakhs, the legal implication of *barimta* as a crime had no meaning." In this instance, the Russian legal system was to triumph over the nomadic customs, mainly because the narrowing of Kazakh grazing lands meant that many nomads actually did take to *barimta* for monetary gain (that is, they committed robbery), while some Kazakhs used *barimta* specifically in a show of defiance to the Imperial Russian regime (McDaniel 2017). Somewhat oddly, an informal legal mechanism was corrupted by formal institutions and became the thing that it was (wrongly) originally perceived to be.

In addition to brushing aside (and transforming) this fundamental tenet of frontier justice, other portions of the regulations demonstrated how St Petersburg was moving towards transplanting its own institutions onto the Kazakhs. Chapter III of the regulations noted that senior sultans received their right to local management only through Russian administration, explicitly detailing how the sultans were obliged to keep the peace; they were even given the rank of major within the Russian military (Malikov 2019). Moreover, the Russian transplantation of norms via the 1822 regulations did not stop with political and judicial mechanisms, as they also set in place some unfamiliar economic institutions. Paramount among these was the description of land as property, designating all traditional Kazakh land as belonging to the Tsar (Kassymova et al. 2012). As part of this seizing of the land, there was both a territorial redrawing and the release of a series of articles related to the apportionment of land for agricultural purposes (but with the caveat that land that had not been used in the past five years could be arbitrarily seized and redistributed), outlining how the land was to be distributed in order to enable agricultural production.[8] Similarly, with an eye to generating economic rents, the laws also focused on fiscal administration; the Russian authorities regarded the new steppe lands as a source of revenue, as well as raw materials, and they imposed a large number of new duties on the Kazakh population and transformed in-kind duties to payment only via currency (Otepova 2014).[9] Finally, as a harbinger of things to come, the last articles of the laws noted that the "Siberian defensive lines," i.e. the borders of the Russian Empire on the Kazakh steppe, were not permanent and could be moved at will in order to bring order to the Kazakhs (Malikov 2019).

The attempt to transplant Russian norms over existing Kazakh ones, coupled with the continued reluctance of the Russian administration to rule directly (rather than by proxy), meant that opposition continued to fester in the Kazakh lands, spilling over into outright rebellion in 1837. Led by Kenesary Kasymov from the Middle Horde, the ostensible beginning of the rebellion began as early as 1824, when the official post of Khan was abolished (Kasymov's official title was "Sultan") and the Middle Horde had been absorbed into the Russian administrative structure as part of the 1822 regulations. According to Malikov (2005), in 1825, Kasymov's father (also known as Sultan Kasym) wrote to the Russian authorities in Orenburg in an attempt to dissolve the *okrug* administration and to continue abiding by Kazakh customary law; this request, when summarily turned down by the Russian administration, ushered in a period of armed rebellion, first led by Kasym's elder son Sarzhan in 1825 and 1826, and, after his death at the hands of Uzbeks, passed to Kenesary. At first, the rebellion had the character of traditional Kazakh raids on sedentary populations (Sabol 2003), and occurred during times of other forms of unrest, such as the incursion into traditional lands across the Ural River following the harsh winter of 1826–1827 and pushback by the Inner Horde against Russian regulations (Olcott 1995). But from 1837 onward, the youngest Kasymov was able to rally disparate elements from each of the three Kazakh hordes in existence against the Russians, finding that there was common ground in the hatred of Russian taxation, arbitrary justice, and land reallocation, and, most egregiously, the expropriation of traditional pasturelands (Oskolkov and Oskolkova 2004).

The Kenesary Rebellion lasted for approximately ten years and restored the title of Khan to Kasymov in 1841, only to see it disappear again when Kasymov was killed by the Kyrgyz in 1847. Given its importance in terms of unified (if not necessarily united, see Malikov 2005) resistance against Russian encroachment, the extant literature has placed considerable emphasis on understanding the reasons behind the rebellion. Of course, we have just mentioned the proximate drivers of the rebellion, above all Russian restrictions on grazing and the attempt to sedentarize the nomads. However, the deeper question comes down to what the rebellion hoped to accomplish, and, as is common in academia, researchers remain highly divided on this point, with interpretations coloured by current events and ideological lenses: for example, Soviet historiography such as Bekmakhanov (1947) framed the rebellion as one of "national liberation," while Sabol (2003) argued that it was an attempt at restoration of nomadic routes, Malikov (2005) countered that Kenesary was a modernizer and thus was attempting to form a new state, and Olcott (1995) was not sure exactly how to characterize the rebellion. In any event, the rebellion itself failed at all three of these potential goals, in that the nomadic lifestyle of the Kazakhs was to slip away even more as Russian settlers continued to pour in over the coming decades, a liberated nation was still out of reach due to the horrendous infighting among the hordes (Sabol 2003), and the dream of a new European-type state was dashed by the further entrenchment of Russian military power (Olcott 1995). In fact, in many ways, the Kenesary Rebellion was the last hurrah for the Kazakh Khanate as an independent entity, separate from the Russian Empire, as the dread of more unrest pushed the Russians to dismantle the Greater Horde in 1848, introducing the "position of *pristav* [in this context, an adviser] … in order to govern the Kazakhs in the southern region of Kazakhstan" (Sultangalieva 2014:62). The dismantling of the rebellion also led to a greater push south and the founding of Fort Vernii by the Russians in 1854 at the base of the Tian Shan mountains, a site which would later be named Alma-Ata and then Almaty (Rahul 2000).

Concurrent with the physical moves into all of modern-day Kazakhstan (which linked two separate military lines and incorporated all the Kazakh lands by 1864; see Erofeeva 2004), the Russian pacification of the steppe via institutional transplantation – or, more accurately, absorption – proceeded apace in the second half of the 19th century, as "between the 1820s and 1860s, the Kazakhs lost their political independence" (Dzhunusova 2004:25). While there were sporadic rebellions against the Russian expansion, including a major uprising in 1856–1857 in the Lesser Horde by nomads who had been displaced from their land twice by Cossacks (Olcott 1995), for the most part resistance became much more localized and, thus, easier to overcome, just as the Russians had intended (Barisitz 2017). In terms of institutional reforms, the next largest, signalling the end of the Kazakh lands as an independent entity, was to come during 1867–1868, as the situation on the ground (Russian military control) was codified:

> The colonial apparatus of the Kazakh region was established by the Turkestan Statute of 1867, which applied to the oblasts of Semirechye and Syr Darya; and the Steppe Statute of 1868, which applied to the remainder of the Kazakh territory; Semipalatinsk and Akmolinsk Oblasts, which were administered as military possessions of Western

> Siberia, and Uralsk and Trugai Oblasts which were administered by the Ministry of the Interior.
>
> (Olcott 1981:13)

These statutes came about after a period of considered study, led by the Steppe Commission of 1865, constituted in order to analyse the Kazakhs and suggest a new basis for their administration; while it concluded that the Kazakhs were too primitive to understand the nuances of Russian law, in time the goal was to supplant the nomadic customary law with the Russian legal code (Martin 2001). Perhaps not surprisingly, in light of the deficiencies in relying on proxies (and their lack of legitimacy among the nomads), the Commission also recommended that a Russian administration, led by Russians, was instituted along the lines of the homeland proper, creating a *guberniya* (governorate) and dividing up the lands into oblasts (Olcott 1995). While the Kazakhs were still involved in the administration of their lands, they were at the lowest levels of governance, with Russian military officers at the highest levels; in yet another way to divide the Kazakh populace, the Russians engaged in "military-popular administration" (Bregel 2003), whereby the local authorities comprised Kazakhs, who were voted in by their compatriots, but who were ultimately responsible for tax collection (Barisitz 2017) – hardly a way to ingratiate themselves with their co-ethnics.

Much as elsewhere in the Russian Empire (especially in Poland after the uprising of 1863; see Hartwell 2016), assimilated Kazakh lands were to undergo a process of "Russification," which was done in two ways: the first was similar to elsewhere in the empire, where cultural Russification proceeded via a dedicated policy of educating the masses (in similar parlance to other imperialist contemporaries, it was linked to a mission to civilize the barbarians – see Sabol 2017 – but also meant so much more than that). The pace of Russification, also as elsewhere in the empire, was slow to unravel during the first decades of Russian rule over the former Kazakh Khanate, with only a few Russian-language educational institutions opened for local elites and the families of Russian settlers (Abašin 2008). However, "in the Kazakh territories, by the end of the 19th century, 162 Russian-Kazakh schools offered instruction to 3,560 boys and 962 girls" (Pavlenko 2011:342). As Olcott (1995) points out, the first half of the 19th century was dedicated to destroying the traditional Kazakh elite but without replacing it with anything tangible, while the second half of the century was dedicated to creating a Russified elite able to handle colonial administration. It is likely that such a narrow view of the educational system was behind what Stevens (2020:1164) has observed, namely that "Russian colonization brought educational, financial and technological resources, from which some Kazakh scholars benefitted," but "Russian control of these resources limited the autonomy of scholars in this phase and did not affect the masses." Unfortunately, this deliberately limited approach did not in fact graduate a whole host of Russified Kazakhs, as leaders sent their children to these schools to learn the

Russian language but not the Russian ways, and the schools themselves appeared to be a better means for Russians to understand Kazakhs rather than the other way around (Olcott 1995).

The push for Russification also touched upon the use of the Russian language, a point which was much more dominant in the European portion of the empire but also reared its head in Central Asia. Searle (2005) has noted that language is perhaps *the* meta-institution, the one commonality which binds groups together (or sets them apart, as in the story of the Tower of Babel from the Bible), and a foundation upon which other institutions are built. Perhaps unsurprisingly, given this reality, the spread of Russian-language instruction in an attempt to supplant the Kazakh language was (and still is) a contentious one in Kazakh history, and the creeping Russification of the steppes in the mid- to late 19th century showed how central language was for both the occupiers and the colonized. Indeed, supporters of Kazakh instruction used the Kazakh language as a way to both preserve cultural norms and to oppose tsarist and Russian domination (Olcott 1985). There was an additional wrinkle to this debate, however, and that was the simple fact that the Kazakh language was by its design heavily reliant on oral (rather than written) propagation, again befitting a nomadic people, and thus the Kazakh population in the 19th century was mostly illiterate – even though the country had a rich literary tradition (Fierman 2005). At the same time, written Kazakh was produced not in Cyrillic or a Latin alphabet, but in a modified Arabic script, used for religious documents until Abay Kunanbayev, a poet now revered in the country of Kazakhstan, began to utilize the language for more literary purposes in the late 19th century (Kirchner 2015). Thus, one could learn Russian well enough to survive but continuing to retain the oral tradition of Kazakh; indeed, much of the push to "Russify" under the Russian Empire was focused precisely on bypassing language (which was also intimately tied in with the economic activities of the Kazakhs) and instead focusing on more practical institutions such as political ones, e.g. administration and leadership.[10] As we will see in the chapters that follow, this approach of minimizing language policy was abandoned under the Soviet Union, as the communists realized that language was a critical barrier to realizing other institutional reorderings, but in Tsarist Russia of the 19th century pursuing an oral tradition was subsumed to other institutional goals.

It is important to remember that the move towards moulding Russian administrators via educational policy co-existed with another imperial policy, mainly the spread of Islam, which led to the proliferation of madrassas to teach the children of elites (Duisembayeva 2019). While not specifically a policy of Russification, as mentioned above, the support of Islam in the Kazakh lands was done explicitly to create some semblance of order, and Tatar and Bashkir clergy (already Russian subjects) were brought in specifically as loyal servants of the Tsar. Yemelianova (2002) points out that Russia had its own clash of institutions with this policy, as the Russian Orthodox

Church had (and still does have) no love of competition, and thus the Church pushed for state interference in madrassas, including the inclusion of obligatory Russian-language classes in Islamic schools as part of Russification. However, despite the best intentions of the Russian colonizers, the spread of Islam over the Kazakh steppe in the late 19th and early 20th centuries was driven mainly by the Kazakhs themselves, finding Islamic education more "useful" than anything on offer from the Russians (Frank 2001). Indeed, Frank (2017:66) makes a compelling argument that Kazakh "Muslims adapted Islamic law to Russian rule, and … they deployed it to solve new problems arising from the Kazakh steppe's integration into the expanding Russian (and global) commercial sphere." In this sense, Islamic law took the place of (or rather, absorbed) customary law at the same time that Russian jurisprudence was attempting to absorb Kazakh customary law, providing a new basis for issues related to nomadic life.[11]

The Russians Arrive En Masse

The second channel by which Russification was achieved was more direct – and, like the issue of the language, has ramifications even today – and that was via the direct settlement of Russians on Kazakh lands, a tidy way to achieve the other institutional goals mentioned above. As Ó Beacháin and Kevlihan (2011:2) aptly put it, "domination was followed by colonization." This approach, starting almost immediately with Russian encroachment into the region in the 18th century (Kendirbaeva 1997) and spanning the period both before and after the abolishment of serfdom in Russia in 1861, fulfilled several policy desires within St Petersburg. In the first instance, the influx of Russians in the form of the military and Cossacks helped to pacify the steppes and to remove a potential source of trouble from closer to the seat of power (Kendirbaeva 1997), thereby introducing a permanent local counterweight to the Kazakhs. The second, and perhaps least important goal (in terms of immediacy), was to increase agricultural production in the south of the empire, using settlers from European Russia to import relatively advanced farming technology (Yan et al. 2020); while the increase in yields was a welcome outcome for the Tsar, the increase in agricultural land also helped to rein in the Kazakh nomads and force them towards less nomadic activities (see below).

However, the tsarist colonization policy on the steppes was to accelerate exponentially in the late 19th century, driven by both structural changes within the Russian economy and the exigencies of global events (including the well-explored "Great Game" in Central Asia between the Russian and British imperia).[12] The extension of Russian power over the future Kazakhstan proceeded at the same time that Russia itself was undergoing industrialization and a shift towards more capitalist modes of production. It must be noted, however, that it was much more of a state-directed capitalism similar to the fascist economic thinking of the 1920s and 1930s, with large-scale state involvement and authoritarian planning, than a true "capitalist" economy. In fact, the Russian variant of industrialization – predicated less on entrepreneurship, laissez-faire policies, the beginnings of a vibrant middle class with income mobility, and a focus on innovation and more on the political needs of the Tsar and the geopolitical posturing of Russia in general – followed closely in line with the overall Russian approach to internal and external policy since the time of Peter the Great. To paraphrase an Italian leader of the early 20th century, the Russian economy was everything with the monarchy, nothing against the Tsar, and nothing outside of Russia's interests (defined as those of the Tsar).

While this book is unequivocally *not* the place to delve into Russia's economic transformation in the late 19th century, it is crucial to note that this substantial reordering of the Russian economy, even though it showed remarkable continuity with previous Russian policies, was bound to have consequences in the empire as well. In particular, the increasingly imperial character of the empire, its increasing desire for raw materials, and the march towards urbanization pushed even harder at Kazakh customary institutions and turned Kazakh lands into almost a pure "settler" colony rather than an equal administrative division of Russia (Brower 2012). The policies of colonization, now focused exclusively on settlement of Russians from the European part of the country, reached a climax in the years prior to the First World War, serving the purpose of creating living space for Russians and generating economic activity needed for the development of the Motherland.[13]

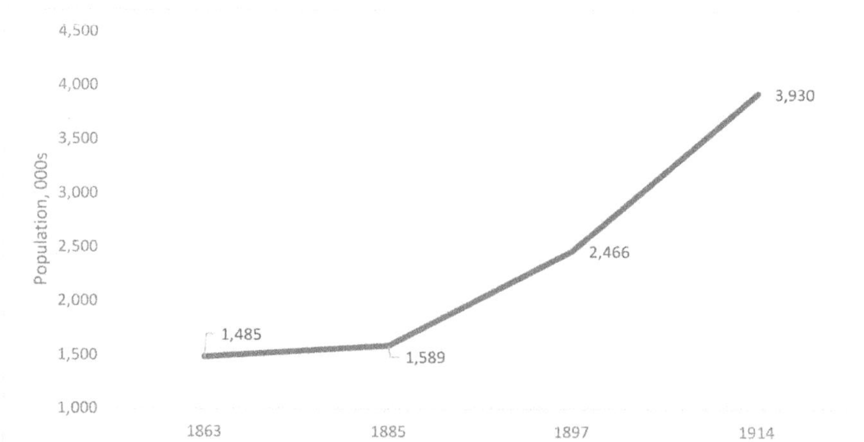

Figure 2.1 Population in the Steppe Lands of Imperial Russia, 1863–1914
Source: based on data in Mitchell (1975). "Steppe lands" refers to the Urals, Turgai, Akmolinsk, and Semipalatinsk.

The precursor to the increased "Russianization" of the Kazakh lands was the "Steppe Statute" of 1891 (officially the "Statute on Administration of Akmolinsk, Semipalatinsk, Semirech'e, Ural'sk, and Turgai Oblasts"), a revamp of the 1868 laws (and a follow-on from similar legislation in Russia proper from 1889) which increased the power of Russian administration over the local Kazakh administration (Martin 2012). The most egregious way in which this was done was by allowing the Russian authorities to seize and distribute land as they saw fit, expropriation which was enabled by the definition of "excess land" contained in the Statute; deeming that each Kazakh had the right to 40 acres, all land after that amount which had been distributed was considered excess and was made part of the "Public Land Fund" to be distributed to settlers (Olcott 1981). This policy had two benefits from the point of view of the Russian administration: first, it reserved land for future Russians migrating to the steppe, but second, it also forced Kazakhs to adopt a more sedentary lifestyle, as the amount allotted was nowhere near enough to sustain a nomadic existence (and, as Sabol 2017 notes, in practice, Kazakhs who settled in agriculture actually received more land than those who were "bitter clingers" to their nomadic ways). Olcott (1981:15) goes so far as to assert that "the sedentarization of the Kazakh nomads was now a conscious policy of the regime," a policy made easier by the introduction of settlers – as Bekmakhanova (1986) points out, the proportion of Kazakhs on the steppe fell by 5.72 percentage points from 1870 to 1897, and land needed to be found for the incoming Russians. A glance at the overall increase in the population of the steppe *krai* (lands), shown in Figure 2.1, is further evidence of this pressure for more land.

In order to ease the flow of Russians to the steppe, the Tsar created a *Pereselencheskoe Upravlenie* (Resettlement Administration) in 1896 to assist Russians who wished to emigrate to the Kazakh lands, as well as to act as an emigration promotion agency and sell the benefits of settlement to European Russians and Ukrainians (Olcott 1995). In many ways, the Administration was merely reacting to facts on the ground, as settlers had been moving illegally to Kazakh lands for years, farming alongside Kazakhs and in many instances taking the land that had been allotted for them (Sabol 2017). But the mission of this new agency, approaching the issue of resettlement as a technocratic challenge to be overcome (Holquist 2010), was to administer the legally permitted settlement of (generally wealthy) emigrants, as well as to attempt to manage the settlers seeking refuge from the famines in Russia in the early 1890s (Wendelken 2000). At the same time, the Administration was also an instrument for the sedentarization project, promoting the farmstead as a model for settlers and even thrusting the benefits of agricultural production onto Kazakhs who were also petitioning for land (Campbell 2020).

Ironically, as Olcott (1995) points out, there was also a fundamental inconsistency in the Resettlement Administration's promotion function, as the total legality of movement throughout the empire was not established until 1904 (although restrictions were eased in 1898; see Sabol 2003). Practically, this meant that the true purpose of the Administration was merely to seize lands for the future, a fact for which it was pilloried in the press and in official government investigations in 1908 and 1909 (see Holquist 2010). Indeed, Count Konstantin Konstantinovich Pahlen led a commission that investigated the Turkestan Government during these two years and found that the Resettlement Administration (like so many government programmes before and since) actually served as a government jobs programme: he charged that the Administration was nothing more than "wretched attempts to settle a few immigrants of dubious character on some strip of land gave rise to bombastic reports which were dispatched to St Petersburg accompanied by columns of padded figures" (quoted in Williams 1972).

The reality of internal movement to a region which had a carefully considered, but increasingly outdated, administrative apparatus meant that St Petersburg (and especially local administration in Orenburg) were eager to reform the oversight of the Kazakh lands. The 1891 Statute made a first attempt to further subdivide the region into various smaller units (*uezds* and *volosts*) and to create some form of "home rule" for the Kazakhs, allowing for the election of local leaders within the Russian administrative framework, while expanding and reinforcing the dual court system at the local level (Wendelken 2000). However, the local system was already crumbling under the weight of a familiar trait of the Russian bureaucracy, namely the pervasive spread of corruption. The continued assault on the livelihoods of native Kazakhs meant that, even when accepted into leadership roles, Kazakh officials remains poor; thus, "in central regions of Kazakhstan, officers accepted bribes because of a lack of financial stability, whereas in the border regions of Russia [Kazakhs] provoked and encouraged bribery to oppose the local government to the colonial one' (Kaliyeva 2013:128). This corruption among the Kazakhs was undoubtedly aided and abetted by the Russians' own lackadaisical attitude to corruption, including the widespread involvement of Russian officials in local elections and their use of bribery. According to Uyama (2015:685), there was "systemic corruption related to elections of *volost* [administrative units comprising between 1,000 and 2,000 households] heads: candidates (Kazakhs) bribed the peasant captain (usually a Russian) and his companions, and they together manipulated the numbers of voters and vote results."

Coupled with the already poor state of the Russian administration on the periphery – including the reality that settler administration and Kazakh administration were often in conflict when they were not colluding (Sultangalieva and Seitz 2020) – and in order to accommodate the sudden surge of Russians into the Kazakh lands enabled by the 1891 Statute, additional reforms were to come in 1897, 1898, and over the coming years for specific oblasts and for overall administrative structures throughout the General Governorships in the region (modern-day Kazakhstan was mainly located in the Steppe Governorship but also had some portions in the Governorate of

Turkestan). However, many of these reforms had little to do with improving the plight of the Kazakhs, such as the extension of the tsarist edict on Kazakh land to forests, making all forests (and many tracts of land which had absolutely no trees) the property of the Tsar under the purview of the Russian Forest Administration (Sabol 2003). If anything, the reforms were meant to accelerate the sedentarism and settlement of Russians, doing so in a way which continued to undercut Kazakh self-governance:

> On 2 June 1898, a year after the proposal by [Baron Maxim] Taube [Governor-General of the Steppe], Emperor Nicholas II approved the Provisional Regulation on Peasant Nachalniks for the management of peasant populations. These new peasant nachalniks were modelled after the zemskii nachalniks of European Russia, and their purpose was to consolidate peasant management and prepare the peasants to live in the new socio-economic conditions of post-reform Russia … the government decided to correct what it saw as the shortcomings of peasant self-government in the simplest way: by increasing its interference in local affairs.
>
> (Sultangalieva and Seitz 2020:168)

These policies resulted in an influx of three million Russians to the steppe by the eve of the First World War (Olcott 1981), a policy that ironically displaced military forces as the major landholders in Kazakhstan – as Hanks (1998) points out, by 1880, 90 per cent of Russian-dominated Kazakh land was held by the Cossacks, a dominant position they entirely relinquished just 20 years later. As mentioned above, the influx of immigrants had the added benefit (from the Russian perspective) of removing pastureland and forcing the nomadic Kazakhs into more easily controlled areas, further eroding their customary laws and entirely upending their traditional way of life (Olcott 1995). The shift of millions of Russians to the virgin lands of the steppe also allowed "poverty [to be] redistributed across Russia: from the czar's restive peasant subjects to his defeated nomadic subjects" (Barisitz 2017:255). In this way, the settlement policies were meant to create "a certain socio-economic structure" on the steppe, "a radical socioeconomic transformation with a new political structure" which would ultimately produce "the victory of the city culture over the steppe" (Shaukenov 2013:298).

The difficulty that this influx of Russian settlers and the concomitant policy of sedentarization caused for the nomadic Kazakhs cannot be understated, as "the official government position encouraged [Kazakh] settlement but provided limited opportunities for a successful transition" (Sabol 2003:47). As Olcott (1981:16) notes,

> The decision had been made that the Steppe was to be developed as a region of Russian settlement and the sedentarization of the Kazakh nomads was seen as a necessary prerequisite for this. The Resettlement Administration was quick to make use of its power, seizing over 4

> million hectares of land from the Kazakhs during the years 1900–1907. In addition to the plots awarded to the Russians, the lands that composed the Public Land Treasury were also unavailable to the Kazakhs. In the years of peak migration, 1906–1910, large amounts of Kazakh land were declared surplus and placed in the land treasury, which contained over 30 million hectares of land by 1910. The amount of land seized from the Kazakhs was far in excess of the current needs of the population of European settlers and was secured in order to guarantee sufficient parcels for later settlements.

Similarly, as Smagulova (2006:305) notes, in the late 19th century, "waves of Russian peasants began to migrate into Kazakhstan, appropriating the best fertile lands near rivers and lakes and pushing the nomad Kazakh from the north and north-east to the south and east." Hoerder (2017) also argues that the wave of Russians also had the effect of exacerbating class tensions among the Kazakhs themselves, as wealthier Kazakhs with larger herds saw increased demand and thus increased prices; smaller herders, with less power to resist and less to offer the Russians, were more likely to be forced off of their lands and rehired by wealthier Kazakhs, upending the entire traditional socio-economic ordering which predominated on the steppe. And Aldashev and Guirkinger (2012) provide evidence to show that the Russian settlement policies had a massively deleterious effect on women in particular, as the scramble for scarce resources occasioned by Russian colonialism meant that families were more likely to route those resources to boys (resulting in high levels of female excess mortality). By any metric, the "land rush" (Wendelken 2000) which the Russians unleashed – and which the Resettlement Administration wildly encouraged and exacerbated – was exceedingly harmful for the Kazakhs and did in fact go a long way towards eradicating their way of life. As Sabol (2003:47) notes, "so successful had this effort become that by 1910 nomadism was almost nonexistent in some uezds of Akmolinsk and rapidly disappearing elsewhere."

The Beginning of "Kazakhstan" and the Run-up to the Revolution of 1905

The Russian policy towards the Kazakhs also had an additional complication, one driven by the structure of the tsarist edifice and its own domestic troubles. From the point of view of St Petersburg, shipping off settlers to the remote reaches of the empire also acted as a "safety valve" against peasant unrest at home (Habib 2003). The pace of internal exile was to increase after serfdom was ended in Russia, as the displacement of farmers and the slow progress in actually dismantling the feudal system meant that there was still a large amount of discontent and peasant uprisings continued to emerge sporadically (Kudaibergenova et al. 2017; for a chronological list of uprisings, see Hartwell 2020). The effects of introducing an already dissatisfied populace into the steppe were as predictable as they were avoidable, as new settlers often continued to agitate upon arrival, "develop[ing] contempt toward the Kazaks, who, they felt, were being maintained on the land at the settlers' expense … [in fact, a]nyone who held coveted land, including indigenous peasants, Cossacks, and settled Kazaks, was seen as a stumbling block" (Wendelken 2000:81).

Moreover, the remoteness of the Kazakh frontier from St Petersburg and Moscow also made the region a favourite for the Tsar to deposit undesirables who had already made their undesirable status well known, i.e. through political activities, secret societies, or dissent against the Tsar. The settlement of Semipalatinsk became the preferred spot for sending oppositionists, dissidents, and those who ran afoul of the imperial *Okhrana* (secret police) in the second half of the 19th century (Campbell 2017), and these exiles actively contributed to the scientific and social life of the region (Aliyassova et al. 2016).[14] The Kazakh steppe (as well as Siberian settlements to the north) also began to receive troublemakers from elsewhere in the empire, most prominently from Poland in two waves (after the 1830 and 1863 uprisings); as Wysocki and Kawalec (2011) note, the Poles did not just play the role of prisoners but also sometimes participated in the military and/or civilian administration of the steppe. In any event, the use of Kazakh lands as a Central Asian jail for dissidents meant that politics were also being imported from the Motherland, helping to disseminate European ideas on various political institutions such as democracy, socialism, and anarchism (Gentes 2017 notes how Poles deported to Siberia in 1830 tried to join forces with Kazakhs to overthrow the Russians).

Indeed, and in an incredibly ironic twist, the Russians may have made administration easier in the Kazakh lands by compressing the former hordes together and overwriting Kazakh institutions (even if done with a lighter touch than elsewhere in the empire), while allowing for mass Russian settlement also may have created a safety valve for unrest in the Motherland; however, the extension of illiberal political institutions and the introduction of waves of oppositionists planted the seeds of further rebellion. As in the case of Islam, the Russian colonization and dumping of exiles kick-started the creation of another set of Kazakh institutions to deal with everyday life, a life which was now become more complex and multifaceted than the simple rigours of nomadism. In other words, having discovered each other as a nation, the Kazakhs began to take up the banner of discontent elsewhere in the empire and to harness the idea of nationalism (in Marxist terms, to develop a "national consciousness").

The key to this development of the idea of a "Kazakhstan" was the creation of a native Kazakh intelligentsia, a group of Kazakhs who were able to think critically about their experience under Russian rule and what it meant to be Kazakh. This book is not the place to tackle this weighty subject, as others have written much more extensively about the creation of the intelligentsia and their process of radicalization in Central Asia, and particularly in Kazakhstan (Sabol 2003, for example devotes a chapter to the beginnings of Kazakh intellectual life). However, it is important to note for the purposes of institutional genesis and evolution that there were two important forces shaping both this move towards an intelligentsia and then, by extension, the creation of counter-institutions. In the first instance, the Russian emphasis on education and Islam laid the basis for allowing the Kazakhs to conceptualize and express their discontent with Imperial Russian policies. With their pastureland taken and given to settlers, and with a younger generation moving through Russian-Kazakh schools, the oral tradition and institutions of the steppe began to be formalized into thought along the lines of Western philosophy, rooted in secular traditions and reflecting on (and utilizing the tools from) the Russian occupation (Olcott 1995). At the same time, while the Russian policy changed abruptly in 1891 to try and de-emphasize Islam, the inculcation of Islamic thought in a more formal manner led to a separate branch of important Kazakh thinkers arguing from Islamic precepts and applying them to the disorienting events of the day (Kendirbay 1997). Although the two schools may have been at odds in their recommendations as to where Kazakhs should direct their energies (the secular school was much more pro-Russian), they both gave voice to the tangible issues facing Kazakh society and how they should be approached within a quasi-modern Eurasian state (rather than, as in eras now past, in a tribal confederation).

In tandem with this intellectual awakening at the highest levels, grappling with questions of what it meant to be "Kazakh," was an awakening at the more basic level, as the codification of the Kazakh language in a modified Cyrillic script made textbooks and religious material available to all (Sabol 2003). As noted above, there was a lack of a dedicated language policy in the Kazakh lands, unlike elsewhere in the Russian Empire, meaning that much of the impetus for national language work came from below rather than above. Of course, the Russian-language instruction subsidized by the Tsar and the extension of Russian as the lingua franca meant that any upwardly mobile Kazakhs would be forced into a Russian language track, but this was more of a passive assimilation rather than the overt Russification seen in the western parts of the empire (i.e. Poland, Belarus, and Ukraine). But just as the printing press set off the Enlightenment in Western and Central Europe, so too did the work of Ibrahim Altynsaryn to produce a Kazakh grammar based on spoken Kazakh make a massive contribution to the written language, thereby creating a native movement for Kazakh language instruction in addition to Russian (Kreindler 1983). When combined with the development of a young intelligentsia – and especially the spread of the intelligentsia's ideas within families and across regions due to Kazakh-language publications (Berdyguzhin et al. 2020) – the core of a Kazakh "nation" had been formed.

In fact, the sum total of the effects of increasing literacy, increasing education, increased access to Islamic religious schooling, and continued discontent with Imperial Russian policies was, as elsewhere in the empire, expressed through increasingly political discourse and the beginnings of a national movement. As noted above, this manifested itself mainly in the writings of Islamic scholars, who were quick to blame every suffering and setback as part and parcel of the Russian occupation (Olcott 1995), but who also were instrumental in advancing debates on nomadism versus sedentarism, the role of Islam in the new Kazakh political structure, and the economic challenges facing Kazakhs (Kendirbaeva 1999). Many of these issues were also touched upon by the secular writers, who became less pro-Russian over time, especially as the climate changed in Russia proper. For example, Alikhan Bukeikhanov, a descendant of the Khan of the Bukei Horde, was raised in Omsk but taught Kazakh children later in life and entered Russian politics as a result of the 1905 Revolution. Having a direct link to Kazakh aristocracy yet steeped in the institutions of the Russian Empire, Bukeikhanov noted in his famous 1910 work on his people (Bukeikhanov 1910) that the policy of Russification and its twin, sedentarization, was explicitly done to break the nomadic spirit of the Kazakhs and to destroy their culture, a type of "national antagonism" by Russia which manifested itself in a condescending colonial attitude in addition to the concrete policies of sedentarism.

Such sentiments were common at the turn of the 20th century, as the waves of terror unleashed by socialists and anarchists across Russia agitating for reform gave a push to various national movements as well (Geifman 1993). With multiple currents of political discontent bubbling underneath the tsarist edifice, the events of 1905 burst forth as a geyser of violence and bloodletting (Galai 2002), a major institutional reform (the creation of the Duma, the first elected parliament in Russia's history), and a severe conservative backlash resulting in more discontent (Sohrabi 1995). The Revolution of 1905 was in many ways a surprise not only to the Tsar but also to the far-flung colonies on the Kazakh steppe, which had seen the beginnings of debates on "Kazakh-ness" but was much less developed than other revolutionary or reformist movements elsewhere in the empire; as Olcott (1995) correctly notes, there is not much available in the writings of Kazakh intellectuals before 1905 which would suggest a revolutionary fervour, while the group of intellectuals exposed to anti-colonial and revolutionary ideas was quite small indeed prior to 1905 (Kendirbay 1997). This does not mean that there was no revolutionary violence during 1905, as rural violence spread rapidly in the middle of the year in tandem with disturbances across Russia, but it does mean that, rather than being protagonists and drivers of the events of 1905, the Kazakhs instead saw an opportunity in the turmoil and reforms being forced upon St Petersburg and seized it (Olcott 1995). As Sablin and Korobeynikov (2016:215) note, "in late October 1905, Kazakh intellectuals translated the October Manifesto (the Manifesto on the Improvement of the State Order, October 17, 1905) into Kazakh and sent '10,000 copies to the Steppe,'" and local newspapers extolling the virtues of territorial autonomy and calls to political action began publishing regularly (one main one for the secular-aligned group and one for the Islamists; see Kendirbaeva 1999). Although tsarist-era censorship was still prevalent, the slight thaw following 1905 meant that 30 newspapers began to be published in Orenburg alone, and while many of them were destined to fail, the lid was off Pandora's box (Sabol 2003).

The key institution which drove forth Kazakh interests was the creation of political parties, a term I use in the plural because Kazakh intellectuals were to make their mark both in national organizations and via representation in the Russian Duma. With regard to the Duma, during 1905–1908, national minorities were allowed to stand for election to the parliament, and ultimately eight Kazakhs were elected, aligned with the Russian Constitutional Democratic Party (Sabol 2017). The shift which occurred with this representation was accurately described by Ohayon (2015:622) thus: "from 1905 to 1928, national elites were no longer simply relaying the discourse and priorities of the central authority to their own societies but also their own ideas in the interest of those societies." Although a rift was to develop between the Kazakhs and their Russian compatriots, mainly over the question of national representation and whether or not the Kazakhs should have a separate state or remain within an indivisible Russia, for the first three years following the Revolution there was broad agreement on issues related to Russian colonialism and especially to the development of democratic norms (Kendirbay 1997). However, as Olcott (1995) elucidates, the main issue from the point of view of the Kazakhs, namely the land issue, was never actually addressed in the Duma, despite Kazakh insistence, fiery oratory, and a proposed Commission (which was denied by the Council of Ministers). The changes in the voting system engineered by the dissolution of the Second Duma in 1907, masterminded by Prime Minister Pyotr Stolypin in order to reduce antimonarchical and liberal tendencies, further weakened any chance of land reform, as the role of non-Russian minorities was greatly reduced, if not prohibited outright (Krasnozhon and Bunyk 2019).

The inability of Kazakhs to influence policies across Russia was perhaps understandable, as the closed tsarist system was always at odds against reformers, and it was difficult even for classical liberals in Russia to oppose policies which undoubtedly benefited them (i.e. the settlement of Russians on the steppe). Perhaps more important for building a Kazakh national consciousness was thus the work done on the steppe itself, as the Alash Orda movement, a national liberation movement led by Russian-educated elites and treading the fine line between nomad and sedentary, Islam and secular, rose to prominence during and especially after the 1905 Revolution (Kesici 2017). Indeed, Alash stood out precisely because of this successful balancing act, offering something to revolutionaries and conservatives alike, opposing the Russian land policy and "the antipopular stance of administrative bodies" (Amanzholova 1997:10). Alash was behind the limited circulation (but outsized impact) newspaper *Qazaq*, started in 1913 and presenting a fairly strident stance against all Russian policies: "First of all the Kazakh people are subject to Russia and have no rights ... Taxes collected from the whole people (several millions) are being spent on absolutely useless things for the people" (Myrzhaqyp Dulatov, quoted in Kendirbay 1997:495).[15] Harnessing discontent with the same critical thinking of the Enlightenment, the Alash movement made deep inroads among Kazakh intelligentsia, while also finding a following among conservative elements who despised the Russian influence in overturning Kazakh traditions.

However, a key point adopted by the Alash movement, and echoed in the various publications supporting Kazakh nationhood, was an eventual acceptance of the Russian policy of sedentarism. From nearly every quarter of the intelligentsia came the realization that Kazakhs should come to terms with the reality that their future was to be more sedentary than nomadic (Olcott 1995). Olcott (1981:20) makes this point explicitly, using an institutional analysis ahead of its time, noting that "the internal support structures of nomadism had been destroyed and an irreversible process of economic change had begun which could only end in the sedentarization of the Kazakh nomads." From other viewpoints, for example in terms of pure economics, the truth was that a sedentary lifestyle actually afforded more opportunities for farmers and herders than free-range grazing, due to the availability of fodder and shelter from the harsh climate of the northern steppes, and this argument was made in its favour in public and in the pages of influential newspapers (Olcott 1981:20). But even with this justification, this did not mean that the issue did not continue to rear its head, and in the Kazakh press there was a heated debate generally in favour of sedentarism but with divergence on how the transition should occur – for example, the editors of *Aiqap*, the main Islamic-oriented paper, argued that sedentarism should be accelerated, because this would allow for a greater role for Islam in Kazakh life (Kendirbaeva 1999). In any event, it appeared that the Russian policies had won this round in terms of institutional transplantation, as, even though nomadism was to survive in some form even through to today, the past of a free-roaming Kazakh people was rapidly coming to an end.

Unfinished Revolution and the Eve of Bolshevism

The first decade and a half of the 20th century saw far-reaching changes in the political organization of Kazakhs and the reordering of their economic institutions, but the Russian authorities unfortunately continued their destructive settlement policies. In fact, after the Revolution of 1905, settlement of Russian farmers actually increased and the pace of land expropriation accelerated: from 1906 to 1912, at the same time that the intelligentsia was arguing in St Petersburg against Russian land policies and coming to terms with their own approaches to land, the number of Russian settlers increased threefold, while that of the Kazakh population rose by just 14 per cent, with regions such as Akmolinsk seeing Russians suddenly leaping into the majority (Sabol 2003). With land being given away in massive amounts to Russians, Kazakhs found that their own land was in short supply, and "by 1907 the Kazakhs were requesting three times more land than the Resettlement Administration could provide" (Olcott 1981:20). This persistent policy, coupled with the brief glimmer of hope for greater representation (snuffed out in 1907 and 1908) meant that, like elsewhere in the Russian Empire, there was little outlet for Kazakhs other than violence.

Much as in 1905, the onset of the First World War also provided an opportunity for Kazakhs to attempt to take advantage of Russian weakness. Economic conditions on the steppe had been in decline prior to the war. As the transition to sedentarism was not complete, the Kazakh population was undergoing a demographic decline (Olcott 1995), and, most importantly, the effects of famine, loss of land, and the Russian destruction of the traditional way of life led to a decrease in food consumption (Cameron 2018). The onset of the war exacerbated these pre-existing trends and pushed the steppe to the brink of economic collapse, as market linkages within the empire were torn asunder and material was reserved for the war effort (Kazakhs were obliged to provide horses for the war effort), while thousands of prisoners of war were sent to the steppe to keep them far away from the fighting (Gatrell 2005). At the same time, taxes were increased, livestock was seized, land expropriation did not cease, and the Kazakhs were even forced to "donate" labour on the farms and homesteads of ethnic Russians who had been conscripted and were fighting thousands of miles away (Olcott 1995).

In the early years of the war (1914 and 1915), there was at least one bright spot for the Kazakhs, as Muslims from the Kazakh lands were themselves exempt from conscription, meaning that while they laboured under a feudal, quasi-slavery system which seized their production and forced them to work on land which was not their own, at least they did not have to take up arms in a faraway land of which they knew nothing. Unfortunately, even this minor perk was soon to be removed in mid-1916, as the continuing needs of the meat grinder on the Eastern Front, including labour shortages and rapidly depleting manpower in critical industries (diverted to munitions), led the tsarist administration to reverse course and introduce conscription for Kazakhs (Tomohiko 2013). Although they were not technically "military," and were used for construction activities far from the front, the thought of having their lives (in addition to their lands and their livelihoods) expropriated by the Tsar proved too much for nearly all the peoples of Central Asia; indeed, an attempt at mediation by Kazakh elders in Petrograd was meant to barter Kazakh labour for a series of concessions related to land policy, but this mission failed when the tsarist authorities (and in particular the Russian Minister of War Alexei Polivanov) held firm to the policies of expropriation and conscription (Sabol 2003). As a result, Kazakhs, Kyrgyz, and Uzbeks rose up in violent and protracted rebellion against the tsarist authorities (Gatrell 2005).

Starting in Samarkand (Uzbekistan) and Khodjent (modern-day Khujand in Tajikistan) on 4 July 1916, the revolt spread within a week to Tashkent and then on to the Kazakhs of the Syr Darya. An interesting study by Ueda (2013), using geographic information system (GIS) data, shows that nomads were the most engaged in the rebellion, and even though the rebellion began in sedentary areas, it spread rapidly onto the steppe (not uncoincidentally the same rural areas which were the prime location for settlers; see Morrison 2015). Soviet historiography (summarized in Carmack 2014), and much Western scholarship (see, for example, Hallez and Ohayon 2019) argue that the rebellion was more accurately described as a paroxysm of rage following years of pent-up frustration at tsarist policies, a manifestation of discontent which was off-loaded onto Russian troops, Russian settlers, Russian infrastructure (especially the Tashkent–Orenburg railroad), and even locals who collaborated with Russian authorities in an attempt to execute the conscription orders (Olcott 1995). However, Tomohiko (2013) astutely notes that rebellions were far and few during the second half of the 19th century in Central Asia, and that the surprise of the tsarist *ukase* was in reality the spark that kindled the conflict. In reality, both sides may be right on this point, as a beaten-down population had seen its hopes of retaining its cultural identity dashed time after time and thus was more likely to be quiescent in the face of further depredations; in this way, it was only the size of the Tsar's edict (drafting all men between the ages of 19 and 43) and the surprise nature of it which precipitated the crisis. On the other hand, Hallez and Ohayon (2019) argue that the seeds of the revolt were intimately connected not only to the legitimate grievances of the Kazakhs but also the longer-term shift in Kazakh perceptions of political leadership under Russian colonialism, from "khan" to "warrior," meaning that leaders are defined less in terms of their followers and more as resisters of established orders (the authors focus on the idea of banditry to make this point). I would add to this that the move towards creating an indigenous intelligentsia mirrored the shift towards a warrior class, one which was equipped with ideas much as their countrymen were equipped with *shokpar* (maces), and one which gave voice to the discontent with Russian policies but through a uniquely Kazakh lens. Morrison (2015) adds some evidence to this interpretation, showing how the revolt of 1916 was not necessarily an isolated incident but instead was part of a growing wave of violence which had started a few years previously. Thus, both interpretations – of a unique event but also one which had deep roots - carry some weight in explaining the virulence of the 1916 rebellion.

And virulent the rebellion was, as the attacks on Russian troops resulted in thousands of deaths on both sides and a diversion of men and material away from the front when the Imperial Army could least support it. The Russian authorities, none too happy about this state of events, imposed martial law and massive punitive raids on the Kazakhs, in many cases going from village to village, arresting draft resisters, and burning down the yurts of suspected dissidents (Olcott 1995). Liberal Russians were outraged about this treatment of the Kazakhs and other Central Asians – Alexander Kerensky (future head of the Russian Provisional Government formed after the abdication of the

Tsar in February 1917) famously lashed out at the Tsar in the Duma after the rebellion had been quashed and made a case that the suppression was "an atavism of barbarism unfit for a modern European state" (Payne 2019) – but the die had been cast: not only had the Kazakhs not achieved any political gains related to land or settlement policy, instead they had witnessed hundreds of thousands of their co-ethnics fleeing from their homeland (mainly to China), many never to return (Zardykhan 2004). At the same time, the Russians enacted a series of cruel reprisals (Demenko 2019) such as the destruction of Kazakh property and animals, imposing a "harsh peace and again plac[ing] the needs of the empire before the needs of its subject populations" (Olcott 1995:125). The lesson that the Russians learned during the rebellion was not that their policies were misguided, although Alexei Kuropatkin, the Governor-General of Turkestan, did note that dispossession of Kazakh land probably played a hand in the uprising; more important, in tsarist eyes, was the fact that the Kazakhs were "inherently untrustworthy" because of their ethnicity, and they needed to understand that "the Russian Empire is great and powerful, but the main role in its formation, strengthening, and expansion is played by the Russians" (Kuropatkin, quoted in Gatrell 2005:192).

Such an attitude, characteristic of the entire Russian bureaucracy, the Russian aristocracy, and especially the Russian colonial administration (on its "civilizing mission" to save the steppe barbarians, see Sabol 2017), was to prevent any reconciliation with the (once again) conquered Kazakhs, and tensions continued to mount both on the steppe and at home in Petrograd and elsewhere in Russia proper. Indeed, Russia had larger problems internally and externally than rebellion on its periphery, as the continued strains of the war led to shortages of fuel and food throughout Russia and, by February 1917 (old style calendar, early March 1917 in the new calendar), a haphazard series of bread riots in Petrograd and massive strikes (at one point, 306,000 workers, or 80 per cent of Petrograd's workforce, were on strike; see Zajda 2014). A rapid agglomeration of shifting political organizations, competing power poles, and absolute exhaustion with a war which was perceived as lost a year and a half earlier (Gatrell 2005) merged into what Lockhart (1957) called the "unanimous revolution," and imperial troops shifted sides to join the protestors on 25 February 1917 (Yi Meng 2021).[16] This move sealed the fate of the monarchy, and the Tsar, sensing that he had no more allies to call on, abdicated his throne in favour of a Provisional Government led by Prince Lvov. The forces which had been building in Russian society and which were unleased by the war had finally overtaken the tsarist edifice, bringing with it hope for an institutional transformation for the better. This same hope was shared on the steppe, along with the possibility that the Kazakhs would once again be able to determine their own fate – if even the Russians did realize that the system was dilapidated and not working for the people, perhaps reform could spread to the steppe as well?

Notes

1 Of course, even this is not sufficient for institutional transplantation, as discovered by the United States and Russia in many of their Cold War and post-Cold War interventions.
2 The centralized administration of the Mongols also promoted commerce in less savoury ways as well, including the outsourcing of tax collection to Central Asian trading partnerships, resulting in ruthless extraction from local populaces in pursuit of revenue (of which a portion accrued to business; see Barfield 1992).
3 The Uzbek Khanate itself is dated as lasting from 1428 to 1506, when it transformed itself into the Khanate of Bukhara. It endured until the 19th century when it was conquered by the Russian Empire and became a protectorate (Wilde 2017).
4 Stein (2011) notes that even this description might be too much, asserting that the Khanate was not a "fixed state" but was held together by identity.
5 As we will see below, Russia aided the Kazakhs against the Dzungars, but in reality it was the rearguard actions of the Chinese which led to the expulsion of the Dzungars from Kazakh lands by 1758 (Baipakov and Kumekov 2003). As will be detailed, however, the damage was already done.
6 Unfortunately, as the Kazakhs were soon to find out, the Empress did not view the oath in the same light. This mistake has been repeated dozens of times by countries that have sought Russian "assistance."
7 This letter raises a point which I have glossed over to this point, insomuch as it is not strictly relevant for the development of institutions in the Kazakh Khanate, but which may cause some confusion: while the Kazakhs were named that way based on their attributes (as noted above), the correspondence and legislation of the Russian Empire used "Kirghiz" and "Kazakh" interchangeably and (more often than not) incorrectly. In this instance, the Tsarina was clearly referring to the Kazakhs, with her direct mention of "Nurali Khan."
8 Contra Kassymova et al. (2012), Article 179 of Chapter III of the laws explicitly allows for the permanent inheritance of land allocated for agriculture. However, the idea that this conferred a real property right is one which is not necessarily supported in Russian law or history, despite the unambiguity of the Article (see Pipes 1994).
9 Shaukenov (2013) blames the Russian move towards extraction via taxation on the steppe on "capitalism," which he expands on to suggest that capitalists captured the state apparatus in tsarist Russia for their own ends (thus pushing colonization as a result of economic incentives). This neo-Marxist interpretation, besides being utterly wrong about the relationship of capitalists and the state *and* the relationship of taxes to a free market (i.e. they are antithetical), also appears to not apply in the Kazakh case, where strategic imperatives were driving the shift towards colonization.
10 Yemelianova (2002) notes that Russian schools in the former Kazakh Khanate adopted a mixed-native approach with local languages used for instruction instead of forcing a total immersion into Russian.
11 Frank (2017) relates a tale from Sadwaqas Ghilmani's collection of Islamic biographies, where Islamic authorities had a vigorous discussion on the use of marmot, given that Kazakhs hunted a great many marmots on the steppe. Oddly enough, the status of the marmot was never definitively settled, with different scholars arguing over whether the marmot *could* be hunted under Islamic law.
12 The Great Game has been covered amply elsewhere and has no immediate bearing on the institutional evolution of the Kazakh lands, even though the rivalry with the British was a key determinant of Russian incursions into Central Asia in the 19th century. Put another way, while the Great Game may have provided an impetus for Russian policy and even set broader outlines for the institutions that

Russia wanted to introduce (i.e. for ease of administration), there was nothing unique about this particular great power rivalry that changed the arc of institutional change in Central Asia vis-à-vis other Russian colonial adventures.

13 The policy also utilized the steppe as a dumping ground for undesirables, a point we will turn to below.

14 One only need look at Fyodor Dostoevsky, arguably Russia's greatest novelist, who was exiled to the steppe in the mid-19th century, where he struck up a friendship with the Kazakh intellectual Valikhanov and encouraged him to be an ambassador of "Kazakh-ness" to the Russia people (Sabol 2017).

15 In many ways, this same charge could be levelled at any government in any country at any time in history.

16 This is based on the old (Julian) calendar for the rest of the world this event occurred on 10 March 1917.

References

Abašin, S. N. et al. (2008). *Central'naja Azija v sostave Rossijskoj imperii* [*Central Asia in the Russian Empire*]. Moscow: Novoe literaturnoe obozrenie.

Abazov, R. (2008). *The Palgrave Concise Historical Atlas of Central Asia*. New York: Palgrave Macmillan.

Afinogenov, G. (2019). Languages of hegemony on the eighteenth-century Kazakh steppe. *The International History Review*, 41(5), 1020–1038.

Akhmedov, B. (1998). CA under the rule of Genghis Khan's successors. In M. S. Asimov and C. E. Bosworth (Eds.), *History of Civilizations of Central Asia*. Vol. IV: *The Age of Achievement, A.D. 750 to the End of the Fifteenth Century* (pp. 265–272). New York: UNESCO Publishing.

Aldashev, G. and Guirkinger, C. (2012). Deadly anchor: Gender bias under Russian colonization of Kazakhstan. *Explorations in Economic History*, 49(4), 399–422.

Aldashev, G. and Guirkinger, C. (2017). Colonization and changing social structure: Evidence from Kazakhstan. *Journal of Development Economics*, 127, 413–430.

Aliyassova, V. N., Ilyassova, A. S., Sirlibaev, M. K., and Temirtasov, D. K. (2016). Development of regional studies and collecting in Kazakhstan (in the late 19th century and early 20th century). *Indian Journal of Science and Technology*, 9(42), 104229–104229.

Allworth, E. A. (1994). *Central Asia: One Hundred Thirty Years of Russian Dominance: A Historical Overview*. Durham, NC: Duke University Press.

Alshorbagy, A. A. (2012). On the failure of a legal transplant: The case of Egyptian takeover law. *Indiana International & Comparative Law Review*, 22(2), 237–266.

Amanzholova, D. A. (1997). Kazakh autonomy and Russia: The history of the Alash Movement (sxcerpts). *Anthropology & Archeology of Eurasia*, 36(3), 10–23.

Asadov, F. (2000). Oil caravans of the 21st century on the Great Silk Road: What the future has in store for Azerbaijan and Kazakhstan. *Central Asia and the Caucasus*, 6, 179–185.

Ashrafyan, K. Z. (1998). Central Asia under Timur from 1370 to the early fifteenth century. In M. S. Asimov and C. E. Bosworth (Eds.), *History of Civilizations of Central Asia*. Vol. IV: *The Age of Achievement, A.D. 750 to the End of the Fifteenth Century* (pp. 323–349). New York: UNESCO Publishing.

Ayupova, Z. (1998). Concise essay on the history of state and law development in the Republic of Kazakhstan, A. *Tulsa Journal of Comparative and International Law*, 6 (1), 49–63.

Baipakov, K. and Kumekov, B. (2003). The Kazakhs. In A. H. Dani and V. M. Masson (Eds.) *History of Civilizations of Central Asia.* Vol. 5: *Development in Contrast: From the Sixteenth to the Mid-nineteenth Century* (pp. 90–109). New York: UNESCO.

Baipakov, K., Kumekov, B., and Pischulina, K. (1997). *Istoria Kazakhstana v srednie veka* [*History of Kazakhstan in the Middle Ages*]. Almaty: Rauan Publishers.

Barfield, T. (1992). *The Perilous Frontier: Nomadic Empires and China, 221 BC to AD 1757.* Oxford: Blackwell Publishers.

Barfield T (2001) Steppe empires, China and the Silk Route: Nomads as a force in international trade and politics. In A. Khazanov and A. Wink (Eds.), *Nomads in the Sedentary World* (pp. 234–249). London: Routledge.

Barisitz, S. (2017). *Central Asia and the Silk Road.* Berlin: Springer.

Becker, S. O., Boeckh, K., Hainz, C., and Woessmann, L. (2016). The empire is dead, long live the empire! Long-run persistence of trust and corruption in the bureaucracy. *The Economic Journal*, 126(590), 40–74.

Beisembayeva, A. R. (2021). The reasons for the weakening of the institution of the Khan's power in the Kazakh Steppe in the context of the regional policy of the Russian Empire at the end of the 18th century and the beginning of the 19th century. *Bulletin of the Karaganda University*, 1(101), 6–14.

Bekmakhanov, E. B. (1947). *Kazakhstan v 20–40 gody. XIX veka* [*Kazakhstan in the Years 1820–1840 of the 19th Century*]. Almaty: Kazakh University Press.

Bekmakhanova, N. E. (1986). *Mnogonatsional'noe naselenie Kazakhstana i Kirgizii v epokhu kapitalizma, 60-e gody 19v.-1917* [*The Multinational Population of Kazakhstan and Kyrgyzstan in the Era of Capitalism, 1860–1917*]. Moscow: Nauka.

Berdyguzhin, L. B. (2016). New insights into the history of the Kazakh Khanate formation. *Analele Universitatii din Craiova-Seria Istorie*, 30(2), 17–26.

Berdyguzhin, L. B., Nagimov, S., Sarsenov, A., Jambaulova, G., Khamidullina, D., Nigmetov, B., and Kaluova, S. (2020). Formation of Kazakh national elites in the late 19th and early 20th centuries. *Codrul Cosminului*, 26(1), 57–72.

Bikenov, A., Abdrakhmanova, G., Zharkenova, A., Muratbekkyzy, B., Erdenbekova, Z., Baibulsinova, A., and Kolumbaeva, Z. (2016). Ethno-cultural aspects of the state of Eurasian nomads. *The Anthropologist*, 26(1–2), 34–39.

Bira, S. (1998). The Mongols and their state in the twelfth to the thirteenth century. In M. S. Asimov and C. E. Bosworth (Eds.), *History of Civilizations of Central Asia.* Vol. IV: *The Age of Achievement, A.D. 750 to the End of the Fifteenth Century* (pp. 248–264). New York: UNESCO Publishing.

Bodger, A. (1980). Abulkhair, Khan of the Kazakh Little Horde, and his oath of allegiance to Russia of October 1731. *The Slavonic and East European Review*, 58 (1), 40–57.

Bodger, A. (1991). Change and tradition in eighteenth-century Kazakhstan: The dynastic factor. In S. Akiner (Ed.), *Cultural Change & Continuity in Central Asia* (pp. 354–370). New York: Routledge.

Bodger, A. (1993). On the extent and nature of Kazakh participation in the Pugachev revolt, 1773–75. *Central Asian Survey*, 12(4), 497–524.

Bregel, Y. (2003). *An Historical Atlas of Central Asia.* Leiden: Brill Publishing.

Brower, D. (2012). *Turkestan and the Fate of the Russian Empire.* New York: Routledge.

Bukeikhanov, A. (1910). Kirgizy. In A. Kastelansky (Ed.), *Formy natsional 'nogo dvizheniia v sovremennykh gosudarstvakh* [*Forms of National Movements in Modern States*] (pp. 575–600). St Petersburg: Public Benefit Publishers.

Burton, A. (1997). *The Bukharans: A Dynastic, Diplomatic and Commercial History 1550–1702*. New York: Routledge.

Cameron, S. (2018). *The Hungry Steppe: Famine, Violence, and the Making of Soviet Kazakhstan*. Ithaca, NY: Cornell University Press.

Campbell, I. W. (2017). *Knowledge and the Ends of Empire: Kazak Intermediaries and Russian Rule on the Steppe, 1731–1917*. Ithaca, NY: Cornell University Press.

Campbell, I. W. (2020). Nationalizing violence in a collapsing empire: A view from the steppe. *Ab Imperio*, 2020(3), 98–113.

Carmack, R. J. (2014). History and hero-making: Patriotic narratives and the Sovietization of Kazakh front-line propaganda, 1941–1945. *Central Asian Survey*, 33(1), 95–112.

Crews, R. D. (2014). Moscow and the Mosque: Co-opting Muslims in Putin's Russia. *Foreign Affairs*, 93(2), 125–134.

Crowe, D. M. (1998). The Kazaks and Kazakstan: The struggle for ethnic identity and nationhood. *Nationalities Papers*, 26(3), 395–419.

Davidovich, E.A. (1998). The Karakhanids. In M. S. Asimov and C. E. Bosworth (Eds.), *History of Civilizations of Central Asia*. Vol. IV: *The Age of Achievement, A. D. 750 to the End of the Fifteenth Century* (pp. 125–149). New York: UNESCO Publishing.

De Jong, M., Lalenis, K., and Mamadouh, V. D. (Eds.). (2002). *The Theory and Practice of Institutional Transplantation: Experiences with the Transfer of Policy Institutions* (Vol. 74). Berlin: Springer Science & Business Media.

Demenko, O. (2019). The revolt of 1916 and its influence on the formation of Kazakh national identity. *Problems of World History*, (8), 55–66 (in Ukrainian).

DeWeese, D. (1994). *Islamization and Native Religion in the Golden Horde: Baba Tükles and Conversion to Islam in Historical and Epic Tradition*. University Park, PA: Penn State University Press.

Diener, A. C. (2002). National territory and the reconstruction of history in Kazakhstan. *Eurasian Geography and Economics*, 43(8), 632–650.

Diyarbekirli, N. (1992). Turkish contributions to cultural and commercial life along Silk Road. *Senri Ethnological Studies*, 32, 171–192.

Duisembayeva, N. B. (2019). Education in Kazakhstan in the late 19th and early 20th centuries and Kazakh intellectuals. *News of the Academy of Sciences of the Republic of Kazakhstan, Series of Social and Human Sciences*, 4, 91–96.

Dzhunusova, Z. (2004). The democratic tradition of Kazakhstan in historical context. *Democracy and Pluralism in Muslim Eurasia* (pp. 13–30). London: Routledge.

Erofeeva, I. (2004). The evolution of the traditional governing elites of Kazakhstan within the Russian Empire between the middle of the 18th and the beginning of the 20th centuries. In G. Rasuly-Paleczek and J. Katschnig (Eds.), *Central Asia on Display: Proceedings of the VIIth Conference of the European Society for Central Asian Studies* (pp. 67–80). Münster: LIT Verlag.

Esenova, S. (2002). Soviet nationality, identity, and ethnicity in Central Asia: Historic narratives and Kazakh ethnic identity. *Journal of Muslim Minority Affairs*, 22(1), 11–38.

Fierman, W. (2005). Kazakh language and prospects for its role in Kazakh "groupness.". *Ab Imperio*, 2005(2), 393–423.

Fisher, A. W. (1968). Enlightened despotism and Islam under Catherine II. *Slavic Review*, 27(4), 542–553.

Fleet, K. (1999). *European and Islamic Trade in the Early Ottoman State: The Merchants of Genoa and Turkey*. Cambridge: Cambridge University Press.

Frank, A. J. (2001). *Muslim Religious Institutions in Imperial Russia: The Islamic World of Novouzensk District and the Kazakh Inner Horde, 1780–1910*. Leiden: Brill Publishing.

Frank, A. J. (2017). Sharī'a debates and fatwas among nomads in northern Kazakhstan, 1850–1931. *Islamic Law and Society*, 24(1–2), 61–76.

Galai, S. (2002). *The Liberation Movement in Russia 1900–1905* Cambridge: Cambridge University Press.

Gatrell, P. (2005). *Russia's First World War: A Social and Economic History*. London: Pearson Education.

Geifman, A. (1993). *Thou Shalt Kill*. Princeton, NJ: Princeton University Press.

Gentes, A. A. (2017). *The Mass Deportation of Poles to Siberia, 1863–1880*. London: Palgrave Macmillan.

Gilomen, H.-J. (2014). *Wirtschaftsgeschichte des Mittelalters*. Munich: C. H. Beck Publishers.

Golden, P. B. (2011). *Central Asia in World History*. New York: Oxford University Press.

Grosfeld, I., Rodnyansky, A., and Zhuravskaya, E. (2013). Persistent antimarket culture: A legacy of the pale of settlement after the Holocaust. *American Economic Journal: Economic Policy*, 5(3), 189–226.

Grosfeld, I. and Zhuravskaya, E. (2015). Cultural vs. economic legacies of empires: Evidence from the partition of Poland. *Journal of Comparative Economics*, 43(1), 55–75.

Guinnane, T. W. (1994). A failed institutional transplant: Raiffeisen′ s credit cooperatives in Ireland, 1894–1914. *Explorations in economic history*, 31(1), 38–61.

Habib, I. (2003). Colonialism and Central Asia. In A. H. Dani and V. M. Masson (Eds.), *History of Civilizations of Central Asia*. Vol. 5: *Development in Contrast: From the sixteenth to the Mid-nineteenth Century* (pp. 338–345).New York: UNESCO.

Hallez, X. and Ohayon, I. (2019). Making political rebellion "primitive": The 1916 rebellion in the Kazakh steppe in long-term perspective (c. 1840–1930). In A. Chokobaeva, C. Drieu, and A. Morrison (Eds.), *The Central Asian Revolt of 1916* (pp. 256–288). Manchester: Manchester University Press.

Hanks, R. R. (1998). Directions in the ethnic politics of Kazakhstan: Concession, compromise, or catastrophe? *Journal of Third World Studies*, 15(1), 143–162.

Hartwell, C. A. (2016). *Two Roads Diverge: The Transition Experience of Poland and Ukraine*. Cambridge: Cambridge University Press.

Hartwell, C. A. (2020). *Terrorism, Political Violence, and Political Instability in Russia: 1788 to 1914*. Ann Arbor, MI: Inter-university Consortium for Political and Social Research. https://doi.org/10.3886/E117682V1.

Hiro, D. (2009). *Inside Central Asia: A Political and Cultural History of Uzbekistan, Turkmenistan, Kazakhstan, Kyrgyz stan, Tajikistan, Turkey, and Iran*. New York: Peter Mayer Publishers.

Hoerder, D. (2017). Introduction to the Special Issue on migrations in Slavic, Tsarist Russian and Soviet history. *Journal of Migration History*, 3(2), 173–178.

Holquist, P. (2010). "In accord with state interests and the people's wishes": The technocratic ideology of Imperial Russia's Resettlement Administration. *Slavic Review*, 69(1), 151–179.

Jackson, P. (2005). *The Mongols and the West: 1221–1410*. New York: Routledge.

Jacoby, T. (2007). Hegemony, modernisation and post-war reconstruction. *Global Society*, 21(4), 521–537.

Kadyrbekov, A. and Veselov, D. (2019). *Migration of Russian Settlers and the Legacy of Inter-Regional Development in Kazakhstan.* HSE working papers, WP BRP 210/EC/2019, Moscow: National Research University Higher School of Economics.

Kaliyeva, G. (2013). Corruption onset in the nineteenth century in Kazakhstan. *CBU International Conference Proceedings*, 1, 125–128.

Kassymova, D., Kundakbayeva, Z., and Markus, U. (2012). *Historical Dictionary of Kazakhstan*. Lanham, MD: Scarecrow Press.

Kauz, R. (2009) Zerstörung, Eroberung, politische Umstrukturierung: Zentralasien. In T. Ertl and M. Limberger (Eds.), *Die Welt 1250–1500*. Essen: Magnus Verlag.

Kaynar, M. and Sakhitzhanova, Z. (2016). Pre-Islamic beliefs of the Kazakhs and the spread of Islam in Kazakhstan. In A. Rogusk and A. Antas-Jaszczuk (Eds.), *Transformations in Cultural, Social and Educational Activity: Challenges Towards Contemporary Europe* (pp. 111–116). Siedlce: Siedlce University of Natural Sciences and Humanities Press.

Kazemzadeh, F. (1974). VI Basin. Rossiia i kazakhskie khanstva v XVI–XVIII vv. (Kazakhstan i sisteme vneshnei politiki rossiiskoi imperii) [Russia and the Kazakh Khanates in the 16th to 18th Centuries (Kazakhstan and the System of Foreign Politics of the Russian Empire)].(Institut Istorii, Arkheologii i Etnografii im. Ch. Ch. Valikhanova an KazSSR.) Alma Ata: Izdatel'stvo "Nauka" Kazakhskoi SSR. 1971 (book review). *American Historical Review*, 79(1), 195–196.

Kendirbaeva, G. (1997). Migrations in Kazakhstan: Past and present. *Nationalities Papers*, 25(4), 741–751.

Kendirbaeva, G. (1999). "We are children of Alash…" The Kazakh intelligentsia at the beginning of the 20th century in search of national identity and prospects of the cultural survival of the Kazakh people. *Central Asian Survey*, 18(1), 5–36.

Kendirbay, G. T. (1997). The national liberation movement of the Kazakh intelligentsia at the beginning of the 20th century. *Central Asian Survey*, 16(4), 487–515.

Kendirbay, G. T. (2020). *Russian Practices of Governance in Eurasia: Frontier Power Dynamics, Sixteenth Century to Nineteenth Century*. New York: Routledge.

Kesici, Ö. (2017). The Alash movement and the question of Kazakh ethnicity. *Nationalities Papers*, 45(6), 1135–1149.

Khazanov, A. M. (2019). Nómadas de la Estepa en el Comercio Eurasiàtico [Nomads of the Steppe in Eurasian Trade]. *Chungará (Arica)*, 51(1), 85–93.

Khodarkovsky, M. (2002). *Russia's Steppe Frontier: The Making of A Colonial Empire, 1500–1800*. Bloomington: Indiana University Press.

Kiliç, E. (2018). The concept of "commercial Law" in the Golden Horde state according to archival resources. In Y. Öztürk and N. Kavak (Eds.), *Concepts, Sources and Methodology in Eastern European Studies* (pp. 443–475). Kyiv: Platform of International Eastern European Studies.

Kilic-Schubel, N. (2004). 1.1. Balancing "Yasa" and "Shariat" in the Shibanid-Uzbek Khanate in the 16th century. In G. Rasuly-Paleczek and J. Katschnig (Eds.), *Central Asia on Display: Proceedings of the VIIth Conference of the European Society for Central Asian Studies* (pp. 17–30). Münster: LIT Verlag.

Kim, S. C. (2009). The changing of Central Asian traditional communities by the cultural succession and discontinuation. *International Area Review*, 12(3), 79–96.

Kirchner, M. (2015). Kazakh and Karakalpak. In L. Johanson and É. Á. C. Johanson (Eds.), *The Turkic Languages* (pp. 318–332). New York: Routledge.

Kovács, S. (2020). Taydula: A Golden Horde queen and patron of Christian merchants. In *Along the Silk Roads in Mongol Eurasia* (pp. 194–212). Berkeley: University of California Press.

Kovalev, R. K. and Mako, G. (2016). Kimek Khaganate. In J. M. MacKenzie (Ed.), *The Encyclopedia of Empire* (pp. 1–2). London: Taylor and Francis.

Kradin, N. N. (2002). *The Xiongnu Empire*. Moscow: Logos Publishing.

Krasnozhon, L. and Bunyk, M. (2019). Liberalism and great upheaval: What did classical liberals do in the Tsarist Russia? *Constitutional Political Economy*, 30(1), 96–113.

Kreindler, I. (1983). Ibrahim Altynsarin, Nikolai Il'minskii and the Kazakh national awakening. *Central Asian Survey*, 2(3), 99–116.

Kudaibergenova, A., Zhugenbayeva, G., Apendiyev, T., Chatybekova, K., Bissembayeva, L., Aynagul, K., Amran, Z., and Kymbat, S. (2017). Influence of migration processes on changing in the ethnic composition of the population of Kazakhstan (end of the XIX-end of the XX centuries). *Man in India*, 97(2), 47–64.

Kumekov, B.E. (2013). Kipchakovedenie: konceptual'noe nauchnoe napravlenie evraziyskogo masshtaba [Kipchak Studies: Conceptual and Scientific Tendencies from a Eurasian Perspective]. In *The Kipchaks of Eurasia: History, Language and Written Records* (pp. 10–17). Nur-Sultan: Kazakstan Rspublikasy Medeniet zhane akparat ministrliginiag Til komitet. Retrieved 30 April2021, http://kazneb.kz/bookView/view/?brId=1559550.

Kundakbayeva, Z. (2021). *The History of Kazakhstan from the Earliest Period to the Present Time*. Vol. I. Moscow: LitRes Publishing.

Kupbaeva, R. M., Beisembaev, M., Kadirgalieva, A. T., and Maulenkul, N. A. (2018). Kazakhstan in Ancient Times. In *Sovremennyye Tendentsii Razvitiya Nauki I Obrazovaniya* [*Modern Trends in the Development of Science and Education*] (pp. 150–154). Prague: Scientific Publishing Center "World of Science."

Lazzerini, E. J. (2016). Kazakh Khanate. In J. M. MacKenzie (Ed.), *The Encyclopedia of Empire* (pp. 1–2). New York: John Wiley & Sons. https://onlinelibrary.wiley.com/doi/abs/10.1002/9781118455074.wbeoe303.)

LeDonne, J. P. (2004). *The Grand Strategy of the Russian Empire, 1650–1831*. Oxford: Oxford University Press.

Levi, S. C. (2002). Hindus beyond the Hindu Kush: Indians in the Central Asian slave trade. *Journal of the Royal Asiatic Society*, 12(3), 277–288.

Lewis, M. E. (2012). *China's Cosmopolitan Empire: The Tang Dynasty*. Cambridge, MA: Harvard University Press.

Lincoln, W. B. (2007). *The Conquest of a Continent: Siberia and the Russians*. Cornell, NY: Cornell University Press.

Lockhart, R. B. (1957). "The unanimous revolution:" Russia, February 1917. *Foreign Affairs*, 35(2), 320–333.

Malikov, Y. (2005). The Kenesary Kasymov rebellion (1837–1847): A national-liberation movement or "a protest of restoration"? *Nationalities Papers*, 33(4), 569–597.

Malikov, Y. (2019). *Modern Central Asia: A Primary Source Reader*. New York: Lexington Books.

Margulan A. K. (1975). *Kassym khannyn kaska zholy* [*The Bright Way of Kassym Khan*]. Almaty: KSE Press.

Marker, G. (2014). *Publishing, Printing, and the Origins of the Intellectual Life in Russia, 1700–1800* (Vol. 32). Princeton, NJ: Princeton University Press.

Martin, V. (1997). Barimta: Nomadic custom, imperial crime. In D. R. Brower and E. J. Lazzerini (Eds.), *Russia's Orient: Imperial Borderlands and Peoples, 1700–1917* (pp. 249–270). Bloomington: Indiana University Press.

Martin, V. (2001). *Law and Custom in the Steppe: The Kazakhs of the Middle Horde and Russian Colonialism in the Nineteenth Century.* New York: Routledge.

Masselos, J. (Ed.) (2010). *Imperien Asiens: Von den alten Khmer bis zu den Meiji.* Stuttgart: Konrad Theiss Verlag.

Mattingly, G. (1955). *Renaissance Diplomacy.* Boston: Houghton Mifflin.

McDaniel, S. (2017). "Our greatest riches": Horses at the intersection of settler and Kazakh society in the late imperial period. *Journal of Migration History*, 3(2), 210–228.

Mearns, R. (1993). Territoriality and land tenure among Mongolian pastoralists: Variation, continuity and change. *Nomadic Peoples*, 33, 73–103.

Mitchell, B. R. (Ed.) (1975). *European Historical Statistics, 1750–1970.* Berlin: Springer.

Morgan, D. O. (1986). The "Great Yāsā of Chingiz Khān" and Mongol law in the ⊠lkhānate. *Bulletin of the School of Oriental and African Studies*, 49(1), 163–176.

Morgan, D.O. (2007). *The Mongols: The Peoples of Europe* (2nd ed.). Oxford: Blackwell Publishing.

Morrison, A. (2012). Metropole, colony, and imperial citizenship in the Russian Empire. *Kritika: Explorations in Russian and Eurasian History*, 13(2), 327–364.

Morrison, A. (2015). Peasant settlers and the 'civilising mission' in Russian Turkestan, 1865–1917. *The Journal of Imperial and Commonwealth History*, 43(3), 387–417.

Mukminova, R. G. (1998). The Timurid states in the fifteenth and sixteenth centuries. In M. S. Asimov and C. E. Bosworth (Eds.), *History of Civilizations of Central Asia.* Vol. IV: *The Age of Achievement, A.D. 750 to the End of the Fifteenth Century* (pp. 350–366). New York: UNESCO Publishing.

Nedashkovskii, L. F. (2009). Economy of the Golden Horde population. *Anthropology & Archeology of Eurasia*, 48(2), 35–50.

Nichols, P.M. (1997). The viability of transplanted law: Kazakhstani reception of transplanted foreign investment code. *University of Pennsylvania Journal of International Economic Law*, 18(4), 1235–1280.

Noda, J. (2016). *The Kazakh Khanates between the Russian and Qing Empires: Central Eurasian International Relations during the Eighteenth and Nineteenth Centuries.* Leiden: Brill Publishers.

Noonan, T. S. (2007). Some observations on the economy of the Khazar Khaganate. In P. B. Golden, H. Ben-Shammai, and A. Róna-Tas (Eds.), *The World of the Khazars* (pp. 207–244). Leiden: Brill Publishers,.

Normatov, S. M. (2020). Analysis of new approaches to foreign economic relations of Sogdiana (on the example of the era of the first Middle Ages). *Theoretical & Applied Science*, 1, 729–731.

Norel, P. (2009). *L'Histoire économique globale.* Paris: Editions du Seuil.

Ó Beacháin, D. and Kevlihan, R. (2011). *State-building, Identity and Nationalism in Kazakhstan: Some Preliminary Thoughts.* Working Papers in International Studies. Dublin: Centre for International Studies, Dublin City University. http://doras.dcu.ie/16243/1/1101.pdf.

Ohayon, I. (2009). *Sedentarizatsija kazahov SSSR pri Staline: Kollektivizatsija i sotsialnyje izmenenija (1928–1945 gg)* [*Sedentarization of the Kazakhs of the USSR under Stalin: Collectivization and Social Change (1928–1945)*]. Almaty: Sanat Publishers.

Ohayon, I. (2015). Foreword: Mediators of the empire in Central Asia (1820–1928). *Cahiers du monde russe*, 56(4), 621–624.

Olcott, M. B. (1981). The settlement of the Kazakh nomads. *Nomadic peoples*, 8, 12–23. www.waunet.org/iuaes/comm/cnp/wp-content/uploads/2020/06/The_Settlement_of_the_Kazakh_Nomads_M_Olcott_No-8_1981.pdf.

Olcott, M. B. (1985). The politics of language reform in Kazakhstan. In I. T. Kreindler (Ed.), *Sociolinguistic Perspectives on Soviet National Languages* (pp. 183–204). Berlin: De Gruyter Mouton.

Olcott, M. B. (1995). *The Kazakhs.* Palo Alto, CA: Hoover Institution Press.

Olcott, M. B. (2010). *Kazakhstan: Unfulfilled Promise.* Washington, DC: Carnegie Endowment.

Omarov, Y. S. (2006). Civilization and economics of Kazakhstan. In A. Vogiatzis (Ed.), *Festschrift in Honor of Maria Negreponti-Delivanis* (pp. 153–182). Thessaloniki: University of Macedonia Press.

Omelicheva, M. Y. (2011). Islam in Kazakhstan: A survey of contemporary trends and sources of securitization. *Central Asian Survey*, 30(2), 243–256.

Oskolkov, V. and Oskolkova, I. (2004). *Istoria Kazakhstana (Spravochnik)*. Almaty: Oner Baspasy Publishers.

Ostrowski, D. (2016). Sibir', Khanate of. In *The Encyclopedia of Empire* (pp. 1–3). New York: John Wiley & Sons. https://onlinelibrary.wiley.com/doi/abs/10.1002/9781118455074.wbeoe190).

Otepova, G. Y. (2014). The history of Kazakhstan in the legislative sources of the Russian Empire in the 18th–the early 20th century. *Life Science Journal*, 11(9), 96–101.

Pavlenko, A. (2011). Linguistic Russification in the Russian Empire: Peasants into Russians? *Russian Linguistics*, 35(3), 331–350.

Payne, M. J. (2019). "Do you want me to exterminate all of them or just the ones who oppose us?": The 1916 Revolt in Semirech'e. In K. A. Goff and L. H. Siegellbaum (Eds.), *Empire and Belonging in the Eurasian Borderlands* (pp. 65–79). Ithaca, NY: Cornell University Press.

Pelenski, J. Z. (1967). Muscovite imperial claims to the Kazan khanate. *Slavic Review*, 26(4), 559–576.

Pelenskj, J. Z. (1974). *Russia and Kazan: Conquest and imperial ideology (1438–1560s)*. Berlin: de Gruyter.

Perlman, B. J. and Gleason, G. (2007). Cultural determinism versus administrative logic: Asian values and administrative reform in Kazakhstan and Uzbekistan. *International Journal of Public Administration*, 30(12–14), 1327–1342.

Pipes, R. (1994). Was there private property in Muscovite Russia? *Slavic Review*, 53 (2), 524–530.

Polek, K. (2013). The role of the Khazar Khaganate in the Economic system of the early Middle Ages. *Quaestiones Medii Aevi Novae*, 18, 335–363.

Rahul, R. (2000). *March of Central Asia.* New Delhi: Indus Publishing.

Raskin, D. I. (Ed.) (2004). *Vysshie i tsentralnye hosudarstvennye uchrezhdeniia Rossii, 1801–1917* [*Higher and Central State Institutions of Russia, 1801–1917*] (Vol. 4). St Petersburg: Sankt-Peterburgskaia izdatelsko-knihotorhovaia firma "Nauka."

Riasanovsky, V. A. (1948). Mongol law: A concise historical survey. *Washington Law Review and State Bar Journal*, 23(2), 166–177.

Roland, G. (2004). Understanding institutional change: Fast-moving and slow-moving institutions. *Studies in Comparative International Development*, 38(4), 109–131.

Rossabi, M. (2014). *From Yuan to Modern China and Mongolia: The Writings of Morris Rossabi*. Leiden: Brill Publishers.

Ruskulovna, A. R. (2019). "Jeti-jarga" as the basis of Kazakh khanate legislation. *Uzbekistan Journal of Oriental Studies*, 1(1), 50–64.

Ryszhanova, G. S. and Cëmplak, K. (2018). The main law of traditional Kazakh society originating from the Kazakh Khanate. *Colloquium Journal*, 8(4), 70–72.

Sablin, I. and Korobeynikov, A. (2016). Buryat-Mongol and Alash autonomous movements before the Soviets, 1905–1917. *AlterNative: An International Journal of Indigenous Peoples*, 12(3), 211–223.

Sabol, S. (2003). Kazak resistance to Russian colonization: Interpreting the Kenesary Kasymov revolt, 1837–1847. *Central Asian Survey*, 22(2–3), 231–252.

Sabol, S. (2017). *"The Touch of Civilization": Comparing American and Russian Internal Colonization*. Boulder: University Press of Colorado.

Saira, S., Aigul, T., and Kanshayuma, D. (2015). Mental types of the Kazakh and Mongolian women. *Procedia-Social and Behavioral Sciences*, 205, 373–380.

Schamiloglu, U. (2018). The rise of urban centers in the Golden Horde and the city of Ükek. *Golden Horde Review*, 6(1), 18–40.

Shalgimbekov, A. B., Gulyaev, I. I., and Moldabayeva, S. A. (2020). Russian military fortifications on the eve of including the northern Region of Kazakhstan into the empire. *3i: intellect, idea, innovation – нтеллект, идея, иннёвация*, 4, 82–86.

Scott, J.C. (2009). *The Art of Not Being Governed: An Anarchist History of Upland Southeast Asia*. New Haven, CT: Yale University Press.

Searle, J. R. (2005). What is an institution? *Journal of Institutional Economics*, 1(1), 1–22.

Shaukenov, A. (2013). Changes in the political and legal system of Kazakhstan in the process of its incorporation into the Russian Empire from the second half of the 18th century to the end of the 19th century. *Journal of Asian and African Studies*, 22(2), 279–301.

Smagulova, J. (2006). Kazakhstan: Language, identity and conflict. *Innovation*, 19(3–4), 303–320.

Sohrabi, N. (1995). Historicizing revolutions: Constitutional revolutions in the Ottoman Empire, Iran, and Russia, 1905–1908. *American Journal of Sociology*, 100(6), 1383–1447.

Stein, M. (2011). Connecting to the Khans: Shaping national identity of the next generation through education in Kazakhstan. *Current Issues in Education*, 14(2), 1–11.

Stevens, C. A. (2020). Russia–Kazakhstan relations in the early post-Soviet era: Explaining the roots of cooperation. *Europe-Asia Studies*, 72(7), 1153–1185.

Sultangalieva, G. (2014). The role of the pristavstvo institution in the context of Russian imperial policies in the Kazakh steppe in the nineteenth century. *Central Asian Survey*, 33(1), 62–79.

Sultangalieva, G. and Seitz, J. B. (2020). "They do not help, only demoralize": Peasant nachalniks and the last imperial Russian reform on the Kazakh steppe, 1902–1917. *Central Asian Survey*, 39(2), 167–184.

Tasmagambetov, I. N. (Ed.) (2005). *Istoriya Kazahstana v russkih istochnikah XVI-XX vv.* 3-t. [*The History of Kazakhstan in Russian Sources from the 16th to the 20th Centuries*. Vol. 3]. Almaty: Dayk Press.

Tomohiko, U. (2013). Two attempts at building a Qazaq state: The revolt of 1916 and the Alash movement. In S. A. Dudoignon and K. Hisao (Eds.), *Islam in Politics in Russia and Central Asia* (pp. 77–98). New York: Routledge.

Trepavlov, V. V. (2018). The Takht Eli Khanate: The state system at the twilight of the Golden Horde. *Revue des Mondes Musulmans et de la Mediterranee*, 143, 235–248.
Tyukhteneva, S. P. (2017). One Hyphen–One Hundred: Revisiting the Issue of Livestock Count among the Turko-Mongolian Peoples. *VESTNIK*, 33(5), 130–140.
Ueda, A. (2013). How did the Nomads act during the 1916 revolt in Russian Turkistan? *Journal of Asian Network for GIS-based Historical Studies*, 1, 33–44.
Uyama, T. (2015). Repression of Kazakh intellectuals as a sign of weakness of Russian imperial rule. The paradoxical impact of Governor AN Troinitskii on the Kazakh national movement. *Cahiers du monde russe. Russie-Empire russe-Union soviétique et États indépendants*, 56(4), 681–703.
Vasyutin, S. A. (2019). Political complexity in nomadic empires of Inner Asia. *Social Evolution and History*, 18(2), 92–114.
Wendelken, R. W. (2000). Russian immigration and its effect on the Kazak steppes, 1552–1965. In A. Bell-Fialkoff (Ed.), *The Role of Migration in the History of the Eurasian Steppe* (pp. 71–101). New York: Palgrave Macmillan.
Wilde, A. (2017). The Emirate of Bukhara. In D. Ludden (Ed.), *Oxford Research Encyclopedia of Asian History*. Oxford: Oxford University Press. https://doi.org/10.1093/acrefore/9780190277727.013.14.
Williams, D. S. M. (1972). Demko, GD "The Russian colonization of Kazakhstan 1896–1916" (book review). *Slavonic and East European Review*, 50(119), 307–308.
Wysocki, W. J. and Kawalec, L. (2011). Golgotha of the East: Polish polity in Imperial Russia. *Dialogue and Universalism*, 21(3), 99–112.
Yan, H., Lai, C., Akshalov, K., Qin, Y., Hu, Y., and Zhen, L. (2020). Social institution changes and their ecological impacts in Kazakhstan over the past hundred years. *Environmental Development*, 34, 100531.
Yemelianova, G. M. (2002). *Russia and Islam: A Historical Survey*. Berlin: Springer.
Yemelianova, G. M. (2014). Islam, national identity and politics in contemporary Kazakhstan. *Asian Ethnicity*, 15(3), 286–301.
Yi Meng, C. (2021). Revolutions never die, they just fade away: The February Revolution through Chinese eyes. *Revolutionary Russia*, 1–26.
Zajda, J. (2014). The Russian Revolution. In G. Ritzer and J. M. Ryan (Eds.), *The Wiley Blackwell Encyclopedia of Globalization Online*. https://doi.org/10.1002/9780470670590.wbeog623.
Zardykhan, Z. (2002). Kazakhstan and Central Asia: Regional perspectives. *Central Asian Survey*, 21(2), 167–183.
Zardykhan, Z. (2004). Russians in Kazakhstan and demographic change: Imperial legacy and the Kazakh way of nation building. *Asian Ethnicity*, 5(1), 61–79.
Zhappasov, Z. E. and Botash, S. (2017). Commercial relations of Kazakhstan and Russia in the XVI-XVII centuries. *International Scientific and Practical Conference World Science*, 4(5), 49–54.
Zhivov, V. M. (2002). *Razyskaniia v oblasti istorii i predystorii russkoi kul'tury* [*Research in the History and Pre-history of Russian Culture*]. Moscow: Iazyki russkoi kul'tury.
Zimonyi, I. (2018). Changing Perceptions of Türk identity among the medieval nomads of Central Eurasia. *Studia Orientalia Electronica*, 6, 79–89.

3 Drawing Conclusions from 1,000 Years of Kazakh Institutional History

Before moving further into the 20th century and the massive dislocations that the Kazakhs and the overall Kazakh institutional milieu were about to experience, it is important at this point to take stock of the massive amount of institutional history we have just waded through. Given the semi-permanence of institutions (as a theoretical construct, if not necessarily in reality), the vantage point of a millennium allows us to better understand the evolution of Kazakh institutions, both political and economic, and to draw some conclusions regarding their development. Indeed, there was remarkable continuity with regard to these institutions over a very long time frame, with structural breaks in overall institutional make-up only manifesting themselves via exogenous shocks imposed from the outside rather than emerging endogenously; in this sense, the Kazakhs saw more institutional *revolution* than *evolution*, a problem which will become more evident in Kazakh history as we move through the 20th century.

In addition to this issue of gradual versus abrupt institutional change, as mentioned in Chapter 1, the Kazakhs also underwent a full range of other institutional issues during their historical evolution, seeing a progression from the informality of the steppe to the formality of various empires and proto-states and the move towards a nation-state (and, of course, the subsequent absorption of the Kazakhs into the Russian Empire). Each step in this transition created complex outcomes in the ecology of institutions within the Kazakh realm, and these interactions – and the weight of history - have also created themes which have persisted (and in turn heavily influenced institutional development) through the 20th and 21st centuries, a point we will explore in later chapters. For now, there are three main conclusions we can draw about Kazakh institutional history up to this point, related to the predominance of economic arrangements, the decentralized nature of political arrangements, and the effects of institutional transplantation.

What Determined Institutional Change on the Steppe?

One of the first lessons which emerges from the Kazakh experience is a challenge to existing theories of institutional influence which tend to

DOI: 10.4324/9781003212508-3

dominate economic thinking, and that is the idea of a "hierarchy of institutions" (Acemoglu et al. 2005). As shown in Figure 3.1, this idea of institutional hierarchy posits that political institutions are the *primus inter pares* of institutions, with the distribution of power within a society determining how formal political institutions constitute themselves and, more importantly, how economic institutions then come to be. This approach, having some Marxist undertones in its thoughts on power relations, believes that economic performance is a third order consequence of economic institutions, which are themselves second order distillations of the prevailing power structure, its political institutions, and the incentives of elites and the powerful. While new institutional economics, led by luminaries such as North (1990), has delved into ways in which economic forces play a significant role in institutional evolution – and, in particular, the role of relative prices in forcing political change – for the most part, the approach taken by Acemoglu et al. (2005) has dominated institutional economic thinking. Put another way, while economic forces in the long term may gradually erode the distribution of resources (and their value) and who has the power in society, in the short and medium term economic events are a consequence of political institutions rather than a driver of them.

This hierarchical approach has been challenged by many authors, including myself (Hartwell 2018), as ignoring the vast literature on the determinants of political institutions and especially the endogeneity inherent in a complex institutional system, where even slight changes in economic conditions can lead to outsize effects on political systems. An excellent example of this is the phenomenon of populism, essentially the marriage of left-wing big government economics and right-wing nationalism (or, as seen recently in the Western world, social conservatism); populist leaders can come to power because of dissatisfaction with economic policy or economic shocks (Stankov 2018), but once in power, they have the ability to introduce substantial institutional changes which can entirely reorder the political institutions of a country (Hartwell and Devinney 2021). In this manner, economics (which may have been the result of previous political institutions) can lead directly to changes in the prevailing power structure and then in political institutions. Similarly, the long-term consequences of profligate monetary policy can cripple nascent political institutions and bring to power much more extreme elements that are willing to use the levers of power for malevolent ends (Hartwell 2019).

The example of Kazakh institutions over 1,000 years supports this second interpretation, as the political and economic institutions of the Kazakhs were tightly interlinked but with a definite chain of causation. As mentioned during our examination of the early years of the Kazakh Khanate in Chapter 2, it appears that economic activity determined the pace and the composition of the creation of political institutions; specifically, the nomadic lifestyle of the proto-Kazakhs and then that of the Kazakhs themselves (who emerged from the Uzbek Khanate in the 15th century) meant that they focused their energies almost entirely on sustaining their herds, and therefore there was an emphasis on mobility and, consequently, a reliance on political institutions which were not tied to location (and which made them more difficult to control from stationary locales, as Scott 2009 notes in another context). At the same time, the economic activities of these nomads meant that they were highly dependent on natural conditions and other factors, namely the sedentary people who produced surplus food and whose lifestyle they derided (Olcott 1995). This reality led to an uneasy integration with sedentary populations in the Kazakh Khanate and, paradoxically, some loss of autonomy, as their reliance on other parts of the economy (in modern parlance, the supply chain) meant that they also had to sacrifice some portions of their nomadic lifestyle in order to survive. While the indigenous political institutions were shifting and always in some sense in flux (as well as tied to geographic location), the meta-political organizations above the tribal or social strata persisted even as the personalities changed – and political success was tied explicitly to how well a leader performed in aiding and abetting the economic activities of nomadism.

This direction of causation, from economic institutions to political ones and contra the hierarchy of institutions proposed by Acemoglu et al. (2005), also had its own hierarchy nested within it, mainly that there was a hierarchy of economic institutions connected with economic activity. As noted above, with nomadic and pastoral behaviour as the centrepiece of the economy, during the early years of the Kazakh Khanate economic institutions were formed to settle issues connected with nomadism but focused on little else: as Sengupta (2017:19) accurately points out, the customary law followed on the steppes was "natural law which had arisen under the nomadic lifestyle and values and ideals of nomadic culture." This meant that any legalization or formalization would be judged on its usefulness in the day to day nomadic life. For example, the legal codification on the use of common lands was one of the centrepieces of the laws of Kasym in the 16th century, while the *Zhety Zhargi* (Seven Laws) of Tauke Khan from the late 17th century (see Chapter

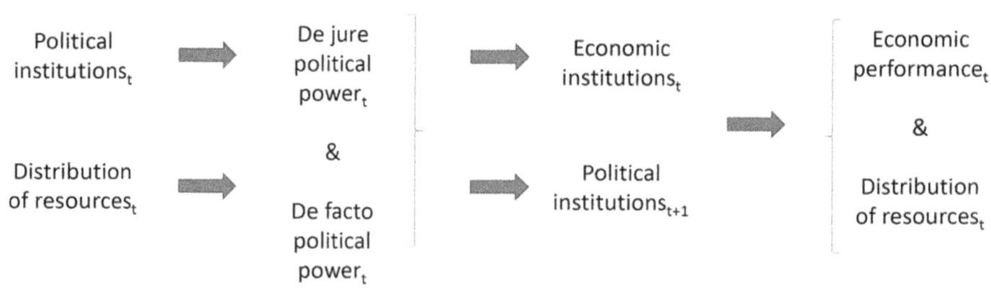

Figure 3.1 The Hierarchy of Institutions
Source: adapted from Acemoglu et al. (2005).

2) dealt specifically with disputes concerning nomads, such as the penalties incurred for stealing a horse (which was in fact its final clause). In between these attempts at formal legalism was a void related to property rights (nomads attributed wealth to herds rather than land, with land never really being "owned"; see Martin 2001) and/or contract enforcement.[1]

Similarly, as the people of the Kazakh steppe were not as engaged in trade as their forebears across the Silk Road, there was little emphasis on providing security or formal institutions related to trade – in fact, as noted in Chapter 2, in the early years of the Kazakh Khanate, trade shifted away from the Kazakh lands due to raids on traders by nomads (an exogenous shock for trade which may have spurred technological development and dissemination in the form of muskets; see Abazov 2008). Trade was also less important in terms of relations with the Russian colonizers, as trade was liable to be disrupted at any point in order to make broader points about Russian policy (practically, this also meant raids on Russian traders). Paradoxically, however, production of crafts for trade was encouraged during the Khanate and codes of conduct enforced, but these codes came not from formal legal strictures but from the informal organizations of guilds (Baipakov and Kumekov 2003). In this way, the value of various trades to nomadism were also reinforced, as the institution of trade was done in a utilitarian manner, in order to procure from sedentary peoples that which nomads could not produce themselves.

As the state of Kazakh life shifted from a purely nomadic organization towards a Eurasian semi-state in the 18th century (beginning the journey to eventual absorption in the Russian Empire but undoubtedly hastened by the presence of Russia's emissaries), so too did Kazakh social and economic institutions. One may say that the "standard" hierarchy of institutions, from political to economic, only began to assert itself in the 18th century – but only because established, foreign political institutions from Russia were able to impose their will on economic ones. But even then, with the Russian attempt to break the nomadic lifestyle of the Kazakhs for ease of administration (and to prevent further rebellion), Kazakh institutions continued to emphasize frontier issues, mainly because (a) nomadism was reduced but never entirely eradicated and (b) Russian judicial institutions left many holes in terms of their treatment of locals, requiring Kazakh codes of conduct to fill the gaps. Moreover, the economic depredations which befell the Kazakhs during the late 19th century (especially the famines in the 1890s) and the early 20th century (coinciding with the First World War) also led to the development of a native Kazakh intelligentsia, one which may have worked within the framework of Tsarism (i.e. by arguing for sedentarism) but which attempted to create their own political groupings and to advocate for indigenous Kazakh political institutions. In this way, once again, economic conditions (brought on by exogenous political institutions) led to the reordering of political organizations and – perhaps if given enough time – to new political institutions.

Roaming Political Institutions

A corollary to the causation of economic institutions to political institutions in early Kazakh life was the effect that this had on political organization in general, in particular in fostering a fairly decentralized and multipolar political system. While the Kazakh political hierarchy was based on the common tribal orderings inherent in and emerging from the Mongol hordes, in its evolution from Khaganates to the Kazakh Khanate of the 15th century the role and function of the executive shifted in a subtle manner. Importantly, as noted in Chapter 2, the political institution of the Khan and his nobility was predicated on frontier life; but as part of this job description came the stipulation that the Khan's rule was not absolute, his powers of compliance were weak, and his tenure was almost directly linked to how well the Khan could actually meet the nomadic Kazakhs' needs. If the Khan was deficient in any of these areas, he was likely to suffer a challenge from other White Bone (*aksuyek*) members of Kazakh society and be deposed, executed, or exiled.

Much of this early set of (extreme) "checks and balances" within proto-Kazakh and Kazakh life was also a holdover of basic tribal relationships predating the Mongols, as power always has suitors and leaders have always faced challengers, pretenders to the throne, and subversion. But the power of the nobility vis-à-vis the Khan was crucial (for the Polish context, see Hartwell 2016) in tempering the worst excesses of tribal hierarchies, making sure that the power of the executive was not used in a manner that was destructive to economic institutions. This should not be overlooked as an important accomplishment, as the hierarchy of institutions thesis shows just how susceptible economic institutions can be to the prevailing political structure – and history shows how the practice of politics (and acceptance of politics as a full-time avenue for gainful employment) almost always subverts and distorts economic institutions for political ends.

To take an analogy from a different time and era, the transition economies of Central and Eastern Europe (and, to some extent, Kazakhstan, as we will see) saw a massive shift in their political and economic institutions simultaneously after the fall of communism. Unfortunately, in many countries, political institutions reconstituted themselves or retained remarkable continuity of their own, thereby hindering economic institutional development before these economic institutions were fully formed. The reasons behind this were mainly related to the inertia of strong executive institutions which then continued through the transition, but indeed some strong legislatures were to blame for voting themselves largesse out of the treasury and stifling economic reforms (Ukraine being the key example, see again Hartwell 2016). In this example, there was not enough of a counterbalancing set of interests (veto points, in the parlance of political science) to prevent career politicians from shaping economic institutions to their own liking rather than for the good of their constituencies; in fact, much of the "opposition" which emerged during these early years throughout the former Soviet Union came down to "you cannot exploit the people! Only I can exploit the people!" With no true checks and balances on the distribution of political power, this power was utilized for politics rather than for economics.

By contrast, the Kazakh political organization we explored in the previous chapter shows how important it is to have an independent opposition comprised of merchants – or, in the case of 1,000 years of Kazakh history, steppe entrepreneurs dealing in herd management – rather than yet more politicians. This is not to downplay the role of economic success in creating political clout in the Khanate and its predecessors, as it is obvious that the Kazakh nobility were also the most well off and of course were able to use their economic prowess to influence the leadership of the various hordes. However, the mere fact that economic activity, spread out over a large area and predating any centralized political apparatus, meant that any political institutions which were to be constituted had to respect the economic necessities of nomadism. The nobility, created by a combination of culture and economic power, was thus sustained by economic success, and kept the Khan in check if they failed to act in the best interests of nomadic peoples. And with the executive of the Khan both constrained in economic institutions and reigning in a manner which was not absolute, there was correspondingly less incentive to actually want to become Khan.

As a final point on the organization of political institutions, there was an additional wrinkle in the Kazakh context, as the inherent fragmentation which came with their nomadic lifestyle and the lack of precisely defined territorial boundaries meant that leaders such as the Khan – if they became too dictatorial – could always simply be abandoned. The history of the Kazakh people prior to the 20th century is one of porous (if non-existent) national boundaries, shifting territories, and the movement of populations not tied down to any particular spot of land; as noted above, the source of a Kazakh person's wealth came not from land ownership but from their herd. Much like political leadership, land was only useful if it sustained the herd, and if the land became unsuitable – or the political leadership too oppressive – the nomad could always pull up his yurt and move elsewhere. Applied to the political realm, this introduced an element of "voting with one's feet" to the process of executive leadership within the Khanate, a reality which was exacerbated by the division of the Khanate into three hordes, each with their own geographic reach and incentives. As the power of a Khan was also gauged by how many able-bodied soldiers he was able to take into battle, the desertion of the nomads also was a consequence to be avoided. Thus, not only was the Khan constrained by the economic institutions which ruled the day and by the nobility which relied on these economic institutions, but even the high and mighty Khan was beholden to the average, Black Bone (*kara-suyek*), Kazakh herder and their judgement of his performance.

Institutional Transplantation: A Success (but the Patient Died)

The first 800 years or so of the Kazakh Khanate were driven by these two issues, that of economic institutional predominance and the corresponding reining in of expansive political impulses. Starting in the 18th century, however, these realities began to shift due to the overarching obstacle facing Kazakh institutional development, an issue that we have already referenced several times: institutional transplantation in the guise of the Russian Empire. The frictions which came from the extension of Russian rule and norms into Kazakh lands at the beginning of the 19th century were a clear case of a clash of institutions, one which the Russians were to win over the longer term (but not before many setbacks).

As noted in the previous chapter, the key approach that the Russian Empire took to vitiate Kazakh institutions was to start from the source of their societal cohesion, namely their economic institutions, and thus dismantling nomadism was the first step towards taming the wild steppe. With the avowed purpose of transforming the Kazakhs from nomads to a sedentary people, the Russians were both attempting to simplify their administration of Kazakh lands while also creating a "surplus" of land for Russian settlers (with the added bonus of keeping the Kazakhs within clearly delineated areas). Sedentarism was not unknown to the Kazakh people, but the identification of "Kazakh-ness" with "nomadism" meant that any move towards externally imposed sedentarism was going to be strenuously resisted across all strata of Kazakh society (in fact, the disruptions that the move towards sedentarism caused helped to give the Kazakhs a sense of unity which hitherto had been lacking in their extended history). The realization that sedentarism was not going to be easy also meant that Russian Empire needed to conduct a multipronged strategy of "Russification," flooding the zone with settlers, and military might.

This pointed attack at the source of Kazakh economic institutions was perhaps far more successful than the Tsar could ever have anticipated, as the removal of the key economic institutions of the Kazakhs exposed the fragmented and contentious nature of their political institutions, underdeveloped for a modern sedentary nation state and somewhat powerless against a military power like Russia. The creeping encroachment of Russia southwards, undertaken by an empire playing "the long game" against those on the other side of the border, was conducted in a slow manner in order to consolidate the new lands into the administration of the empire, absorbing the newly conquered steppe region into a pre-existing institutional matrix. And once sedentarism had been substantially accomplished and the Kazakh economic institutions were in disarray, Russian institutions were thrust into this vacuum. In many ways, Russian institutions could brook no opposition, as the attempt to impose dual-track systems – with some local administration and/or judicial control delegated to Russian-chosen Kazakh leaders – on an indigenous system which operated entirely differently was taken as additional evidence that *more* Russian control was required rather than less. Indeed, the supplanting of the entire code of frontier justice (and especially *barimta*) with a system predicated on formalities (but not derived from the consent of the governed) led to a succession of commissions from St Petersburg/Petrograd which noted that the administrative apparatus needed to be tightened.

With the extinguishing of nomadism and the narrowing of pastureland (and the ability to move geographically away from the Tsar's rule), it was exponentially easier for the Russian colonizers to impose strict and centralized political institutions, overriding the fragmented and informal Kazakh style of governance. In practice, this meant a series of administrative reforms and subdivisions, a parade of important officials through Orenburg, and the creation of a separate steppe *krai* (region) and the Governor-Generalship of Turkestan (somewhat artificially dividing the Kazakh people). In the aggregate, however, it meant bringing Kazakhs into the empire under the Tsar but keeping them at arm's length as full subjects, a reality which was observed after the Revolution of 1905, as Kazakhs were first welcomed into the Duma and then, as part of a reactionary backlash, kept out of successive Dumas. In this sense, the issue of whether institutional transplantation was a success was an odd question for the average Russian bureaucrat and hinged on the difference in what an observer might consider a "success." Put another way, from the point of view of the bureaucrat (and as attested to by several Steppe Commissions), the extension of Russian institutions was prima facie a success because the administrative apparatus was completed, the Kazakh lands were included in the empire's bureaucratic structure, and the lands were pacified. From our point of view, however, this excludes key questions of how this affected the local population, how it contributed to economic and societal development, and whether the institutions thus transplanted were appropriate.[2]

Of course, the transplantation of institutions was not without its problems, in particular becoming an issue when it came to (a) transplanting institutions which were not necessarily indigenous to the Russian Empire or (b) transplanting institutions which it did not actually want to transplant but which came about via the evolution of institutions which actually were transplanted. In the first instance, institutions which were transplanted did not always operate to the benefit of the Russians, and once implanted the institutions took on a life of their own: the most egregious example of this is with Islam, a foreign institution to Muscovy but which became part of the Russian Empire with the conquering of Kazan and Crimea. As mentioned in Chapter 2, Catherine the Great's attempts to use Islam to pacify the population actually created a rival set of jurisprudence and, in some instances, extremism and support of national movements, so much so that Russian policy had to reverse itself in the late 19th century (but by then the damage had been done). The longer-term ramifications of the emphasis on Islam are only now being felt, but it is obvious that the introduction of Islam was a process which very quickly was beyond the control of the colonizers, especially since the Kazakhs had a long experience with Islamic tenets while the Russians did not. At the same time, the policy of sedentarism which broke the backs of the Kazakhs economically also made them much more susceptible to Islamic teachings, another unintended consequence of this institutional operation.

Finally, and perhaps the most monumental consequence for the Russian Empire at the beginning of the 20th century, was the creation of a "national consciousness," the awakening of the Kazakhs within a modern state architecture and a self-definition of the Kazakh people as having a shared past and (importantly) a shared future. The development of a Kazakh intelligentsia, coupled with the backlash against Russia's quasi-capitalist economic institutions, led to a growing revolutionary movement against the particular form of governance enacted by the Russian Empire. Mainly but not necessarily socialist, the ideas of freedom and equality spread from the Motherland out to the Kazakh steppe and were only possible in the particular socio-economic milieu of the day, one which the Russians brought with them. There could be no fertile ground for socialist dogma in a nomadic society, where the promises of socialism have already been met (except perhaps the nomad also had food and freedom) and where the labour of the nomad is seen as corresponding directly with his outputs within an organic market and social structure. Likewise, there would be no need to entertain a philosophical debate on democratic governance in the context of steppe justice, where judicial mechanisms were informal, and the Khan was already highly constrained by his subjects. Only in a state-directed capitalist system, where the health of the economy was a direct interest of the state and where large swathes of the economy were controlled by bureaucrats – and where incentives were absent to allow any improvements for workers or even access to the political system – could the vitriol against the existing system fester. While it is folly to attempt to predict what would have happened in an independent Kazakhstan outside of the Russian Empire, and whether or not it would have entertained socialism in an alternate universe, we can see from this universe that the introduction of Russian institutions also created the soil where the seeds of revolution could spring from.

1917 and All That

The ideological extremism of the late 19th and early 20th centuries, transmitted outwards from the Russian Empire, coupled with the real and understandable grievances of the Kazakh people, created an uneasy melange of institutional change, reform, overthrow, absorption, and transplantation within the Kazakh lands, as the colonizing Russian Empire gyrated wildly through three revolutions in the space of a decade and a half. Unfortunately, as we will see, the entire edifice of Russian life itself was radically transformed during the last revolution, and in European Russia, the clash of old versus new, formal versus informal, and (in the words of Karl Popper), institutions of the open society versus anti-rationality would end in the triumph of the anti-rational and the ascendance of institutions which would go on to slaughter countless millions. And, as with the Russian Empire's incursions into Central Asia over the previous 200 years, the disease of communism was to also to be imposed on the body politic of the Kazakhs of the steppe by their Russian conquerors (assisted by home-grown revolutionaries). For a land which had seen 1,000 years of institutions systematically dismantled over the course of a century, it was going to prove impossible for their nascent and foreign-delivered institutions to resist such an overwhelming exogenous shock. This is the story of our next chapter.

Notes

1 It is this focus of customary law on land use, to the exclusion of land tenure or land registration, which made the Russian prohibitions on grazing and pasturing so effective in picking apart the extant political institutions of the Kazakh Khanate.
2 One can almost hear a large bearded Russian bureaucrat yell out "Nesushchestvenno!" (Immaterial!) to these questions.

References

Abazov, R. (2008). *The Palgrave Concise Historical Atlas of Central Asia.* New York: Palgrave Macmillan.
Acemoglu, D., Johnson, S., and Robinson, J. A. (2005). Institutions as a fundamental cause of long-run growth. In P. Aghion and S. Durlauf (Eds.), *Handbook of Economic Growth* (pp. 385–472). North Holland: Elsevier.
Baipakov, K., and Kumekov, B. (2003). The Kazakhs. In A. H. Dani and V. M. Masson (Eds.), *History of Civilizations of Central Asia.* Vol. 5: *Development in Contrast: From the Sixteenth to the Mid-nineteenth Century* (pp. 90–109).New York: UNESCO.
Hartwell, C. A. (2016). *Two Roads Diverge: The Transition Experience of Poland and Ukraine.* Cambridge: Cambridge University Press.
Hartwell, C. A. (2018). The "Hierarchy of Institutions" reconsidered: Monetary policy and its effect on the rule of law in interwar Poland. *Explorations in Economic History*, 68, 37–70.
Hartwell, C. A. (2019). Short waves in Hungary, 1923 and 1946: Persistence, chaos, and (lack of) control. *Journal of Economic Behavior & Organization*, 163, 532–550.
Hartwell, C. A., and Devinney, T. (2021). Populism, political risk, and pandemics: The challenges of political leadership for business in a post-COVID world. *Journal of World Business*, 56(4), 101225.
Martin, V. (2001). *Law and Custom in the Steppe: The Kazakhs of the Middle Horde and Russian Colonialism in the Nineteenth Century.* New York: Routledge.
North, D. C. (1990). *Institutions, Institutional Change and Economic Performance.* Cambridge: Cambridge University Press.
Olcott, M. B. (1995). *The Kazakhs.* Palo Alto, CA: Hoover Institution Press.

Scott, J. C. (2009). *The Art of Not Being Governed: An Anarchist History of Upland Southeast Asia*. New Haven, CT: Yale University Press.
Sengupta, A. (2017). *Symbols and the Image of the State in Eurasia*. Singapore: Springer Singapore.
Stankov, P. (2018). The political economy of populism: An empirical investigation. *Comparative Economic Studies*, 60(2), 230–253.

4 The Soviet Experiment in Kazakhstan

Long-ago events may exert a profound influence on institutions over time either by having an immediate impact on their creation – thus immediately altering the path of institutional evolution from a previous trend and setting it on a new path to be followed for decades or centuries – or, alternatively, by shifting the external environment in a manner that then forces institutions to adapt. Given that institutions operate in a complex web of other institutions, culture, and policies, shifts in the environment external to a particular institution may nonetheless have far-reaching consequences on the operation and structure of that same institution. As shown in Chapter 2 (and also in the Introduction), this process can be very long indeed, with institutional evolution unfolding over a period of centuries and influencing (and being influenced by) other institutions within a geographic space.

However, despite the persistence of events in shaping institutions and their operation, institutional change often has a more proximate cause than the long ago; like Newton's laws of gravity, objects which are closer may exert more influence and may also be easier to observe. Moreover, given the complexity of institutional change, the further away one moves from a specific event, the more likely it is that other events, other forces, other institutions, or other personalities in the intervening years may also intervene. If the event is sufficiently large – to return to Newtonian mechanics – it could still exert influence over time and space, but if it is smaller, it is likely to be subsumed by the complexity of the eons and overtaken by closer events.

This reality gets to the heart of this chapter, as the October Revolution in Russia was to be both massively outsized in terms of its goal, impact, and extent, while also being much closer to Kazakhstan's present than the distant dealings of Khaganates and nomads. In addition, the Bolshevik triumph in Russia came on the heels of the already substantial alteration of Kazakh institutions that accompanied the incorporation of Kazakh lands into the Russian Empire – and in many ways, continued this process, albeit with a different stated goal (communism) than that vocalized by the Tsar and his bureaucracy. As noted in Chapters 2 and 3, the Russian expansion into Central Asia had already kick-started a process of altering institutional evolution, forcing external autocratic political institutions onto a society which

DOI: 10.4324/9781003212508-4

had focused more in the past on building spontaneous economic and social institutions and whose political institutions were tribal and geographic rather than ideological. The October Revolution of 1917, a cataclysm for the world in general, was to blend the ongoing Russian obsession with authoritarian politics with authoritarian economics, attempting to finish what the Tsar had begun in obliterating native Kazakh and nomadic institutions. And, of course, all of this was done in the name of "the people."

As we will see, even the comprehensive attempts of communism to overwrite Kazakh indigenous economic and cultural institutions had only limited success, meaning that there is a strong persistence from 1,000 years of institutional evolution which lingers even to this day. But "success" is different from "impact," as the Soviet experience looms large in the rear-view mirror, shaping much of the political landscape of the modern-day nation of Kazakhstan. From the tens of millions of lives lost under Joseph Stalin's imperium to the stagnation of Brezhnev and the lost years of generations of Kazakhs, the Soviet experiment may not have erased "Kazakh-ness," but it did leave a massive mark on the evolution of the geographic space which is now known as Kazakhstan. This chapter thus delves into the institutional destruction, creation, and rearrangement which accompanied the (at that time) unprecedented attempt to remake Kazakh institutions in a specific image.

Kazakhstan in the Russian Civil War

The October Revolution, its causes and effects, and the exact form it took, has been discussed at length elsewhere, in fact having its own literature devoted to it (interested readers are counselled to see Pipes 1991 for an excellent overview of the forces which led to the cataclysm). In addition, the Russian Civil War arising out of the revolution, coupled with the early Soviet period after the Bolsheviks emerged triumphant, has also been extensively chronicled (see Pipes 2011). These two facts mean that we can dispense with much of the historical background to home in specifically on the impact that these events had on Central Asia and, particularly, on Kazakh lands.

As noted at the end of Chapter 2, the immediate effect of the February Revolution was to overthrow the Tsar and vest power in the hands of a provisional government in St Petersburg. However, the weakness of this government, and especially the inability of the government to take Russia out of the Great War, led to a further, more violent revolution later in 1917 to overthrow the newly established regime; as Minister-Chairman of the provisional government Alexander Kerensky noted in a hopeful but entirely unapologetic article 15 years after the fact, "it was only the war, with all its material and psychological consequences, that provoked the collapse of the democratic revolution" (Kerensky 1932:2). Dissatisfaction with the progress of reforms and a series of bold strategic and tactical moves by the "Bolshevik" party,[1] led by Vladimir Lenin, culminated in an armed insurrection and takeover of government buildings, defeat of government forces, and proclamation of the Second All Russian Congress of Soviets. Moving swiftly to sideline rival factions (such as the Mensheviks and Socialist Revolutionaries) and to consolidate power as the sole authority, elections to the Constituent Assembly in 1917 returned the Bolsheviks to a minority; as with autocrats everywhere, they simply ignored the results and dissolved the Assembly (Wade 2006). The country, and indeed the empire, then dissolved into a paroxysm of fighting and chaos, as a Civil War between Bolsheviks, Bolshevik-backed local communists, monarchists, nationalists, ethnic minorities, and liberals (clumsily aggregated as "Reds" versus "Whites") bloodied Europe's largest country and its periphery for four years (1918–1922).

In the context of Central Asia, the revolution (and, subsequently, the Civil War) lasted even longer as the run-up to the February Revolution in 1917 unleashed forces which had been suppressed for too long (or, as in the case of nationalism, were actually created as a result of the Russian occupation). In the first instance, the provisional government backed away from Russia's role as a colonizer, decreeing that "all subjects of the Russian empire [were] free and equal citizens, regardless of sex, religion, or ethnicity, and [it] gave them all an equal right to vote" (Khalid 2006: 237). This somewhat radical move towards equal status, following on the heels of the 1916 revolt that spread across the region, opened a Pandora's box which had already been cracked in the preceding decade, unleashing more ethnic and nationalist pride within the region against the Russian authorities.

This nationalism took varying forms: for example, the informal Alash (tribesman or, alternately, sometimes synonymously used with Kazakh) national liberation movement of intellectuals, detailed in Chapter 2, actively participated in the local governance structures of the provisional government (Amanzholova 1997a) and regional religious organizations such as the Tatar Religious Board in Orenburg (Kendirbaeva 1999). At the same time, Kazakh congresses were convened in nearly all the oblasts, with the All-Kazakh Congress of July 1917 establishing Alash as its own formal political party (Tomohiko 2013). Alash spent the autumn months of that year establishing party committees in Semipalatinsk and Omsk (Sabol 2003), and, despite a rather niche demographic of voters, Alash won representation in the short-lived All Russia Constituent Assembly, where it garnered approximately 1 per cent of the vote. A key part of its platform, which set it apart from the more radical elements in St Petersburg (namely the Bolsheviks), was a focus on socio-economic change conducted in a gradual fashion, above all with an anti-colonial stance that started in Russia, was dependent upon the democratization of the Russian government, and was focused on self-governance for Kazakhs (Koigeldiev 2007). Given this difference of emphasis with the Bolshevik revolutionaries, there should be little surprise that the Alash authorities did not welcome Bolshevik organizations on Kazakh territory, and the organizations and workers' councils (Soviets) which did exist had very little Kazakh representation in their ranks (Amanzholova 1997a).

More important, and much more aggressive than participation in local governance, was the eventual proclamation of an autonomous state on Kazakh land in December 1917, a process which Alash had held at bay during the provisional government, but which became imperative in the run-up to and especially after the October Revolution. As Kesici (2017:1144) notes in the context of the broader Turkestan region, "the indigenous population had severe issues with the mainly Russian organizations that had replaced Tsarist rule after the February revolution," a consequence of the "deep Russophobia since the 1916 revolts against the mobilization decree issued by the tsar during World War I, which had been violently crushed in some parts of Central Asia, especially among Kazakh nomads." While there was some hope that the provisional government, especially with its decrees on equality, would redress the grievances of the Kazakhs, the ascension of the Bolsheviks rendered these desires hopeless and accelerated the move towards national autonomy (Amanzholova 1997a). Indeed, it has often been noted that Bolshevik policies, and especially early Bolshevik policies, had a remarkable consistency with tsarist expansionism, and in Central Asia this consistency was evident: as Buttino (2020:199) notes, the October Revolution was "the affirmation of the will to re-establish the old order and Russian supremacy in the colonies."

The first steps towards autonomy came in December 1917, as the ascendant Alash party promised the First Siberian Regional Congress in Tomsk that the Kazakhs would join a Siberian autonomous entity as a junior partner, rejecting proposals to join a separate Turkestan autonomous region based in Kokand (although Kazakh intellectuals were also helpful in creating this autonomy as well; see Tomohiko 2013). In essence, this decision meant that the Kazakhs had proclaimed independence from the Bolsheviks but not necessarily from all parts of the Russian administrative apparatus (Sabol 2003). Facing this reality, the Alash leaders scrambled to hone their party programme, originally published in November 1917, which laid out its own institution-building plans, focusing on the "establishment of native courts and the creation of native military units, which would be independent of central control … [as well as] a graduated tax system and labour laws in accordance with the program of the 'social-democrat Mensheviks'" (Kesici 2014:17). Territorially, the Kazakh lands were divided into two zones, corresponding with the former lands of the Middle and Lesser Hordes (Amanzholova 1997a), while the autonomous Kazakh government replaced the Russian colonial administrative apparatuses operating in Orenburg and Astrakhan (Kesici 2014). Disputes regarding territory remained with the Turkestan autonomous region, with Alash leader Alikhan Bokeikhanov arguing that the Turkestanis were both sedentary and fanatical, a group of zealots who would not mesh well with traditional Kazakh nomads (Kesici 2017). However, for the most part these disputes did not have time to flare up into conflict, as the real threat from Bolshevism remained the priority.

While the Alash programme represented a step towards building the first Kazakh formal political institutions within a modern nation-state, it still did not encapsulate the economic institutions necessary for making the leap towards prosperity nor did it represent much of a break from Russian traditions. In particular, the treatment of property rights was squarely in line with far-left/socialist thinking, although coloured by Kazakh needs: the resolutions coming from the Kazakh congresses in mid-1917 noted explicitly that property owners were the enemies of the poor, and outlined how land should be used and, especially, it placed the Kazakhs into the queue for being allowed to have priority for land distribution over Russians (Martynenko 1992). What was envisioned in reality was a shift back to collective ownership of the commons, as was prevalent before the Russian occupation, rather than a move towards more formalized property rights as they are generally conceptualized today. However, it is too easy to say that Alash was another socialist party, concerned with land as a communal good, when in reality it was more concerned with the long-running tension between sedentarization and nomadism and, in particular, in undoing the seizures of traditional Kazakh lands which the Russian tsarist apparatus had undertaken and transferred to settlers (Sabol 2003). In this sense, underpinned by traditional Kazakh informal property arrangements, Alash was more focused on who supervised and managed the land – and the freedom to use it – rather than bickering about specific land tenure arrangements.

Whether or not the Alash programme would have led to the development of the necessary economic institutions to build a diversified economy in the Kazakh lands is, unfortunately, a moot point, as the Alash movement – and with it, Kazakh autonomy – was not long for the world. Although the Alash movement played an impressive role in generating a true Kazakh identity and unifying Kazakhs under an anti-colonial banner, the movement itself never made the crucial transition from "movement" to "governing party;" still unfamiliar with the issues related to running a modern bureaucratic state, Alash was concerned with both meta (autonomy, territorial boundaries) and micro (land distribution, judicial apparatuses) issues, lacking the administrative wherewithal to implement either of these priorities (Nurmagambetova 2003). But even if it had been able, in a short amount of time, to generate a state apparatus, the reality that political power emanated from the barrel of a gun meant that the Bolsheviks were destined to overwhelm the nascent independent state.

The reabsorption of the Kazakhs into a Russian state, one that this time was led by the Bolsheviks, did not occur immediately and indeed took place in fits and starts. The progress and tenor of relations between the Bolsheviks and Alash was consistently set by the military success that the Bolsheviks enjoyed during the Civil War, however, with periods of success corresponding with much more strident approaches to the Kazakh leadership. The schizophrenia of Moscow's approach to the Kazakhs can be seen in the commencement of a series of negotiations in early 1918 on the "necessity" for

Kazakh autonomy and on how it could be incorporated into a Moscow-directed state as part of a federated Russia. As directed by the Soviet authorities, the Kazakhs had provided Stalin (of all people, in his capacity as Commissar of Nationalities) with their resolutions from the previous year on autonomy and had apparently seen some agreement from Moscow on Kazakh autonomy, conditional on this Kazakh state remaining within a Union of Soviets (i.e. recognizing the ultimate authority of the Bolsheviks).

But at the same time that the Bolsheviks were negotiating, as Amanzholova (1997b) points out, various sections of the Soviet government were issuing warrants for the arrests of Alash leaders as "counter-revolutionaries" and attempting to disrupt meetings in the Kazakh lands with an eye on arrests (forcing Alash leaders to abandon Semipalatinsk for the steppe on more than one occasion). Parallel structures to Alash, i.e. local soviets, were supported by and subordinated to Moscow, but were staffed by Russians and had more of a security function than representative democracy, helping the Military-Revolutionary Headquarters of the Red Guard to keep the peace by watching the Kazakhs closely (as E. A. Samoilov, a lawyer in Semipalatinsk noted, "our soviet of deputies had a great fear of the [Kazakhs] as a people"; quoted in Amanzholova 1997b). Simultaneously, Lenin and Stalin were working on separate plans to subordinate national questions to class questions, overriding any "national bourgeoisie" attempts at autonomy. This longer-term strategy of consolidation of power back in Moscow and away from ethnic and nationalist leaders had predictable consequences for the leaders of Central Asia, including crushing the Kokand Autonomy in January 1918, resulting in 14,000 deaths, as tallied by the British embassy (Bergne 2003). In tandem with this general drift towards centralization, throughout April 1918, the Bolshevik attitude towards the Kazakhs hardened, leading to an outright rift:

> The Soviet center's enmity toward the Alash-Orda proposals concerning the autonomous organization of the krai, alongside the conflicted relations with local soviets and Bolsheviks in the absence of national communist organizations, the "special dictatorial power" hiding behind the name of Bolsheviks locally, the violence, and the robbery and abuses that accompanied, in the words of Baitursynov, the Bolshevik movement in the outlying areas, representing "complete and total anarchy," pushed the Alash movement into the camp of the anti-Soviet forces.
>
> (Amanzholova 1997b:38)

The destruction of Kokand left no doubt as to which method the Bolsheviks were prepared to pursue if the Alash movement did not kowtow to Moscow. But despite being murderers, the Bolsheviks were savvy as well, and incorporated in their own propaganda the very same anti-colonial message that Alash had championed, co-opting the nationalists at the periphery of empire and presenting themselves as the only true, authentic champions of the common man (Dave 2007). The Alash leaders, cognizant of this fact, realized that they needed to hone their message (Amanzholova 1997b) and, more importantly, effect a total break with the Bolsheviks; thus, on 24 June 1918, the Alash government proclaimed that all Soviet directives were null and void on Kazakh territory, beginning the process of arming the populace while at the same time attempting to secure sources of revenue for state-building (Sabol 2003). Coming after several days of attempts by Soviet authorities to head off any coup, including seizing weapons and attempting to arrest any Kazakhs with military experience (thus making them flee to the steppe, which warmly took them in and held them in reserve), the "Whites" seized key buildings and beat the Bolsheviks at their own game, namely subversion under the cover of darkness (Amanzholova 1997b).

The coup against the Bolsheviks forced Alash to make great strides towards becoming a governing force, but both Sabol (2003) and Abazov (2008) note that it is still an open historical question on how effective Alash was as a government (or just how much territory it actually administered). Indeed, Sabol (2003:148) notes that "Alash was never able to resolve the most pressing issue [from its point of view], how to redistribute the land equitably," meaning that it was also exploring a fundamentally similar reform as the Bolsheviks but with the twist of leaving the question to the local authorities (which had been established under the Russians, the *zemstvos*). Externally, too, Alash had suffered several missteps, including incorporating Kazakh units into Admiral Kolchak's Siberian army, an arrangement which lasted up until the point that Kolchak repudiated the idea of having national units in the army and instead tried to subordinate them to Russian units – before he ordered Kazakhs to stop mobilizing (Smele 1996) and attempted to abolish the Alash Orda in its entirety (Kesici 2014).

Seeing its internal and external options dwindling, the Alash leadership reopened negotiations with the Bolsheviks in early 1919, and the Bolsheviks gradually increased the pressure on the Kazakhs with both sticks (military force) and carrots (promise of participation in a new soviet socialist republic via decree in July 1919). In the face of the Bolshevik victory in the Civil War, and with no allies to call upon, this truly was an offer that the Kazakhs could not refuse, and, by 1920, the Alash leadership had all become Bolshevik members (although, in true Bolshevik fashion, there were still arrests of key figures such as Bokeikhanov; see Nurpeisov 1998). More importantly, the Kazakh lands relinquished their short-lived autonomy, while the entire region was absorbed into the new Bolshevik imperial administrative apparatus; although the outcome was inevitable once the Bolsheviks had gained the upper hand against the White Guard, the unfolding of this result was to prove a disaster for the dreams of Alash and the Kazakhs. It was also to upend thousands of years of slowly developing political and economic institutions.

The Kazakh Soviet Socialist Republic: Broken Eggs and No Omelettes

The absorption of Kazakh lands was formalized with the creation of the Kirghiz Autonomous Socialist Soviet Republic (Kirghiz ASSR) in August 1920, an administrative unit with its capital in Orenburg and designed entirely within the broader Russian Socialist Federative Soviet Republic. In addition to being part of Russia proper, the Kirghiz ASSR was named after the erroneous tsarist label applied to the Kazakhs, retaining this name until 1925, when it was correctly named (in terms of ethnicity) the Kazakh ASSR. The final part of its evolution, in line with Stalin's evolving thoughts on the nationalities question and the desire to create ethnic states, was the eventual transformation of the Kazakh ASSR into the Kazakh Soviet Socialist Republic (Kazakh SSR) in 1936 as a separate (i.e. not part of Russia) Union Republic of the Union of Soviet Socialist Republics (USSR).

Over the course of the next 16 years, massive internal institutional changes were to come for the Kazakhs, with (as Buttino 2020 notes) a reassertion of Russian supremacy and a continuation of the plans to sedentarize the Kazakhs, but now overlaid with a massive ideological component to extract resources and rents from the populace en route to achieving a utopia for planners in Moscow (but no one else). While the tsarist imperial policy, and especially its implementation, had generated depredations for the Kazakh nomads, removing their pastureland and attempting to break their nomadic way of life, it was done in a haphazard crescendo, as an explicit goal but as a second order consequence of first order institutional changes. By contrast, the Soviet institutional experiment in Kazakhstan and elsewhere in the Red Imperium had direct first order consequences on human life, destroying livelihoods and eventually lives in the millions. As Nikolsky (2017:186) correctly notes, "the development of the revolution required its spread throughout the empire and vice versa—the preservation of the empire required the further development of the revolution."

The first changes came early on in the life of the Kirghiz ASSR with the dismantling of the skeletal indigenous political structures which emerged under Alash and by "methodically and consistently propagat[ing] the view that the pre-revolutionary Kazakh intelligentsia were some sort of reactionary, counter-revolutionary force that had acted in opposition to the cardinal interests of the Kazakh population on the whole" (Koigeldiev 2007:161). As noted above, the Alash leadership did not make an especially successful transition from an intellectual/revolutionary movement to a governing force, but they did have a start on nascent Kazakh political institutions informed by a burgeoning ethnic identity, an identity which itself had "originat[ed] in political pressure and resistance, culture and social adjustment" (Esenova 2002:14). Moreover, the governing council of the new Kazakh nation was to share executive power across a multi-ethnic committee, with 15 seats held for Kazakhs and ten (unfilled) seats reserved for Russians and other minorities on the territory (and the Chairman of the

Committee selected from these 25 officials). In this way, the executive was to reflect the desires and concerns of the entire nation, but with the recognition that this was a Kazakh state first and foremost. This was to be a first step towards an independent state which consolidated both territory and ethnicity (Auanassova et al. 2018) but was still part of a democratic Russian federation. Carlson (1993:64) puts it best when he notes that the Alash ideal was that "sovereignty was thus to be realized in the body-politic, consisting of the community and the state."

However, as in so much of the Russian Empire, the Bolsheviks had little idea on how to replace the Alash leadership structure, preferring to discredit the past without understanding what was needed for the future. What they did know was that "Bolshevism meant the rule of the workers, soldiers, and peasants; the Kazakh–Kirghiz had no workers, soldiers, or peasants; therefore, the Kazakh–Kirghiz must not rule but be ruled" (Pipes 1964:86). Zardykhan (2004:63) notes how this went in practice, as

> a Kirghiz Revolutionary Committee, *Kirrevkom* … conducted negotiations with the Alash Orda in January 1920. As a result of these negotiations, the Committee announced that 'the Alash Orda had merged with the Kirghiz revolutionary government, that all laws of the Alash Orda were null and void, and that all their property was to be seized.'

While Alash members of government were allowed to continue serving their region in some capacity, they were sidelined; by the late 1930s, they had all been executed during the Stalinist terror waves (Kendirbay 1997). Wiping the slate clean of even the nascent organs of government, however, the Bolsheviks were in a bind, as their own views on how executive power should be organized were in a state of flux, split between the party apparatus and state organs (Smith 1999).

This tension played itself out in the Kirghiz ASSR alongside the nationalities question, namely how much participation was needed from the indigenous population to implement Bolshevik ideas. Cherot (1955) notes that the "nationalities policy" of the Soviets, settled upon in 1922, was theoretically predicated on "nativization," or the inclusion of indigenous populations, a trait which played itself out in the Kirghiz ASSR mainly at the lower administrative levels (i.e. fairly similar to the tsarist system). Indeed, Olcott (1995) notes that the Bolsheviks were able to secure some support in the Kazakh lands via this approach, mainly because the tension in Bolshevik ideology on how an administrative state should appear meant that much of the old tsarist apparatus was retained, but with new names and titles. Much like the Tsar and his emissaries, however, this turning over of some authority to locals was also utilized to play off different groups of Kazakhs against each other in order to retain Bolshevik (Russian) superiority, thus providing window dressing for another massive institutional change: the dismantling of traditional family/clan/tribal relations.

Believing that everything from the past that was not related to class was a prologue to the new communist paradise – and thus needed to be discarded – the Bolsheviks saw traditional kinship ties and lineage among the Kazakhs as an archaic way to enshrine dominant classes, freeze production structures in place, and inhibit the development of class consciousness (Ohayon 2016). Suspicious of the religious overtones of kinship as well, the Bolsheviks believed that the Kazakh focus on lineage was a backdoor way to instil "pan-Islamist" thinking, a threat which would directly challenge Bolshevik power (Guseva and Kristoforov 2019). The Soviet rulers of the Kirghiz ASSR thus made an overt attempt with the Kazakhs (as well as elsewhere) to try to break traditional clan structures along class rather than tribal lines (Ohayon 2016), placing wealthy herders against poorer members of the same clan. This approach meant that tribal relations were torn apart from the inside out, creating new rivalries – especially when combined with political power granted to local authorities – and helping to keep Kazakhs divided. The overall goal was to create a "republican" rather than an "ethnic" identity, and to have loyalties directed towards the overall territorial leader rather than kin or tribe (Zardykhan 2004). In many ways, this was an extension of the sedentarization policy (see below), as it took a political structure which was linked by personal relations and mobile assets and instead replaced it with a structure formed by agglomerating similar people on a carefully delineated geographic space. It also was consistent with early Soviet plans to break up national territories along economic lines, retaining the territorial borders but creating a master-colony dynamic complete with economic specialization (an approach which, if implemented by itself, would not have necessarily attempted to crush nomadism; see Pianciola 2017).

As part of the reorientation of political structures came the necessary move towards substantially reordering economic institutions as well, given that Kazakh political structures prior to Russian imperial conquest (and for some time thereafter) were built on economic relations. The first attempt to superimpose a centralized planning structure on the food supplies of the Kirghiz ASSR was introduced in tandem with a similar massive change across the Soviet republics, the introduction of the *prodrazvyorstka* (food requisition or apportionment) policy. Following the collapse of tsarist economic structures during the back-and-forth of the Civil War, and, after years of wartime rationing and a slowdown in agricultural production with workers at the front (Markevich and Harrison 2011), the Bolsheviks faced the difficult issue of procuring enough food for their urban centres (the base of their support). Ironically, their approach was to shift towards overt coercion and requisition of food from rural areas, a move which hardened the peasantry against the Bolsheviks and led to rural autarky as food became a local (and not a national or even a revolutionary) issue (Channon 1988).

This overriding of market signals and forced requisition led directly to the first famine to befall the Kazakhs in Soviet times, the famine from 1919 through to 1922, with the worst years being 1920 and 1921; according to

Pipes (1964), approximately one million Kazakhs died as a result of poor weather (drought conditions and frigid winters). Places thought of as the most fertile in the ASSR, such as the Akmola *uyezd* in the north on the exposed steppes, suffered catastrophic weather and crop failures, with rural nomads crowding into the city of Akmolinsk in search of a livelihood and, above all, food: as Karsakova et al. (2018) relate, relying on archival materials from Kazakhstan, the level of starvation was so dire that people were reduced to eating cats, dogs, and food substitutes in an attempt to survive. This also led to a massive increase in disease (mainly cholera and typhus) and the number of orphans recorded in the Kirghiz ASSR increased from 128,000 at the beginning of 1921 to a disheartening 408,000 two years later (Churin 1967).

These natural disasters were combined with a fragile social system stressed by years of conflict and upheaval and then pushed over the edge by the food requisitioning strategies demanded by collectivism. While this era in Kazakh history is properly placed within a longer perspective, starting with the 1916 uprising and extending through the Civil War, the excess deaths from the famine alone can be laid directly at the feet of the communist experiment, either in its conquest of the steppe or in its institutional policies. In the first instance, the creation of state-owned farms (*sovkhozy*) was begun in the middle of the famine, an approach which at once failed to solve the "land issue" which Kazakhs were concerned about while providing a disincentive for production. Indeed, in true bureaucratic fashion, their operation was "particularly infuriating to the peasants [as they] were … scandalously inefficient yet coddled … and the way in which food taken from hungry peasants was wasted through incompetent storage and transport" (Lih 1990:206). Even an internal report from the "People's Commissariat of State Monitoring" excoriated the system:

> A whole round of reports, and even more the results themselves of the food-supply apparatus, indicates that the apparatus is completely worthless … The worker detachments and the Committees of the Poor find neither in the center nor in the localities a crystallizing and unifying center and so they lose focus and scatter their efforts, often distorting the economic policy of the Soviet Republic. The food-supply institutions have neither experienced agents, nor a quick, clear accounting system, nor exact statistics. The question arises: what are they doing out there?
>
> If we turn our attention to the center and consider the endless sections, subsections, and directorates of the Food-Supply Commissariat, we will see the same picture: a flood of paper, top officials weighed down with trivial correspondence, bureaucrats who have no initiative, who are bored and oppressed with their work, and who have a strikingly unsympathetic attitude toward visitors.
>
> (Mashkovich 1919:29).

With food requisition occurring in the midst of famine and a *dzhut* (terrible winter) from 1920–1921, food production collapsed, and the Kazakhs were unable to invest in any future production, eating the seeds for the next harvest just to stay alive (Olcott 1995). While food aid was requested, the Bolsheviks were mostly indifferent to the plight of the Kazakhs, with Ivan Tobolin – Chairman of the Turkestan ASSR to the south of the Kirghiz ASSR – famously declaring that Kazakhs were

> economically the weakest from the Marxist's point of view [and so] must die out anyhow. For the Revolution, therefore, it is more important to devote the available means to the maintenance of the front rather than expending it in famine.
>
> (Quoted in Ryskulov 1925:12)

This callous indifference extended to prioritization of other policies that the Bolsheviks found more politically expedient – including the eradication of former White combatants and controlling the population's movements (Talgat et al. 2019) – which, if relaxed, might have slightly eased the plight of the nomads.[2]

Horrifically, the famine of 1919–1922 was not the worst example of collectivism in the Kirghiz ASSR, for that was to come, but it quickly highlighted the shortcomings of a centrally planned economy built on theft and quotas rather than the equilibristic chaos of the market. The replicated failure of an immediate switch to communism across the Bolshevik-conquered areas, and the recognition that something radical needed to be done to stave off total collapse, was the impetus for the introduction of the New Economic Policy (NEP), which restored some modicum of free enterprise to the Soviet system, including regarding property rights, and shelved (for the moment) the proliferation of *sovkhozy*. The NEP attempted to address the most pressing issues in the Kirghiz ASSR and elsewhere, mainly the need to rebuild the economy and population of the regions; the reluctant allowance for land ownership, free enterprise, and even tax relief for nomadic and semi-nomadic lands in the Kirghiz ASSR specifically spurred commerce where it was most needed, specifically in agricultural production (Olcott 1995). As Pianciola (2004) notes, the economic relationships which sprung up as part of the NEP were purely capitalist, based on comparative advantages and relative endowments, as Russian settlers sold grain to Kazakh nomads, who in turn sold animals and animal products to the settlers; this approach naturally incentivized an increase in both grain and cattle (and sheep), both alleviating lingering problems due to famine and also providing for a more robust agrarian economy, at least in the production of meat (Table 4.1)

Ironically, as part of the NEP and its move towards small-scale property rights, the Bolsheviks also pursued a policy the Kazakhs had been clamouring for, mainly "hard decolonization," and the expropriation of lands from Russian settlers (Pianciola 2019). While there was a reluctance in Moscow to

Table 4.1 Cattle and Sheep Production in Kazakhstan, 1896–1927

Year	*Cattle*	*Sheep*	*Total*
1886	n.a.	n.a.	15,293
1895	n.a.	n.a.	17,259
1905	n.a.	n.a.	18,815
1912	n.a.	n.a	22,850
1913	4,954	17,204	25,698
1920	4,103	7,360	13,802
1925	5,258	11,233	19,304
1926	6,444	16,020	27,176
1927	7,592	20,780	35,159

Source: Olcott (1981).

disadvantage Russians merely to improve relations with non-Russians, the move towards decolonization was in line with other Bolshevik initiatives, in that it looked to destroy private property rather than merely redistribute it: put another way, there was enthusiasm among the Bolsheviks for expropriating lands from Russian settlers mainly because there was enthusiasm for expropriating land in general, not because it was an effective way to address Kazakh concerns about previous expropriations of land by the tsarist administration. The expropriation of settler land also had the benefit of playing into emerging Bolshevik thought on nationalities, and, as the removal of Russian land could be seen as a way to harden territorial divisions and further the nationalities policy of the Soviets, it was also supported by Moscow (Thomas 2018).

During the early NEP years (1921–1922), the decolonization policy was implemented in a broad manner, expropriating land in the south-eastern Kirghiz ASSR from somewhere between 8,000 and 10,000 Russian settlers (Pianciola 2017) and redistributing it to Kazakhs and Kyrgyz returning from China (Pianciola 2004). While the land expropriation may not seem to be that large in terms of settlers affected, the actual impact can be seen in population numbers, as the number of Russians in Kazakh lands decreased from 2.7 million to 2.2 million from 1920–1923, driven by a kind of affirmative action (Martin 2001) which gave priority to Kazakhs for land redistribution. However, given that the Kazakhs remained semi-sedentary or semi-nomadic (Ohayon 2014 notes that 23 per cent of the population was classified as "entirely sedentary," while large sections of the ASSR had become semi-sedentary but were still wedded to nomadic economic organization), the redistribution of land did not immediately lead to an increase in grain production, and the acreage under agricultural cultivation dropped by over one-half (50.6 per cent) from 1921–1922 (Martin 1998). Although incentives might have existed for greater grain production for those who stayed, the nationalities policy was creating a disincentive by forcing the Russians off the land. In particular, the paradox of the NEP was that the nationalities policy was punishing precisely those farmers who were more efficient and skilled in working the land (Cameron 2018), and transferring the land to neophytes in the ways of farming.[3]

The unwinding of the NEP in the late 1920s brought additional benefits to the Kazakhs. The first was the more accurate renaming of their administrative unit, changed from the Kirghiz ASSR to the Kazak ASSR (Kazakhskaya Avtonomnaya Sotsialisticheskaya Sovetskaya Respublika) in June 1925. Perhaps more substantive was a concerted move towards decolonization, a welcome step from the Kazakh point of view but one which soon turned into a curse. Decrees were issued throughout 1925 which announced that all *pomeshchiki* (large-scale landowners) who were still occupying their land were to be removed, a step which was taken explicitly with Russian settlers in mind. Within the ASSR, a total of 87 landowners, all of Russia descent, were registered, and in total 82 of them were pushed off of their land (Channon 1987). However, as usual, such a policy was not just utilized against specific "rich" or "wealthy" targets or "kulaks" (peasants who owned land and/or became wealthy at the end of the tsarist era) but soon expanded to include all "elite" Kazakhs (not just Russians) with the aim of eliminating "the wealthiest livestock owners and local power figures who were impeding sovietisation" (Ohayon 2013a:67). An amendment to the Soviet land code was proposed in 1927 in an attempt to shield peasants "from expropriation and redistribution of land, which apparently was quite frequent in Kazakhstan and Ukraine" (Bandera 1963:267), but the thirst for land and control on the part of the Bolsheviks meant that such protections, even if offered, were sure to be tossed aside when no longer needed.

In fact, concurrently with this proposal, the Bolshevik leadership was showing its schizophrenia towards land in general by simultaneously pushing people off the land and hoping to put new ones on it. In 1927, a new commission was formed in Moscow to examine the politics of land in the Kazak ASSR with a focus on peasant resettlement, forcing holdout nomads to become sedentarized in order to double the amount of land under agricultural cultivation; over the subsequent three years, ideologists began to seek Marxist-Leninist support for such policies, while those who supported any form of nomadism were purged, arrested, and/or executed (Cameron 2018). With the move away from a faltering NEP, a push to further expropriate land from the most successful at using it, and a renewed vigour for sedentarization, the Bolshevik bureaucracy was also ramping up in an attempt to control the Kazakhs, including a staged move towards more administrative hurdles and internal passport and identification cards (Talgat et al. 2019). These attempts to further control the Kazakh populace, wedded with similar initiatives across the Union, were to come to a head with the renewed push for collectivization beginning in 1928.

As Olcott (1981) notes, the economic imperatives of increasing grain production while preserving or expanding the livestock sector mingled easily with Moscow's desire to both Sovietize the Kazakhs and break the back of a stubborn political resistance to Bolshevism. These two objectives were wedded via a four-stage plan from 1928 onwards, with each stage meant to increase output via Marxist-Leninist tenets while simultaneously crushing any anti-communist sentiment. According to Pianciola (2001), this plan encompassed various facets, including a decree making Kazakh men eligible for the military and banning Kazakh cultural practices as backward, a further attempt to "de-Kazakhify" the Kazakh lands and bring them under control of Moscow. In addition, in a stunning reversal of previous decolonization policies, the authorities also opened up the steppe to European (that is, Russian) colonists from 1929 onward, keeping an eye on the relative efficiency of Russian settlers but really hoping to once again swamp Kazakh nationalism in a tide of Russians (Pianciola 2019). The relationship between the new settlers and the Kazakhs went the same way as previous waves of migration, with the state of affairs between the two so frosty that in 1937 Trotsky noted that they would not even play chess together (Trotsky 1980). However, the first and most important stage of the change in Soviet policies beginning in 1928 was similar to the fate which befell successful Russian farmers in 1925, and that was a campaign against successful Kazakh farmers.

The richest livestock owners, the *bai* (literally, a type of husband, but used in Turkic-speaking countries to refer to owners of resources) were used during the tail end of the NEP as the institutional core of the semi-settled unit *kolhkozy* (multi-village agglomerations for agriculture, the commune-run analogue to state farms) in the Kazak ASSR, with the *bailar* (the local *bai* or leader of the *kolkhoz*) given the power "to control livestock, migratory movements, and water points" (Kerven et al. 2021:7). Once the decision had been made by Stalin to increase the number and power of the *kolkhozy*, however, the role of the *bailar* was no longer tenable; put another way, if the *bailar* were used to help to attract and organize Kazakhs within the *kolkhozy*, with the entire USSR moving towards mandatory participation in the communes, there was no need for the *bailar* to provide this function. Indeed, as the most successful and wealthiest of a particular *kolkhoz* unit, the *bailar* were instead meant to be singled out and targeted, "neutralized" in the memorable phrase of Ohayon (2013a). This is precisely what happened in the collectivization drives that began in 1928, as the Soviet authorities sent another signal about the perils of being good at one's profession, even if – in reality – the livestock requisitions only amounted to approximately 4 per cent of all livestock in the Kazak ASSR (Olcott 1981). According to Pianciola (2001:239), the point of the attack on the *bais* was, in addition to "what was officially described as the expropriation of the property of approximately 700 owners of large animal herds," actually to create "a cover for the indiscriminate pillaging of the entire rural Kazakh population," in many instances with the collaboration of rival clans of Kazakhs (Ohayon 2013a).

Pianciola (2019) suggests that the Soviet policy during this time oscillated between the eradication of pastoral nomadism and the obsession with collectivization, but in reality these two objectives reinforced and supported each other. Whereas the small-scale herder, still migrating in the summer months but otherwise avoiding long-term, multi-season migration (Kerven et al. 2021), could easily be made sedentary due to their economic precariousness – Hudson (1938) notes that the loss of even a few cattle made a poorer Kazakh easy prey for the depredations of weather and his fellow herders – the wealthier *bais* could only be co-opted if they were deprived of their own livelihoods and kept on the *kolkhozy*. Branded as "kulaks," a social designation that was dreaded throughout the USSR (as it made individuals instant targets for expropriation or death), the wealthier *bailars* were denounced as exploiters and capitalists and stripped of their assets, and their livestock were transferred to the collective farms (Thomas 2018). Thus, two birds were killed with one bloody stone, as collectives were given an infusion of capital (in the form of livestock) while the *bailars* were subdued as a political force (or even, realistically, as any force of their own).

The increase in sedentarism and collectivization which this policy facilitated subsequently had predictable effects on the fragile Kazakh economic institutions related to agriculture. In particular, the sedentarization of most Kazakhs meant that the complex web of social relationships related to survival on the steppe was rent asunder. During the NEP and shortly thereafter, theorists in the Kommunisticheskaya partiya Sovetskogo Soyuza (KPSS –Communist Party of the Soviet Union) suggested that the Kazakhs were nomadic not because they were backwards, but because the harshness of the steppe demanded it; Sergei Shvetsov in particular became known for his writings which predicted that "destroying nomadism in Kazakhstan would not only mean the end of livestock breeding in the steppe and Kazakh economy, it would also turn the arid steppe into uninhabited lands" (quoted in Kindler 2018:40–41). This astute observation was swept away in the "dizzy with success" years from 1929 to 1930,[4] as centralized directives from Stalin himself to accelerate collectivization meant that not only was there an influx of peasants into collectives (Pianciola 2001) but also the remaining agricultural capital and assets were nationalized in an attempt to "permanently silence the private sector" (Kindler 2018:69). In one fell swoop, collectivization would reorder the existing economic institutions, removing all carefully cultivated links embedded in social and historical experience, and superimpose a new form of production, information dissemination, and order. In this manner, the reconstruction of new economic institutions would produce new political institutions, ones which were not wedded to old concepts of clan or family but were instead based on loyalty to the party (Ohayon 2013a).

The proof, as they say, is in the pudding, and the disastrous effects of collectivization in Kazakhstan (as well as elsewhere in the USSR, such as Ukraine) on economic institutions as well as political institutions cannot begin to be understated. The collectivization drive in the Kazak ASSR started on shaky foundations and worsened as the realities of collectivism took hold. Dunmore (1980:63), writing in general about the command economy, accurately states that "it was one thing to get a particular policy enshrined as a leadership priority in plans and decrees; it was quite another to ensure that the apparatus of the command economy obeyed its masters, even in such priority matters." In the Kazakh lands, this was entirely the case regarding the Soviet approach to collectivization. Olcott (1995) notes that, even if collectivization was a good idea, the Kazak ASSR was woefully unprepared for it, as collective farms made up a scant (and inefficient) portion of the Kazakh economy by 1929, with little access to equipment or even a working model of what a collective farm should be. The sudden acceleration of collectivization thus had no best practices to emulate, and even the introduction of "25,000ers" from European Russia and Ukraine, shock troops or assault troops that were intended to provide the benefits of collectivization knowledge, had little effect on the ability of the Kazakhs to collectivize (Olcott 1981).

As it stood, however, collectivization was *not* a good idea in terms of politics or economics, a reality which should have been evident even before collectivization went into hyperdrive. The requisitioning of grain began to accelerate in 1928, and the fact that grain needed to be forcibly taken from farmers – in Marxist terms the labourers were alienated from the fruits of their labour – should have been the first clue that something was amiss with this method of organizing. However, power was the end goal of, as well as the means behind, collectivization. Kindler (2018) relates the story of Stalin personally travelling to Western Siberia to teach "Bolshevist" methods for grain requisition, using maximum pressure and violence on peasants to force them to comply. This approach was done specifically to pressure the governor of Semipalatinsk, where price differentials had existed with Western Siberia, and the demonstration had the effect of launching a wave of expropriation, mainly from Kazakhs (even though the region was densely populated by Russians and Ukrainians).

The expansion of requisition throughout the Kazak ASSR in 1929 led to predictable revolts from the Kazakhs and even more predictable violent repression from the Bolsheviks (Olcott 1981; Ohayon 2013b), while the theft of grain by the state had far-reaching repercussions for livestock: with targets set for requisitioning grain, and afraid of underperforming, the Kazakh authorities actually overfulfilled their quotas in specific geographic regions but only by sacrificing feed for animals (Pianciola 2001). A grand total of one million metric tons of wheat was requisitioned in 1930, one-third of the Kazak ASSR's total production, and, in a bitter irony, the animals that remained were then themselves also requisitioned for the cities (Ohayon 2013b). As Anderson (1997) was to note, the stock of animals collapsed between 1929 and 1934, with the number of sheep and goats alone decreasing from 27.2 million to 2.3 million (a decline of 92 per cent), while Ohayon (2006) shows that requisition of livestock increased to over two-thirds of all animals in the Kazak ASSR by 1931, an increase of 361 per cent compared to the number requisitioned in 1929.

The result of this approach was thus to sacrifice the future for the present, the people for the *nomenklatura*, and, in particular, the countryside for the city. In fact, collectivization and sedentarization were put in place to improve agricultural production (both in terms of grain output and livestock rearing) as a way to support the industrialization of key Russian cities. In the words of Pianciola (2017:86),

> one of the main features of the Stalinist system was … spatial and demographic segmentation, and its readiness to consciously sacrifice, or actively destroy, the population of any geographic or demographic unit for the sake of overall state-building and state security.

This is what occurred in the Kazak ASSR, as the combination of plans designed to support urban Soviet citizens, propelled by a hubris in the efficacy of Soviet bureaucracy, and a misunderstanding of human action in the face of incentives, led to a humanitarian disaster in the form of another, more massive famine from 1929 to 1933.

Several excellent books have been written in recent years detailing the Kazakh famine, many of which have been referenced already (e.g. Cameron 2018 or Kindler 2018), and a detailed retelling of the consequences of the collectivization drive would add nothing to these excellent resources. What concerns us more is the institutional effect that the famine had on the land that was to become Kazakhstan, and it is here that the numbers can only begin to convey the enormity of what actually occurred. The combined collapse of animal stocks and an insatiable hunger for food to requisition (with the amounts demanded only slightly declining during the worst of the famine) meant that the tragedy in Kazakhstan was devastating (Ivnitskiy 2009). In terms of institutional development, it had three main impacts:

Economic Institutions: Loss of Human Capital

As Pianciola (2004:137) states, the direct outcome of collectivization was the "great famine of 1931–1933, in which between 1.3 and 1.5 million Kazaks (between 35% and 38% of the total population, the highest percentage of any nationality in the USSR) lost their lives," while other scholars place the number of deaths as being even higher.[5]Ohayon (2013b) echoes these numbers but also calls attention to the fact that several hundred thousand Kazakhs also left the country, crossing the USSR's borders into China, Afghanistan, and Iran (and many moved onward into Mongolia). Statistics from the All-Union Censuses of 1926 and 1939 show that the number of Kazakhs in the Kazakh ASSR officially decreased by almost 1.3 million people over the course of 13 years, while a secret report from the Statistical Agency of the Kazak ASSR asserted that the rural population of the republic had declined from 5.87 million people on 1 June 1930, to 2.49 million on 1 June 1933, a decrease of 3.38 million people of all ethnicities (Davies and Wheatcroft 2009).

The reality of such a human tragedy meant that both economic and political institutions within the Kazakh lands were bound to suffer. From an economic standpoint, the accumulated human capital of the Kazakh ASSR was diminished considerably, meaning that it was less able to actually produce or innovate. Kremer (1993:681) famously showed that "among societies with no possibility for technological contact, those with larger initial populations have had faster technological change and population growth"; in other words a sufficient basis of human capital was required to drive innovation in physical capital. A direct challenge to standard Solow-type growth models, Kremer's discovery implied that countries with larger populations would experience more growth rather than less, for the simple reason that, statistically speaking, a larger population is likely to comprise more scientists, more engineers, more entrepreneurs, and more innovators. While these people would still require physical capital to innovate – innovation is a capital-intensive exercise, after all – the distributed knowledge would be able to help to bring about economic change.

With human action leading to technological innovation, a sequence of events would be set in motion that would then also force economic institutional change, as "given the existence of a specific technology, institutions are chosen by firms to minimize transaction costs" (North and Wallis 1994:610). While North and Wallis (1994) go further in demonstrating the difficulty in "choosing" institutions based on specific technologies, they prove this point via an examination of the endogeneity of institutions, and highlight the fact that institutional change can be caused by, as well as be a cause of, technological change. Bush (1987:1080) puts it more eloquently, stating that "as new patterns of behavior are required to accommodate the absorption and diffusion of new technology, instrumentally warranted patterns of behavior must change accordingly; and this requires changes in the instrumental values that correlate such behavior," manifested in a country's economic institutions. Technological change would require new ways of dealing with the shifting incentive structures created by innovation, changes which would happen in legislation, in various social relations, and at the private and corporate level.

In the context of Kazakhstan, the loss of such a massive amount of human capital, coupled with the reality of technological destruction – i.e. the loss of herding and grazing technology acquired via hundreds of years of experimentation and local knowledge – meant that Kazakhstan's economic institutions were going to be frozen in place, if not vitiated. Of course, this was the rationale behind collectivization, namely forced institutional change. In the words of Vasili Vodovozov, recalling (perhaps erroneously) conversations with Bolshevik leader Lenin three decades previously (Ellman 2005):

> By destroying the peasant economy and driving the peasant from the country to the town, the famine creates a proletariat and facilitates the industrialization of the region, which is progressive. Furthermore, the famine can and should be a progressive factor not only economically. It will force the peasant to reflect on the bases of the capitalist system, demolish faith in the tsar and tsarism, and consequently in due course make the victory of the revolution easier.
>
> (Vodovozov 1925:176–177)

However, the Bolshevik rationale behind this callous approach was to impose a new institutional structure from above immediately, ending all resistance by breaking the man; there was little thought of the longer-term consequences, which could be more profound than the short-term change from pastoral markets to sedentary collectivism. That is, not only did the Bolshevik collectivization drive "rip out the plumbing" from existing Kazakh economic institutions, it decimated the ability to innovate, to change, and thus to facilitate the development of more successful economic institutions going forward. Of course, as Vodovozov notes, it also made political institutions obsolete, all which were subsumed under the centralized party apparatus. Famine in the Kazakh lands thus served a broader purpose for institutional change, a purpose which began and ended with the naked exercise of power over the Kazakhs (and others in the Soviet Union).

Political Institutions: Russification of the Steppe

Population trends in the Kazakh lands reflect somewhat this loss of human capital in its immediacy. Figure 4.1 shows the average annual population growth rate in the Kazak ASSR from 1858 to 1950. As censuses and other data were only available on an irregular basis, growth is calculated as the change between two available data points, averaged across the years in between. Based on official statistics, from 1926 to 1939 this yielded an average annual population growth rate of 0.09 per cent per year, and during the collectivization drive over the same period, the overall population of the Kazak ASSR increased by just over 1 per cent (1.18 per cent). However, as noted, the population of ethnic Kazakhs declined by approximately 1.3 million during this period, although perhaps not all these deaths can be attributed to famine. What, then, is driving the overall growth in population after such a cataclysm? Poor Soviet bookkeeping? A baby boom after the famine? Or something else?

While Soviet bookkeeping may appear to be a likely culprit, the answer is simultaneously more prosaic and more nefarious. The average annual population growth rate in the Kazakh ASSR during this period was undoubtedly buoyed by a massive increase in the Russian population both prior to the famine, in the aforementioned re-colonization policy, but, more importantly, after the famine. Pianciola (2019) notes the scale and unrelenting pace of these transfers:

> The number of Europeans in the Steppe grew during the first half of the 1930s, since Kazakhstan was one of the main destinations for deported peasants from European Russia. Almost three hundred thousand peasants (mostly Russian peasants and Kuban Cossacks) were brought to Kazakhstan from other Soviet regions in cattle trains between 1930 and 1933, a new form of state-led colonization. Thousands of deportees were put to work in one of the biggest Gulag camps of the Soviet Union, the Karaganda Lager, created in Kazakhstan during the famine years. During the second half of the 1930s, the first victims of Soviet ethnic deportations arrived in central Kazakhstan from Soviet border regions (in 1936, thirty-six thousand Poles and nine thousand Soviet Germans from Ukraine; in 1937, ninety-eight thousand Koreans from the Russian Far East).

According to Soviet census data, this constant influx of settlers meant that, on the eve of war, ethnic Russians outnumbered Kazakhs for the first time in the history of recorded statistics in the region; as of 1939, Russians made up 40 per cent of the total population of the Kazakh ASSR compared to just 37.8 per cent of Kazakhs. Indeed, at the same time as the Kazakh population was plummeting, the number of Russians almost doubled from 1.275 million to 2.458 million, an increase of 93 per cent. In tandem with the famine's devastating effect on the nomadic Kazakhs, the "Russification" of Kazakh

Figure 4.1 Population Growth in the Kazakh Lands, 1858–1950
Source: based on the author's calculations and Global Financial Data, https://globalfinancialdata.com/products#GFDdata.

land was accelerated by the influx of settlers, a matter of policy as well as of circumstance.

This shift in the ethnic make-up of the Kazakh ASSR was bound to have consequences similar to the loss of human capital among the Kazakhs. In particular, while the institutional structures and accumulated knowledge of the Kazakhs were being dismantled person by person, it was being replaced by Russians, who had a distinctly different way of viewing the steppe and the region (and, of course, a different language). The first wave of Russians who came to the steppe under the threat of violence were "kulaks," relatively richer peasants whose property had been expropriated by the Soviet authorities and who were being sent away to develop their own class consciousness (Spehr and Kassenova 2012). This meant that the new arrivals had never been nomads, were already sedentarized, and had a history of land ownership or at least attachment to land; moreover, they were being sent, not as specialists in agriculture or even to supplement the agricultural labour force, but as builders of industry and in particular in mining coal, copper, and iron (Davies and Wheatcroft 2009). They brought with them Russian ways of thinking, Russian language skills, and Russian cultural biases, expectations, and formulations, similar to those in power in the Kremlin, and (in theory), that were easier to control. As Kindler (2018:234) asserts, "Many deported people were settled into existing kolkhozes. This gave the repression apparatus an ever greater influence over the Kazakh population and power over the 'civic' administrations of the regions in question."

The reality in terms of institution-building in the Kazakh ASSR was that the introduction of foreign elements such as European Russians meant that the path of institutional evolution was bound to be altered. Not only had Soviet plans imposed a top-down transformation in the name of the people, *but they had also actually changed "the people" themselves.* Indeed, in the Kazakh case, the transfer of broken and repressed peasants into Kazakh lands created a further hierarchy of peasants, as the "kulaks," undesirable as they were, were actually treated as more valuable to the building of communism than the archaic nomads they were replacing (Pianciola 2001). In fact, the introduction of already-broken peasants to the steppes was also seen as a way to continue the subjugation of the Kazakhs, as "Moscow did not care if the denizens of the steppes became shining examples of the 'New Soviet Man.' Loyalty was not asked of them, only compliance and obedience" (Kindler 2018:233). In short, the Russification of the Kazakh ASSR entailed replacing a rebellious populace with a quiescent one, the better to control the path of institutional development.

Social Institutions: Completion of Sedentarization

Finally, the famine put an end to large-scale pastoral nomadism in the Kazakh lands until it was once again encouraged by the Soviet authorities. Despite the arguments in the literature and indeed within the Soviet leadership about the pace of sedentarism versus collectivism, the collectivization drive was the means by which the nomadic life of Kazakhs was finally ended in a most spectacular way. Cameron (2018:178) explicitly states this, saying that "through collectivization, Moscow sought to destroy nomadic life, a key feature of Kazakh culture and identity." We need not rely on second-hand sources to confirm this, as the Bolsheviks were typically unabashed in their pursuit of destroying the social institutions of the Kazakhs related to their pastoral way of life; Party Secretary Filipp Goloshchekin noted explicitly in a 1931 article that "the old, backward, nomadic and seminomadic aul is dying; it has to die … the old aul is now collapsing, it moves towards sedentarization, haymaking, agriculture" (quoted in Pianciola 2019). The reason for this death of the old was precisely the Soviet authorities' use of hunger as a weapon, in order to break the back of resistance within the Kazakh traditional structures of clan and family and to quell any further rebellion (Ohayon 2013b; Cameron 2018). The famine itself had a "pernicious impact … on social cohesion, codes of morality, and Kazakh societal values" (Ohayon 2013b:9); more bluntly, Yesdauletova et al. (2015:543) states that "collectivization, forced sedentarization and repression of the economically stronger entities all combined to explode the traditional structures of the Kazakh village." And, to come full circle to the Soviets speaking forthrightly about their intentions, the Central Committee of the Kazak Communist Party resolved in 1929 that the "sedentarization" of the nomads was a necessary prerequisite "for the socialist reconstruction of the economy" (quoted in Olcott 1981).

The twin policies of collectivization and sedentarization were indeed effective in achieving these aims, as, out of a pre-famine nomadic population of 564,000 households, Soviet statistics (taken with the appropriate caveats) claimed to have settled a total of 338,685 households by the beginning of 1937 (data extracted from *Gosudarstvennyi Arkhiv Rossiiskoi Federatsii*, quoted in Kindler 2018). While the specific numbers are a source of debate (especially given the possibility of double counting for nomads who were "settled" more than once), the effects of collectivization had precisely the desired effects for a sedentarization policy. In many ways, even seemingly innocuous schemes dedicated purely to economic development also were part and parcel of broader attempt to socially re-engineer the Kazakhs. As with most central planners, the Bolsheviks were enamoured with infrastructure – the bigger the better. Neither the Kazak ASSR nor later the Kazakh SSR were spared from these mega-projects, one of the most important of which was the Turkestan–Siberian railroad (in classic Russian fashion, known as the portmanteau Turksib). The Turksib was an impressive accomplishment of organized and coerced labour, originally covering approximately 1,400 kilometres from Seminpalatnisk in the Kazak ASSR to Frunze (now known as Bishkek) in the Kirghiz ASSR, with additions outside of the Kazak ASSR continuing south to Arys in modern-day Uzbekistan and north to Novosibirsk in Russia (covering a total length of 2,375 kilometres). The "first-born of the Five-Year Plan," begun in 1926 and completed in 1931, The Turksib was

> one of the two top construction priorities in the country, along with the Dnepr hydroelectric plant … In the economic calculus of the late NEP, the Turksib was of all-Union, and not just regional, importance. The Turksib was needed to provide inexpensive Siberian wheat for the peasants of Turkestan to induce them to sow more of their land with cotton.
>
> (Payne 1988:354)

The Turksib, in addition to bringing food to the masses and occupying a crucial spot in the socialist supply chain, also was projected to have another salutary effect, namely bringing "backward" Kazakhs into the proletariat. Despite the proclamations of the *New York Times* that this was "entirely a Russian achievement," the Soviet authorities hired approximately 50,000 Kazakhs as unwilling labourers on the project with an eye to continuing the sedentarization process.[6] However, as Payne (1988:410) points out, "the local population did not share its elite's view that being proletarian was desirable and the Kazakhs only 'turned to' the railroad after their traditional means of livelihood had been shattered by the grain crisis and collectivization," seeing construction work as "culturally alien and spiritually debilitating" (Payne 2001: 121). Moreover, While Payne (1988, 2001) uses this as evidence that the goal of the Turksib as the "forge of a new proletariat" in the Kazak ASSR failed, it can be seen perhaps more accurately that a substantial number of Kazakhs were forced into labour that they would not have done if their nomadic livelihoods had not been taken away from them. In this sense, sedentarization had once again prevailed.

The creation of jobs which required a sedentary populace was mixed with a removal of the livelihoods that the Kazakhs already had. Pianciola (2019) draws our attention to the fact that pastoral routes were shortened as a result of Soviet policies and the creation of infrastructure such as the Turksib and *kolkhozes*, making the very logistics of nomadism more difficult even apart from the official attempts to discourage it as a livelihood. Moreover, the Soviet response to the famine, namely to shroud it in secrecy, had a further effect of "obliterat[ing] … the memory of the famine, and hence of sedentarization," thus obscuring "the nomadic past, forever relegating it to the mists of the remote, folkloric past" (Ohayon 2013b:8).

Purges, Terror, and the Great Patriotic War

As if the famine had not done enough to wipe away the remaining vestiges of large-scale nomadism and the social institutions buttressing these economic and political arrangements, two further shocks were to befall the Kazakh ASSR in the 1930s and extending into the 1940s. Both were common shocks across the territory of the USSR, although the precise extent of the shocks differed in various territories, and both were to have substantial ramifications for the development of the institutions on Kazakh lands: first, the Stalinist Terror of the late 1930s, and second, the "Great Patriotic War" (Second World War) from 1941 to 1945.

By 1936, the Soviet Union had formulated and put into practice a new legislative framework, the so-called Stalin Constitution, which sought to bring the myriad of administrative and bureaucratic strata in the country under the firm hand of Moscow. Part of this evolution in the Union's political institutions was to replace the federation called for in the 1924 constitution (hence, the "Union" of Soviet Socialist Republics) with a much more centralized apparatus; as Getty (1991:35) states, "in 1936, the union republics were stripped of whatever independent authority they had enjoyed." As part of the revamped regional policy, and perhaps in recognition of its sacrifices to the communist cause during the early 1930s,[7] the Kazak ASSR had been transformed once again into the Kazakh SSR. In line with this shift in the overarching legal authority governing the republic, in line with every other SSR, the Kazakh SSR adopted its own constitution, mirroring the overall Soviet constitution. In the Kazakh SSR, the triumph over the old social order was proclaimed, with "the Kazakh constitution ascrib[ing] the political foundation of the state to the overthrow of the power of the 'bai'," explicitly referring to "the destruction of pre-capitalist as well as capitalist relationships" (Collins 1951:22). In this manner, the Soviet authorities completed a forced imposition of top-down and centralized institutional orderings, and a replacement of traditional and informal social bonds with the formal linkages of the state.

Not content with this formal institutional change, however, Moscow and in particular Stalin sought to reinforce the new legal apparatus with informal enforcement mechanisms predicated on bringing every single subject of the USSR into line with his changing whims on the direction of communist development. This of course was the Stalinist Terror, beginning with show trials in 1936 but really accelerating during 1937, which led to the deaths of between 950,000 and 1.2 million people across the entire Soviet Union (Ellman 2002). The Terror has been well documented in terms of its effect on the Russian psyche and the development of institutions across the USSR (Conquest 2018), with the impact on economic institutions in particular showing that "Stalinism … was a double anathema, killing tens of millions between 1929 and 1953 and impoverishing most except those in the inner circle" (Rosefielde 1996:978). Cheremukhin et al. (2017) provide estimates that the welfare of those who survived the Terror was far lower at the end of the period than at the beginning, as measured in per capita consumption. Moreover, the Terror had demonstrable effects on the future evolution of political institutions, as work done by Zhukov and Talibova (2018) shows that groups which were more repressed by Stalin (including deportees) have had persistently lower voter turnout in the post-communist era. Nikolova et al. (2022) elucidate that people who live closer to former gulags also exhibit far lower levels of social trust and engagement, while Levkin (2014) demonstrates that descendants of deportees in particular displayed a (healthy, one might suspect) distrust of centralized authority.

In the Kazakh SSR, the impact of the Terror was in terms of absolute numbers smaller than elsewhere in the USSR, but this was only due to the relative differences in the size and population of the republic. When scaled for these differing traits, the Kazakh SSR was perhaps more harmed by Stalin's willing executioners: for example, Yensenov et al. (2021) calculate that a 105,000 residents of the Kazakh SSR were arrested during this time, of which 22,000 were summarily executed. If this number of arrests is correct, then we can use population numbers to understand the extent of the Terror. However, population estimates from 1939 differ, with the official Soviet statistics perhaps inflated by as much as 13 per cent in an attempt to hide the scale of losses in the territory (Tolts 2006). Using both official and corrected population estimates, we can surmise that anywhere between approximately 1.7 per cent and 2 per cent of the entire population of the Kazakh SSR were incarcerated (compared to approximately 1 per cent of the entire Soviet Union arrested during this time). To take an example of the distribution of this repression, although the Kazakh intelligentsia had long been a favourite target of the Bolsheviks (see above), repression of this specific demographic also intensified, with the Kazakh representation to the First Congress of Soviet Writers in 1934 seeing, by 1937, "33 out of 101 board members … called 'the enemies of the people,' and 180 out of 597 delegates who attended the congress suffer[ed] prosecution" (Tanatarova 2015:104). Olcott (1995:218–219) notes that, by the end of 1937, "a whole generation of Kazakh intellectuals, historians, journalists, poets, and writers were found guilty and executed for the crime of dedication to the Kazakh people."

The infrastructure needed to support such a mechanism of repression meant that, in reality, the Kazakh lands were transformed during the 1930s and 1940s into one giant labour camp, a dumping ground for those who had fallen out of favour with Stalin and needed to be hidden away somewhere. As Wojnowski (2017:1000) notes, "Soviet Kazakhstan was also home to millions of victims of Stalinist deportations and some of the largest Gulag camps." This included the Karagandinskaia lager (known as the KarLag or Karaganda Labour Camp), which was founded in 1931 and covered more than a staggering 6,800 square miles, held 65,000 inmates at its peak occupancy, and eventually saw more than one million inmates passing through its vast expanse (Brown 2001). At the same time, the area outside of present-day Nur-Sultan, Akmolinsk, was home to the largest women's camp in the USSR, the awkwardly named Akmolinskii lager zhen izmennikov rodiny (ALZHIR – Akmolinsk camp for the wives of the traitors of the fatherland), which held approximately 8,000 women in 1938; eventually this number rose to 18,000 (Satymbekova 2017). As time passed, and the camps proved their worth to Stalin and Moscow, additional forms of camps were created, so-called groups of special camps (*Steplag*), predicated on hard labour and housing former Red Army soldiers, fighters captured in the territories the Soviet Union annexed during the Second World War, and other dangerous elements (Barnes 2005).

This vast labour complex, present throughout the Soviet Union and named the "gulag" (a portmanteau for *Glavnoe Upravlenie Lagerei,* or "main camp administration"), was populated by a large number of prisoners, mainly accused "kulaks," political dissidents, "anti-Soviet elements," people who had joked about Stalin, committed Bolsheviks, and many others (Ilič 2006). Indeed, we have already noted the deportations of "kulaks" to the Kazak ASSR during the famine, and Viola (2007) estimates that a total of 261,227 "kulaks" were deported to Kazakhstan during 1930 and 1931 (based on Soviet statistics). Additional massive deportations occurred from the purges onward, reaching a zenith in the early days of the Second World War. According to Brown (2001:20),

> documentary evidence has confirmed survivor accounts that narrate how Soviet security forces, the OGPU [Ob'yedinonnoye gosudarstvennoye politicheskoye upravleniye, Joint State Political Directorate], NKVD [Narodniy komissariat vnutrennikh del, People's Commissariat for International Affairs], MVD [Ministerstvo vnutrennikh del SSSR, Ministry of International Affairs], uprooted millions of peaceful citizens and subjected them to physical and psychological abuse, starvation, and conditions ripe for disease, from which hundreds of thousands of people died.

One of the key sources of supply for the gulags on Kazakh lands included members of undesirable or suspect ethnic minorities, who were transported from across the Union to Central Asia beginning in the early 1930s with an increase in movement during the time of the purges and following the Nazi invasion of the USSR. The institution of a nationalities policy by Stalin in 1937 was a thinly veiled excuse for the persecution of minorities who had failed to integrate into Soviet life, building on the previous waves of deportations of Poles and Germans and growing to encompass nearly all diaspora groups (Biltstein 2006). No ethnic minorities were safe, as each could be accused of harbouring dual loyalties or being in the paid employ of a foreign power: for example, Soviet Koreans, a minority group based predominantly in the Far East, were the first to be targeted for exile in their entirety in 1937. Accused of spying for Japan, Soviet Koreans were deported en masse in three stages, with 95,256 Soviet Koreans sent to Kazakhstan (and a further 76,525 to Uzbekistan; see Pohl 2000). Heady with the rush of success in effectively relocating an entire set of people, the Soviet authorities "exiled the Soviet Finns and Germans in 1941, the Karachays and Kalmyks in 1943, the Chechens, Ingush, Balkars, Crimean Tatars, Crimean Greeks, Meskhetian Turks, Kurds and Khemshils in 1944 and the Black Sea Greeks in 1949 and 1951" (Pohl 2000:279) to Central Asia, with the bulk of them arriving in Kazakhstan (Marie 1995).

Ultimately, the effect of the Terror was to deplete native human capital yet further in the Kazakh SSR, imprisoning or executing the best and brightest, while once again shifting the composition of the population on the Kazakh lands; taken from a purely mechanistic approach, the deportation of many skilled prisoners to the Kazakh SSR (such as the Soviet Koreans) could have improved the overall level of technological knowhow and expertise in the republic. But on balance, the uprooting of peoples sent to an unfamiliar land, barely provisioned for when they arrived (Pohl 2000), with skills that were either unrelated to their new homes (as with Korean rice farmers reaching the arid steppes) or wasted by Soviet imperatives (many labourers were routed into mining) meant that the economic benefit to the Kazakh SSR was negligible. And, as noted by Cheremukhin et al. (2017), the benefits to the entire USSR from the Terror (including collectivization) were wholly evanescent; those who survived the purges, the deportations, and the war, nevertheless experienced a decrease in their standards of living. Finally, to link to recent scholarship on the effects of economic policy uncertainty (Baker et al. 2016), the despotic approach to running an economy generated massive waves of uncertainty for labourers and managers, making loyalty and keeping one's head down more important than fulfilling targets or innovating. Indeed, the Terror had at its core absolutely no concern for the development of any economic institutions. It was not concerned with fashioning better linkages among sectors, fostering productivity, or even improving information dissemination related to a planned economy. It was a naked attempt to (a) place blame for previous failures associated with collectivization and (b) to continue to exercise raw power in order to intimidate and terrorize. Within the Kazakh SSR, the impact it had on economic institutions was directly related to the uncertainty and disruptions it caused, further retarding the development of indigenous economic relations.

While the Terror and its associated purges were entirely unconcerned with economic institution-building, another effect thereof was directly related to the political apparatus that the Soviets were building. The governing apparatus of the Kazakh SSR was already running low on expertise as a result of the famine and the failure of collectivism, as Goloshchekin, his supporters, advisers, and a slew of other local officials had already been dismissed or arrested by 1932 and accused of "sabotaging" the agricultural plans of Stalin (Olcott 1981). This trend also accelerated exponentially from 1937 onward, with Olcott (1995:219) noting that, after the intellectuals had been executed, "the purgers themselves were next [and] before another year had passed, every member of the Kazakh buro of [the] first Congress [of the Communist Part of Kazakhstan in 1937] was arrested and charged." As noted by Rogovin (2009:294),

> the "recruits of 1937" [bureaucratic appointees hired to backfill those arrested] were incomparably less competent and ideological than the people they replaced. With them, the devotion to Bolshevik ideals was replaced with a truly unlimited personal devotion to the leader and a readiness to zealously execute any directives coming from his office.

Olcott (1981:132) takes this further and notes that, predictably, "the constant replacement of personnel and the related fear of arrest stifled any initiative on the part of local leadership to work out solutions for the specific problems which beset their localities." Thus, not only had the very hands needed to build the economic system been crippled by the despotic purges, but the stripping away of bureaucrats into the gulag also decimated any hope of creating a professional civil service.

Finally, as a social catastrophe, the effects of the Terror can be seen in many ways, one of the most important being two semi-fictional novels by Yurii Dombrovskiy, namely *The Keeper of Antiquities* and *The Faculty of Useless Knowledge.* Tracing the life of an archaeologist in Alma-Ata, Georgi Zybin (only named in the second novel) is accused of stealing gold and is hounded through interrogation by a zealous NKVD agent who wants to out-Stalin Moscow with a show trial of his own. Portraying the reality of life on the empire's furthest periphery, the issues faced by citizens of the USSR, and how the most banal trivialities could end up threatening someone's life under Stalinism, the books, given that they are based on Dombrovskiy's own life, also capture the reality of "show trials" being put together simply because Stalin ordered them, searching for scapegoats on any pretext (Degitaeva 1998). In many ways, this tied back into the broader goals of the Terror, which sought to make no one feel safe in the face of an omnipotent state apparatus. And this was also to feed into both political and economic institutional development throughout the Soviet period.

Before moving on to the post-war period, however, something must be said about the second exogenous shock faced by the Kazakh SSR, the Second World War itself. Being situated thousands of miles from the battlefields of Europe, and with Japan and the USSR technically not at war until May 1945, the Kazakh SSR was spared the horrors which were visited upon Ukraine, Belarus, and other countries in the "bloodlands" between Hitler and Stalin (Snyder 2010). Indeed, the main disruptions to the republic have already been noted, mainly the mass deportation of "enemy sympathizers" which took place between 1941 and 1944, including the entire Chechen and Ingush people and the Volga Germans. The strain that these new settlers put on the already struggling economy of the Kazakh SSR was considerable, as, during the first wave of German deportations, "the local authorities in these areas were unprepared for the sudden influx of hundreds of thousands of ethnic German exiles" (Pohl 2000:280). This reality is echoed by Tokhmetova et al. (2014), focusing on the deportation of Germans to Pavlodar, who note that the Soviet authorities were excellent at organizing the deportations, with care taken to ensure an adequate number of trains, disembarkation points, and the like, but paid no attention to what happened when the deportees reached Pavlodar.[8] The inability of the Kazakh SSR authorities to provide for the new arrivals, along with the harsh realities of climate and geography, meant that the losses of human life were also considerable: Bugai (1995) estimates that between 30–50 per cent of the Chechens and Ingush, between

20 and 40 per cent of the Balkars, between 25 and 46.2 per cent of the Crimean Tatars, and a massive but indeterminate number of Volga Germans died either en route to their destination or within the first year and a half after arriving.

For those that did survive the deportation or their first year, there were additional issues in both integrating socially and into the existing informal economic relations which still persisted, albeit that these issues were not evenly distributed. As Hionidou and Saunders (2010) note, Greek exiles from the Caucasus deported to Kazakhstan, actually improved their standing and integrated, contributing to the development of the Kazakh SSR. The same was found with the Koreans, resettled in the first wave of deportations, who brought new crops to the Central Asian heartland and were some of the most productive and educated workers in the entire Soviet Union (Gelb 1995). However, on the whole, the formal administrative apparatus for dealing with these deportees was very thin and not geared towards helping deportees to assimilate: indeed, as Scarborough (2017) details, the law dealing with deportees was not passed until January 1945, a year after the bulk of the deportations had ended, and the actual parameters which deportees were to follow were unclear (and not backed by any administrative instructions). Werth (2006) also notes, in the case of the Chechens, that any official assistance did not come until 1948, but it was packaged along with a strict crackdown on special settlers and an attempt to build a more coherent and punitive administration. Even evacuees coming from western Soviet areas under attack by the Germans found that there was very little support given for their evacuation, with emphasis placed on rescuing materials rather than people (Zharkynbayeva et al. 2020). As with so many of the Soviets' economic policies, the success of deportees and even evacuees to weather their environment came down to the individual and his/her ability to overcome the system, rather than success being attributable to the system itself.

Beyond the influx of "settlers," there was also a substantial outflow of Kazakh soldiers, shipped off to the front to die for Soviet internationalism and against the Soviet Union's former ally, Nazi Germany. The Kazakh SSR provided a relatively high per capita contribution to the war effort: Sarsenbekov and Sagatova (2021) provide estimates not broken down by ethnicity, claiming that 1.366 million people were mobilized during the war years from the SSR, with the number of fatalities totalling 410,000, including both Russian and Kazakh deaths (these figures also appear in Ismailov 2011). Taking a more granular view of the impact of the war, Carmack (2019) estimates that over one million people were mobilized from the Kazakh SSR, including 450,000 Kazakhs, with at least 125,000 Kazakhs becoming casualties (including dead, wounded, or missing soldiers) of the war. Much as with the deportees who came to the Kazakh SSR to find an alien land, Kazakh conscripts into the Red Army also found themselves alone, often torn from their villages and with only a scant knowledge of the Russian language (Schechter 2012). While the Soviet administration was aware of the need to better integrate the non-Russian conscripts into the army, "the centralized nature of the Soviet propaganda machine was a key factor hampering attempts by Kazakhstan's party organizations to deliver agitprop materials to Kazakh political workers" (Carmack 2014:98).

Despite these hurdles, the Kazakhs also furnished the Soviet army with personnel who would go on to become "heroes of the Soviet Union," including sniper Aliya Moldagulova and machine gunner Manshuk Mametova, honoured for their exploits against the Germans (Rees 2020). Kazakhs were also to be found fighting the Germans in resistance movements around Europe, especially in France, Belgium, Italy, and Yugoslavia (Mendikulova et al. 2019). However, the "Great Patriotic War" (the Soviet designation of the conflict, meant to deflect from the Russian-Nazi alliance from 1939 to 1941) also assumed a mythic status in Kazakh history, elevated as it was throughout the Soviet Union and especially in Russia; as part of this elevation also came with it the need to root out "collaborators" who "assisted the enemy," and the immediate post-war era was replete with examples, even in the Kazakh SSR, of trials and executions of Izmenniki rodiny (betrayers of the motherland) at the hands of the Soviet authorities (Kaiser 2014). Although less affected than the occupied territories, the combined effect of conscription, wartime fatalities, and absorption of deportees was to further handicap the development of economic and social relations within the Kazakh SSR. As with collectivization and famine, the war and the change in the composition of the Kazakh populace also made the Kazakh SSR easier to control from Moscow.

A Post-Mortem on Stalinist Economic Development in the Kazakh SSR

As noted above, the objective in the Kazakh economy during the time of famine, purges, and war was to build the SSR into an agricultural powerhouse, providing sustenance for the cities and ensuring its own place in the broader industrialization schemes for the Soviet Union. But despite the push for improving output in the Kazakh SSR (and, as an afterthought, the living conditions of its citizens), the record of economic development on the Kazakh lands remained poor, much as it did throughout the Soviet Union. Even after the unfortunate passing of Stalin (in the sense that he never saw justice for his crimes), the deleterious consequences of collectivization and sedentarization remained. Economic statistics on the development of the Kazakh SSR are scarce before 1950, and few data are available on the aggregate success or failure of Stalinist development schemes. Thus, in order to judge their effects, we must instead focus on areas for which data are available while also zooming in on the contemporary accounts of worker concerns in the Kazakh SSR.

In the first instance, the drive within the Kazak ASSR and the Kazakh SSR to supplant livestock rearing with more sedentary forms of agriculture did not succeed, and in fact it only served to devastate the number of livestock without any concomitant increase in the efficiency of wheat or grain output. Holdsworth (1952:266) notes explicitly that "the sown area at 5,124,000 hectares in 1935 in Kazakhstan was an increase of 20.5 per cent on that of 1913. Wheat had been extended and the cultivation of sugar beet established." Similarly, during the communist era from 1918 to 1940, the amount of land dedicated to wheat production increased by approximately 83 per cent, but yields rose by just 35 per cent, a record of accumulation without efficiency, especially when compared with later successes in the Kazakh SSR without collectivization (Abugaliyeva and Morgounov 2016). On the other hand, by 1940, 11 years after the collectivization drive had started, many collective farmers still did not have a cow of their own (Olcott 1995). Holdsworth (1952:266) also contrasted the increase in the amount of land under cultivation with the effect of livestock, noting that "the cattle situation remained disastrous and the overall pre-collectivization totals had not been attained by 1940." In fact, increases in the number of livestock during this period also came about through the accumulation of capital rather than any technological breakthroughs, as the evacuation of livestock from the German war machine in the west meant that the Kazakh SSR's stock of animals expanded by approximately two million between 1941 and 1942 (Pianciola 2019). Much as with the rest of the USSR's industrialization policy, which entailed moving a massive amount of labour to the capital (Allen 2001), agricultural policy in the Kazakh SSR was a process of accumulation rather than of technological improvement.

Perhaps a more damning indictment of the effect of Stalinist economic policies is the counterfactual, which could be seen in livestock management in the post-collectivization era (from 1941 onward). Indeed, it was only the volte-face that Soviet authorities made on the issue of sedentarism in 1941 which spurred the technological change needed in this area, bringing long-distance livestock husbandry back as a technique in its own right (Kerven et al. 2021). With the official adoption of long-range livestock management as Soviet policy, the reconstitution of livestock herds came about in spite of previous Soviet policies rather than because of it, with advances made because of the "spontaneous experimentation and diffusion" of knowledge from individual Kazakh herders (Alimaev and Behnke 2008:163). Without admitting defeat in the ability of the collectivization or sedentarization drives to boost economic productivity, the Soviet authorities instead shifted towards "a form of industrialized nomadism, in which the latest modern technical assets were coupled with ancient pastoralist skills, to adapt to and exploit the variable environment of Kazakhstan's pasture wealth" (Kerven et al. 2021:8).

Of course, this change in policy can be viewed in a very different light, namely as the triumph of Soviet policies rather than their defeat. Pianciola (2019) notes that "after the early-1930s collectivization drive, never again did the Soviet government attempt to eradicate pastoral mobility." However, this was not due to any uptick in learning on the need to prepare nomadic populations for sedentarization (Olcott 1995), rather it was because they had little need to do so. Although Soviet status was no longer tied to being sedentary (with initiatives actually undertaken to support nomadic life; see Kindler 2018), much of this acquiescence was due to the fact that the broader social institutions supporting nomadism had already been demolished. To put it another way, the nomadism that could be countenanced after the Second World War was occurring in the framework of Soviet social institutions, and thus could be encouraged, rather than the nomadism which occurred in the framework of traditional clan and family relations. Nomadism and/or mobile animal husbandry was effective as an economic institution so long as it contributed to the increase of output within a Soviet planned economy, and thus it could once again be supported officially. From this point of view, the inefficiency in output was a small price to pay for the destruction of hated pre-capitalist and capitalist social institutions.

With regard to the daily concerns of Kazakh labourers, there was also ample evidence of economic stagnation related to the "shock troop" approach to economic development. Wojnowski (2017) notes that the complaints of Kazakh workers in the wake of de-Stalinization in 1956 were less focused on the broader issues of repression and terror and more on bread-and-butter issues. These included the lack of decent housing and basic items, as well as the inability to access services such as healthcare without travelling hundreds of kilometres. Pohl (2004:60), reflecting on female labourers on state farms in the same year, notes that "workers experienced severe and prolonged shortages of all basic food supplies. In extreme instances workers went hungry for days," a decided lack of progress for a region that had already suffered famine, purges, and war. In fact, these same concerns could easily have been voiced 20 years earlier (albeit with greater fear of repression) and corresponded with the "alternative" economic estimates of Russian economist G. I. Khanin during the 1980s of very low multifactor productivity growth in the entire USSR (Harrison 1993).[9]

As a final point regarding the effect of Stalinist economic policies, while the intention of collectivization and the deportations was to develop the Kazakh rural economy, in particular to expand grain and wheat production, there was a concurrent push towards industrialization similar to that in other regions of the USSR (more on this below). The war itself spurred industrial development: according to Rybakovskii (1995), at least 1,500 factories relocated to the east ahead of Nazi advances, with approximately 100 settling in the Kazakh SSR. According to a self-serving but informative article by Mots (1964:523) – Mots was a staff member on the "national economic council" of the USSR – the Kazakh SSR saw "industry, virtually non-existent until the Revolution, now cover[ing] all the main branches, and production per head of many items is considerably greater in the Kazakh SSR than in the Soviet Union as a whole." Data provided by Mots (see Table 4.2), while possibly off in terms of its magnitude, does show the timing of this structural change, which started tentatively around 1940 but truly began to take off by 1950 (i.e.

Table 4.2 Industrial Output in the Kazakh SSR, 1913–1950

Product	*Unit*	*1913*	*1928*	*1940*	*1950*
Steel	thousand metric tons	–	–	–	131.00
Rolled ferrous goods	thousand metric tons	–	–	–	107.00
Coal	million metric tons	0.09	0.04	7.00	17.40
Oil	million metric tons	0.12	0.25	0.70	1.10
Electricity	billion kWh	0.00	0.01	0.63	2.60
Cement	thousand metric tons	–	–	–	16.00
Woollen textiles	million metres	0.14	0.13	0.41	2.20
Cotton textiles	million metres	–	–	0.07	4.92

Source: Mots (1964:523).

the post-war era). Additional statistics from the Soviet leadership (Tsentralnoe statisticheskoe upravlenie, 1956) reveal that industrial production in the Kazakh SSR increased by 322 per cent from 1940 to 1955 (more on this below). Coupled with massive capital investment throughout Central Asia, more so than in Russia (Scarborough 2021), the next stage of economic development was the move towards heavy industry in a place that had no experience of it.

This too could be a consequence of "success" in the collectivization drives, especially with sedentarization. Much like the example of the Turksib, by divesting the populace of their nomadic ways, the economic machinery of the Soviets then began to create jobs in areas appropriate for Soviet men, i.e. sedentary and urbanized, rather than for nomads. Once again, this was an example of top-down economic planning, in that there was no ecosystem of institutions generating jobs according to the complex web of supply and demand; instead, it involved the creation of jobs which required the altering of the populace to fit them. In this sense, the shift towards urbanization and industrialization was another example of the Kazakh SSR being used as a vast laboratory to engineer human souls (in the immortal words of Škvorecký 1977).

Khrushchev, Virgin Lands, and Industrialization

For the most part, the tale of institutional evolution in the Kazakh ASSR has already been told, mirroring the changes in the Soviet Union: the catastrophes of communism, collectivization, famine, and war played a massive role in uprooting many of the formal and informal institutions which had been painstakingly built in Kazakh lands over the previous centuries. The extreme centralization demanded by communism, an extension of the policies started under Tsarism, coupled with the Russification of the region and the wholesale movement of peoples, made such a fundamental change to social and political orderings within the land set to become Kazakhstan that it was difficult to imagine any further changes having as important an effect. To again return to our analogy of gravity, while the distant past looms large over the present of Kazakhstan, exerting a strong pull on institutional paths, the period from 1918 to 1945 might be the body with the most mass in Kazakh history, distorting all around it.

However, as I have mentioned already and will mention repeatedly in this book, history is not destiny, and other countries, while influenced by the persistence of the communist era, have somehow managed to reach terminal velocity in escaping the worst depredations of the 1920s, 1930s, and 1940s, including Ukraine (Hartwell 2016) and the Baltic states (Smith et al. 2002). Moreover, just because the largest institutional influences came early in the Soviet period, setting the stage for the manner by which the political and economic institutions within the USSR were to conduct themselves, this does not mean that the influence of the Soviet Union was done in moulding the Kazakh SSR. In fact, much of what was to happen in the post-Stalinist era, including the gradual thaw of de-Stalinization instituted by his successor Nikita Khrushchev, allowed for some reconstitution of lost institutional pathways. Indeed, given the persistence of informal alternatives to the Soviet system, and the manifest failure of the Soviet apparatus to extinguish all opposition, even during its darkest and most oppressive times, the 1950s and 1960s within the USSR helped to enable more traditional Kazakh institutional orderings to reappear, albeit in different forms. In many ways, the post-Stalin era is a tale of how institutions can survive even a massive cataclysm such as Stalinism and/or how they are altered by such an event.

According to most economic historians, the 1950s can be said to be the only decade during which the Soviet Union actually "worked," in the sense that the destruction of capital during the war needed to be replaced, massive amounts of investment were placed by the party into the economy, and, surprisingly, technical efficiency did improve somewhat (Khanin 2003). But the investment during this time did not follow market tenets and was still done as part of a centralized command economy, meaning that the emphasis of investment was still determined by Moscow and not closer to where the actual relations, orderings, and productive capacity were located. This reality was to impact Central Asia again, as the death of Stalin and the ending of his reign of terror in 1953 did not mean that the Soviet planners were done with the Kazakh SSR, and in particular there was a renewed emphasis on expansion of agriculture on Kazakh territory in the post-war years. The next "great leap forward" institutionally that the region was to take was the Virgin Lands campaign of the 1950s and early 1960s, which focused on making Kazakhstan the agricultural powerhouse that it patently had not become prior to the war.

Agriculture in the Kazakh SSR had not improved even with the end of the war and the demobilization of the populace, with productivity continuing on a downward trajectory and a contraction in the actual number of collective farms; at the same time, however, the population farming collectively remained constant, meaning that the number of households per farms had almost exactly doubled (Olcott 1995). In response to this state of affairs in the Kazakh SSR and throughout most of the Soviet Union, the Virgin Lands campaign was devised by Soviet leader Nikita Khrushchev in 1954 to "embark upon a project of ploughing up and putting under crop several million hectares of virgin and fallow land in Kazakhstan, Siberia, the Urals, and the north Caucasus" (Durgin 1962:255). In the Kazakh lands, this meant once again de-emphasizing livestock rearing in favour of sedentary agriculture (Pianciola 2019), with the focus shifting instead towards increasing the amount of land under cultivation to the maximum extent possible, even over the heads of Kazakh party officials who agreed in principle with the overall scheme (Mills 1970).

The economic rationale for the programme was once again questionable: Olcott (1995:224) notes that "these so-called virgin lands were underutilized only from the point of view of Moscow, since the Kazakhs had for generations made good use of them as pasturelands." Elie (2015:260) goes even further and accurately states that "settlers replaced on an enormous area a potentially highly profitable and far more sustainable grazing animal production with a low-yield wheat monoculture." However, this mattered little to the central planners in Moscow, who were more interested in what the Kazakh SSR could do for the Soviet Union. Indeed, two separate strands united the planners with regard to the Virgin Lands project. First, in his book retelling his experiences in the Kazakh SSR, General Secretary Leonid Brezhnev summarized the almost mystical obsession that the party had with the transformation of agriculture across the Soviet Union, especially within the Kazakh SSR:

> Grain has always been the staple product, the very basis of life. Even in our age of great scientific and technological advance it has remined the bedrock of the life of nations. People have broken through into outer space, they tame rivers, seas, oceans, they extract oil and gas from the bowels of the earth, they have mastered the energy of the atom, but grain is still grain.
>
> (1979:1)

Beyond this fascination with grain, there were much more tangible goals in undertaking the Virgin Lands scheme, including, most importantly, securing the food demands of the Soviet Union in perpetuity (something that the party thought it had done in 1952 on the back of a bumper harvest; see Mills 1970), as well as achieving parity with the USA in grain production (Rowe 2011). To this end, the original plan called for the cultivation of an additional 6.3 million hectares of land in the Kazakh SSR, with the vast bulk of this land being allocated to *kolkhozy* – approximately 5.01 million hectares –

and with the largest allocation (1.17 million hectares) located in the Kostanay region in the north-west of the Kazakh SSR (Durgin 1962). Recognizing that collectivized land being toiled on by individual farmers (all united in their love of socialism) might not be entirely sufficient to achieve the massive goals set by the Kremlin, the Virgin Lands programme also relied on the state taking charge directly, via the creation of 492 state farms (*sovkhozes*) from 1954 to 1963, with the average farm aggregating up to 30,000 hectares of agricultural land (Petrick et al. 2013); 300 of these farms were created in the first year of the plan alone (Olcott 1995).

The results of the Virgin Lands programme were mixed throughout, depending upon which metric one uses to judge "success." In terms of its impact on the Kazakh SSR, the programme once again showed the heavy-handedness of Moscow's planners versus the Kazakhs who had to implement their directives. The Soviet authorities invested massive sums in the programme, including a grand total of 44 billion roubles for land reclamation between 1954 and 1960, an amount equal to approximately 10 per cent of the annual budget of the entire Soviet Union (Durgin 1962).[10] Perhaps because of this gigantic financial stake, it might have been felt that the success of the programme was far too important to leave to the locals. As noted above, Mills (1970) relates how Khrushchev's planning in setting targets for the Kazakh SSR went over the heads of local leaders, who were consulted for their acquiescence in the scheme but not at all in the scope or scaling of it. Moreover, when local leaders (not necessarily Kazakh) were shown to be deficient in their zeal for the programme, they were replaced, with future General Secretary Leonid Brezhnev (born in Ukraine) becoming the General Secretary of the Communist Party of the Kazakh SSR in 1955, allowing him to experience the crucial nature of grain at first-hand. Finally, in preparation for the Virgin Lands project, the Kazakhs were again subjected to a large wave of migration; in this instance between 1.5 million and 1.7 million Russian and Ukrainian settlers responded to the call to help to reclaim the lands of the Kazakh SSR for agricultural purposes (Turekulova et al. 2016). This latest wave of settlers meant that Kazakhs now only constituted 30 per cent of the population of the Kazakh SSR.

With regard to the stated aims of the Virgin Lands programme, namely to improve the output of Soviet farming, there was somewhat more success, but once again it was success that probably could have been achieved faster under a more market-oriented economy. Early accomplishments in the programme included the rapid expansion of land under cultivation: Petrick et al. (2013) provide data from Soviet and Kazakh sources that show that the amount of land used for spring wheat rose from approximately 2.75 million hectares in 1953 to 13.5 million hectares just three years later, eventually reaching a high of approximately 14 million hectares in 1958 (and then again in 1963). In the most authoritative piece on the subject, McCauley (1976) notes that in 1954 grain production in the Kazakh SRR more than doubled compared to its 1949–1953 average, hitting record highs of more than 10

Table 4.3 Agricultural Performance in the Kazakh SSR under the Virgin Lands Programme

	Grain production (thousands of metric tons)	*Yields (centres per hectare)*	*Average yields, USSR*
1949–1953	3,942	6.2	7.7
1954	7,658	7.8*	7.8*
1955	4,737	8.4*	8.4*
1956	23,803	9.9*	9.9*
1957	10,557	8.4*	8.4*
1958	21,978	9.4	11.1
1959	18,997	8.7	10.4
1960	18,710	8.5	10.9
1961	14,604	6.6	10.7
1962	15,913	6.5	10.9
1963	10,618	4.4	8.3
1964	23,889	9.8	11.4
Mean	14,617.17	7.51	10.18
Standard deviation	7,100.75	1.87	1.38

Source: Based on the author's calculations and McCauley (1976). Yields from 1954 to 1957 are for the USSR as a whole, as data were not available specifically for the Kazakh SSR.

million metric tons in the Virgin Lands alone during 1962 and making impressive gains throughout the republic (Table 4.3). At the same time, however, the Kazakh SSR had some of the least productive land in the USSR (see too Table 4.3), with yields below those of even the Urals and only barely surpassing those of the Far East at the very beginning of the programme. Indeed, for every year of the programme, the Kazakh SRR recorded lower absolute and far more volatile yields than the rest of the USSR, with production itself extremely volatile (a standard deviation of 50 per cent of the mean). While this situation was reversed in the late Soviet era, at least with reference to standard deviations of production (Craumer 1991 shows that volatility decreased in the 1970s), for approximately 20 years, the Kazakh lands saw much more variable production than in Russia proper.

Part of this volatility can be attributed to normal weather patterns, including sunspot activity, a point to which McCauley (1976) draws our attention. However, the nature of Soviet planning must bear some of the brunt of the blame, as

> in the early years of the program the Soviets used methods ill-suited for such dry conditions, partly because large numbers of the agricultural

> workers who came to work here from other moister parts of the country simply adopted the methods with which they were already familiar.
> (Craumer 1991:3)

Indeed, although both McCauley (1976) and Craumer (1991) attempt to downplay the role of Soviet agriculture in crop yields, there was a more troubling effect of the Virgin Lands programme, and that was "soil degradation, reduced soil organic matter, extensive salinization, and dust storms" (Yan et al. 2020:7). The decline in grain production and yields (see Table 4.3) from 1960 to 1963 was occasioned by dust storms that turned most of the virgin lands of the Kazakh SSR into a dust bowl. In reality, the physical elimination of agronomists under Stalin had reduced knowledge of erosion substantially, and even where there was scientific acumen warning of the dangers of various techniques transplanted to the steppe, Soviet authorities simply ignored their scientific advisers (McCauley 1976). Elie (2015:276) puts it bluntly:

> Fallowing, mould-board ploughing, disking, rolling: all these techniques weakened the light-textured soils (clay sand, argil sand, loamy sand and others) especially common in the Pavlodar region. Practiced on millions of hectares, they were the central factor underlying the severe dust storms which, beginning in 1955, would amount to a self-inflicted plague in the mid-1960s.

According to Rowe (2011), approximately 40 per cent of the virgin land cultivated in both Russia and the Kazakh SSR was subjected to wind erosion due to these sub-optimal techniques, in combination with other climatic features (in particular, droughts).

Finally, in terms of return on investment, McCauley (1976) is careful to hedge that a cost analysis of the Virgin Lands programme is one of incredible complexity, and unfortunately he stays within a narrow lane in juxtaposing expenditures and stated costs (although his analysis is rich in other ways, especially regarding weather). Using data gleaned from the Soviet authorities, he concludes that, as a financial investment, it worked well from 1954 to 1960, with incomings keeping pace with outgoings, while also crediting the programme with spurring on productivity elsewhere in region (a point that Durgin 1962 also stressed). McCauley (1976) also takes pains to state that it is difficult to prove the counterfactual, i.e. what would have occurred in terms of Soviet grain production in the absence of the Virgin Lands programme. However, on balance, the figures provided by McCauley (1976) definitively show that yields were lower; moreover, it cost much more to produce a metric ton of grain in the Kazakh SSR than to produce the same amount in Russia: in 1960, grain cost 41 roubles per ton in Russia compared to 46 roubles per ton in the virgin lands of the Kazakh SSR. From 1961–1964 the cost in Russia rose to 46 roubles per ton, while across all of the

Kazakh SSR it rose to between 66 and 68 roubles per ton (approximately 47 per cent more). During the entire period of the Virgin Lands programme, McCauley (1976:151) notes that Kazakh grain cost approximately 20 per cent more than it did in Russia.

Again, these figures are based on the accounting and methods utilized by Soviet planners but do not, in the words of Fredric Bastiat (1850), reflect the cost of that which is unseen. On the whole, the Soviet plans "worked" in that they increased grain production and helped to achieve the planners' goals of increasing food security; in 1952, grain from Kazakh lands accounted for only 4 per cent of the total produced in the Soviet Union, while by 1956 it accounted for 30 per cent, mostly coming from Akmola and Kostanay (Ketenci 2012). At the same time, although no longer an explicit goal of Khrushchev and the Politburo, the ongoing Russification and sedentarization of the Kazakh SSR was an added bonus, one which Kazakhs living in the northern territories today still resent (Koch 2013). Taken from an objective standpoint, i.e. did the long-term benefits outweigh the inefficiencies and long-term costs, however, the Virgin Lands programme was not sustainable nor was it particularly beneficial for the Kazakhs. Indeed, it forced animal husbandry into arid and semi-arid lands and pushed for more land reclamation to support livestock, in order to take the place of the lands which were now being used for wheat and other grains, thereby fostering long-term ecological pressure (Yan et al. 2020). And, importantly, the forcing of land into agriculture "withdrew" the land from use for the Kazakhs themselves, taking away any form of property rights (formal or informal) from the localities.

In short, the Virgin Lands programme would not have occurred in any other system but the centralized communist bureaucracy of the Soviet Union, and it definitely would not have occurred in an independent Kazakhstan, mainly because the impetus for the programme came from the need to feed elsewhere, i.e. the rest of the Soviet Union. An independent Kazakh nation, or at least a self-governing unit, would never have tried to radically transform the structure of the economy, especially given that the pasturelands which were converted were crucial to the region's emphasis on animal husbandry; in modern economic terms, given the exigencies of the steppe and the demands of the dwellers living there, the comparative advantage of the Kazakhs remained in livestock rearing and using the land for this purpose. Going against these economic pathways meant a misallocation of resources, even if (as McCauley 1976 and especially Craumer 1991 assert) the actual balance sheet and effects of the grain programme were salutary for the USSR as a whole in the short term. Instead, while the Virgin Lands programme did transform the landscape of modern-day northern Kazakhstan in particular, it had a deleterious effect on institutional development, once again placing the needs of (mainly) Russia above those of the Kazakhs.

Alongside the Virgin Lands experiment was, as noted above, a push towards industrialization of the Kazakh SSR, an initiative which worked in tandem with the Soviet emphasis on large-scale development projects throughout the 1950s and 1960s. Of course, "industrialization" in the broader sense had been ongoing in the republic since the end of the NEP, as the approach towards agriculture was industrial, that is, aggregating farms for higher production (collectivization) and building large-scale, state-owned farms to create economies of scale (nationalization). Moreover, as noted above, proper industrialization – that is, an emphasis on heavy manufacturing and large-scale factories – was also underway in the Kazakh SSR with the advent of the war, as factories were evacuated east to escape the Nazi onslaught. Prociuk (1961), using Soviet sources, provides data on the increase in the productive capacity of the republic: using brick production as a proxy for industrial development, he finds that production increased from a low of 98.3 million units in 1945 to an astounding 622.4 million in 1955, second in Central Asia only to the Uzbek SSR (which produced 721.8 million) and even higher than that produced in Stalingrad during its reconstruction (432.2 million units).

However, from 1953 onward, the shift towards heavy manufacturing within the Kazakh SSR increased dramatically, a change from the previous plans, which used Kazakh agriculture as a means to support industrialization elsewhere in the Union. The increase in industrial might also presaged a major shift in the social relations within Kazakh daily life, as it further severed the link between the land and the individual and instead shifted it towards capital investment and management (Brown 2001). This is reflected in the increasing urbanization of the Kazakh SSR after the collectivization policies and into the post-war years, with the urban population increasing from 8.3 per cent of the total population in 1926 to 44 per cent in 1959 (and growing at a rate twice that of the Soviet Union in general; see Lewis et al. 1975). In many ways, urbanization was part and parcel of the changing composition of demographics in the Kazakh SSR, as the influx of deportees from other regions tended to be attracted towards urban rather than rural environments, when they were allowed to choose (Rather and Abdullah 2018). Indeed, Kazakhs only comprised about 17 per cent of the urban population of the Kazakh SSR during the 1950s and 1960s (concentrated mostly in the north), while Russian settlers made up 50 per cent of the republic's cities (Akiner 1998). At the same time, the increase in industrial workers throughout the SSR came mainly from settlers, as Russian migrants also tended to concentrate in industry and made up the vast majority of industrial workers in the Kazakh SSR up until the end of its existence (Glenn 1999). The increasing ethnic stratification within the republic was to have long-term ramifications, the effects of which are felt even today.

An additional portion of the Kazakh SSR's industrial push which was to have substantial ramifications for the region was the drive for increased resource extraction. As mentioned above, during the Stalinist era, mining and basic resource extraction commenced throughout the Kazak ASSR, and focused mainly on lead, zinc, and coal (Jäger 2014), while oil had been discovered in the Kazakh territories in 1907, in the Dossorskoye field in the Atyrau region, with additional exploration carried out in Aktobe in the 1930s. But alongside the push for greater industrialization in 1953 was a directive from Moscow to increase "the development of existing fields of mineral resources and to search for new sources of oil, gas, and other ferrous and non-ferrous metals, in order to create new possibilities for the industrial development of the Soviet Union" (Ketenci 2012:69). In this, the Kazakh SSR was highly privileged (cursed?), as there were "major coal basins at Karaganda and Ekibastuz, iron ore at Kustanay, copper deposits at Dzhezkazgan and Balkhash, major re- serves of non-ferrous metals in the Altai Mountains, and petroleum along the littoral of the Caspian Sea," all of which contributed to "the establishment of major industrial centers in Kazakhstan" (Lewis et al. 1975:291).

During the 1950s and 1960s, mining and exploration activities increased substantially, with the lead, copper, and zinc mining already noted ramping up more intensely, making up the vast bulk of investment from the centre to the periphery (Figure 4.2). In the eastern Kazakh SSR, for example, in the main industrial cluster of Ust-Kamenogorsk, zinc and lead concentrate were processed at a major regional metallurgical centre established specifically for this purpose, leading to a 70 per cent increase in zinc-lead ore from 1960 to 1970 and an overall increase of 475 per cent from 1950 to 1970; at one point, it accounted for 69 per cent of total production in the Kazakh SSR (Ketenci 2012). These staple resources were also joined by an expansion into gold and other metals or minerals deemed crucial for the Soviet economy: in fact, massive gold discoveries in the Mugodzhar Range in Aktobe in 1964 in particular were trumpeted by the Soviet authorities as proof that the Union was not running out of gold. The Ust-Kamenogorsk centre was also instrumental in processing the gold found in this region of the Kazakh SSR, proving its worth as a multifaceted facility (Sagers 1998a). However, as Sagers (1998b) notes, gold production in the Kazakh SSR often took a back seat to the other metals being mined with gold recovered as a by-product of zinc-lead and copper mining rather than as an industry in its own right. This is another reason why the Ust-Kamenogorsk centre (along with another facility in Shymkent) was so important to the mining industry in the SSR. As we will see later in the book, this heavy industry was also to have an incredibly deleterious effect on the environment in the region (Pryde 2009).

Alongside the more familiar riches of gold and other base metals, the 1950s and the dawn of the atomic age also made radioactive materials valuable to the Soviet nation-building effort, and here the Kazakh SSR was to play a leading role, mainly in the mining and extraction of uranium. Uranium deposits in the Tian Shan mountains were discovered as early as 1928, while additional deposits were found in the Karatau mountains in 1940 and 1941 (Shimkin 1949); with the requirements for uranium increasing as part of the nuclear arms race, there eventually came to be discoveries of more than 30 separate uranium deposits throughout the south of the Kazakh SSR,

Table 4.4 Oil and Gas Production in the USSR and the Kazakh SSR, 1940–1965

	1940	*1945*	*1950*	*1951*	*1952*	*1953*	*1954*	*1955*	*1956*	*1957*	*1958*	*1959*	*1960*	*1965*	*1969*
Kazakh SSR	0.70	0.80	1.10	1.30	1.40	1.40	1.40	1.40	1.40	1.40	1.50	1.50	1.60	2.02	10.12
As a percentage of the USSR	2.25%	4.12%	2.90%	3.07%	2.96%	2.60%	2.36%	1.98%	1.67%	1.42%	1.33%	1.15%	1.11%	0.83%	3.08%
RSFSR	7.00	5.70	18.20	21.80	26.10	31.40	38.20	49.30	61.30	74.60	88.00	103.00	116.00	199.93	265.65
USSR	31.10	19.40	37.90	42.30	47.30	53.80	59.30	70.80	83.80	98.30	113.00	130.00	144.00	242.88	328.29

Gas production, millions of cubic metres

	1940	*1943*	*1950*	*1955*	*1956*	*1957*	*1958*	*1959*	*1965*
Kazakh SSR	4.00	10.00	7.00	25.00	33.00	39.00	42.00	n.a.	60.00
As a percentage of the USSR	0.12%	0.54%	0.12%	0.28%	0.27%	0.21%	0.15%		0.04%
RSFSR	210.00	730.00	2867.00	4290.00	5659.00	8773.00	13728.00	19800.00	84960.00
USSR	3219.00	1852.00	5760.00	8979.00	12069.00	18583.00	28063.00	37200.00	150000.00

Source: Lydolph and Shabad (1960) and Hopkins et al. (1973).

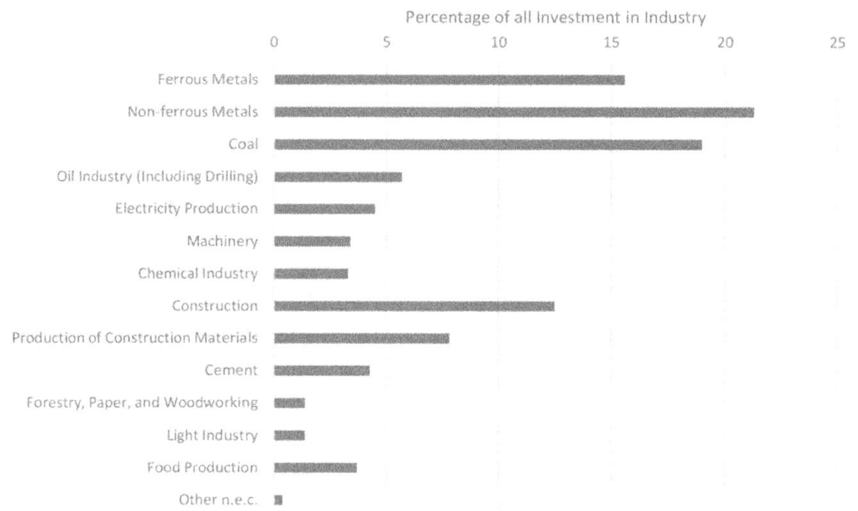

Figure 4.2 Capital Investment in Industry in the Kazakh SSR, 1958
Source: compiled using Neishtadt (1960). The figures shown are a percentage of all investment in industry.

with concerted exploration efforts beginning in 1954 yielding significant finds (Fyodorov 2002). In tandem with the Kyrgyz SSR (Alekhina et al. 2008), a series of massive plants and processing facilities were built across the region, refining and making the suddenly valuable uranium available for both civilian and military use.

Both uranium extraction and more regular mining operations also contributed to the further sedentarization and urbanization of the Kazakh SSR through the creation of "monotowns" or "company towns," new settlements built around a single factory or enterprise. For example, the nuclear industry was also to create its own form of colonization throughout the SSR, with the settlement of "Shevchenko" (modern-day Aktau) on the Caspian Sea being touted as "home to the world's first industrial-scale breeder reactor and the largest atomic-powered water desalination plant ever built," an example of "atomic-powered Communism" (Guth 2018:94). Throughout the republic, monotowns were built near the minerals or raw materials they were meant to extract/refine/process, with the town populations growing through both voluntary internal migration and via the addition of deported "settlers," creating odd ethnic enclaves in remote and barren areas of the SSR (Junussova and Beimisheva 2020). Although these monotowns were well supported by government subsidies, their reliance on a single enterprise also made them highly susceptible to both commodity price shocks and, especially, to changes in the plan or exogenous economic conditions (as these towns were to find out in the post-Soviet world). However, from the Soviet point of view, this was not an issue as, indeed, monotowns were part of the plan, meant to create an ersatz form of comparative advantage among spatial units in order to serve the greater plans of the USSR.

While the mining of base, ferrous, and non-ferrous metals was undoubtedly important to the economy of the Kazakh SSR – and indeed it did help to spur industrial development, as well as further urbanization – the oil and gas revolution was slow to reach the region. As can be seen in Table 4.4, even with such a push towards increased extraction of key resources, the Kazakh SSR was not as productive in oil and gas as elsewhere in the USSR (especially when compared to Azerbaijan, which led most production in the Soviet Union during this period). Indeed, gas production within the SSR was only 0.03 per cent of that in Russia at its peak, while oil never contributed much more than 3 per cent of the total production of the USSR during the 1950s. It was only from the late 1960s that oil production was able to reach substantial amounts of production, but even then it only hit modest peaks. As with the rest of the centralized economy, part of the explanation for this unsatisfactory performance was that the extraction of resources was plagued by low technological prowess and poor accounting methods, all of which accounted for as much as 50 per cent loss of materials during extraction (Turkebaev and Sadikov 1988). Exploration was also halting, with only approximately 20 boreholes drilled per year in the 1950s; however, some of these were to pay off in later years with the discovery of the Uzen and Kenkiyak oilfields in the 1960s, namely the Karachaganak, Karazhanbas, and Kalamkas fields, discovered in the 1970s, and in particular the Tengiz oilfields, discovered in 1980 (Bealessio et al. 2021). In sum, Soviet discoveries in oil revealed reserves of approximately 20.1 billion barrels of oil, not including post-Soviet exploration (Campbell and Wöstmann 2013). Indeed, the persistence in searching for "black gold," and the success had in finding it, was to energize the economy of the SSR, but in a way that would only become apparent towards the end of the Soviet Union (as we will see).

Interestingly, and entirely contra the approach utilized in agriculture, the industrialization of the Kazakh SSR in the post-Stalin period did have a salutary effect on the development of the indigenous Kazakhs, in that it was controlled almost entirely locally rather than from the central party apparatus. Part of this was due to benign neglect, in that the emphasis in the Kazakh SSR remained on agriculture and natural resource extraction rather than the overt industrialization seen elsewhere in the Soviet Union (Scarborough 2021). But this was also part of a concerted effort throughout the USSR to reduce "economic supervision by other control organs (the procuracy, the ministry of state control, and departmental control organs). In other words, the control system … was to a significant degree dismantled in the 1950s" (Khanin 2003:125). While Khanin (2003) notes that this was to create headaches for the planners in the longer term, in the short term, the relaxation of control led to local leaders overseeing the economy: in the Kazakh SSR, this resulted in a shift from 34 per cent of local control in 1953 to an almost-complete 98 per cent of control in 1957 (Ketenci 2012).[11] This was even more important with the ascendancy of Brezhnev in 1964 to the leadership of the Soviet Union, as from 1964 to 1986 the Kazakh SSR was run by an actual ethnic Kazakh, First Secretary Dinmukhamed Kunaev.

While the tacit decentralization of planning to the Kazakh SSR may have helped to create a cadre of leaders skilled in economic governance (an argument made by Dave 2007), the reality remains that much of the emphasis in the republic remained on agriculture and natural resources and was not destined to move any further during the rest of the Soviet Union. As Adamchuk and Dvoskin (1968) show, the six blocks of industry in the Kazakh SSR, delineated by regions within the country, did not stray far from the distribution of spending shown in Figure 4.2, with a focus on mining, metallurgy, chemicals, oil, and construction. As several commentators at the time noted, the difficulty in creating a "Kazakh industry" came down not to a lack of local control but more simply to a lack of skilled labourers (Dunn and Dunn 1967) or, in many places, a lack of population in general (Prociuk 1961). With industry being run by imported Slavic labourers and Kazakhs remaining for the most part rural, the economy of the Kazakh SSR was wholly stratified along ethnic lines (Lewis et al. 1975).

Brezhnev, Soviet Stagnation, and the End of the Union

The end of Khrushchev's time in power in 1964 and the ascendance of Leonid Brezhnev as General Secretary – he of the fascination with grain and having experience in running the Kazakh SSR – ushered in an era of contrasts in Soviet life. From a Western perspective, the Soviet Union in the late 1960s and 1970s was on the move globally, having impressive successes in turning newly de-colonized countries to communism, while expanding its own reach on its borders (Afghanistan) or in military interventions-by-proxy abroad (Angola, Ethiopia, Vietnam, Cambodia). But from an economic standpoint, if the 1950s had been the "triumph of the Soviet economy" (as Khanin 2003 called it and even American economists such as Paul Samuelson seemed to believe), the 1960s and especially the 1970s were to devolve into an era of stagnation; put simply, the massive capital accumulation of the late 1940s and 1950s which backfilled the capital and labour losses of the Second World War now approached a steady state, with heavily declining marginal returns (Krugman 1994). The unlimited promise of the space race, the nuclear arms race, and the battle for hearts and minds that the Soviet Union appeared to be winning was slowing measurably, as the economy could no longer provide for either the daily needs of the population or the massive investments needed to sustain the Soviet image abroad (Tompson 2014). Most importantly, the increases in productivity that characterized the 1950s – capital investment can beget innovation – disappeared as the political elite sought to freeze the status quo of the Khrushchev years. Indeed, Leonid Brezhnev "carefully avoided the experimentation of structural reforms in the economy" in favour of spending on the military, keeping the Soviet gaze on global competition while ignoring the accumulating problems internally (Hyland 1979:51).

This schizophrenia was to replicate itself in the Kazakh SSR during the late Soviet years. Some authors cheekily called the 1970s the "golden age" of the Kazakh republic, but "only in comparison with what came before and immediately after" (Keller 2019:212). The Kazakh SSR was squarely involved in the extension of Soviet power, both hard and soft, globally, with two specific programmes taking place on Kazakh soil and feeding the perception of the Soviet Union as a country on the move. First, the Baikonur Cosmodrome in the southern Kazakh SSR, founded in 1955 as the top-secret Tyuratam Missile Range, began its space-related operations in 1957 with the (also secret) launch of Sputnik. Over the years, it became renowned for being the launching pad for Yuri Gagarin, Luna 1, Valentina Tereshkova, and countless other symbols of Soviet power (Gerovitch 2011). The complex itself was a testament to Soviet engineering feats, built into the steppe and fashioning its own monotown nearby (the city of Leninsk), the size of the Cosmodrome was staggering:

> fifteen active launch pads for different rocket engines and ballistic missiles, eleven vehicle assembly and testing buildings, three fueling stations, a cryogenic oxygen–nitrogen plant, a 60-MW combined heat and power station, two runways (one over a mile long), almost 300 miles of rail lines, more than 4,000 miles of power lines, and almost 800 miles of roads.
>
> (Kopack 2019:559)

The other, original use for the Cosmodrome, however, is the second programme that the Kazakh SSR contributed to the Soviet Union. While the space launches were the most visible part of Baikonur's activities, in reality it spent the largest proportion of its time testing intercontinental ballistic missiles capable of reaching the United States (Gruntman 2019). Indeed, much of the Kazakh SSR became instrumental in the Soviet drive for nuclear parity (and then superiority), with both the testing at Baikonur and, perhaps more importantly, the Semipalatinsk nuclear test site becoming synonymous with Soviet nuclear might. The remoteness of the steppe – from Moscow, which was the only "remoteness" that mattered – meant that many of the testing grounds for Soviet nuclear weaponry were "sacrifice areas," closed military sites that were meant to be destroyed and never utilized for any other purpose (Kopack 2019), a destructive legacy which has persisted to this day. The Semipalatinsk site in particular witnessed more than 110 nuclear tests carried out as atmospheric explosions from 1949 to 1963, including the first ever test for the USSR and a hurried 49 tests in 1962 in anticipation of an international ban (Kassenova 2016). Underground testing continued up until the eve of the Soviet Union's collapse in 1989 (Bauer et al. 2013), a total of 456 tests in all (Kassenova 2016).

However, despite the centrality of the Kazakh SSR in Soviet power projection abroad, it was once again just a cog in a much larger machine. The imperial administration of both Baikonur and Semipalatinsk made it clear that the land and the people were being utilized for the greater good of the USSR rather than to advance development within the Kazakh SSR itself (Kassymbekova and Chokobaeva 2021); Kassenova (2016) notes how 40 Kazakhs were forced to remain within the blast zone of the first thermonuclear device tested in the USSR in August 1953 specifically to test the effects of radiation on humans.

This relegation of the Kazakh lands to be another laboratory for Soviet experiments did not, ironically, extend to the economic sphere, as internally (much as with the greater USSR), the Kazakh SSR was also facing economic sclerosis. As mentioned above, the structure of the economy within the Kazakh SSR had been fully put in place by the 1950s and was to change little, in fact becoming a victim of its own success as oil discoveries increased the specialization of the republic. As Glenn (1999) notes, while the Kazakh SSR was the most industrialized of the Central Asia republics, by 1990 it had only reached 22 per cent of the workforce employed in industry. The only structural change to occur was in the areas where the state was loosening its reins, as the Kazakh SSR (along with the Uzbek SSR) saw an increasing number of labourers move into the non-state economy, setting up small-scale family enterprises in the services sector, and absorbing perhaps as much as 10 per cent of the population (Abazov 1997).[12] But for the overwhelming majority of the formal sectors of the economy, even those such as mining, the emphasis on satisfying quotas and national goals meant that stagnation was the order of the day, with waste and inefficiency pervading Kazakh industry. As Ketenci (2012) notes, examining Soviet statistics, whereas industrial production was still growing at a healthy pace at the beginning of the 1970s – a 47 per cent increase in output was recorded from 1970 to 1975 – by the time the 1980s had rolled around, industrial production was growing by just 18 per cent (from 1980 to 1985).

Perhaps as a result of this stagnation, and the increasing perception that the Kazakh SSR was a mere outpost of the USSR, devoid of dynamism, during the 1970s, another interesting demographic trend was to occur. The lack of economic opportunities in the Kazakh SSR vis-à-vis Russia created a pull for many Russians to return "home" (Kaiser and Chinn 1995): by the mid-1970s, Russians were leaving the Kazakh SSR faster than they were arriving (Olcott 2010), a reversal of longstanding migration patterns. The trend was aided by the fact that Kazakh birth rates were on the rise compared to those in the Russian communities (Zardykhan 2004), but overall, the shift was slow-moving, and on the eve of independence in 1989 Kazakhs made up only 40 per cent of their country (and were still a distinct minority in the northern territories; see Olcott 2010). Still, it did represent a tangible change in the region, a shift away from the colonial purpose which the Kazakh SSR had fulfilled for so long in Russian political planning, even if the actual shift away from the republic being an economic colony was still in the future.

This creeping "Kazakhification" came in tandem with the leadership of an ethnic Kazakh of the republic's Communist Party, with Dinmukhamed Kunaev working to increase Kazakh representation in the administrative apparatus of the SSR and improving the political visibility of Kazakhs in both their own republic and in the USSR more broadly (Stefany 2013). As he was to write in his own memoirs, long after the fact,

> Are there no good administrators among the local party members? In my opinion, such personnel policies had nothing to do with Leninist principles. It seems that Moscow is not ready to give up its imperial ambitions and will keep ruling in the old way: "We appoint those who we want. And your business is to approve our decisions unanimously." And we did vote.
>
> (Kunaev 1994:105)

Kunaev was able, in his long tenure as First Secretary and in the manner of the Khans of old, to substitute local patronage networks spurred on by the Soviet system with his own clientelism (Olcott 1995), creating new ethnic-based patronage within the more relaxed Brezhnev machine and even increasing the number of Kazakhs within the Communist Party (Stefany 2020). Indeed, according to Willerton (1987), Kunaev had one of the largest patronage networks within the Politburo, allowing him to advance Kazakh interests in the USSR and within his own SSR with a relatively free hand, especially when compared to his predecessors.

Unfortunately, there were two countervailing forces pushing against Kunaev's tenure (three, if one thinks of the overall stagnation in the USSR). The first was, from the point of view of Moscow, that the Kazakhs were taking greater control of their republic but not delivering economically (see especially the aforementioned stagnation in the Kazakh SSR by the early 1980s). From the vantage point of the Kremlin, this was a damning critique of the indigenization of the Kazakh SSR (Brown 1988), as cultural autonomy was not paying off in economic gains as it should have (Shelekpayev 2021). The second headwind that Kunaev faced was intimately connected with this first one. Kazakh culture and language in particular had been thoroughly "Sovietized," subsumed under Russian instruction, and, in fact, Kazakhs seemed to be proud of this greater entity more so than feeling a national affinity (Akiner 1995). This meant that even with the increase in Kazakh representation, it was not in indigenous institutions, but rather an ascendance into the Russian-run and Soviet-built centralized planning apparatus. It was akin to the difference between being promoted at a Fortune 500 company and starting one's own Fortune 500 company: in the former, one is the master of their domain and can choose their personnel, while in the latter one ascends through the ranks of an established organization, with its own policies and procedures (and where room for manoeuvre is limited).[13]

Where these two issues combined to create a headache for the Kremlin was the ingenuity of Kazakhs in pushing back against the Sovietization of their culture by using the Soviet system against itself. To return to the Fortune 500 analogy, in order to make one's mark within an established organization, even one as centralized as Soviet central planning, it calls for creativity. In the Kazakh SSR, with the loosening of Moscow's grip and the hands-off approach of Brezhnev, managers survived and even prospered via the creation of internal networks, organizations within organizations: in the Kazakh lands, this manifested itself in the hiring of relatives for state enterprises, allowing kin and clan to enjoy the benefits of state employment whether or not the employees hired were actually suitable for the job. Actually, in most instances, the family hires were not at all suitable, leading to a decrease in factory productivity (Kalyuzhnova 2016), a situation which was sustainable because of soft budget constraints, meaning that the Soviet administrative apparatus covered the losses of enterprises so that they could continue producing (Ketenci 2012). This also then contributed to poor aggregate performance in the Kazakh SSR, making Soviet planners even more suspicious.

In this way, Kazakhs began a slow reassertion of their identity from within the Soviet system – Stefany (2020) called it a *reconquista* – as Moscow had its gaze elsewhere. When Moscow did turn its gaze back to the Kazakhs, however, leading to the removal of Kunaev in 1986 (dealt with in the next chapter), a clash between the centre and a reassertive periphery was in the making. Indeed, even after 60 years of Soviet trauma, perhaps Kazakh culture was not as far below the surface as assumed. And, as unexpected events less than a decade away were to show, this reassertion of traditional culture would soon be making a much bigger return in the governance and economy of Kazakh lands.

Conclusion

This chapter has shown the history of institutional development in the geographic space which was to become Kazakhstan during its long dark period under Soviet rule. From the Bolshevik revolution, civil war, collectivization, famine, purges, labour camps, world war, and eventually stagnation, the institutions in the Kazakh SSR were thoroughly reordered from their previous trajectories, with social institutions destroyed or supplanted entirely and economic institutions subordinated to centralized political ones, run by Moscow. The Kazakh SSR simply became a cog in a giant machine, with its people and its resources used as part of a supply chain for elsewhere in the Soviet Union. During times when the machinery within the Kazakh republic did not turn quickly enough, the Soviet authorities simply sought to change the people, encouraging Russian settlement, deporting undesirables to the steppe, and making the Kazakhs a minority on their own lands.

All these issues combined to create a clear and unwanted deflection in the path of institutional evolution in the Kazakh SSR. In order to understand the full impact of the Soviet era on the Kazakhs, however, this requires an even broader look, focusing on the counterfactual of what would have happened if the Soviet experiment had *not* occurred on the Kazakh lands. Counterfactuals are hazardous undertakings at the best of times and one that is of course fraught with its own pitfalls, but understanding the path not taken by the Kazakhs is crucial to making sense of the path that *was* taken. As I have already noted, and in the first instance, massive plans such as the Virgin Lands programme would not have occurred under a more market-oriented economy, nor would it have arisen under a Kazakh-dominated economy, mainly because of the economic waste associated with the abrupt change from nomadic husbandry to sedentary agriculture. Reclamation of lands from the semi-arid steppe might have occurred in tandem with changes in irrigation technology, but it would have proceeded at its own pace, with its own tensions (the pre-existing tensions between sedentary and nomadic Kazakhs noted in Chapter 2) and its own solutions. In any event, it would have been a much smaller-scale effort, not informed by Soviet gigantism and not driven by the imperatives of Moscow.

Along these lines, one can also argue (as Kunaev 1994 does) that other events in the history of the Kazakh SSR would not have occurred if it had not been for the Soviet dominion over these lands: the nuclear testing at Semipalatinsk, for example, nor the continued use of the Baikonur Cosmodrome. Chosen as sites that could literally be discarded, with little heed to local populations, other country experiences with innovation and research and development show that these processes can occur without the destruction of large swathes of the environment. At the same time, the emergence of Kazakh industry and in particular the development of monotowns would also not have occurred under any system but the Soviet one (despite the prevalence of company towns in early industrializing societies in Europe). without the rush to extract minerals and forcibly industrialize the Kazakh SSR, again in pursuit of providing benefits for the whole USSR, industrial development could also have proceeded at its own pace. In fact, company towns connected with extractive industries had already started disappearing from the landscape of countries such as the United States in the 1930s and had almost disappeared by the 1950s, victims of changing market conditions, automation, and especially the realization that diversification was necessary (Shifflett 1991). The only areas where "company towns" survived were those that were either protected by government regulation (similar to the Soviet approach) or those that actually provided a benefit to the populace and were able to innovate and compete (Agrawal et al. 2010).

The danger with counterfactuals is that we can go too far down the rabbit hole in fashioning them, ending up at an idealized point, a halcyon existence, which also would not have come to pass because of the exigencies of reality. And there is no need to suggest that the Soviet experience irrevocably crippled the Kazakh lands, shifting it into an unsustainable equilibrium. As Dave (2007) and others have argued, the late Soviet era was good for the Kazakhs, providing them with stability, security, and, with the slow out-migration of Russians, opportunities for advancement. If we are to argue that an industrialized society is also crucial to compete in the global marketplace, then a debate can be had on the benefits of the industrialization which took place under the Soviets, especially when related to the 1960s and 1970s, when it occurred under Kazakh control (albeit within the Soviet system). Finally, it can be argued that the Soviet investment and intellectual firepower brought to bear in exploration and extraction of natural resources (above all, oil) and in developing agriculture was a major boon for the Kazakh economy and set up the country for growth when it finally rid itself of the Soviet system.

Despite these arguments – and that they ignore the fact that the Soviet way was not the only means by which Kazakh institutions could have evolved – the purpose here is to not dwell on the relative benefits or costs of the Soviet experiment to the Kazakh economy (we have already made it clear where the impacts have been problematic, to say the least) but instead to note that it did in fact occur. And because it did occur, the Soviet experiment was to have a crucial impact on the development of Kazakh political and economic institutions going forward. To take another quick counterfactual, it was apparent that the inefficiency of the Soviet apparatus in the Kazakh SSR meant that institutional change was necessary; by the 1980s, Soviet planners were focused on a shift towards machine-building and tightening up overall control of the republic, a move which would have signalled small-scale institutional change and, in many ways, a reduction in Kazakh participation in the governance of the republic (Ketenci 2012). If events in 1991 and 1992 had never unfolded in the way that they did, we would have thus been able to show definitively the effects of the Soviet experiment on Kazakh institutions, because the Kazakhs would still be living under them. However, as we know, massive changes were to come in the near future, changes which were to upend the institutional order once again. This is where the rest of the book will take us.

Notes

1 I have put the word "Bolshevik" in quotation marks because *Bolshevik* literally means "majority" or "one of the majority," a moniker which Lenin applied to refer to the Bolsheviks' status in the Russian Social Democratic Party but also to make them appear as if they had greater support nationally then they actually did. They were never actually a majority in a contested election.

2 In theory, the ability to move across borders could have helped the Kazakhs move to places where there was food from places where there was none. However, internal movement likely would not have made much of a difference, as the famine was widespread across the Bolshevik-conquered lands (including Tatarstan, the Volga region, and Turkestan), and it was likely only international travel (i.e. very long distances) which would have allowed Kazakhs to escape the failures of central planning (and even then, others, such as Persia, had their own famines to deal with).

3 This precise reason was given by the ASSR's Central State Executive Committee for attempting to end nomadism in the Republic, a finding echoed in at least two

studies created in 1930 (Cameron 2018). However, these documents also did not address the issue of expropriation and how this might affect incentives concerning (and ability to) farm the steppe.

4 Stalin (1930) famously wrote an article in *Pravda* in March 1930 entitled "Dizzy with Success," in which he extolled "[t]he Soviet government's successes in the sphere of the collective-farm movement." On later reflection, a more appropriate title probably would have been "dizzy because of malnourishment."

5 Professor Talas Omarbekov of Kazakhstan State University claimed to have seen the Soviet archives in the 1980s and the documentation related to Soviet policies during this time, numbering a total of 2.3 million Kazakhs (excluding other ethnicities) alone killed during the famine; see Pannier (2007). Unfortunately, these archives are now off-limits to researchers.

6 The *New York Times* headline of 29 April 1930 erroneously proclaims, "TURKSIB RAILROAD OPENED BY SOVIET; 1,700-Mile Link Between Siberia and Turkestan Makes Way for Great Development. MAY END COTTON IMPORTS Scores of Settlements Spring Up Along Line, Built by Government at Cost of $100,000,000. Entirely a Russian Achievement. Brings Soviets Closer to China." See full article at www.nytimes.com/1930/04/29/archives/turksib-railroad-opened-by-soviet-1700mile-link-between-siberia-and.html.

7 Of course, this was not actually the case. As Uibopuu (1979) argues, the administrative divisions in Central Asia were part of a divide and conquer strategy, to forestall any pan-Turkic movements, and the 1936 constitution made these divisions permanent with an eye towards perpetual subjugation.

8 Even where Tokhmetova et al. (2014) caution us to note that some provisions had been made in Pavlodar for deportees, the numbers they quote – for example, the building or acquisition of some 2,748 homes in the entire Kazakh SSR – were woefully inadequate to handle the torrent of deportees.

9 Khanin, a Russian economist from Novosibirsk, carried out a wide-ranging recalculation of official Soviet statistics from 1928 to 1987 and provided meticulous detail on his methodology. His work is referenced elsewhere in this chapter.

10 Frühauf et al. (2020) quote this number from Dugin and note that it was "20 percent" of the "national budget," but it is not clear if they meant the Kazakh SSR or the Soviet Union. In any event, the number of 44 billion roubles comports more closely with 10 per cent of the Soviet budget in terms of expenditures, which were consistently around 450 billion roubles in the 1950s; see, for example, Harrison (1986).

11 This tacit decentralization may have been the first steps towards the salutary effects which Dave (2007) attributes to Soviet management, especially in relation to the development of a Kazakh ethnic elite. However, the history of central planning in the Kazakh SSR shows that most (if not all) of the gains it achieved could have been done better under a different system, and it is probable that this is the case with the decentralization of industrial policy. Indeed, the absence of a centralized policy generating better results does not exactly make a sound case for the superiority of that centralized policy.

12 Abazov (1997) references Polyakov (1989), who gave an upper bound of 15 per cent employment in the non-state sector but, based on research done by the European Bank for Reconstruction and Development in the transition period, an upper bound of 10 per cent for Uzbekistan (and perhaps 5 per cent for Kazakhstan) is much more plausible.

13 This is in no way to suggest that the Soviet Union was as efficient or productive as the average Fortune 500 company.

References

Abazov, R. (1997). Formation of the non-state sector and privatisation in Kazakhstan and Uzbekistan. *Communist Economies and Economic Transformation*, 9(4), 431–448.

Abazov, R. (2008). *The Palgrave Concise Historical Atlas of Central Asia*. New York: Palgrave Macmillan.

Abugaliyeva, A., and Morgounov, A. I. (2016). The history of wheat breeding in Southern Kazakhstan. In A. P. Bonejan and W. J. Angus (Eds.), *The World Wheat Book: A History of Wheat Breeding* (Vol. 3, pp. 311–330). Paris: Lavoisier,.

Adamchuk, V. A., and Dvoskin, B. A. (1968). *Problemy Razvitiya Promyshlennykh Uzlov SSSR, na primere Kazakhstana* [*On the Problems of Developing Industrial Hubs in the USSR, Using the Example of Kazakhstan*]. Moscow: Mysl.

Agrawal, A., Cockburn, I., and Rosell, C. (2010). Not invented here? Innovation in company towns. *Journal of Urban Economics*, 67(1), 78–89.

Akiner, S. (1995). *The Formation of Kazakh National Identity, from Tribe to Nation-State*. London: The Royal Institute of International Affairs.

Akiner, S. (1998). Social and political reorganization in Central Asia: Transition from pre-colonial to post-colonial society. In T. Atabaki and J. O'Kane (Eds.), *Post-Soviet Central Asia* (pp. 1–34). London: I. B. Tauris (Bloomsbury).

Alekhina, V. M., Vasiliev, I. A., Idrisova, S., Mamatibraimov, S., and Tolstikhin, G. M. (2008). Quantitative assessment of the man-induced uranium in the tail disposal of Kara-Balta mining plant. In B. Salbu and L. Skipperud (Eds.), *Nuclear Risks in Central Asia* (pp. 167–172). Dordrecht: Springer.

Alimaev, I. I., and Behnke, R. H. (2008). Ideology, land tenure and livestock mobility in Kazakhstan. In K. A. Galvin, R. S. Reid, R. H. Behnke, and N. T. Hobbs (Eds.), *Fragmentation in Semi-Arid and Arid Landscapes: Consequences for Human and Natural Systems* (pp. 151–178).Berlin: Springer.

Allen, R. C. (2001). The rise and decline of the Soviet economy. *Canadian Journal of Economics*, 34(4), 859–881.

Amanzholova, D. A. (1997a). Kazakh autonomy and Russia: The history of the Alash movement (excerpts). *Anthropology & Archeology of Eurasia*, 36(3), 10–23.

Amanzholova, D. A. (1997b) The Alash movement and the Bolsheviks: From attempts at compromise to confrontation. *Anthropology & Archeology of Eurasia*, 36(3), 24–49.

Anderson, J. (1997). *The International Politics of Central Asia*. Manchester: Manchester University Press.

Auanassova, A., Auanassova, K., Zhumagulov, B., and Karasayev, G. (2018). The Alash party on Kazakh statehood. *Astra Salvensis*, 11, 129–136.

Baker, S. R., Bloom, N., and Davis, S. J. (2016). Measuring economic policy uncertainty. *The Quarterly Journal of Economics*, 131(4), 1593–1636.

Bandera, V. N. (1963). The New Economic Policy (NEP) as an economic system. *Journal of Political Economy*, 71(3), 265–279.

Barnes, S. A. (2005). "In a manner befitting Soviet citizens" An uprising in the post-Stalin gulag. *Slavic Review*, 64(4), 823–850.

Bastiat, F. (1850). *Ce qu'on voit et Ce qu'on ne voit pas* [*That Which is Seen, and That Which is Not Seen*]. http://bastiat.org/fr/cqovecqonvp.html.

Bauer, S., Gusev, B., Belikhina, T., Moldagaliev, T., and Apsalikov, K. (2013). The legacies of Soviet nuclear testing in Kazakhstan: Fallout, public health and societal issues. In D. Oughton and S. O. Hansson (Eds.), *Radioactivity in the Environment*: Vol. 19. *Social and Ethical Aspects of Radiation Risk Management* (pp. 241–258). North Holland: Elsevier.

Bealessio, B. A., Alonso, N. A. B., Mendes, N. J., Sande, A. V., and Hascakir, B. (2021). A review of enhanced oil recovery (EOR) methods applied in Kazakhstan. *Petroleum*, 7(1), 1–9.

Bergne, P. (2003). The Kokand Autonomy, 1917–1918. In T. Everett-Heath (Ed.), *Central Asia: Aspects of Transition* (pp. 30–44). New York: RoutledgeCurzon.

Biltstein, P. A. (2006). Cultural diversity and the interwar conjuncture: Soviet nationality policy in its comparative context. *Slavic Review*, 65(2), 273–293.

Brezhnev, L. I. I. (1979). *Virgin Lands: Two Years in Kazakhstan, 1954–5*. Oxford: Pergamon Press.

Brown, B. (1988). The Kazakhstan riots. In V. Mastny (Ed.), *Soviet-East European Survey, 1986–1987*. New York: Routledge.

Brown, K. (2001). Gridded lives: Why Kazakhstan and Montana are nearly the same place. *The American Historical Review*, 106(1), 17–48.

Bugai, N. F. (1995). *Soglasno vasetu ukazaiyu* [*According to Your Instructions*]. Moscow: Associasija issledovatelej rossijskogo obshchestvo XX veka.

Bush, P. D. (1987). The theory of institutional change. *Journal of Economic issues*, 21 (3), 1075–1116.

Buttino, M. (2020). Revolution in the borderlands: The case of Central Asia in a comparative perspective. In D. Orlovsky (Ed.), *A Companion to the Russian Revolution* (pp. 197–210). London: Wiley & Sons.

Cameron, S. (2018). *The Hungry Steppe: Famine, Violence, and the Making of Soviet Kazakhstan*. Ithaca, NY: Cornell University Press.

Campbell, C. J., and Wöstmann, A. (2013). *Campbell's Atlas of Oil and Gas Depletion* (p. 788). New York: Springer.

Carlson, C. F. (1993). The concept of sovereignty in Kazakhstan from Kültegin. In B. Kellner-Heinkele (Ed.), *Altaica Berolinensia: The Concept of Sovereignty in the Altaic World* (pp. 57–67). Berlin: Springer Verlag.

Carmack, R. J. (2014). History and hero-making: Patriotic narratives and the Sovietization of Kazakh front-line propaganda, 1941–1945. *Central Asian Survey*, 33(1), 95–112.

Carmack, R. J. (2019). *Kazakhstan in World War II: Mobilization and Ethnicity in the Soviet Empire.* Lawrence: University Press of Kansas.

Channon, J. (1987). Tsarist landowners after the revolution: Former pomeshchiki in rural Russia during NEP. *Soviet Studies*, 39(4), 575–598.

Channon, J. (1988). The Bolsheviks and the peasantry: The land question during the first eight months of Soviet rule. *The Slavonic and East European Review*, 66(4), 593–624.

Cheremukhin, A., Golosov, M., Guriev, S., and Tsyvinski, A. (2017). The industrialization and economic development of Russia through the lens of a neoclassical growth model. *The Review of Economic Studies*, 84(2), 613–649.

Cherot, R. A. (1955). Nativization of government and party structure in Kazakhstan, 1920–1930. *American Slavic and East European Review*, 14(1), 42–58.

Churin, X. (1967). *Сквёзь Бурю* [*Through the Storm*]. Alma-Ata: Academy of Sciences of Kazakhstan.

Collins, H. H. (1951). The constitutions of the Soviet republics. *Science & Society*, 15 (1), 17–30.

Conquest, R. (2018). *The Great Terror: Stalin's Purge of the Thirties.* New York: Random House.

Craumer, P. R. (1991). *Land Use and Agricultural Productivity in the Soviet Virgin Lands* [Doctoral dissertation, Columbia University].

Dave, B. (2007). *Kazakhstan: Ethnicity, Language and Power.* London: Routledge.

Davies, R. W., and Wheatcroft, S. G. (2009). *The Industrialisation of Soviet Russia:* Vol. 5. *The Years of Hunger.* London: Palgrave Macmillan.

Degitaeva, I. (Ed.) (1998). *Politicheski e repressii v Kazakhstane v 1937–1938 gg* [*Political Repression in Kazakhstan, 1937–1938*]. Almaty: Archive of the President of the Republic of Kazakhstan.

Dunmore, T. (1980). *The Stalinist Command Economy: The Soviet State Apparatus and Economic Policy 1945–53.* London: Macmillan.

Dunn, S. P., and Dunn, E. (1967). Soviet regime and native culture in Central Asia and Kazakhstan: The major peoples. *Current Anthropology,* 8(3), 147–208.

Durgin, F. A., Jr. (1962). The Virgin Lands programme 1954–1960. *Europe-Asia Studies,* 13(3), 255–280.

Elie, M. (2015). The Soviet dust bowl and the Canadian erosion experience in the new lands of Kazakhstan, 1950s–1960s. *Global Environment,* 8(2), 259–292.

Ellman, M. (2002). Soviet repression statistics: Some comments. *Europe-Asia Studies,* 54(7), 1151–1172.

Ellman, M. (2005). The role of leadership perceptions and of intent in the Soviet famine of 1931–1934. *Europe-Asia Studies,* 57(6), 823–841.

Esenova, S. (2002). Soviet nationality, identity, and ethnicity in Central Asia: Historic narratives and Kazakh ethnic identity. *Journal of Muslim Minority Affairs,* 22(1), 11–38.

Frühauf, M., Meinel, T., and Schmidt, G. (2020). The Virgin Lands campaign (1954–1963) until the breakdown of the former Soviet Union (FSU): With special focus on western Siberia. In M. Frühauf, G. Guggenberger, T. Meinel, I. Theesfeld, and S. Lentz (Eds.), *KULUNDA: Climate Smart Agriculture* (pp. 101–118). Berlin: Springer.

Fyodorov, G. V. (2002). *Uranium Production and the Environment in Kazakhstan.* International Atomic Energy Agency Report, No. IAEA-CSP–10/P. Vienna: International Atomic Energy Agency.

Gelb, M. (1995). An early Soviet ethnic deportation: The far-eastern Koreans. *The Russian Review,* 54(3), 389–412.

Gerovitch, S. (2011). "Why are we telling lies?" The creation of Soviet space history myths. *The Russian Review,* 70, 460–484.

Getty, J. A. (1991). State and society under Stalin: Constitutions and elections in the 1930s. *Slavic Review,* 50(1), 18–35.

Glenn, J. (1999). *The Soviet Legacy in Central Asia.* New York: Palgrave Macmillan.

Goloshchekin, F. I. (1931). *Yeshche Raz o Putyakh Razvitiya Zhivotnovodstva i ob Opportunistakh* [On the ways of developing animal husbandry and the opportunities on this front]. *Narodnoye Khozyaystvo Kazakhstana* [*National Economy of Kazakhstan*], 8–9, 20.

Gruntman, M. (2019). From Tyuratam missile range to Baikonur Cosmodrome. *Acta Astronautica,* 155, 350–366.

Guseva, Y. N., and Kristoforov, V. S. (2019). Kazakhskoye Obshchestvo i Elita 1920-kh gg v Fokuse Sovetskikh Spetssluzhb: Politicheskiye Klishe i Sotsial'noye Konstruirovaniye [Kazakh society and elite of the 1920s in the focus of Soviet intelligence services: Political clichés and social construction]. *Elektronnyy Nauchno-obrazovatel'nyy Zhurnal "Istoriya" [Electronic Scientific-Educational Journal "History"*], 1, 17–34. https://history.jes.su/s207987840002546-9-1/.

Guth, S. (2018). Oasis of the future: The nuclear city of Shevchenko/Aqtau, 1959–2019. *Jahrbücher für Geschichte Osteuropas*, 66(1), 93–123.

Harrison, M. (1986). The USSR State budget under late Stalinism (1945–55): Capital formation, government borrowing and monetary growth. *Economics of Planning*, 20(3), 179–205.

Harrison, M. (1993). Soviet economic growth since 1928: The alternative statistics of GI Khanin. *Europe-Asia Studies*, 45(1), 141–167.

Hartwell, C. A. (2016). *Two Roads Diverge: The Transition Experience of Poland and Ukraine.* Cambridge: Cambridge University Press.

Hionidou, V., and Saunders, D. (2010). Exiles and pioneers: Oral histories of Greeks deported from the Caucasus to Kazakhstan in 1949. *Europe-Asia Studies*, 62(9), 1479–1501.

Holdsworth, M. (1952). Soviet Central Asia, 1917–1940. *Europe-Asia Studies*, 3(3), 258–277.

Hopkins, G. D., Korens, N., Schmidt, R. A., and Trexel, C. A., Jr. (1973). *Analysis of Energy Resources and Programs of the Soviet Union and Eastern Europe*: Appendix C. *Oil.* Menlo Park, CA: Stanford Research Institute.

Hudson, A. E. (1938). *Kazak Social Structure.* New Haven, CT: Yale University Press.

Hyland, W. G. (1979). Brezhnev and Beyond. *Foreign Affairs*, 58(1), 51–66.

Ilič, M. (2006). The forgotten five per cent: Women, political repression and the purges. In M. Ilič (Ed.), *Stalin's Terror Revisited* (pp. 116–139).Basingstoke: Palgrave Macmillan.

Ismailov, A. I. (2011). On the issue of human losses during the Great Patriotic War, 1941–1945. *Journal of Slavic Military Studies*, 24(2), 232–237.

Ivnitskiy, N.A. (2009). *Golod 1932–1933 v SSSR: Ukraina, Kazakhstan, Severnyy Kavkaz, Povolzh'ye, Tsentral'no-Chernozemnaya oblast', Zapadnaya Sibir', Ural [The Famine of 1932–1933 in the USSR: Ukraine, Kazakhstan, the North Caucasus, the Volga Region, the Central Black Earth Region, Western Siberia, the Urals*]. Moscow: Sobranije.

Jäger, P. F. (2014). Flows of oil, flows of people: Resource-extraction industry, labour market and migration in western Kazakhstan. *Central Asian Survey*, 33(4), 500–516.

Junussova, M., and Beimisheva, A. (2020). Monotowns of Kazakhstan: Development challenges and opportunities. In A. Koulouri and N. Mouraviev (Eds.), *Kazakhstan's Developmental Journey* (pp. 211–247). Singapore: Palgrave Macmillan.

Kaiser, C. P. (2014). Betraying their motherland: Soviet military tribunals of *Izmenniki Rodiny* in Kazakhstan and Uzbekistan, 1941–1953. *The Soviet and Post-Soviet Review*, 41(1), 57–83.

Kaiser, R., and Chinn, J. (1995). Russian-Kazakh relations in Kazakhstan. *Post-Soviet Geography*, 36(5), 257–273.

Kalyuzhnova, Y. (2016). *The Kazakstan Economy: Independence and Transition.* Berlin: Springer.

Karsakova, G. B., Saktaganova, Z. G., Abuev, K. K., Bukanova, R. G., and Mazhitova, Z. S. (2018). The struggle of the Soviet government against famine and the increase of the homeless children in the Akmola governorate in 1921–1923. *Space and Culture, India*, 6(2), 46–54.

Kassenova, T. (2016). Banning nuclear testing: Lessons from the Semipalatinsk nuclear testing site. *The Nonproliferation Review*, 23(3–4), 329–344.

Kassymbekova, B., and Chokobaeva, A. (2021). On writing Soviet history of Central Asia: Frameworks, challenges, prospects. *Central Asian Survey*, 40(4), 483–503.

Keller, S. (2019). *Russia and Central Asia: Coexistence, Conquest, Convergence*. Toronto: University of Toronto Press.

Kendirbaeva, G. (1999). 'We are children of Alash …' The Kazakh intelligentsia at the beginning of the 20th century in search of national identity and prospects of the cultural survival of the Kazakh people. *Central Asian Survey*, 18(1), 5–36.

Kendirbay, G. T. (1997). The national liberation movement of the Kazakh intelligentsia at the beginning of the 20th century. *Central Asian Survey*, 16(4), 487–515.

Kerensky, A. (1932). The policy of the provisional government of 1917. *The Slavonic and East European Review*, 11(31), 1–19.

Kerven, C., Robinson, S., and Behnke, R. (2021). Pastoralism at scale on the Kazakh rangelands: From clans to workers to ranchers. *Frontiers in Sustainable Food Systems*, 4, 590401.

Kesici, Ö. (2014) *Territory and the Kazakh Nation: Bordering the Alash Orda*. CIBR Working Papers Series (26), 1–23. www.qub.ac.uk/research-centres/CentreforInternationalBordersResearch/Publications/WorkingPapers/CIBRWorkingPapers/Filetoupload,481367,en.pdf.

Kesici, Ö. (2017). The Alash movement and the question of Kazakh ethnicity. *Nationalities Papers*, 45(6), 1135–1149.

Ketenci, N. S. (2012). *Kazakhstani Enterprises in Transition: The Role of Historical Regional Development in Kazakhstan's Post-Soviet Economic Transformation*. Stuttgart: ibidem-Verlag/ibidem Press.

Khalid, A. (2006). Backwardness and the quest for civilization: Early Soviet Central Asia in comparative perspective. *Slavic Review*, 65(2), 231–251.

Khanin, G. I. (2003). The 1950s: The triumph of the Soviet economy. *Europe-Asia Studies*, 55(8), 1187–1212.

Kindler, R. (2018). *Stalin's Nomads: Power and Famine in Kazakhstan*. Pittsburgh, PA: University of Pittsburgh Press.

Koch, N. (2013). The 'heart' of Eurasia? Kazakhstan's centrally located capital city. *Central Asian Survey*, 32(2), 134–147.

Koigeldiev, Mambet (2007). The Alash movement and the Soviet government: A difference of positions. In T. Uyama (Ed.), *Empire, Islam, and Politics in Central Eurasia* (pp. 153–184). Hokkaido: Slavic Research Center of Hokkaido University.

Kopack, R. A. (2019). Rocket wastelands in Kazakhstan: Scientific authoritarianism and the Baikonur Cosmodrome. *Annals of the American Association of Geographers*, 109(2), 556–567.

Kremer, M. (1993). Population growth and technological change: One million BC to 1990. *The Quarterly Journal of Economics*, 108(3), 681–716.

Krugman, P. (1994). The myth of Asia's miracle. *Foreign Affairs*, 73(6), 62–78.

Kunaev, D. (1994) *Ot Stalina do Gorbacheva* [*From Stalin to Gorbachev*]. Almaty: Sanat.

Levkin, R. (2014). *The Effect of Stalin's Deportations on Distrust in Central Authority*. https://papers.ssrn.com/sol3/papers.cfm?abstract_id=2484925.

Lewis, R. A., Rowland, R. H., and Clem, R. S. (1975). Modernization, population change and nationality in Soviet Central Asia and Kazakhstan. *Canadian Slavonic Papers*, 17(2–3), 286–301.

Lih, L. T. (1990). *Bread and Authority in Russia, 1914–1921*. Berkeley: University of California Press.

Lydolph, P. E., and Shabad, T. (1960). The oil and gas industries in the USSR. *Annals of the Association of American Geographers*, 50(4), 461–486.

Marie, J.-J. (1995). *Les peuples déportés d'Union soviétiques*. Brussels: Editions Complexe.

Markevich, A., and Harrison, M. (2011). Great War, Civil War, and recovery: Russia's national income, 1913 to 1928. *The Journal of Economic History*, 71(3), 672–703.

Martin, T. (1998). The origins of Soviet ethnic cleansing. *The Journal of Modern History*, 70(4), 813–861.

Martin, T. D. (2001). *The Affirmative Action Empire: Nations and Nationalism in the Soviet Union, 1923–1939*. Ithaca, NY: Cornell University Press.

Martynenko, N. (1992). Postanovlenie Vcekirgizskogo C'ezda v Orenburge 21–28 Iulia 1917 Goda [Resolution of the All-Kyrgyz Congress in Orenburg 21–28 July 1917]. In N. Martynenko (Ed.), *Alash Orda: Sbornik Dokumentov* [*Alash Orda: Collection of Documents*] (pp. 116–117). Alma-Ata: "Aikap."

Mashkovich, A. P. (1919). *Deyatel'nost' prodovol'stvennoy organizatsii (Po dannym Chrezvych. revizii Soveta oborony)* [*Activities Related to Food Organization (According to the Special Audit of the Defence Council*). Moscow: People's Commissariat of State Monitoring [Digital scan]. http://lib.urfu.ru/mod/data/view.php?d=110&mode=single&page=20.

McCauley, M. (1976). *Khrushchev and the Development of Soviet Agriculture: Virgin Land Program, 1953–64*. Berlin: Springer.

Mendikulova, G., Nadezhuk, E., and Akatayeva, A. (2019). New Documents on Kazakhs in the European Resistance Movements during World War II. *Journal of Modern Turkish History*, 15(29), 205–226.

Mills, R. M. (1970). The formation of the Virgin Lands policy. *Slavic Review*, 29(1), 58–69.

Mots, A. (1964). Industrialisation and technical training in the Kazakh SSR. *International Labour Review*, 90, 521–543.

Neishtadt, S. A. (1960). *Ekonomicheskoye Razvitiye Kazakhskoy SSR* [*Economic Development of the Kazakh SSR*]. Alma-Ata: Gosizdat KazSSR.

Nikolova, M., Popova, O., and Otrachshenko, V. (2022). Stalin and the origins of mistrust. *Journal of Public Economics*, 208, 104629.

Nikolsky, S. A. (2017). The October Revolution and the constants of Russian being. *Russian Studies in Philosophy*, 55(3–4), 177–193.

North, D. C., and Wallis, J. J. (1994). Integrating institutional change and technical change in economic history a transaction cost approach. *Journal of Institutional and Theoretical Economics (JITE)/Zeitschrift für die gesamte Staatswissenschaft*, 150(4), 609–624.

Nurmagambetova, R. K. (2003), *Dvijenie Alash i Alash-Orda: Istoriographia Problemy 1920–1990-e Gody XX Veka* [T*he Alash Movement and Alash-Orda: Historiography Problems in the 1920–1990s of the XX Century*]. Almaty: Ministerstvo Obrazovania i Nauki Respubliki Kazakhstan, Institut Istorii i Etnologii Im. Ch. Ch. Valikhanova [Ministry of Education and Science of the Republic of Kazakhstan, Institute for History and Ethnology named after Sh. Sh. Valikhanova].

Nurpeisov, K. (1998). The Alash party's role and its place in the social and political life of Kazakhstan. In M. K. Kozybaev (Ed.), *History of Kazakhstan: Essays* (pp. 124–

141). Almaty: Ministry of Science-Academy of Sciences of the Republic of Kazakhstan - Institute of History and Ethnology Named after Ch. Ch. Valikhanov.

Ohayon, I. (2006). *La sédentarisation des Kazakhs dans l'URSS de Staline.* Paris: Maisonneuve & Larose.

Ohayon, I. (2013a). Loyalty, solidarity and duplicity: Clan systems in the 1928 drive against rural elites in Kazakhstan. In P. R. Bullock, A. Byford, C. Nun-Ingerflom (Eds.), *Loyalties and Solidarities in Russian Society, History and Culture* (pp. 67–79). London: UCL-SSEES Press.

Ohayon, I. (2013b). The Kazakh famine: The beginnings of sedentarization. *Science-PO: On-Line Encyclopedia of Mass Violence.* www.sciencespo.fr/mass-violence-war-massacre-resistance/en/document/kazakh-famine-beginnings-sedentarization.

Ohayon, I. (2014). Formes et usages du territoire à la période coloniale: La première sédentarisation des Kazakhs. *Cahiers d'Asie centrale*, 23, 183–244.

Ohayon, I. (2016). The Soviet state and lineage societies: Doctrine, local interactions, and political hybridization in Kazakhstan and Kirghizia during the 1920s and 1930s. *Central Asian Affairs*, 3(2), 163–191.

Olcott, M. B. (1981). The collectivization drive in Kazakhstan. *The Russian Review*, 40(2), 122–142.

Olcott, M. B. (1995). *The Kazakhs.* Palo Alto, CA: Hoover Institution Press.

Olcott, M. B. (2010). *Kazakhstan: Unfulfilled Promise.* Washington, DC: Carnegie Endowment.

Pannier, B. (2007). Kazakhstan: The forgotten famine. *Radio Free Europe/Radio Liberty*, 28 December. www.rferl.org/a/1079304.html.

Payne, M. J. (1988). The TurkSib: First born of the Five-Year Plan. *Russian History*, 15(2/4), 353–414.

Payne, M. J. (2001). *Stalin's Railroad: Turksib and the Building of Socialism.* Pittsburgh, PA: University of Pittsburgh Press.

Petrick, M., Wandel, J., and Karsten, K. (2013). Rediscovering the Virgin Lands: Agricultural investment and rural livelihoods in a Eurasian frontier area. *World Development*, 43, 164–179.

Pianciola, N. (2001). The collectivization famine in Kazakhstan, 1931–1933. *Harvard Ukrainian Studies*, 25(3/4), 237–251.

Pianciola, N. (2004). Famine in the steppe: The collectivization of agriculture and the Kazak herdsmen 1928–1934. *Cahiers du monde russe. Russie-Empire russe-Union soviétique et États indépendants*, 45(1–2), 137–192.

Pianciola, N. (2017). Stalinist spatial hierarchies: Placing the Kazakhs and Kyrgyz in Soviet economic regionalization. *Central Asian Survey*, 36(1), 73–92.

Pianciola, N. (2019). Nomads and the State in Soviet Kazakhstan. In D. Ludden (Ed.), *Oxford Research Encyclopedia of Asian History.* https://doi.org/10.1093/acrefore/9780190277727.013.314.

Pipes, R. (1964). *The Formation of the Soviet Union: Communism and Nationalism, 1917–1923.* Cambridge, MA: Harvard University Press.

Pipes, R. (1991). *The Russian Revolution.* New York: Vintage Books.

Pipes, R. (2011). *Russia under the Bolshevik Regime.* New York: Vintage Books.

Pohl, J. O. (2000). Stalin's genocide against the "repressed peoples". *Journal of Genocide Research*, 2(2), 267–293.

Pohl, M. (2004). Women and girls in the Virgin Lands. In M. Ilič, S. E. Reid, and L. Attwood (Eds.), *Women in the Khrushchev Era* (pp. 52–74). Basingstoke: Palgrave Macmillan.

Prociuk, S. G. (1961). The territorial pattern of industrialization in the USSR: A case study in location of industry. *Europe-Asia Studies*, 13(1), 69–95.

Polyakov, S.P. (1989). *Традициёнализм в сёвременнём среднеазиатскём ёбществе* [*Traditionalism in Contemporary Central Asian Society*]. Moscow: Znanie.

Pryde, P. (2009). *Environmental Management in the Soviet Union*. Cambridge: Cambridge University Press.

Rather, Z. A., and Abdullah, D. (2018). Russian migration and structural change in Kazakh SSR with special reference to agricultural developments (1917–1991). *The Journal of Central Asian Studies*, 25(1), 25–44.

Rees, K. M. (2020). Recasting the nation: Transforming heroes of the Soviet Union into symbols of Kazakhstani patriotism. *Central Asian Survey*, 39(4), 445–462.

Rogovin, V. Z. (2009). *Stalin's Terror of 1937–1938: Political Genocide in the USSR*. Oak Park, MI: Mehring Books.

Rosefielde, S. (1996). Stalinism in post-communist perspective: New evidence on killings, forced labour and economic growth in the 1930s. *Europe-Asia Studies*, 48(6), 959–987.

Rowe, W.C. (2011). Turning the Soviet Union into Iowa: The Virgin Lands program in the Soviet Union. In S. Brunn (Ed.), *Engineering Earth* (pp. 236–237). Dordrecht: Springer.

Rybakovskii, L. L. (1995). Migratsionnyy Obmen Naseleniyem mezhdu Tsentral'noy Aziyey i Rossiyey [Migration Exchanges between Central Asia and Russia]. *Sotsiologicheskie issledovaniia*, 9, 89–95.

Ryskulov, T. (1925) *Revolyutsiya i Korennoye Naseleniye Turkestana. Chast' 1. 1917–1918 (Sbornik Glavneishikh Statey, Dokladov, Rechey i Tezisov) s Predisloviyem Avtora* [*The Revolution and the Indigenous Population of Turkestan. Part 1, 1917–1918. (The Collection of the Most Important Articles, Reports, Speeches and Theses) with a Foreword by the Author*]. Tashkent: Uzbek State Publishing House.

Sabol, S. (2003). *Russian Colonization and the Genesis of Kazak National Consciousness*. Berlin: Springer.

Sagers, M. J. (1998a). The nonferrous metals industry of Kazakhstan. *Post-Soviet Geography and Economics*, 39(9), 495–517.

Sagers, M. J. (1998b). Gold production in Central Asia. *Post-Soviet Geography and Economics*, 39(3), 125–150.

Sarsenbekov, N. Z., and Sagatova, A. S. (2021). The existential reflection in Kazakhstan society during the Great Patriotic War. *Bulletin of the Karaganda University*, 3 (103), 188–196.

Satymbekova, R. (2017). *The Gulag Camp "Alzhir": Memorialization Practices*. [Doctoral dissertation, Central European University].

Scarborough, I. (2017). An unwanted dependence: Chechen and Ingush deportees and the development of state–citizen relations in late-Stalinist Kazakhstan (1944–1953). *Central Asian Survey*, 36(1), 93–112.

Scarborough, I. (2021). Central Asia in the Soviet Command Economy. In *Oxford Research Encyclopedia of Asian History*. https://doi.org/10.1093/acrefore/9780190277727.013.504.

Schechter, B. (2012). The People's Instructions: Indigenizing the Great Patriotic War Among Non-Russians. *Ab Imperio*, 2012(3), 109–133.

Shelekpayev, N. (2021). Rethinking transfers of power and public protest in Kazakhstan, 1959–1989. *Europe-Asia Studies*, 1–15. https://doi.org/10.1080/09668136.2021.1990213.

Shifflett, C. A. (1991). *Coal Towns: Life, Work, and Culture in Company Towns of Southern Appalachia, 1880–1960*. Knoxville, TN: University of Tennessee Press.

Shimkin, D. B. (1949). Uranium deposits in the USSR. *Science*, 109(2821), 58–60.

Škvorecký, J. (1977). *The Engineer of Human Souls*. Ontario, CA: Collins Press.

Smele, J.D. (1996). *Civil War in Siberia: The Anti-Bolshevik Government of Admiral Kolchak, 1918–1920*. Cambridge: Cambridge University Press.

Smith, J. (1999). *The Bolsheviks and the National Question, 1917–23*. New York: St. Martin's Press.

Smith, D. J., Pabriks, A., Lane, T., and Purs, A. (2002). *The Baltic States: Estonia, Latvia and Lithuania*. Hove: Psychology Press.

Snyder, T. (2010). *Bloodlands: Europe between Hitler and Stalin*. New York: Basic Books.

Spehr, S., and Kassenova, N. (2012). Kazakhstan: Constructing identity in a post-Soviet society. *Asian Ethnicity*, 13(2), 135–151.

Stalin, J. V. (1930). Golovokruzhéniye ot Uspékhov. K Voprósam Kolkhóznogo Dvizhéniya [Dizzy with success: On questions of the collective farm movement]. *Pravda*, *2*, 198.

Stefany, M. G. (2013). Kazakhization, Kunaev and Kazakhstan: A bridge to independence. *Orta Asya ve Kafkasya Araştırmaları*, 16, 49–72.

Stefany, M. G. (2020). On the road to insurrection: The Soviet nationalities problem, the Kazakhs, and Zheltoksan in Kazakhstan. *The Journal of Central Asian Studies*, 26/27, 1–14.

Talgat, M., Omarbayev, Y., and Zhandos, K. (2019). Activities of the passport bodies of the Bolshevik government in Kazakhstan in the 1920s. *The Journal of Slavic Military Studies*, 32(3), 435–442.

Tanatarova, Z. T. (2015). Repressions of 1937–1938 in Kazakhstan and their consequences. *IJHSSE*, 2, 100–106.

Thomas, A. (2018). *Nomads and Soviet Rule: Central Asia under Lenin and Stalin*. London: Bloomsbury Publishing.

Tokhmetova, G. M., Tokhmetova, G. M., and Kanzhigalina, M. M. (2014). On the material and living conditions of German special settlers during the deportation (on the example of the Pavlodar Region). *Terra Sebvs*, S, 259–274.

Tolts, M. (2006). Ethnic composition of Kazakhstan on the eve of the Second World War: Re-evaluation of the 1939 Soviet census results. *Central Asian Survey*, 25(1–2), 143–148.

Tomohiko, U. (2013). Two attempts at building a Qazaq state: The revolt of 1916 and the Alash movement. In S. A. Dudoignon and K. Hisao (Eds.), *Islam in Politics in Russia and Central Asia* (pp. 77–98). New York: Routledge.

Tompson, W. J. (2014). *The Soviet Union under Brezhnev*. London: Routledge.

Trotsky, L. (1980). National aspects of politics in Kazakhstan, March 11, 1927. In N. Allen and G. Sanders (Eds.), *Trotsky: The Challenges of the Left Opposition (1926–1927)* (pp. 210–213). New York: Pathfinder.

Tsentralnoe statisticheskoe upravlenie (1956). *Narodnoye khozyaistvo SSSR M. 1956*. Moscow: Central Statistical Directorate.

Turekulova, D. M., Mukhambetova, L. K., Kapenova, A. Z., Ospanova, A. T., Nukesheva, A. Z., Burlakov, L. N., and Chimgentbayeva, G. K. (2016). Migration processes in Kazakhstan: Peculiarities, consequences, prospects of the development. *International Journal of Economic Perspectives*, 10(4), 274–283.

Turkebaev, E. A., and Sadikov, G. X. (1988). *Kompleksnoye ispol'zovaniye syr'ya i otkhodov promyshlennosti* [*Integrated Use of Raw Materials and Waste Materials in Industry*]. Alma-Ata: Kazakstan Publishers.

Uibopuu, H. J. (1979). Soviet federalism under the new Soviet constitution. *Review of Socialist Law*, 5(1), 171–185.
Viola, L. (2007). *The Unknown Gulag: The Lost World of Stalin's Special Settlements.* New York: Oxford University Press.
Vodovozov, V. (1925). Moyo znakomstvo s Leninym [My relationship with Lenin]. *Na Chuzhoy Storone* [*On the Other Side*], 12, 174–181.
Wade R. A. (2006) The October Revolution, the Constituent Assembly, and the end of the Russian Revolution. In I. D. Thatcher (Ed.), *Reinterpreting Revolutionary Russia*. London: Palgrave Macmillan.
Werth, N. (2006). The "Chechen problem": Handling an awkward legacy, 1918–1958. *Contemporary European History*, 15(3), 347–366.
Willerton, J. P., Jr. (1987). Patronage networks and coalition building in the Brezhnev era. *Soviet Studies*, 39(2), 175–204.
Wojnowski, Z. (2017). De-Stalinization and the failure of Soviet identity building in Kazakhstan. *Journal of Contemporary History*, 52(4), 999–1021.
Yan, H., Lai, C., Akshalov, K., Qin, Y., Hu, Y., and Zhen, L. (2020). Social institution changes and their ecological impacts in Kazakhstan over the past hundred years. *Environmental Development*, 34, 100531.
Yensenov, K. A., Saurykova, Z. S., Naimanbayev, B. R., Bakhtorazov, S. U., and Nurbekova, R. K. (2021). History of persecution of the intellectual class in Kazakhstan during Stalin's Repression. *Analele Universitatii din Craiova-Seria Istorie*, 25(2), 65–75.
Yesdauletova, A., Yesdauletov, A., and Kakenova, S. A. A. G. (2015). Famine and Kazakh society in the 1930s. *The Anthropologist*, 22(3), 537–544.
Zardykhan, Z. (2004). Russians in Kazakhstan and demographic change: Imperial legacy and the Kazakh way of nation building. *Asian Ethnicity*, 5(1), 61–79.
Zharkynbayeva, R., Abdirayimova, A., and Dadabaeva, G. N. (2020). The evacuation policy of the Soviet Union during the Second World War. *The Journal of Slavic Military Studies*, 33(3), 403–419.
Zhukov, Y. M., and Talibova, R. (2018). Stalin's terror and the long-term political effects of mass repression. *Journal of Peace Research*, 55(2), 267–283.

5 The Political Development of Post-Soviet Kazakhstan

When we left off at the close of the last chapter, the Soviet Union was facing economic sclerosis, a state of affairs which was also prevalent in the Kazakh Soviet Socialist Republic (SSR) albeit in microcosm (and, realistically, one that occurred because of the issues afflicting the broader Union). But both the Union of Soviet Socialist Republics (USSR) and the Kazakh SSR were also undergoing a political evolution of sorts, unlike anything seen under the tightly controlled centralized Soviet system, with the monopoly on power held by the Kommunisticheskaya partiya Sovetskogo Soyuza (KPSS – Communist Party of the Soviet Union). The 1980s saw the USSR finally starting to open up its political system and, tentatively, its economy, under the twin policies of glasnost and perestroika; instituted by new the General Secretary of the KPSS, Mikhail Gorbachev, these changes had the electrifying effect of "engag[ing] a traditionally conservative society – a society used to secrecy, following orders, and unquestioning obedience in a far-ranging debate over the need for openness, innovation, and democracy" (Battle 1988:367).

These changes could not be contained within Moscow alone, and in the hinterlands of Alma-Ata and Shevchenko, things were also beginning to shift, as the political system moved from closed to slightly less closed. In the first instance, after years of subordination, the Kazakhs were beginning to tentatively re-emerge as a potent political force in their own land, even as the centre tried to reassert its authority over the Kazakh SSR. But the centre itself was soon to collapse, leaving the Kazakhs to go their own way as an independent nation-state for the first time in their history. As this chapter will show, the removal of Dinmukhamed Kunaev by Gorbachev, the growing environmental and anti-nuclear movement, and, finally, the collapse of the Soviet Union at the end of 1991 changed the whole political dynamic which existed in Kazakhstan, as the now-independent country sought to build a political system using bits of the past while looking to the future. Where could political institutions emerge and would they be based on traditional Kazakh methods of governance, as shown in Chapter 2? Would they basically be Soviet institutions, just in an independent country? Or would they be a hybrid of both?

This chapter examines the political end of the USSR and, more importantly, the development of political institutions in the new and independent

DOI: 10.4324/9781003212508-5

Kazakhstan once the Soviet Union had passed into the pages of history. The difficulty of constructing a new institutional structure from a blank slate cannot be understated, even as we comfortably look back from 30 years (or more) of experience and confidently assert what should have been done; as the last leader of the Kazakh SSR and the first leader of independent Kazakhstan noted well after the fact, the pressures of the time made such deliberation a luxury. Indeed, the events of 1991 and 1992 transformed the institutional landscape in the Kazakh lands so profoundly that the only way to describe it comes from the character Bulat in Victor Robert Lee's book *Performance Anomalies* (set in Kazakhstan): "History is running very fast in my country" (Lee 2012).

This reality meant that mistakes were made, and in the early years, *many* mistakes were made. However, how Kazakhstan handled these mistakes in fashioning its political institutions – or, more accurately, how it entrenched these mistakes – can explain a great deal of its transition experience. Together with the next chapter examining the development of Kazakhstan's economy (the very reason for this book), this chapter will set the stage for understanding how Kazakhstan arrived at the point where it is today, and what hope lies ahead for the future.

The Denouement of the USSR

The overall decline of the USSR has been treated in thousands of papers and hundreds of books, a reality which corresponds to the fact that many scholars are still trying to grapple with *what just happened.* From a nearly impregnable fortress which seemed to be on the move everywhere simultaneously in the 1970s, and one which was attempting to adapt in the 1980s and address its many (hidden and overt) failings, the Soviet Union just sort of fizzled out. Of course, we know that centrifugal forces were in place throughout the entirety of the Union's history, attempting to pull apart the stitched-together USSR:

- There was never an adequate reconciling of all nationalities within the Union, allowing them to be both distinct (with their own national language and culture, for example) yet still Soviet (Marples 2016).
- The stark division of labour which the centre imposed on its periphery created alienation from the greater project of the Soviet Union and overrode local desires (as noted in Chapter 4). Additionally, this approach led to the Soviet Union's corresponding absence from the international division of labour (i.e. allowing the country to play to its comparative advantages rather than follow an artificial plan; see Miller 2016).
- Extreme bureaucratization and centralization made the system inefficient as well as burdensome (Laqueur 1996), relying on terror for compliance.
- A crisis of legitimacy descended upon the USSR once other alternatives to the stifling edicts of communism were presented (Aron 2011).

Added to these long-simmering issues in keeping the Union together were new ones discovered in the 1980s[1]: first, the failure of the Soviet Union to subdue Afghanistan and the approximately 15,000 dead soldiers which accompanied this defeat marked a turning point in the USSR's fortunes. The once mighty emperor was shown to have no clothes, defeated by a technologically backward resistance (funded by the United States), and discrediting the Red Army in the process (Reuveny and Prakash 1999). At the same time, the protracted nature of the conflict and Soviet attempts to keep the war secret, despite the body bags flowing back from the south (Kamrany 1986), opened up new forms of political protest to challenge the regime and its legitimacy (Reuveny and Prakash 1999). Second, the inability of the planned economy to provide for its citizens was a constant factor throughout the Soviet Union's existence, but, as Suesse (2018) shows, this was immensely exacerbated once member republics started declaring their intention to leave the Union. This secessionist drift only came about in the 1980s when Gorbachev (finally) eschewed the same use of violence that Leonid Brezhnev or Joseph Stalin would readily have embraced (Aron 2011), but once it picked up momentum, it had a massive feedback effect on the country's economic decline. In both of these instances, ironically, the relaxation of omnipresent threats of terror, arrest, or the gulag led to an immediate weakening of the state's position.

The impending economic collapse and the threat to the party's monopoly exposed the third fault line in Soviet politics, namely the ideological schism in Moscow between liberalizers and hardliners. Like the idea of secession or protest, this schism emerged only in the 1980s mainly because suddenly there were liberalizers to oppose the old guard (again, such a thing would not have been tolerated under previous Soviet leaders, including the short-lived Yuri Andropov, much less Lenin or Stalin). This political tension, playing out in party meetings and in the press in the late 1980s (Minaev 2015 provides an excellent insider's account of these meetings), exploded into the open with the botched coup attempt against Gorbachev in August 1991. A three-day affair executed in the most spectacularly inept fashion, the coup resulted in "both Gorbachev and the credibility of the Soviet political system … fatally weakened by the attempted coup … and the fabric of Soviet political control began to unravel with astonishing speed" (Shevtsova 1992:5).

More importantly for our purposes, the failed coup and the rise of Boris Yeltsin – and the concurrent rise of a "Russian" leader against a "Soviet" leader (Huskey 2016) – marked the denouement of the USSR not just in terms of political institutions but also in terms of geography, as it spurred already-existing secessionist movements in the Soviet Union. The uneasy policies conducted in pursuit of a fundamentally Russian project to incorporate the nationalities at its fringes, absorbed via imperialism and bloodshed and co-opted through massive amounts of terror and far fewer rewards (Jowitt 1997), were showing their lack of suitability by the 1980s (Hajda 1988). With Gorbachev further relaxing Moscow's grip on the other constituent republics of the USSR (Walker 2003), secession, once unthinkable, was already under way (Tuminez 2003): in the Baltic states, Estonia declared its sovereignty in 1988 and Latvia and Lithuania followed a few months later, with Lithuania declaring its independence in March 1990 and Estonia and Latvia in May (Emizet and Hesli 1995). Similarly, and surprisingly, in the Caucasus, Azerbaijan declared its sovereignty in September 1989. However, the failed coup accelerated the move towards the door for the hesitant republics, and a mere two days after the coup was quashed, Ukraine had declared its independence (24 August 1991), followed by five other republics in the next 16 days. Notably, the Kyrgyz SSR was one of these five republics, but the Kazakh SSR was not, and indeed it held on until the very end (in fact, for four days the entirety of the Soviet Union was reduced to Kazakh borders).

The Kazakh SSR in the Waning Days of Empire

This reluctance on the part of the Kazakh SSR's political leadership to break up the Union in the waning days of the Soviet Union was directly due to the political events which occurred within the republic during the period 1986–1991, including the monumental shift of leadership that occurred in Alma-Ata. Despite the fact that, five years hence, there would be a revival of nationalism across the USSR, the Kazakh SSR in the mid- to late 1980s saw moves from Moscow which did not appear to presage a revival of "Kazakhness" and in fact tried to bind the Kazakh SSR closer to the Kremlin. However, these very attempts to reimpose control from the centre also helped to spark the revival of nationalism in the Kazakh lands which would underpin independence, as well as elevate the leadership which would take over after independence was won.

The main event which showed how much things had changed in the SSR under Brezhnev was the removal of its leader, Dinmukhamed Kunaev, in 1986. While Gorbachev would eventually move towards a looser nationalities policy, early in his tenure he sought to clear out many of the Brezhnevites who remained in the Kremlin and elsewhere, thereby tightening his own personal control over the leadership on the periphery. As noted in the previous chapter, long-serving First Secretary of the Kazakh Communist Party Dinmukhamed Kunaev owed his position as leader of the SSR to his close ties with Brezhnev, and thus was a prime target of Gorbachev's initiative. Unfortunately for the Kremlin, Kunaev had been a member of the Politburo since 1971, making him more difficult to shift; instead, in 1985, Gorbachev dismissed the first secretaries of the Kirghiz, Tajik, and Turkmen Communist Parties and waited over a year to target the Kazakh SSR (Olcott 1989). At the same time, the Kremlin attacked the Kazakh leadership in official party organs and by late 1985 and early 1986, several Kunaev allies within the Kazakh SSR had been dismissed, with further vilification of the leadership carried out at the 27th Party Congress held in Moscow (Olcott 1995).

Although Kunaev was re-elected First Secretary at the 16th Congress of the Kommunisticheskaya partiya Kazakhstana (KPK – Communist Party of Kazakhstan) in February 1986, by December, Gorbachev believed that he had the necessary support to force Kunaev into retirement, and he replaced the long-serving (since 1964) Kunaev with a relative newcomer, Gennady Kolbin, a functionary from Ulyanovsk who had never worked in or even been to the Kazakh SSR before (Olcott 1981).

The removal of Kunaev and his replacement with an ethnic Russian led to something not seen in the Kazakh lands since the 19th century, namely unrest against Russian (Soviet) rule. As news of Kunaev's dismissal spread in the Kazakh SSR, shock and disbelief (Stefany 2020) quickly turned into discontent (Stefany 2013), with Gorbachev's move seen as a national insult (Ó Beacháin and Kevlihan 2013). Taking to the streets from 17–19 December 1986, demonstrations now known as Zheltoqsan (Kazakh for December) grew to encompass some 60,000 people, mainly students, and acted as a focal point for dissatisfaction with the way in which Kazakhs were handled within the Soviet system – as well as dissatisfaction with this particular event and the implications it had for the system that Kunaev had built. Ro'i (1991a) notes that the mobilization of students and other protestors had an inherently political nature, as the demonstrations were targeted almost exclusively at public buildings representing Soviet power. Caron (2019:185) saw in the riots a nascent pushback against the entire Soviet system and not just an internecine struggle confined to the Communist Party: in his words, the protestors "demanded local autonomy regarding power and the end of the Soviet dictatorship. Kazakhs demonstrated to express their dissatisfaction with Soviet governance and demanded recognition of their national identity." Ó Beacháin and Kevlihan (2013:349) also note that "there is little doubt that at least a sizable minority was inspired by nationalist sentiment: 'Every people deserves their own leader' was one banner held up by demonstrators, for example." This assertion of national identity also contained an ethnic component which had been repressed during the Soviet rule, as protestors attacked Russians specifically due to their ethnicity (and also the fact that the Russians had either remained silent or tacitly supported the ouster of Kunaev and accused their Kazakh neighbours of being "anti-Russian"; see Sarsembayev 1999).[2] As Stefany (2020) correctly notes, the Zheltoqsan demonstrations were the first ethnic uprising under Gorbachev, and, as time would show, they would not be the last.

At a different level, for the elite in the Kazakh SSR, the removal of Kunaev "threatened the clientele network drawn disproportionately from the first secretary's own tribal group; it threatened the career prospects of the indigenous nationals who had tied their careers to the local leadership; and it brought a wave of violent protest" (Roeder 1991:222).

In many ways, Brezhnev's benign neglect of the Kazakh SSR had enabled the traditional Kazakh political organization of nomads to reassert itself, and, by deferring to the local authorities and stitching together kinship networks for support – as well as keeping lower-level chieftains happy via dispensation of state largesse – Kunaev was able to build a power base independent of the machinations of Moscow (Collins 2004). Following Kunaev's removal, it appeared that Moscow was attempting to cut off the ability of locals to act independently, ironically recentralizing in order to reform a project which had fallen into disrepair precisely because of the de facto decentralization of the Brezhnev years (Willerton 2007). Not only did Kunaev's removal result in the loss of rents but also the loss of power, neither of which politicians are ever eager to cede. As Olcott (1989:406) asserts,

> many of the rioters were communists who wanted to protest [against] Moscow's redefinition of the power relationships between center and periphery … The Alma Ata riots were so serious because they were a violent manifestation of the Central Asian party elite's disapproval of official party policy.

Taken aback by the demonstrations and relying on old established ways, Gorbachev, like his predecessors (and his successors), was not above using the army, the special forces, and violence in order to quell dissent. Apprised of events on the ground from his handpicked protégé Kolbin, aided and abetted by representatives from the security forces, Gorbachev ordered the demonstrations to be forcibly dispersed and provocateurs to be arrested. According to official estimates, as a result of this action over 2,000 protestors were detained and more than 50 were hospitalized in order to clear the disturbance (Shelekpayev, 2021), with the exact number killed by the Soviet suppression unknown (Sarsembayev 1999) but estimated at between one and 200 (Ó Beacháin and Kevlihan 2013). While this ended the immediate problem for Moscow (the demonstrations), the suppression of the discontent that Kazakhs felt was to only grow; as Phillips and James (2001:31) note, "the fact that military tanks overwhelmed a peaceful demonstration, with a number of demonstrators killed and many subject to long-term imprisonment, confirmed for many Kazakhs a history of enmity rather than 'great friendship' between themselves and the Russians."

In many ways, the December 1986 protests were eerily similar to Russian-Kazakh relations during the 18th and 19th centuries, tinged with imperialism and colonialism but revolving around the exact same issues: the scale of local autonomy for the Kazakhs; the right to do with their land as they saw fit; and the limits of local governance vis-à-vis a centralizing authority. With Kunaev having returned some autonomy to the region, both in terms of political structures and nationalism, the removal of the native Kazakh emissary to the red court of Moscow was bound to revive these latent struggles. More importantly from the point of view of a region which was to become independent just five years later, the demonstrations played a key role in awakening informal organizational structures which were independent from the formal Soviet apparatus. In a political system which claimed to countenance no institutions outside of the purview of the state, the Zheltoqsan demonstrations not only provided an anchor point for nationalist desires (Phillips and James 2001) but also helped to spark the development of civil society.

It is an understandable failing in the political science, sociology, and even the history literature that it is difficult to pinpoint the precise moment that discrete bouts of unrest such as the Zheltoqsan demonstrations actually turn into the development of a sustainable civil society distinct from formal political apparatuses. Indeed, perhaps historians have the most to offer here, as they have the luxury of seeing what came before and after and can speak about how various specific events contributed to social movements and what shape these movements were to take. But even then, while we can trace various facets of civil society back to specific events, in the moment, it is impossible to see the institutional evolution which may occur after a milestone. As an example from the post-Soviet space shows, the act of protesting itself often dictates how civil society is to develop and what path it will take: Ukraine's Euromaidan civil unrest in 2014[3] was characterized by dissatisfaction with the status quo, the fostering of non-state civic organizations, and the emergence of order via spontaneous processes, including self-organization (Onuch 2014). Shifting from informal to more formal in the years following the Euromaidan protests, these traits of self-organization also were evident during the Russian Federation's disastrous military invasion of Ukraine that took place in February 2022, as Ukraine forced heavy losses on a Russian invader which was ossified into a hierarchical and staid approach to warfare. From the vantage point of late 2013, the events of 2022 would have been unthinkable, as would have been the prospect of Ukraine resisting a Russian invasion based on the strength of its informal organizations. And yet, here we are.

In the Kazakh SSR, the Zheltoqsan demonstrations did not inflict the same level of trauma as is currently (at the time of this writing) being endured by Ukraine, but it had a similar catalysing effect in terms of paving the way for the formation of civil society, including providing a way for Kazakhs to coalesce around nationalist sentiment. As they say, it is difficult to "unring the bell," and the cracks that opened in the formal institutional edifice during the Brezhnev years allowed the light of civil society to shine through when given an opportunity such as the 1986 demonstrations. Indeed, while the Zheltoqsan demonstrations were the first major disruption in Soviet rule over Kazakh lands since the Russian Civil War, they prized open the spaces in the Soviet system even further to allow the Kazakh SSR to take another nascent step towards civil society: the environmental movement.

From the vantage point of 30 years, the environmental devastation of the communist political and economic apparatus is indisputable (Mazurski 1991; Peterson 1993), an eventuality which could easily have been predicted by economic theory (Coase 1937). The presence of "closed cities" and tight security surrounding military installations meant that there was little incentive or accountability for environmental protection, while extremely centralized planning from Moscow and a hyper-obsession with industrial development meant that local concerns were regularly passed over, including any potential environmental impact. At the time it was occurring, this degradation was little observed from the outside due to the USSR's obsession with secrecy; for those inside the USSR, however, the environmental degradation could be seen on a daily basis, as disregard of the natural environment in pursuit of either industrial or military objectives led directly to an impact on daily life. These effects were sometimes large and catastrophic, as in the Chornobyl (Chernobyl) nuclear disaster in 1986 or the gradual disappearance of the Aral Sea on the border between Kazakhstan and Uzbekistan, but more often they were smaller and more nefarious in their human toll, such as in the cumulative effect of air and water pollution (Carter and Turnock 1996).

Given the proximity to the problem, "environmental movements were the first non-governmental or independent organizations to emerge throughout the Soviet Union" (Luong and Weinthal 1999:1268), providing an outlet for a seemingly anodyne concern (the environment) but using organizational means unfamiliar to Soviet life. According to Kuzembayeva et al. (2019:95), the environmental movement began in the Kazakh SSR as "informal public formations – the nonconventional, alternative organizations and movements which worked outside official structures, leaning only on the initiative of citizens and without applying for official status," creating pushback against these same official structures and their policies on the environment in a rare space that was not policed by the Soviets (Schatz 1999). Using these unconventional methods, the environmental movement began to focus on small-scale goals such as nature conservancy in the late 1970s and early 1980s but became emboldened by the Zheltoqsan demonstrations and the Chornobyl disaster. In one of the first organized moves towards raising environmental awareness, a public committee on "the problems of Aral, Balkhash, and the ecology of Kazakhstan" was started by poet (and former People's Deputy) Mukhtar Shakhanov in 1987 (Alimbaev et al. 2017). Unfortunately, it had little success in its efforts, even though it was elevated to formal status in 1989, mainly because it was prevented from pointing the finger too vigorously at Moscow (Schatz 1999). Moreover, it was also prevented from blaming the true culprit for environmental disaster, a Marxist-Leninist system which rewarded apparatchiks for their transformation of nature rather than its conservation (Penati 2019).

As with the Zheltoqsan demonstrations, the precipitating factor for the widespread acceptance of the environmental movement in the Kazakh SSR was a crisis and the reality that, sometimes, the environmental degradation was so spectacular that it could not be ignored. As noted in the previous chapter, the Kazakh SSR's place of honour in the Soviet hierarchy as the Union's nuclear testing ground was accompanied by wanton destruction of

Kazakh land and callous indifference to human life. Indeed, the nuclear testing and storage of radioactive materials made the environmental question in the Kazakh SSR "extremely loud and incredibly close" (in the words of Jonathan Safran Foer). While nuclear testing had moved underground in 1963 as part of the Test Ban Treaty, there was scientific evidence that approximately one-third of the radioactive gases from the 370 tests conducted since 1965 had escaped into the atmosphere and landed in nearby villages and cities (Purvis-Roberts et al. 2007). Although public health information related to nuclear testing was a closely guarded state secret and the Soviet government did not release epidemiological data, there had been undeniable evidence around the Semipalatinsk "polygon" that something was seriously amiss: as Peterson (1993:202–203) notes, there were "numerous anecdotal reports … on continuing high rates of cancer, miscarriage, infant mortality, hair loss, skin disorders, depression, and suicide among the region's population, conditions many doctors have labeled collectively 'Semipalatinsk AIDS.'"

In February 1989, the Soviet authorities in Semipalatinsk accidentally vented not once, but twice, radioactive material – first reported by Soviet leadership as "inert noble gases" of no consequence but in reality Xenon-133 and Xenon-135 gas (Kassenova 2016) – over neighbouring villages. This malfeasance, and especially the subsequent cover-up, was exposed by Olzhas Suleimenov, a poet and candidate for the Congress of People's Deputies, during a televised speech at the Kazakh Writer's Union, where he tore up his prepared remarks and readings and addressed the issue directly (Rozsa 2020). Within two days, Suleimenov had registered Nevada-Semipalatinsk, an environmental umbrella group, as a non-governmental organization (NGO) which had as its goal the closure of Semipalatinsk as a test site, and that same day thousands of demonstrators took to the streets in Alma-Ata. More peaceful than the paroxysm of rage which accompanied the removal of Kunaev, environmental activists in the Kazakh SSR handed petitions bearing over a million signatures to the government and kept up the pressure on Moscow to cancel all testing entirely (Kassenova 2016).

While taking advantage of the same discontent manifested by the Zheltoqsan demonstrations, Nevada-Semipalatinsk (and the environmental movement in general) was far less nationalist in their outlook, focusing first on the Kazakh territory and then on global actors for change (hence the "Nevada" in the name; see Schatz 1999). The results of this discontent with specific Soviet policies perhaps unsurprisingly manifested in a similar way to the Zheltoqsan uprising, with mass rallies and, in the slightly more open atmosphere of perestroika, grassroots civic action. As Peterson (1993:203) notes, "by 1991, Nevada-Semipalatinsk had become the largest and most influential public organization in Kazakhstan, drawing its support from a broad range of people – from the intelligentsia to the working class." More importantly, the weakening resolve of the Kremlin to assert its policies by force led to much greater success in changing Moscow's policies, first resulting in accommodation with local authorities (by promising to cut back planned testing from 18 tests to one) and then, after this test was undertaken, promising funding for development in the Semipalatinsk area, and then, finally, to a cessation of all testing in the area from November 1990 on (Kassenova 2016).[4] The ripple effect from Nevada-Semipalatinsk spread to Russia proper, as the shift of nuclear testing from the polygon to Novaya Zemlya on the Barents Sea was also protested by environmental activists in 1991 (Peterson 1993).

The demonstrations that accelerated Kunaev's removal and the growing environmental movement surrounding Semipalatinsk (and, it must be noted, the Baikonur Cosmodrome as well) under his successor Kolbin were a visible manifestation of the emergence of a critically important informal political institution, civil society. In the Soviet Union, with all manner of organizing subsumed beneath the state, the emergence of any other power pole was a welcome institutional shift, providing a veto point which had been absent. Of course, civil society is often canonized in the policy and politics literature as a good unto itself, which is not always the case; a group of people operating outside of government may push for policies just as deleterious as those enacted by government, especially when they push for government to act in an even more ruthless manner. But in general, countries with strong civil society can see this act as a check on government power, creating a set of values outside of the transactional realm of the political (Gellner 1994), and the two events just discussed did in fact plant the seeds of civil society in the Kazakh SSR. However, as noted above, Kunaev's rule and in particular the late Brezhnev era gave rise to another, less visible informal institution, one which operated within the Soviet system itself, namely the rise of clientelism and the dispensation of largesse based on tribe, clan, and family. In many ways, the Soviet era's failures may have been just as damning as its successes, as the inability of the system to control all means of production and, in particular, to make humans behave as if they were angels, generated opportunities where political leaders were able to exploit the all-encompassing government for their own means. Thus, not only were the cracks in the institutional edifice used for good from the outside (civil society), but in the case of patronage, they were to be used for less salutary ends.

As I and others have already asserted (Dave 2007), Kunaev's actions during his long tenure were in one sense beneficial for the Kazakh SSR within the broader Soviet machine, as he helped to win back some autonomy from Moscow for Kazakhs. Moreover, his creation of a political/patronage system in parallel with the Soviet apparatus also harkened back to earlier Kazakh times, where (as shown in Chapter 2) they were an effective way of organizing a mobile populace. Unfortunately, the Kazakh populace at this point in its history were no longer the nomads that they once were (the result of previous Russian and Soviet policies), meaning that the tribal approach to maintaining group cohesion where exit costs were low was instead grafted onto the sedentary lifestyle of Soviet man (where exit costs were prohibitively high). Put simply, there was little risk of defection from the tribe of *Homo Sovieticus* among the Kazakh people, and thus there was little reason to dispense largesse. In fact, the only risk of defection was from supporting Kunaev and thus the diversion of assets and favours to a client network represented a deadweight loss for those not in that inner circle (and/or paying into it via their labours).

Perhaps more importantly, Kunaev's alternate power structure was not an additional power pole in society but occurred within the confines of the Soviet system, where a monopoly on power was guaranteed by violence. One of the redeeming features of the clan/tribal system in the pre- and early Russian years on Kazakh lands was that it generated competition, with ineffective leaders removed when they could not provide the grazing lands for the clan. As noted in Chapter 3, the system also favoured a somewhat restrained executive, balanced by nobles who did not want a leader who was too powerful, and with mechanisms to transfer power if the current leader was problematic. The Soviet system removed that widespread element of competition, especially with the appointment of leaders from Moscow. With no local competition and masters 3,120 kilometres away (as the crow flies), patronage networks could become entrenched in formal Kazakh political institutions, especially when Brezhnev had little inclination to examine what was happening in the Kazakh SSR too closely.

From Kazakh SSR to Kazakhstan

The development of informal clan networks within a formal institutional structure – a structure which wielded far too much power over the daily life of Kazakhs anyway – had an impact on the Kazakh SSR's political institutions which continues to this day. But these patronage networks would have remained local and within the Soviet system, subjected (as during the Gorbachev years) to a tug of war between the centre and the periphery and bounded by the ossification of Soviet institutions, if it were not for the greatest geopolitical victory for mankind of the 20th century – the collapse of the Soviet Union.[5]

The broader issues surrounding the collapse of the USSR have already been noted at the beginning of this chapter, but from the Kazakh side, the collapse of the Union came somewhat as an unwanted surprise, especially to the Kazakh SSR's new leader, Nursultan Nazarbayev (Elliot 1993). Much has been written about Nazarbayev (and much will be written about him in this book), mainly because he looms large in post-communist Kazakhstan as the "Father of the Nation" (*Elbasy*; see the Introduction to this volume). Without delving too deeply into his biography, it is important to understand his rise to power in the context of the way in which the Kazakh SSR responded to the collapse of the Soviet Union and, eventually, what path its political institutions were to take. Born in Chemolgan (now known as Ushkonyr), a rural village north-west of Almaty, Nazarbayev ascended through the ranks of the Communist Party to become the youngest Chairman of the Council of Ministers of the Kazakh SSR, appointed in 1984 at the age of 42. However, his rise to the top was perhaps signalled most clearly in his well-known denunciation of Askar Kunaev, Head of the Academy of Sciences (and the brother of Dinmukhamed Kunaev), in a proxy attack on the First Secretary in 1986 (Olcott 1995). With Nazarbayev's greater political ambitions now out in the open (and even before), Kunaev had made several attempts to remove Nazarbayev from his post (Alexandrov 1999), but the steel worker from Chemolgan proved himself a survivor (and with some support from Gorbachev) and was one of the main beneficiaries of Kunaev's dismissal.

Of course, as we know, Nazarbayev's aspirations did not end there, and he set his sights on Kunaev's successor, Gennady Kolbin. Kolbin was viewed as a transitional figure in the Kazakh SSR and, with time, proved to be more in tune with Gorbachev's early incremental moves towards reform than with the bolder pace adopted later in his term (Olcott 1995). The relative lack of flexibility in adapting to the times, combined with his challenge from the environmental protests detailed above, made Kolbin a prime target for the Kazakhs in their republican Communist Party (Alexandrov 1999). The events of June 1989 in Tbilisi provided an opening for the Kazakhs, as protests and heavy-handed Soviet repression led to the massacre of 16 protestors by Soviet troops and the wounding of hundreds in an eerie echo of the riots of December 1986 in Alma-Ata. Sensing their opportunity, the Kazakhs (led by Nazarbayev) threatened Moscow with constituting a second (Kazakh) commission to look into the events of 1986 if changes were not made in the structure of the Kazakh SSR's leadership. With Tbilisi burning, Gorbachev quickly acquiesced to the proposed bargain, namely the removal of Kolbin, and – after a suspiciously timed episode of ethnic unrest in the town of Novy Uzen, perhaps stoked by the Kazakh authorities and which began to spread across much of the northern Kazakh SSR (Ro'i 1991b) – Nursultan Nazarbayev became leader of the KPK (Alexandrov 1999).[6]

Nazarbayev's tenure as head of the KPK, the highest position in the Kazakh SSR, was soon superseded by an even more important post, as the waves of change across the Soviet Union rolled towards representative democracy and greater civic participation in politics (Olcott 1995). In this atmosphere, the Kazakh Supreme Soviet elected Nazarbayev to the newly created post of President of the Kazakh SSR on 24 April 1990; as the Ministry of Information and Communication of independent Kazakhstan was to declare years later (Ministry of Information and Communication 2010), the realization that the Communist Party in both Kazakhstan and across the Soviet Union was losing its grip on power – in many ways loosened deliberately by policies of glasnost in other ways going far beyond what Mikhail Gorbachev had imagined – required an additional post at the top of the state apparatus to defend the sovereignty of the region. For Nazarbayev, this post had the added bonus of allowing him to "remain at the top of the power structure" (Nurumov and Vashchanka 2019:222), an important position to be in as more and more sovereignty was being devolved at the level of the republic. Indeed, just two months later, the Russian Soviet Federative Socialist Republic (RSFSR) adopted a declaration on state sovereignty, setting in motion the adoption of similar initiatives by other republics and culminating in the Kazakh SSR issuing a similar declaration in October 1990. This assertion of sovereignty recognized that the centrifugal forces within the USSR were accelerating (Clemens 1993) and the document emphasized the voluntary nature of the Union (thus allowing for secession). Also included in the document was a compromise approach to ethnic issues, the outcome of lengthy discussions among leaders, which put Kazakhs as first among equals in "their" SSR but respected the equal rights of all ethnicities (Elliot 1993).

At the same time as the push for state sovereignty was taking place, draft amendments to the constitution of the republic were passed in November 1990, which streamlined the executive branch by eliminating Vice-Chairs and linked power within the republic formally to the President (Nurumov and Vashchanka 2019). Similar moves were taking place throughout the Soviet Union, building momentum for a much looser association of states than the strict centre-periphery model which had existed since the earliest days of the Bolsheviks but guaranteeing that the prevailing elites could maintain their power. Indeed, moving the USSR towards complete dissolution was not necessarily the goal of Nazarbayev or other Central Asian and Caucasus leaders (with the exception of Georgia): indeed, there were considerable perks to being the head of a republic within the USSR, especially if there was to be a combination of great autonomy (as Kunaev had during the Brezhnev years) and economic subsidization from Moscow. In short, Nazarbayev and many of his other compatriots looked to have the best of both worlds, security within the Soviet system but with autonomy to run their republics as they saw fit. In this sense, it was an analogue to what was happening in the economy at the time, namely the so-called spontaneous managerial privatizations, whereby state-owned enterprise managers carved up state assets for themselves, generating incipient property rights in a system where the assets were being provided by the coercion of the state rather than from the marketplace (Johnson and Kroll 1991). Applied to the political sphere, these spontaneous privatizations were similar to what the late Soviet era meant for republic leaders, as the Soviet system coerced political power from its citizens, creating an overweening apparatus for the benefit of elites, and providing the power and spoils for republic leaders. Republic leaders then used this existing political system for their own benefit within the borders of their republics, much as managers used their own factories as rent generators.

It was this reality which caused many a leader not from Ukraine, the Baltic states, or Georgia to resist the "Slavic" accords being hammered out throughout 1991 which attempted to minimize the role of the Union in its entirety; no Union meant no spoils and an uncertain future, and only with a strong Union apparatus could very autonomous leaders thrive in their own backyards (at least until their own internal political institutions were functioning). In March 1991, an all-union referendum on the future of the Soviet Union showed this very tendency, as the question on the ballot – for a renewed Soviet Union of sovereign republics – was overwhelmingly approved by 76 per cent of voters across the USSR (Austin 1996). Perhaps cognizant of the benefits that benign neglect would bring to them, the inhabitants of the Kazakh SSR were on the whole even more enthusiastic than other republics, with a turnout of 88 per cent of the population and an overwhelming 94 per cent of citizens voting "yes" to preserve the Union (Gleason 1997). However, as White and Hill (1996:153) note, "events over the next few months, partly in consequence of that referendum, made the exercise redundant," as the hardliners in Moscow launched the August coup precisely to avoid any loosening of the Kremlin's reins over its colonial territories. Thus, while the leaders and their subjects in Central Asia and other parts of the USSR were in favour of greater autonomy but preserving the Union, nostalgic communists in Moscow were in favour of recentralizing power in the Kremlin. It was perhaps ironic that this tug of war between "autonomy within the Union" versus "no autonomy within the Union" would result in "no Union at all."[7]

While the Central Asian republics were "amenable to continuing a great degree of dependence on the USSR," and in fact supported the framework of the March referendum, this trajectory was "broken by the August 1991 military *putsch* in Moscow" (Slipchenko 1997:116). Sensing that autonomy could only come via the removal of Mikhail Gorbachev, his office, and, indeed, the entire central apparatus of the Soviet Union, the Slavic trio of Russia, Belarus, and Ukraine sought to dissolve the ties that bound them. Much of this was due to the recognition that the Central Asian republics were acting precisely in ways that would further their own interests: as Wilson (2017) comments in the context of Boris Yeltsin, there was widespread sentiment among the Russian reformers that the non-Russian (and, in practice, non-Slavic) republics were more of a burden to Russia than anything else. This desire for greater autonomy but less involvement with the poorer republics to the east led the Slavic troika to draw up and sign the Belovezh (Minsk) Accords in December 1991, the defining document in dissolving the Soviet Union. Coming on the heels of votes on independence held in the Soviet Union in the previous months – the Baltic states had already voted in favour before the August coup, while Armenia voted in favour afterwards and the Ukrainians voted by 92 per cent in favour of independence just one week previously – the Belovezh Accords declared that the Soviet Union had ceased to exist and that the three signatories had withdrawn from the Union, setting up instead a "Commonwealth of Independent States" (CIS; see Libman and Vinokurov 2012).

The month of December 1991 was a fraught one for the region rapidly becoming known as Kazakhstan and its leader, Nursultan Nazarbayev. The fait accompli of the Belovezh Accords presented a challenge, as Kazakhstan was not quite ready for full sovereignty (Slipchenko 1997), but it would soon have no choice in the matter. Throughout 1991, Nazarbayev had been actively involved in designing a new Union treaty (the so-called Novo-Ogaryevsk agreement, which would have created a confederation of sovereign states) and, after the August coup, was pushing hard for formalizing economic relations among the separating republics. According to Smith (2016), Nazarbayev was committed to a new confederate Union treaty as late as 6 December 1991, two days before Russia, Belarus, and Ukraine formally withdrew from the USSR; however, Smith (2016:32) also notes that Nazarbayev was not naïve about the way in which the tide had turned:

> Nazarbayev was not a mere observer in this process, he was actively seeking to not only preserve some kind of union, but to shape it to his republic's own advantage, securing greater rights but also a coordinated economic system which he saw as absolutely necessary for the future prosperity of all of the republics. At the same time as supporting Gorbachev's project, however, Nazarbayev hedged his bets by paying careful attention to relations with the RSFSR and its President Boris Yeltsin … he also worked to develop bilateral relations between Kazakhstan and Russia. Nazarbayev and Yeltsin met in Almaty on August 16–17, 1991, just two days before the coup began. Following this meeting they issued a joint statement of cooperation which included an early commitment to the principle of territorial integrity.

Domestically, Nazarbayev cleaved closely to the Soviet political institutional heritage, even as referendums were being held and more popular (and direct) participation in politics was opening up. Nowhere was this more evident than the first popular presidential election in Kazakhstan, announced in October 1991 and scheduled to be held on 1 December. It is important to recall that Nazarbayev was in his post after being selected by the Supreme Soviet, not because of a popular election; as Nurumov and Vashchanka (2019) note, this meant that Nazarbayev could have been removed by the legislature that elected him, and thus a popular electoral victory would make him much harder to dislodge. At the same time, in a bid to bolster his victory – and also dictated by the fact that the Soviet Union was falling apart – a deliberately short time frame was put in place between the announcement of the election and the election itself (in hindsight, waiting any longer for the election would have meant that the election would have taken place already after the USSR ceased to exist). This tactic would be used by Nazarbayev several times during his tenure, as short electioneering campaigns are advantageous for the party in power, which benefits from the state apparatus and all that comes with it (Kurtov 2007).

With the date for an election set, Nazarbayev set about whipping up support across the soon-to-be country at the same time as others had the same idea; in fact, even before the election was announced, one of the nascent political institutions of democracy was emerging, namely the political party.

Already in 1990, several parties were being formed, including the Sotsial-demokraticheskaya partiya Kazakhstana (Social Democratic Party of Kazakhstan), a party that drew its support almost exclusively from the intelligentsia in Alma-Ata, and the Natsional-demokraticheskaya partiya "Zheltoksan" (Zheltoqsan National Democratic Party), led by Khozen Murzakhmetov, a party formed from the December 1986 protests but with an explicitly nationalist and independence-minded agenda (Olcott 1990). Other parties attempted to link specifically to Kazakhstan's past, most prominently the Alash party, which was deliberately named as a harkening back to the Alash Orda movement of the early 20th century, focusing on continuity and national revival through Islam (Babak 2004); similarly, the Azat movement was overtly nationalist, focusing on the "decolonization" of Kazakhstan and supporting the supremacy of the Kazakh language and culture (Abdelal 2003). As a backlash against this growing Kazakh nationalism, a Russian ethnic party was also formed, named Edintsvo (Unity) but with an idiosyncratic (Russian) idea of unity which called for "strikes, rallies, and civil disobedience" if Russian was not retained as a state language (Alexandrov 1999:25).

Within this churning of political organizations, by late 1991 four political parties had been officially registered with the authorities (Karmazina 2008), the first of which was the Sotsialisticheskaya partiya Kazakhstana (SPK – Socialist Party of Kazakhstan) in September 1991, followed by the Respublikanskaya partiya Kazakhstana (RPK – Republican Party of Kazakhstan, also in September 1991), the People's Congress of Kazakhstan (NKK – Narodnii Congres Kazakhstana, in October 1991, incorporating the Nevada-Semipalatinsk movement and regarded by Nazarbayev as a possible vehicle for his own ambitions), and the KPK, also in October 1991 but declared illegal at the end of the year and not legalized again until 1993). Many of the parties which had been formed one year earlier remained unregistered, but this did not mean that they were not interested in contesting the election. In fact, the opposition party Zheltoqsan, and its candidate Hasen Kozhakhmetov, was the main rival to Nazarbayev for this historic first election, but, officially, the party was unable to secure the necessary 100,000 signatures to appear on the ballot (Olcott 1995). Unofficially, in what can be seen as a precedent for subsequent elections in the country, there were substantial allegations by Kozhakhmetov that the government took measures to prevent any opposition (Akkuly 2009), including a police raid during which 40,000 signatures mysteriously disappeared (Kurtov 2007). With Zheltoqsan sidelined as an effective force, and the only other viable candidate (Olzhas Suleimenov of the Nevada-Semipalatinsk movement and the officially registered NKK) withdrawing from the race, Nazarbayev ran unopposed in the first presidential election in the history of Kazakhstan, garnering a whopping 98.78 per cent of the vote (Yang 2020).

Oddly enough, with Belarus, Russia, and Ukraine withdrawing from the Union by 12 December 1991, President-elect Nazarbayev was actually the leader of the Soviet Union for four days until Kazakhstan withdrew on 16 December 1991 (the last republic to leave the USSR). But once the Soviet Union was officially disbanded on 26 December 1991, after the last Soviet leader Mikhail Gorbachev had resigned on Christmas Day, and after all the declarations of sovereignty and independence had been proclaimed, the hard work of building political institutions from scratch was to begin in earnest. As noted, Nazarbayev had been laying the groundwork for his own reign over a sovereign and independent Kazakhstan, but he was also forward-looking enough to consider the structure of Kazakhstan's political institutions in a post-Soviet world. Indeed, despite having the collapse of the USSR thrust upon him, Nazarbayev was to "emerge as the central figure responsible for guiding Kazakhstan through its incipient years of independence" (Isaacs 2010a:438).

Kazakh Political Institution 1: A Constitutional Basis

The first issue that Kazakhstan faced was defining its foundational document, a constitution, which literally set out the rules of the political order within the country, as well as its political institutions (specific institutions such as the executive and the legislature are dealt with in more detail below, however). As with every other post-Soviet state, in theory the Soviet constitution of 1977 (the so-called Brezhnev Constitution) was still in force, even though it had ceased to have a territory to be enforced on since 16 December 1991. More importantly for the development of a post-Soviet state, the reliance on the Soviet constitution meant that new institutions were operating under a document which adhered to the idea of "democratic centralism," but which professed fealty to socialist law and which had the Communist Party as the sole representative of the people. It was understood by political elites quite early on in the transition that this document needed to be replaced, in order better to reflect realities on the ground in the newly independent country, and, even before Kazakhstan became independent, competing groups had been studying a reform of the constitution. Nazarbayev established a commission as early as December 1990 to fashion a new constitution (with little progress), while a parallel process within the Supreme Soviet also explored alternatives to the 1977 document; as Anderson (1997:302) mentions, "both groups studied the constitutions of foreign states, drew in advisers from other CIS countries and consulted widely with international groups such as Amnesty International" and even had a roundtable discussion in May 1991 to discuss the draft which came out of these processes. However, the drafts which had been in discussion, while slowly moving away from the Soviet legal principles of the Brezhnev Constitution, were still predicated on Kazakhstan remaining a part of a country which no longer existed by late 1991 (the USSR), and thus the earlier drafts were for the most part discarded in favour of a necessarily different approach (Kanter 1993).

After independence, and with the imperative of not only defining the Kazakh state's *raison d'être* but also its entire political system, Nazarbayev continued to be deeply involved in drawing up the new constitution. Appointing a new working commission in 1992 to complete the process, he stressed that the new document should reflect a strong executive in order to successfully navigate the economic challenges that the country faced after its internal linkages to Russia and other Central Asian states suddenly became external ones (see Chapter 6). As Partlett (2012:231) notes, "Nazarbayev was not a proponent of pluralistic electoral democracy. Instead, he envisioned the president as the manager of political life and valued economic reform before democratic reform." This meant that Nazarbayev, as well as others in the pre-independence elite, believed that it would be prudent to eschew experimentation in the political system and to focus first and foremost on the overall transformation; in their eyes, attempting to move towards a suddenly open and pluralistic political system would lead to avoidable delays in the country's transition, threatening the work already being done by Nazarbayev in consolidating power for reform (and other, less savoury, goals – see below). Olcott (2010:95) echoes this sentiment, stating that, even in the early 1990s, "the ruling elite set strict barriers on those engaged in independent political actions," believing that this would set the stage for gridlock and confusion when bold initiatives were needed.

In addition to concentrating power to be able to push through economic reforms, a key goal of Nazarbayev with regard to the constitution was to build the new country as a functioning and effective state with a clearly delineated territory, "ensuring that Kazakhstan actually remains Kazakhstan" (Bremmer and Welt 1996:179). This was no passive goal, as, despite the out-migration of Russians in the 1980s, at independence, only 39.7 per cent of the population of Kazakhstan was actually Kazakh, with Russians comprising 37.8 per cent and other ethnic minorities making up the remaining 22.5 per cent (including 5.4 per cent Ukrainians and 5.8 per cent Germans, according to the 1989 Soviet census). This ethnic imbalance generated two specific issues with regard to creating a Kazakh state and, by extension, codifying it into a constitution: first, the problem of territory, as Russia was hinting even before independence that it had designs on bringing Russian speakers into the Russian Federation proper (i.e. not by having them migrate but by annexing Kazakh land); and second, the problem of a national language, defining how the functions of state would be communicated.

On the point of territorial integrity, as mentioned earlier, even before the Soviet Union fell apart, Russian President Boris Yeltsin had expressed his thoughts on Kazakhstan's northern territories. In particular, Yeltsin hinted that Kazakhstan's borders might need to be "revised," given the preponderance of Russians in its north, moving the territories around Tselinograd back under Russian control (Smith 2016).[8] This view, that Russians outside of Russia needed to have their lands incorporated into Russia proper, was a popular one before the collapse of the Soviet Union (and beyond), with even former dissident Alexander Solzhenitsyn arguing that Kazakhstan was not a valid state because its borders included "Russian provinces" (Solzhenitsyn

1995). Fighting this Russian irredentism, Kazakh historiographers relied on the sort of analysis we utilized in Chapter 2, focusing on the historical Kazakh claims on the lands which comprised the new country. In particular, the Kazakh state apparatus enlisted academics to trace the ancestral lands of Kazakh nomads back several centuries in order to show a more concrete claim to all of the territories of independent Kazakhstan than the colonizers had, "establishing the illegality of previous annexation/conquest of Kazakh lands" (Diener 2002:639). Unfortunately, the historiography approach made little difference in the face of waves of Russian nationalism – including a movement in 1999 to declare a Russian puppet "Republic of Altay" in Eastern Kazakhstan, one which was quickly suppressed by the authorities (Zardykhan 2004) – and the territorial issue has continued to be utilized by Russian politicians as a cudgel with which to threaten Kazakhstan (with a land border between Russia and Kazakhstan stretching for more than 7,000 kilometres, it is in Russia's best interest to keep this threat in its pocket).

In the end, the only real resolution of Kazakhstan's territorial integrity, at least during the early years of transition, came about from international law (i.e. that the borders were recognized as binding in the treaty dissolving the Soviet Union) and the fact that Boris Yeltsin (realizing his flirtation with redrawing the map of Kazakhstan was a blunder) abandoned any Russian claims to the northern territories (Hanks 1998). The example of Yugoslavia was also perhaps instructive, as Nazarbayev himself warned that the consequences of redrawing Soviet borders would lead to a situation worse than the bloodshed which accompanied Yugoslavia's collapse (Nazarbayev 1991). But a more tangible assertion of Kazakhstan's control over the territories also came from the very public move of the capital from Almaty in the south to Astana in the north, within the Akmola region, one of the areas which Russian nationalists continue to pine for. As Diener (2002:644) notes,

> The relocation of Kazakhstan's capital to Astana from the historically Russian-dominated Almaty, however, suggests a firm belief that history alone will not avert a territorial loss. If possession is in fact nine-tenths of the law, then the positioning of the Kazakh capital in the middle of the disputed territory and the consequent shift of ethnic Kazakhs to the region will only strengthen the state's assertions of territorial integrity.

Another lever was included in the fashioning of the country's first constitution to attempt to neutralize any sectarian or ethnic unrest delineated by geographical boundaries: the creation of Kazakhstan as a unitary state (Busygina et al. 2018). While other countries emerging from communism (notably Russia but also Czechoslovakia and, infamously, Yugoslavia) attempted to institute a federalist structure, giving some measure of political and fiscal power to various regions, Kazakhstan stayed in line with the vast majority of transitioning economies in elevating the centre above all: as

Melvin (2001:165) notes, "rather than accommodating regional interests and identities, a powerful centralizing impulse developed in Central Asia that led to the construction of formally strong unitary states," with Kazakhstan being the most developed in terms of its administrative apparatus. This unitary nature was meant to preclude any regions developing their own ethnic identity and institutions (i.e. so as to make the Russian north distinct from the Kazakh south): as Kukusheva et al. (2019: 933) points out, "the ethnic groups of Kazakhstan are united into one political entity of the Republic of Kazakhstan and do not have the right to act as a separate international legal entity." This mechanism to keep Kazakhstan's borders intact was enshrined in the new constitution, with "republic interests placed above regional ones" (Olcott 2010:96). The centralization of powers even encompassed religion, again, in a nod towards forestalling breakaway regions, directed at the schism between Orthodox Russians and Muslim Kazakhs, as the constitutions declared Kazakhstan to be a secular state.[9]

The second point regarding the creation of a state/administrative apparatus in an independent Kazakhstan was somewhat more problematic than the issue of borders, as it was less about clearly delineated territory – lines which could be drawn on a map and had a definite beginning and end – and more about the hazy mélange of languages which existed in the country. A large debate ensued before the end of the Soviet Union on the role of language in all the Central Asian republics (Anderson 1997), as language was somewhat entwined with the demographic challenges that the country faced. More importantly, as John Searle (2005) has noted, language is the "ur-institution," the institution which colours how we discuss, conceptualize, and frame all other institutions within a country (and how we conceptualize the animating framework of these institutions, through words such as "freedom," "constraints," and "responsibilities" and how they are defined). Despite the fact that the Kazakhs were an ethnic minority in their own country at independence, the authorities and Nazarbayev in particular pushed for a process of Kazakh ethno-nationalization and laid the groundwork for the reality that an independent Kazakhstan was meant to be for Kazakhs, eschewing a "Kazakhstani" identity for a "Kazakh" one (Ó Beacháin and Kevlihan 2013).

Diener (2016) notes that this push for "Kazakhization" was done in an inclusive (if awkward) manner but showed up perhaps nowhere more prominently than in the language solution which was hit upon in the run-up to the codification of the new constitution. In 1989, Kazakh was proclaimed the official language of the republic, while Russian was promoted as the language of "inter-ethnic communication," meaning that Kazakhs and Russians were encouraged to speak to each other in Russian (although, as a Kazakh writer has noted, the state should have had no right to intervene in people's private conversations; see Anderson 1997). In an early draft of the country's Declaration of Sovereignty from 1990, this distinction was emphasized by noting that Kazakh was the "state" language while Russian was an "official" language (Lee 2004), a distinction which was scrubbed from the final document in favour of silence (Fierman 1998). In reality, while Nazarbayev was trying to create a strong state, the only way in which this could be achieved was by treating the issue of language in a deliberately vague manner, leaving the definition of a "state" versus an "inter-ethnic" or "official" language ambiguous and open to interpretation (Schatz 2000a) – as Lee (2004) notes, even the original Law on Language(s) left vast areas unsettled, as the name of the law in Russian was in plural but in Kazakh it was singular (i.e. language versus languages). The only unambiguous clause was entirely self-serving for Nazarbayev, and that was Article 114 of the final constitution which required the President of Kazakhstan to speak Kazakh (Ó Beacháin and Kevlihan 2013). Apart from this one measure, the delicate compromise in pursuit of larger goals thus attempted to create a multicultural state for Russians, making any Russian irredentist claims farcical while soliciting their buy-in during the crucial early days of independence (Cheskin and Kachuyevski 2019), and at the same time also ensuring that Kazakhstan became the homeland for, of, and by Kazakhs (Holm-Hansen 1999).

What do these issues, of territory and language, have to do with the foundational legal document of the country's political system? With the Kazakhs a minority in their own country, there was a worry (which appeared manifestly justified, given what was happening in Nagorno-Karabakh, Abkhazia, Tajikistan, Trans-Dniester, and Yugoslavia) that a weak political system could lead to ethnic strife and a collapse of the country into warring factions, with Kazakhstan as an "ethnic tinderbox" (Schatz 2000b:71). This was also part of the delicate balancing act which Kazakh policymakers faced, as the first article of the 1993 constitution was to note that the republic itself was "the expression of the Kazakh nation in the form of the state," meaning that "Kazakhs were accorded a specific and privileged status" (Peyrouse 2007:485). This precise formulation was due not just to the raw ratio of Russians to Kazakhs, where Russians settled within Kazakhstan, or what language people spoke, but also about the access to the levers of power, the very issue which was tearing other newly independent countries apart.

As Elliott (1993:1247) notes, under the Soviet Union,

> Kazakhs were allowed to occupy many government positions, but they had little power, as the real power was in the hands of the party organisation [*sic*] controlled from Moscow. With independence and the disappearance of the party, these jobs have become more important.

Melvin (1993:208) makes a similar point, stressing that

> under the Soviet system, [Russians] had dominated political and economic life in the republic. Although the highest political positions were occupied by ethnic Kazakhs, the personnel in these positions were always heavily Russified and normally shadowed by a European –

> usually an ethnic Russian – in the number two position. Industry was also dominated by the European population, as were most of the cities in the republic.[10]

Theorists such as Khazanov (1995) also argue that the fact that Russians held the commanding positions within the economy was going to be a prime motivator in ethnic grievances in Kazakhstan, generating animosity towards Russians and instability going forward.

However, arguing against the likelihood of such internecine conflicts was the reality that ethnicity was not the only factor causing fractionalization in the new country. Lee (2004:103) correctly notes that, at the onset of independence, Kazakh society was

> stratified by residence as well as the traditional clan system. According to the stratification by residence, there was discord even among Kazakhs themselves; for instance, between those in urban residence who mostly speak Russian with a poor command of Kazakh and those in rural residence who usually speak Kazakh with a poor knowledge of Russian.

Similarly, Kolossov (1999) cites marriage statistics to show that, by the 1980s, a full 20 per cent of Kazakh marriages were ethnically mixed, making it more difficult to put people into one category or another. In any event, the worries about ethnic conflict were highly prevalent at independence, making another case for structuring a constitution which focused more on the executive than the legislature – and then using that executive to promote a "supra-ethnic" identity, based on patriotism, focused on supporting the Kazakh state (Kolstø 1996).

Understanding the fears, omnipresent in the early 1990s, about loss of territory, the need to build a national character, and avoiding the bloody strife engulfing the transition space, make the move towards a strong administrative state somewhat justifiable, at least in terms of creating a "caretaker state" for economic reforms. Were it that all the goals of the Kazakh elite were so noble, however, as more prosaic and nakedly political objectives were also at play in 1992 and 1993. Among these, the most powerful was the desire to use the constitution as a mechanism to enshrine the prerogatives of the existing elite and to avoid a fate similar to that which had already befallen Central and Eastern European leaders. From the unthinkable execution of the deposed Romanian dictator Nicolae Ceausescu and his wife to the fairly milquetoast removal of the communists in Czechoslovakia and Poland, around the former Warsaw Pact, the last thing that Nazarbayev or any of the communist holdovers wanted was a reckoning on their complicity in the crimes of communism or even just their removal in favour of a fresh start. While the working groups charged with drafting the constitution were notable for their youth (Kanter 1993), the process of creating new political institutions also allowed for the entry into politics of established "clan notables" in addition to Nazarbayev himself, allowing the parliamentarians of the new Kazakhstan – already elites in regional politics – to "gain access to state resources" (Collins 2004:257). Part of this process of entrenchment was due to the fact that the constitution and the electoral process did not work in tandem, meaning that the members elected to the Supreme Soviet of the Kazakh SSR in 1990 not only oversaw the process of drafting a new constitution but were in power as the country became independent and operated under this new constitution. Rather than dissolving the parliamentary mechanism which was designed for a region of a country that no longer existed and allowing a new parliamentary elite to helm the constitutional reforms, the existing elites oversaw the process themselves. Perhaps not surprisingly, this led to remarkable continuity in the composition of political elites: as Murphy (2006) shows in an exhaustive empirical analysis, by 1995, at least 90 per cent of the Kazakh elite was drawn from those who had been members of the Communist Party, while the business elite had both business experience and large amounts of time spent in government employ. Put simply, the constitution did not facilitate clearing house from the past, but instead allowed the pre-transition elite to continue unmolested.

The sum of all these political objectives meant that "the Constitution of 1993 represented a certain compromise between old and modern times and did not correspond to all of the demands of an independent Kazakhstan" (Sayabayev 2016:96). While it was passed by an overwhelming majority in the Kazakh parliament on 28 January 1993, the compromises which had to be made during the drafting process to reach that point did not fully satisfy any actors in the newly independent nation. Indeed, almost from the moment it was passed, Nazarbayev was undertaking preparations to create a more permanent and even more centralizing document; the worry, as during the earlier constitutional working groups, was that the constitution as formulated would lead to instability and far too many legal and political "collisions" which required an even stronger hand to resolve (Nurumov and Vashchanka 2019). In reality, as in many other post-communist transitioning economies (Hartwell 2016), the constitution's provisions on the development of political institutions provided for a balance of power between parliamentary mechanisms (undergoing a cosmetic change from being called the Supreme Soviet to its new name as the Supreme Council) and the President (more on this below). While, on paper, this created an admirable set of checks and balances within a semi-presidential system, in practice, this meant that there were now two power poles of politicians, "manifest[ing] institutional competition between the president and the parliament" (Isaacs 2010b:11). In this situation, as in Russia during the same period (and as was to be seen Ukraine), Nazarbayev's power was less than complete, with parliamentarians – as already noted, pre-independence elites in their own right – attempting to take an active role in setting the policies of the nation.

The new constitution of 1995 came about after a deadlock in late 1993 between Nazarbayev and the parliament (and in particular Speaker Sergei Abdildin) regarding the economic reforms which Kazakhstan needed, ironically vindicating the worries of Nazarbayev that reform would stall without strong guidance. Adhering to the letter of the law (although patently not its spirit), Nazarbayev argued in late 1993 that the Supreme Council was not a democratically elected body of Kazakhstan (since it had been elected under the Kazakh SSR), and – with no power of his own to dissolve the parliament – he suggested vociferously that the Supreme Council should "voluntarily" resign en masse. On the legal point, Nazarbayev was probably correct, as the continuing parliamentary body should have been dissolved upon independence, but this legal nicety was subsumed under an attempt to centralize further, and the Council did actually resign in December 1993 (Cummings 2005). However, on its way out, the Supreme Council passed a special decree giving Nazarbayev "extraordinary" powers, including the right "to declare a state of emergency, initiate referendums, and appoint personnel" (Ibadildin and Pisareva 2020:105).[11] With the policies he had coveted in place, the next year and a half witnessed a series of crises regarding a replacement parliament – including a call for and the holding of new elections to the parliament in early 1994, a seating of the parliament, and then a further dissolution of the parliament in 1995 on legal grounds (see below) – creating an opening for a new constitution to be passed to cement the emergency laws that had allowed Nazarbayev to rule almost exclusively by decree.

With parliament dissolved and no successor in place, Nazarbayev took his case directly to the Kazakh people. After three short months of preparation (Mishra 2008) and relying only on the President and a small group of close associates (Cummings 2005), a new draft of the constitution was submitted to and approved by popular referendum in August 1995. The 1995 constitution created a "super-presidential" system in Kazakhstan (Nurumov and Vashchanka 2019), taking the "extraordinary" lawmaking powers that had been granted to the executive by the outgoing Supreme Council in 1993 and codifying them into law. The differences between the 1993 and 1995 documents were stark: while the 1993 constitution envisioned checks and balance, the 1995 constitution eschewed these by elevating the President outside of the normal political process, making the office-holder not only the head of state but charging him or her with the typically modest role of "guarantor of the people's unity and of state power" (cited in Cummings 2005). As a parliament would only interfere with such lofty goals (as they are wont to do), the constitution made sure that it "expanded presidential power at the expense of the legislature, which became a largely consultative body, with legislation initiated by the president" (Olcott 2010: 111–112). Part of this process included codifying the major overhaul of parliament which Nazarbayev had begun after dissolving the body in 1993, dividing it into two houses (the Majilis and the Senate) and slimming it down considerably (from the 360 seats of the communist era to 177 seats in total), including an allowance for appointments by the President in the upper house (Cummings 2005). Perhaps underscoring how the Kazakh nation had moved on to more pressing things, since the President was guaranteeing the people's unity, the ethnicity issue was quickly resolved in the 1995 constitution by allowing for the use of Russian and Kazakh in state and local official dealings (Zardykhan 2004).

As of the writing of this book, the 1995 constitution continues to remain in force in Kazakhstan, although its form is somewhat unrecognizable from what it was upon its approval in a popular referendum in 1995. In particular, the constitution has been amended six times since then (in 1998, 2007, 2011, 2017, 2019, and 2022), in many different ways, ranging from the merely cosmetic – the amendment in 2019 changed the name of Astana to Nur-Sultan – to the easily predicted – the 2007 amendments removed term limits for the first President of the republic, thus allowing Nazarbayev to stay in power as long as he wanted (Yang 2020) – to the massively consequential, as in 2017, where there was an attempt to effect far-reaching changes to the Kazakh political system and a retreat from super-presidentialism (see below). In each case, however, the constitution has been less of a codification of the fundamental values and rules of the game of the Kazakh republic but instead has been a reflection of political whims and expediency; in this sense, the constitution has been a "living document," tossing aside institutional mechanisms when they did not suit the ruling party and changing them frequently in pursuit of short-term goals. While constitutional processes are not above normal cultural and sociopolitical processes within a country, being born into a specific milieu which determines the constitution's shape (Thornhill 2017), there is an anticipation that constitutions concern the higher orders of the state and, crucially, which institutions matter, and which are limited (Ginsburg 2010). As the reality in Kazakhstan was that the executive began to matter more and more, the constitution's importance in the development of Kazakhstan's political institutions was subordinated to institutional change rather than vice versa.

Kazakh Political Institution 2: Elections and Political Parties

Given the role of the constitution as a mirror rather than a rulebook, we thus turn our attention to the other political institutions of the Kazakh transformation, starting with elections and their main actors, political parties. Elections are the mechanism of all forms of democracy, in that they are discrete events which choose a country's leadership across administrative levels, with their operation governed both by constitutional frameworks and more mundane operational regulations. Elections also have immense importance for the setting of economic policy (as I tell my advanced macroeconomics class every year, fiscal policy is what we fight about in a democracy) in the short term; elections can also set the trajectory of a country for the longer term, as well, by having chosen governments enact institution-changing policies which then rearrange the rules of the game.[12] We have already touched upon elections in general with regard to the executive, and those with even a passing acquaintance of Kazakhstan know that Nazarbayev was in power for many years, elected in the Soviet way with amazing turnout and implausibly high majorities (in 2015, for example, after 24 years in office, when most polities would be tired of their leaders, Nazarbayev "won" 97.7 per cent of the vote). But there is much more to the institutional development of Kazakhstan's political apparatus than the ceremonial re-anointing of Nazarbayev, including the development of legislative and executive political parties and the way in which they crafted their message to the people.

A large literature explores why authoritarian countries go through the charade of elections and why they seek to legitimize their rule in a way which is obviously fraudulent (see, for example, Tolstrup 2015 or Von Soest and Grauvogel 2017). In the case of Kazakhstan, it appears that this was not the intent from the outset: as Olcott (2010:2) notes, part of the move towards independent political institutions included an elite that "at least flirted with the idea of a transition to democracy," a path that could have resulted in a more liberal democracy "if its leaders had only shown the will to discipline themselves." In the heady days of 1992 and 1993, however, the lack of restraint had not yet become apparent, and it appeared that the new country would be on the road to experimentation with various political mechanisms, including using elections as a valid method for settling political differences.

As noted above, elections pre-dated Kazakhstan's independence, with the Supreme Soviet being elected by territorial district vote in 1990, although the elections were both incredibly messy (Bowyer 2008 notes that there were over 2,000 candidates for the 360 seats in the Soviet) and somewhat preordained (even though these were the first contested elections since 1925, the Communist Party retained 342 of the 360 seats; see Olcott 1995). It was not until Nazarbayev's push to have the Supreme Council dissolve itself in 1993 that independent Kazakhstan was to have its first elections under a democratic regime (unburdened by being part of a foreign assembly), with the (now-reduced) parliamentary elections occurring in March 1994. In theory, these elections should have returned a diverse group of new lawmakers to the Supreme Council, furthering political diversity and allowing for competitive pressures to create, if not better policies, then at least more representative ones. Like Ukraine (Hartwell 2016), Kazakhstan had kept a "holdover" parliament in place for far too long (Bowyer 2008) and would need fresh initiatives in order to press ahead with its transformation.

A digression is necessary here before we discuss the 1994 elections and the ones that followed. While elections are the mechanisms of democracy, political parties are the vehicles, and elections cannot be discussed without understanding the participants. A quite recent invention in human history, political parties are merely a collective action and organizational response to the difficulties inherent in getting oneself elected, Indeed, if elections were ever presented as an example of a marketplace, the sheer amount of "failures" in political markets – asymmetrical information, start-up costs, externalities, spatial and other transaction costs – would lead to Econ 1 students around the world baying for government intervention to fix these massive "market failures."[13] Instead, as with nearly every other "market failure" that has ever existed, an organizational and institutional work-around has been found to mitigate these issues, and this is the political party. Of course, in a world of second-best solutions, political parties create their own problems (famously, the American Founding Fathers warned against "factions" that could harm the fledgling republic), and much of the contribution of political parties to democracy in general comes down to how they themselves are organized (Stokes 1999), and this once again is an organizational/institutional (rather than fundamental) issue.

In Kazakhstan, the organizational form of political parties started as theoretically envisioned, as an institutional experiment, with parties designed to both serve as vehicles to help their leaders to attain prominence and as a means to advance ideological and policy goals. However, as in other post-Soviet successor states, the goal of parties soon became inverted, with political parties being organized to support particular personalities and, specifically, to create an administrative apparatus for re-electing the leader rather than opposing him (see, among others, Magaloni and Kricheli 2010). While the concept of a political organization predated the Soviet experiment in Kazakhstan – with the Alash movement being a proto-political party in the years leading up to the Bolshevik Revolution, as noted in Chapter 2 – the first political parties during the waning years of communism were single-issue advocacy organizations. Ranging across the Nevada-Semipalatinsk environmental awareness campaigns, the Zheltoqsan movement, and the mobilization of Russians in the north under the Respublikanskoye obshchestvennoye slavyanskoye dvizheniye (Lad-ROSD – the Republican Official Slavic Association) banner, these early parties were ideological or policy-oriented platforms in search of an organization. Even the parties brought together to contest the presidential election in 1991, including the Zheltoqsan movement (which, as noted, was disqualified from having a candidate stand against Nazarbayev) and the parties allowed to register (the SPK, the RPK, the NKK, and the QKP), were just rough drafts of what the party system would look like under full-fledged democracy, often hastily assembled to provide a particular person with an entrée to politics. With this in mind, the churning of political parties which had begun before the December presidential election was not unexpected, with the Narodno-kooperativnaya (National-Cooperative Party of Kazakhstan) coming to fruition in December 1994, and the Partii vozrozhdeniya Kazakhstana (Party of Revival of Kazakhstan) registering in time for the next presidential election in January 1995 (Karmazina 2008). Existing parties also merged, split, and recombined, with the Grazhdanskoye dvizheniye Kazakhstana "Azat" (Azat Nationalist Party), Zheltoqsan, and the RPK becoming one in 1992 (and promptly splitting again near the end of the year; see Olcott 2010), and the Soyuz promyshlennikov i predprinimateley Kazakhstana (Union of

Industrialists and Entrepreneurs) being formed seemingly to support the president's economic ambitions (Vladimir 2005). Keeping up with the melange of parties which were spawned, died, or were resurrected during this period is far beyond the scope of this book, but the key point to note is that, while interference had already been afoot during the last Soviet elections, there was a glimmer of hope that the formal institution of political parties would result in coherent channels for voters to express their preferences.

Arrayed against the alphabet soup of emerging parties in the early 1990s was another, perhaps more important phenomenon. The Party of National Unity of Kazakhstan (alternately translated as the People's Unity of Kazakhstan Union and known by its Russian name and acronym, Soyuz Narodnoy Edinstvo Kazakhstana – SNEK) was registered in February 1993 and was widely seen as President Nazarbayev's third attempt to secure a political administrative apparatus of support: having failed to keep the socialist bloc together with his desires for rapid economic liberalization and having lost the NKK to Olzhas Suleimenov of the Nevada-Semipalatinsk movement (with the party eventually going into "constructive opposition"), the SNEK remained loyal to the President and was widely regarded as a way for Nazarbayev to attempt to have his wishes enacted through the legislature (Curtis 2003; del Sordi 2016a). As Magaloni and Kricheli (2010) noted in a broad survey of the reasons why authoritarians utilize political parties, Nazarbayev also could have been attempting to create a formal apparatus to co-opt the emerging elites in Kazakhstan (especially those from rival parties or who were starting to benefit from economic reform) while at the same time mobilizing mass support for his initiatives for transformation. It is important to remember, as well, that during 1992 and the beginning of 1993, as Olcott (2010) noted, the flirtation with democracy was in full swing and Nazarbayev had not gone fully authoritarian, and thus a party could have appeared to be an effective hedge against political uncertainty.

With this landscape set, we can now turn back to the 1994 elections, as they were to represent a key point in the development of the balance of power in Kazakhstan (as mentioned above and as we will see); they are also of immense importance in being the first elections to be held under a non-Soviet regime. As part of the changes ordered by Nazarbayev in the wake of the dismissal of the Council in 1993, in addition to the parliament being pared down to 177 seats, a further

> 42 of the 177 deputies were elected on the basis of the so-called presidential list, in which three officially nominated candidates stood in each of the 42 oblasts and the cities of Almaty and Leninsk, with two to be elected in each constituency.
>
> (Anderson 1997:30)

This meant that, in reality, only 135 seats were being contested in the race, a point which was emphasized by international observers (including the

International Foundation for Electoral Systems and the erstwhile Conference for Security and Cooperation in Europe – CSCE) as one of the main issues during the run-up to the elections. In short, while political parties had proliferated and joined forces and gone through different processes of formation, the limiting of the legislature made actual access to the levers of power difficult for the vast majority of parties. Moreover, beyond this point, other irregularities were noted in the actual conduct of the election, and the CSCE was scathing in its post-election report: in particular, it noted that unethical practices such as transporting ballot boxes to voters' homes to get them to vote occurred, as well as rampant arbitrary closing of polling stations, and thus the CSCE refused to certify the elections as acceptable for a member state (CSCE 1994).

The 1994 elections, set up as they were, should have returned a legislature which was amenable to President Nazarbayev's wishes but, even with the restrictions on competition, the parliament was mostly dominated by "undecided" voters, followed only then by pro-presidential members and, finally, opposition members of parliament (MPs) (Cummings 2005). The former Communist Party, reborn as the SPK, registered as a party at the end of 1991 and still holding the property of the Communist Party of the Kazakh SSR – but not to be confused with the Communist Party of Kazakhstan, which was formed by "ideologically unrepentant deputies and elites" (Isaacs 2022:66) – won 15 per cent of the vote and eight seats. Combined with the NKK and a smattering of communist-affiliated parties, enough votes could be cobbled together to create a stalwart opposition to the President's plans (Isaacs 2010b). In fact, the opposition held together strongly enough to force a vote of no confidence against Nazarbayev's Prime Minister, Sergei Tereshchenko, a staunch supporter of radical economic reform, in May 1994, winning the vote with a lopsided majority of 111 votes to 28; however, since the 1993 constitution had no mechanism for removing a Prime Minister via a vote of no confidence, Tereshchenko remained in place until October, leading disgruntled deputies to form a formal opposition bloc called Otan-Otechestvo (Fatherland in both Kazakh and Russian; see Higashijima 2022).

The continued recalcitrance of the parliament, however (including holding up passage of the budget for 1995), meant that it was not long for the world, and Nazarbayev used a legal manoeuvre to dissolve the body for a second time. In March 1995, Tatyana Kvyatkovskaya, a failed candidate in the 1994 elections (and, notably, a Russian journalist), brought a case before the Constitutional Court which alleged that the elections were unfair because of the way in which the electoral districts were drawn, a Kazakh version of "gerrymandering" that meant that legislators were not representing equally sized constituencies; five days after accepting the case, the court agreed with the plaintiff but gave the solution of annulling the elections, an outcome which Nazarbayev readily agreed with (Kembayev 2011). Demanding the resignation of his government, but then immediately reappointing the Prime Minister by presidential decree, Nazarbayev dissolved the parliament (Olcott

1995) and scheduled elections for a new, Nazarbayev-controlled legislature for December 1995: leaving nothing to chance, "candidates were arbitrarily banned, Russians were underrepresented on the candidate list, and Nazarbayev supporters dominated" (Bremmer and Welt 1996:193). The dissolution of parliament also set in motion a referendum on the extension of the President's term in office to 2000 (it was meant to expire in 1996), and (as noted), a popular referendum was held to approve the new version of the constitution (Kembayev 2011, 2017). Facing the choice of possible political conflict, "most elites agreed to Nazarbayev's demand for power consolidation and weakening of legislative power, not unlike in Russia where Boris Yeltsin was facing similar problems with the Duma" (Ibadildin and Pisareva 2020:105), while the average Kazakh in the street also cast their lot in with the President, who guaranteed stability and a way forward (Kembayev 2011).

The new constitution, guaranteeing substantial powers to the President, made the role of political parties and especially of elections far less important than they had been at the dawn of the republic. In the first instance, presidential elections were now to take a five-year hiatus, meaning that the jockeying for the most powerful post in the country was now also to enter hibernation. Moreover, the concentration of power within the presidency meant that any pretenders to the throne, who were going to use the long run-up to the election as a chance to build a power base to rival Nazarbayev, could also be dealt with before they became too powerful. Instructive is the case of Akezhan Kazhegeldin, Nazarbayev's Prime Minister from 1994 to 1997 (replacing Tereshchenko, who eventually had to resign due to scandal), who made it clear that he wished to stand against Nazarbayev in the elections of 2000. Resigning from his post in October 1997 ostensibly due to health reasons but facing accusations of corruption and misuse of his office (Gleason 1999), Kazhegeldin fled Kazakhstan in 1998 and lived in exile in the United Kingdom; still harbouring ambitions to challenge Nazarbayev in the 2000 elections, he was convicted in absentia of tax evasion and soliciting bribes, thus making him ineligible to register his candidacy (Ibadildin and Pisareva 2020). Instead he became a scathing critic of Kazakhstan's "democracy" (Kazhegeldin 2000), but from the outside.

Kazhegeldin's removal allowed Nazarbayev to bring up the date of the presidential elections from December 2000 to January 1999. The decision was made in October 1998, one day after constitutional amendments had been accepted by the Constitutional Council (replacing the Constitutional Court) which removed age limits for the presidency, increased the President's term from five to seven years (Oka 2009), and allowed the President to serve for more than two terms; these decisions thus allowed Nazarbayev to run again, once he had satisfied the statutory bare minimum for candidacy (Gleason 1999).

With the presidency out of reach, and with the legislature now operating under the 1995 constitution, the role of political parties also began to change immensely. Isaacs (2010b:14) describes the political landscape after the early era of post-Soviet development had ended in Kazakhstan:

> Nazarbayev reacted … by seeking to manage and control the situation to reflect his political interests, which principally was to ensure and consolidate his political rule. It was not permissible to have autonomous parties and groups provoking institutional conflict and proselytizing an alternative discourse, as this created uncertainty and instability for those in power. Therefore, pluralism had to be controlled from above through the creation of a personal political pro-presidential party (as in SNEK), which is illustrative of the personalization of politics in neopatrimonial systems, through cooption and the establishment of patron-client relationships (as in NKK) and through criminalization (as with the KPK [Communist Party]). Informal forms of political relations and behavior were employed to ensure party development from above would succeed whether through electoral manipulation … in ensuring SNEK won the most seats in the legislative elections, or through offering rewards for loyalty.

The political landscape had now irreversibly shifted towards several pro-regime parties who provided legislative cover for the executive branch (ironically, this occurred after Nazarbayev had made a big show in late 1998 of calling for a strengthening of political parties; see Nurumov and Vashchanka 2019). Party fatigue was pervasive among the population, as a poll in 1997 showed that at least 40 per cent of the population distrusted political parties in general (Olcott 2010). Thus began another round of consolidation, as the SNEK first rebranded itself as the Partiya Narodnogo Edinstva Kazakhstana (PNEK – Party of People's Unity of Kazakhstan) for the 1995 parliamentary elections and then merged with several other pro-presidential parties for the 1999 parliamentary elections (Higashijima 2022), forming the Otan party under the leadership of former Prime Minister Tereshchenko.[14] At the same time, in addition to the refusal to allow Kazhegeldin and his party stand for election (Kembayev 2011), and not satisfied with one vehicle for legislative success, two additional pro-government parties were created in time for the 1999 elections, the Grazhdanskaya partiya Kazakhstana (Civic Party of Kazakhstan) and the Agrarian Party (Higashijima 2022). Of the two elections held in 1999 – first the presidential elections in January and the parliamentary elections in October – the regime did unsurprisingly well: Nazarbayev was re-elected President with purportedly 81 per cent of the vote and a turnout of 87 per cent, with his lone opponent, the communist holdout and former Speaker of the Parliament, Serikbolsyn Abdilin, garnering just 11 per cent of the vote. With the OSCE once again noting that the presidential elections were not free and fair (OSCE 1999), an undeterred Nazarbayev roared into the October parliamentary election, with Otan, the Civic Party, and the Agrarnaya partiya Kazakhstana (Agrarian Party) collectively winning 39 of the 77 seats, ironically only the most paper-thin of majorities (50.6 per cent). The communists did not fare any better in parliament, winning just three seats, while the largest bloc apart from the pro-regime lists was the

Federation of Trade Unions (11 seats). Unaffiliated or independent representatives made up the rest, with 23 seats (or the same number as won by Otan).[15]

The period from 1999 to the next presidential and parliamentary elections was characterized by some notable changes, many of which will be dealt with below and in the next chapter. Paramount among these was the ruling by the Constitutional Council that Nazarbayev was realistically only starting his first presidential term as of 1999 (as the previous ones occurred under different constitutional regimes), and thus could run for unlimited terms as the First President of the Republic (Kembayev 2017). Further solidifying presidential power continued to prevent the emergence of political parties as mass organizations, and the use of parties as conduits of support for the ruler rather than as a "civic training ground" meant that politics remained the purview of a select few (Olcott 2010:95). However, the fragmentation of Kazakh elites, starting with the Kazhegeldin affair and accelerating after the 1999 elections, introduced a little more competition into the electoral process; as Ibadildin and Pisareva (2020) note, the elites who amassed wealth during the privatization processes of the 1990s were seeking to enter politics after the 1999 elections and created the first party not openly affiliated with the regime, Democraticheskiy Vibor Kazakhstan (DVK – Democratic Choice of Kazakhstan), which was originally constituted to combat not Nazarbayev but the power of the deputy head of the National Security Committee, Rakhat Aliyev (Olcott 2010). While the "big tent" nature of the party meant that it soon fractured into pieces, including splitting into the Ak Jol (Bright Path) party in 2002, which then broke into another party, Nağyz Ak Jol (True Bright Path) in 2005, it also suffered from political persecution, as some founders of DVK were jailed on the direct orders of Nazarbayev (Ibadildin and Pisareva 2020) while Ak Jol and Nağyz Ak Jol Co chairman (and former Minister of Information) Altynbek Sarsenbayev was assassinated in 2006 (Tipaldou 2021).

Despite the emergence of parties which were actually opposed to the government, the 2004 parliamentary elections – perhaps due to the backlash which actual pluralism engendered – were even less competitive at the formal level. According to Roberts (2012:322),

> initially, the government adopted several seemingly "democratic" changes to the election law. They allowed for political party representatives on the seven-person local election commissions that run the polling stations. They also pledged to post results publicly outside each polling station and to allow observers access to the vote count.

However, other moves from the government counteracted these tentative steps, including voter intimidation, denial of airtime or space to the opposition (Roberts (2012), and denial of full access for observers to the counting process (perhaps trying to avoid a repeat of the tale told in endnote 15). The reality of these moves meant that Otan increased its number of seats in the Majilis from 23 to 42, an unqualified majority, while the Civic Party increased its representation to 11 seats. A new entry on the political scene, the party Asar (literally meaning "all together"), also garnered four seats during the elections; born of social movements focusing on low-income Kazakhs, Asar was perhaps more notable for being led by Nursultan Nazarbayev's daughter Dariga (Dave 2005). The only victory for the opposition was a paltry seat won by Ak Jol, meaning that the government and its supporters held a 76:1 advantage in the Majilis. As noted by the Republican Network of Independent Monitors (RNIM), an NGO based in Almaty which had been observing elections in Kazakhstan since 1999,

> when compared with the results of RNIM's monitoring of the 1999 elections to the Majilis and the 2003 elections to Maslikhats (local councils), this election was by no means a step forward in the development of democracy in Kazakhstan, but rather demonstrated a significant regression.
>
> (RNIM 2004:1)

Roberts (2012) disagrees with this contention somewhat; not in terms of the rampant problems with the elections or the reality that the government kept its thumb on the scale long after it was necessary, but with the assessment that the electoral process was less competitive in 2004 than in 1999. As he notes, in many ways it was *more* competitive, but this competition was behind the scenes and informal rather than playing out in the political marketplace and during the tournament which is an election. In particular, the elite rivalry which had begun after 1999 (and which had created Ak Jol) had intensified at the beginning of the millennium, with various actors stepping forward, ostensibly in support of the President but with their own agendas (del Sordi 2016a). The electoral process in 2004 thus showed the organizational response of these several different elite groups, with their parties nominally allied with the President, coming into their own, with power struggles within clans and even possibly within the Nazarbayev family. Indeed, worries about the presidential daughter becoming too independent – along with anxiety about the Civic Party's growing popularity – led to both the Asar and the Civic Party being merged into Otan in 2006, creating the super-presidential party Nur Otan (Light of the Fatherland) as a successor to Otan (Isaacs 2013). As del Sordi (2016a:86) notes, the creation of Nur Otan "sent a signal to the elites that their political ambitions now had to be channeled through the super party to have any credible chance of success."

Nazarbayev was to enjoy additional electoral success after the relative competition of the 2004 legislative elections, with a new presidential election being scheduled for December 2005 (Nazarbayev's seven-year term was set to end in January 2006, so, for once, the election schedule was not unduly manipulated in a manner to favour the ruling party). In another innovation distinct from earlier elections, Nazarbayev had at least three competitors for the coveted post of President, including the head of Ak Jol, Alikhan Baimenov, a former Minister and head of the Presidential Administration, and – perhaps the most formidable opponent – Zharmakhan Tuyakbai, the nominee of the electoral grouping Za Spravedlivyy Kazakhstan (ZSK – For a Just Kazakhstan). ZSK encompassed a motley crew of parties across the political spectrum, including the Communist Party from the far left and the Nağyz Ak Jol party from the liberal-minded right, but coalesced around a campaign that focused on alleviating poverty and making better use of Kazakhstan's oil riches (Kennedy 2006). Alas, neither the notoriety of his opponents nor the worthiness of their cause could keep Nazarbayev from the top spot again, and he won more than 90 per cent of the vote in an election that once again was marred by irregularities, particularly in respect to the vote-counting procedures (Knox 2008). However, as Kennedy (2006) notes, even widespread fraud, more so than that which Nazarbayev was accused of, would not have resulted in such a lopsided win, and even the control which Nazarbayev exerted over the commanding heights of the economy (see Chapter 6) did not prevent the opposition from making its case; indeed, the real issue might have been the inability of the opposition to mobilize voters, as the call for stability which Nazarbayev continued to campaign on appeared to resonate far more with the Kazakh electorate than taking a chance on the unproven.[16] With Kazakhstan in a much better position economically by the mid-2000s, there was a real sense that Nazarbayev had delivered.

Building on his additional assumed mandate as newly elected President and the creation of Nur Otan, Nazarbayev further augmented his administrative power through a series of amendments to the constitution in 2007. Sold to the public as an attempt to improve both the operations of parliament and the political parties (Kanapyanov and Kaliyev 2015), one of the key provisions was the removal of restrictions on state representatives becoming members of political parties. While apparently a means of strengthening parties as formal organizations (another amendment made it so that an MP who was thrown out of a party would also lose their standing in the Majilis), the practical result was to strengthen support for Nur Otan; in particular, allowing bureaucrats and ministers to join a political party effectively enlisted a whole new cadre of loyalists to ensure consistency at the legislative level with the President's priorities (Isaacs 2013). This change to the constitution also meant that, importantly, the President of the Republic of Kazakhstan was now no longer floating above party politics but was now a player as well, as Nazarbayev became the head of the Nur Otan party.

As a further step towards "party-based authoritarianism" (Bader 2011), the constitutional changes of 2007 also allowed for an increase in the size of the Majilis, from 77 to 107 seats, and the legislative elections following these changes resulted in Nur Otan winning every single seat. As it had in previous elections, the OSCE returned a determination that the legislative elections were not "free and fair," due to ever-present irregularities, but, in perhaps authoritarian solidarity, the CIS observers found the process to be completely transparent (Kanapyanov and Kaliyev 2015). As a result of this resounding electoral triumph, even the pretence of opposition was swept away, as Ak Jol lost its token seat (perhaps due to its leader having the temerity to oppose Nazarbayev at the polls), and the 98 contested seats all went to the President's party (the remaining nine seats were selected by the otherwise-unremarkable Assembly of the People of Kazakhstan). In the words of Bowyer (2008:12), "one could argue that the Majilis building itself serves as a de facto second headquarters for the party," as the sweep of the legislature meant that Nur Otan ended up controlling all committees and organs of the parliament as well (Isaacs and Whitmore 2014). For the entire legislative term, from 2007 to 2012, only one political party mattered in Kazakhstan, meaning that the era of elite rivalry had effectively come to an end – or at least was now in a deep slumber, as, "in general, already by the mid-2000s Kazakhstan was a consolidated authoritarian regime" (Ibadildin and Pisareva 2020:108).

This consolidation of power was confirmed in both the grandfathering of Nazarbayev as the term-unlimited First President of the Republic but also in the reality that Nazarbayev did not have to worry in the short term about contested elections or an intransigent parliament (Nurumov and Vashchanka 2019). With such a groundswell of confidence, over-the-top measures such as parliament's debate in 2010 to make Nazarbayev "President for Life" did not seem necessary and thus were eschewed in favour of a more "normal" electoral cycle (Roberts 2012). The success of this approach was confirmed via the next round of elections, with the presidential election called a year and a half early in April 2011 and regular parliamentary elections scheduled for January 2012. Part of the reason for the early elections was to play up the recurrent theme of Nazarbayev as the bulwark against instability, especially after neighbouring Kyrgyzstan's second revolution in five years in 2010 (del Sordi 2016a); moreover, the global financial crisis had eaten into Kazakhstan's economic success story, making Nazarbayev's economic record less attractive than it was in 2007. Reverting to old tricks, the snap election was thus "a government operation to undermine the opposition by ensuring that only Nazarbayev would have the resources, organization and time to mount a serious campaign" (Ambrosio 2015:156).

With superior organizational abilities coming from control of the Majilis and every other formal political (and many economic) institution in the country, Nazarbayev cruised to victory again (Isaacs 2013), winning 95.5 per cent of the vote, according to official figures. The President faced three challengers in this round, belonging to the Communist Party, Tabığat (the environmental party), and the newest entry, the Partiya patriotov Kazakhstana/Qazaqstan patriottary partiasy (QPP – Party of Patriots of Kazakhstan), which fared the best – their leader, Gani Qasymov, a long-time confidant of Nazarbayev, garnered nearly 2 per cent of the vote. With Nazarbayev in his seventies, rumours had begun to swirl that he might step aside, but the snap elections were widely seen as a means to buy time (until 2016, when his term expired) to sort out any issues of succession (Ambrosio 2015). The parliamentary elections in January 2012 merely confirmed that Nazarbayev was not going anywhere in the short term, as Nur Otan once again won the lion's share of the vote, although it did lose ground to Ak Jol (back in parliament with eight seats) and the communists (who won seven seats).[17] In what was becoming a tradition, the OSCE and other international observers condemned the election as being marred by illegal activities and pressure from the government; in perhaps a sign of the healing of a rift in the Nazarbayev family, however, presidential daughter Dariga Nazarbayeva was welcomed back and won a seat as an MP in the Majilis after her absence from politics since 2007 (Roberts 2012).

At the same time, the Nur Otan party was moving beyond merely being a "big tent" political party of the executive to a transmission belt from the populace and elites to the governing regime. A series of initiatives, including regular discussions with other political parties and, more importantly, the Khalyktyn dauycy – Golos Naroda (KDGN – People's Voice) project in 2011, which placed boxes around the country in the hope of eliciting complaints, suggestions, and innovations from the Kazakh people. As del Sordi (2016a) notes, however, the project turned out to be cosmetic in nature, as many of the "suggestions" which were published were merely missives of praise for the ruling party and the President, and the project slipped into oblivion once the economic situation in the country improved. In addition to the promised civic improvements, the party apparatus also proved itself adept at adopting other parties' platforms, for example working under Nazarbayev to refine a message of responsibility to the nation in achieving Kazakhstan's development goals; as part of broader attempts to help raise up the most disadvantaged in society, the party co-opted the opposition's platform from 2007 but connected it to the duty of Kazakhs to create their own opportunities (Omelicheva 2016).

Unfortunately for Nazarbayev, the country's close ties to Russia were to create even more headaches in the economy, as Western sanctions on Russia following the illegal annexation of Crimea and the invasion of eastern Ukraine in 2014 led to substantial economic pressure on Kazakhs (as well as a massive contraction in Russia's own economy). As Ibadildin and Pisareva (2020:109) note, "much of the regime's legitimacy during the late 2000s came to rest on its economic performance, which largely depended on high oil prices and left the economy vulnerable to macroeconomic volatility." Sensing that the stability card needed to be played in the face of uncertainty, Nazarbayev called snap elections for early 2015, meaning that the issue of succession was once again postponed to a later date. Perhaps feeling less secure than in 2011 (and with two elections occurring in the face of political turmoil and, as we will see, the after-effects of the Zhanaozen massacre in December 2011), Nazarbayev and the government were not permitted the luxury of concerted opposition, and thus turned to Turgyn Syzdyqov of the

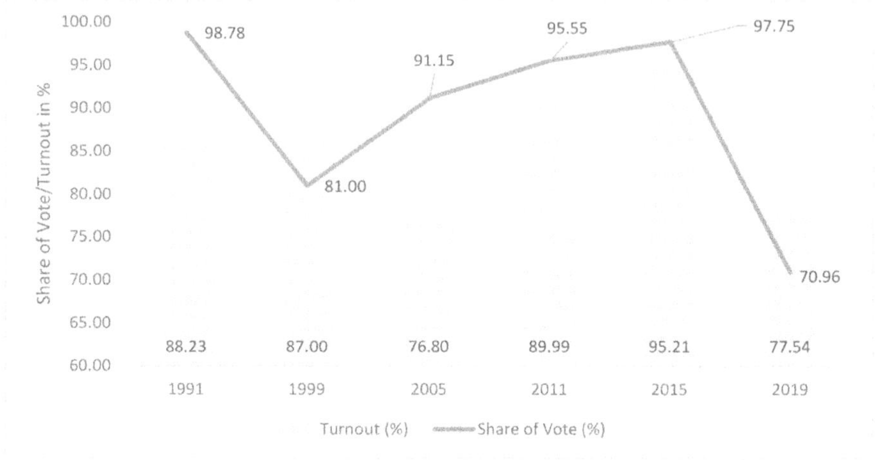

Figure 5.1 Nazarbayev's Electoral "Successes," 1991–2019
Note: In 2019, it was Tokayev who stood for President with Nazarbayev's backing.
Source: Compiled using data from the Central Election Commission of the Republic of Kazakhstan, www.election.gov.kz/eng/information-on-elections-and-referenda-in-the-rk/.

Communist Party, an old-line Marxist who railed against capitalism in campaign speeches, as the second candidate to run. The Communist Party had actually been banned intermittently from 2011 to 2012 to keep the party's support in the presidential and parliamentary elections low, a ploy that was probably not needed but appeared to work anyway (Smagulov et al. 2017). Alongside Syzdygov ran independent candidate Äbilgazy Qusaiynov, who appeared to not have much of a platform at all but instead spoke of "ecological education" and "industrial safety" (Taubayev 2015). In true Soviet fashion, even facing these formidable adversaries, Nazarbayev was able to increase his share of the vote to over 97 per cent, a highly implausible result given the economic duress that Kazakhstan was under but continuing his remarkable run of success (see Figure 5.1).

This success was followed by another excellent result for Nur Otan in the 2016 Majilis elections, with Ak Jol losing a seat and the communists retaining their seat for a total opposition result of 14 versus 84 for the ruling party. Perhaps tired of the same complaints going unheeded, "2016 was also the last year of parliamentary elections to be closely observed by the OSCE mission" (Ibadildin and Pisareva 2020:109). There was a proliferation of tinier parties contesting seats in the Majilis in 2016, including Birlik, a party that focused on social justice issues, the Jalpyūlttyq Sotsial-Demokratialyq Partia (Nationwide Social Democratic Party), focused on ending the economic crisis, and the "Auyl" Halyqtyq-demokratialyq patriottyq partiasy (Auyl People's Democratic Patriotic Party, more commonly referred to as Auyl), which came about as a merger of the QPP and the Krest'yanskaya partiya Kazakhstana "Khalyk zher" (Peasant's Party), and which focused on social democracy. However, as Smagulov et al. (2017:87) note, "the 2016 elections changed practically nothing in the party sector." The "big tent" approach of Nur Otan and the organizational machine which had delivered such fantastic results for over a decade had no reason to change, and it would require a massive shift in the relationship between the executive and the legislature to actually create such a change. This was to happen in two stages, in 2017 and especially in 2019, but to address these monumental events, we first need to understand what the parliament of Kazakhstan was actually envisioned as doing.

Kazakh Political Institution 3: The Legislature

If the constitution sets the rules of the game and political parties are the players (and elections the qualifying tournaments), then the legislature is the stadium.[18] It is impossible to separate the players from the game, the game from the tournaments, and the tournaments from the venue, and we have already spoken at length about the development of the Kazakh parliament in the constitutional process in the late and post-Soviet era. Indeed, we have looked in-depth at the composition of parties during electoral campaigns, at the seating of parties after elections, and how these parties affected the operations of the legislature. But before we jump ahead to the real power base in Kazakhstan – the executive – we need to understand the actual conception of the legislature as an institution within an independent Kazakhstan, as opposed to how it operated in practice and during elections. This will also help us understand where it fits in with Kazakh history and in determining the trajectory of Kazakhstan's political and economic transformation.

Legislatures as a concept in transition economies (as well as elsewhere) are a tricky institution to examine, as there are various schools of thought on how they should function during an economic transformation. In one corner is the almost mythical attachment to democracy above all, elevating the legislature into the institutional expression of the will of the voters, operationalized via elections but implemented via representation. This approach marries the political transformation towards liberal democracy with the transformation towards economic liberalism, positing that the two must go hand in hand and thus a freely elected legislature is crucial for completing both transformations (Olson and Norton 1996). Beyond the belief that democracy is the highest institutional ordering for political institutions, there are also practical mechanisms via which a strong legislature can contribute to better economic outcomes: in the first instance, there is a well-established literature on the power of checks and balances and veto power in constraining the executive (Gehlbach and Malesky 2010 are an excellent illustration of this literature). For example, when thinking of post-Soviet transitions as in Kazakhstan, Wright (2008) argues that binding legislatures, even in authoritarian settings, can help to check the confiscatory impulses of the leader, and thus they contribute to economic growth in the longer term. In this way, not only is representation of popular sentiment assured, it also helps to create an institutional counterbalance to a too-strong executive; the corollary to this is that a strong legislature is necessary with appropriate and robust "mechanisms required to aggregate and channel the preferences of legislators" lest the institution itself fall prey to policy incoherence (Chaisty 2006:3).

On the other hand, the evidence in favour of stronger legislatures in transition (as elsewhere) is not good (Hartwell 2013). First, legislatures are there to generate laws, and there is no guarantee that they will take this mandate as a limited one, i.e. they can far overshoot the optimal number of laws necessary to implement a successful transition, devoting their time to peripheral issues instead of advancing what needs to be done to effect transformation. Again, this is not a failing specifically of transition, as developed countries with standing legislatures (i.e. they are not convened for specific amounts of time or for specific issues) seem to concern themselves with areas that government should patently not be involved in. In the second instance, as was seen in the former Soviet Union (including Kazakhstan), many legislatures at the beginning of transition were communist holdovers who had no love of the capitalism they had spent their lives denouncing, and thus remained implacably opposed to overseeing a successful transition in the first place. Having attempted to hold elections before the Soviet Union actually fell, countries such as Russia, Kazakhstan, Ukraine, and other Soviet republics saw (perhaps unsurprisingly) that adherents of the old system were elected; contrast this with countries such as Poland, which held fresh elections once the monopoly of the Communist Party was revoked, meaning that real political opposition could compete – and win. Just as firms cannot be expected to adapt to a market economy when they do not live in one, politicians should not be expected to act like democrats when they are not in a democracy.

Third, and perhaps as a pointed rejoinder to the "democracy above all" school, modern legislatures have become less rule-making bodies and more redistributive factories. In words attributed to the Scottish jurist Alexander Fraser Tytler,[19] "a democracy will continue to exist up until the time that voters discover that they can vote themselves largess from the public treasury," meaning that (a) legislatures can actually pose a threat to democracy, and (b) private gain rather than public service characterizes the incentives of most politicians and bureaucrats.[20] With a standing parliament of representatives making laws year-round, each representative has an incentive to redistribute economic largesse to their constituents, their followers, or, in too many examples, themselves, in order to increase their power base. In this sense, their interest is not in increasing the size of the pie but in shuffling pieces around, a reality which means that there is less pie to go around for everyone who is *not* a politician. Put another way, a legislature which enables growth-enhancing legislation (low taxes, a favourable business environment, checking the power of the executive) will assist in a transition, but a parliament filled with communists is likely to just keep appropriating funds for the state. In this case, overriding the parliament is perhaps the only way to move a transformation forward.

These countervailing effects played themselves out in Kazakhstan and, indeed, avoidance of the downsides of legislative strength was a key justification by Nazarbayev for his un-democratic moves. Russia (Chaisty 2006), Ukraine (Hartwell 2016), and Kazakhstan all faced power struggles between a parliament opposed to rapid economic change and an executive pushing for quicker transformations away from communism. While the "gradualist" versus "big bang" argument was somewhat vapid – the evidence was and is overwhelmingly in favour of rapid transformation (Hartwell 2013) – stronger legislatures comprised of pre-democratic holdouts tended to put in place much larger speedbumps for reform than those legislatures which were given a popular mandate at the beginning of independence. Perhaps Nazarbayev understood this intuitively (and sold his decisions as such), or perhaps it was just a smokescreen for a desire to remain the Khan of the newly independent country, but in any event, the history of the legislature in post-independence Kazakhstan is a series of moves intended to lessen the power of the body.

In fact, the 1993 constitution was constructed as a reaction to the atmosphere of supreme executive power (i.e. the Soviet Union) which had been the reality in Kazakhstan for too long and was envisioned as a way to avoid such politics continuing in their Soviet manifestation. Independent Kazakhstan's first constitution in 1993 was intended precisely as a way to institute separation of power and in particular to combat the public perception that the President held too much authority (Anderson 1997), drifting towards an American style of presidentialism (Ludwikowski 1993) which had multiple veto points strewn throughout the system. Key among these veto points was the independence of three separate branches of government, with no one branch having the right to remove members from the other branches (Kembayev 2011). Formed as a unicameral body with members chosen on the basis of territory, the parliament had the responsibility for approving ministers and contributing to policy debates (Olcott 2010), as well as veto power over the President and the responsibility of members of the Cabinet to the Supreme Soviet as in a parliamentary system (Kanapyanov 2018). More importantly, the legislature was expected to be active in the politics of the nation (Amandykova 2014), and a lively debate among elites on the exact composition of parliament (unicameral versus bicameral, strong parliamentary committees) showed how serious the parliament's role in a post-Soviet Kazakhstan was taken (Anderson 1997). However, Kanter (1993) notes that such debates on the "proper" role of parliament were often limited to the elites, as popular opinion was fixated on the language and ethnic issues related to Russian-speakers, meaning that policies concerning a key institution often took a backseat to policies concerning the passions of the day.

It is of course not necessary that grand issues of political institution-building are debated at the tavern and town hall level – as proved by the

American experiment from the late 1700s – but the unfortunate fact of the matter in Kazakhstan is that even the intellectual ferment among the elite was short-lived. The 1993 constitution did not end the President's prerogatives of power in relation to the legislature, and in fact some specific quirks of the document enabled the executive to exert some power in the legislative process. In particular, Article 78 facilitated the addition of amendments by the President after a bill had been passed by the legislature, with one final round of voting to confirm or deny these presidential amendments. Unlike most other countries, however, in Kazakhstan, any presidential amendments are enacted automatically unless both chambers of the parliament vote to reject them, thus keeping momentum on the President's side (Tsebelis and Rizova 2007).

Even this lever was not enough to keep an unruly parliament in line and, as noted above, the flirtation with representative democracy which began in 1991 was effectively ended in 1993 with the "self-dissolution" of the Supreme Council in 1993, a major step towards shifting power away from any legislative body and towards the executive and "in effect, the beginning of the end of parliamentarism in Kazakhstan" (Nurumov and Vashchanka 2019:227). The first step in the redefinition of the legislature's role came with the streamlining of the parliament down to 177 seats and, more importantly, the inclusion of 42 seats which were directly appointed by Nazarbayev. Reserving nearly 24 per cent of the seats in parliament for the executive meant that Nazarbayev had far less work to do in achieving parliamentary majorities, as the "power of patronage" (Isaacs 2010b) allowed the executive to reward supporters with seats in parliament (and then demand further loyalty via votes). Contrary to the spirit of the 1993 constitution, this move towards super-presidentialism effectively pushed checks and balances far to the margins, allowing for only the slimmest of counterbalancing to the President's policies. Indeed, the reality of the post-1993 world in Kazakhstan was that Nazarbayev tolerated parliament so long as it was not actually checking or balancing his power and took steps to undermine it – or eliminate it entirely – when it actually did. Thus, short-term political imperatives (and, to be fair, medium-term economic imperatives) took precedence over longer-term political institutional imperatives in Kazakhstan's post-Soviet development.

This was accelerated with the dissolution of parliament in 1995. Hanks (1998:162), in a bit of an understatement that academics are not normally known for, notes that the effect of parliamentary dissolutions was to "cast doubt on [Nazarbayev's] commitment to democratic institutions." In a more descriptive (and powerful) retelling of the events of 1995, Partlett (2012:233) relates how Nazarbayev "disbanded parliament, turning off its power, water, and telephone, and sending in workmen to begin remodeling the building." In all fairness, the elected parliament from 1994 to 1995 was spectacularly inefficient, especially in the midst of a major economic disruption, only passing seven pieces of legislation during the year it existed, but on the other hand, it was actually developing as a counterbalance to Nazarbayev (Olcott

2010). The dissolution of parliament via court order and the creation of the People's Assembly in 1995 as a consultative body (but with members selected by the President himself) installed an ersatz legislature in place of an actual legislature and allowed Nazarbayev to rule by decree for the better part of 1995. When the return to a popularly elected legislature under the 1995 constitution was allowed, it only worked within the confines of the expansion of presidential powers which occurred in the interregnum. From the point of view of parliament, the 1995 constitution shifted the legislature from a unicameral to a bicameral body, changing the structure of the Majilis, and creating a byzantine series of arrangements in the Senate (upper house):

> all the provinces of Kazakhstan and the city of Almaty, which had provincial status, had two senators, chosen for four-year terms by the joint sessions of the provincial legislative bodies. An additional seven senators were appointed directly by the President. In addition, ex-Presidents automatically receive the status of senators-for-life.
>
> (Mishra 2009:318)

It is quite possible that this move by Nazarbayev was done in a way to restrain the legislature, as political scientists note that bicameral legislatures can have a dampening effect on the amount of legislation which is produced, especially if there is discord between the two houses (Hicks 2015); on the other hand, and more probably, the move was done to ensure that the legislation which was produced was amenable to the President, with the upper house acting as a veto player for legislation not favoured by Nazarbayev (Tsebelis and Money 1997).

Since 1995, the parliament in Kazakhstan has played a far less important role as a formal political institution, with Isaacs (2010b:17) noting that, "from this point onwards Kazakhstan moved away from democratization to a form of durable authoritarianism." While the Majilis retains the institutional form of a Western democratic parliament – including committees, factions, onboarding for new members, and contact with foreign parliaments (Bowyer 2008) – from 1995 to 2017 it was far less involved in building the other institutions of a transitioning Kazakhstan. Indeed, instead of becoming a functioning legislative body with responsibility for passage of laws, the key mechanisms through which Nazarbayev has ruled have been political parties (as shown in the last section) and informal mechanisms such as patronage (Isaacs 2010a), which we will explore in the next section.

Changes to the constitution such as the 2007 amendments institutionalized the shift away from parliament being the key institution to the players (i.e. the parties) being more important organizational mechanisms for political progress in Kazakhstan (Isaacs and Whitmore 2014). But even in basic documents such as the 1995 constitution, which lays out the concept of checks and balances, the legislature as the key institution of legislation in the country was downplayed. In fact, the status of the President was elevated in the 1995 constitution to ensuring the functioning of all state bodies (as well as the ability to declare martial law), meaning that assertions of lack of functionality should be all it takes legally to challenge the operations of the parliament and replace them with more executive-friendly ones (Kanapyanov 2018). Similarly, the legislative powers which Nazarbayev had in the 1993 constitution (i.e. the ability to add amendments after a bill had been passed) expanded greatly, with the executive taking on the role of the legislature as well (Olcott 2010). This comported well with the philosophy expressed by Nazarbayev of "economics first, politics second," whereby "efficient government is one that has the opportunity and knowledge to introduce complicated economic reforms unbound by an electoral cycle" (Tutumlu and Rustemov 2021:127), allowing for his initiatives to be rubber-stamped rather than debated (Olcott 2010).

The relegation of the legislature to an approving body rather than an initiator of legislation allows us to revisit the debates from the beginning of this section. In the first instance, if a democratic transition was desired, the vitiation of parliament meant that it was unlikely to be achieved but, as just noted, this was part of the design rather than a flaw of Nazarbayev's strategy. Similarly, the point of successive moves by the executive and in the constitution was the removal of checks and balances, again as part of a concerted strategy. The question is thus whether the sidelining of the parliament led to better outcomes than would have been expected with a fully functioning standing parliament, i.e. avoiding communist obstruction, over-production of laws, and a hyper-obsession on redistribution. In one sense, the history of the Majilis is one of avoiding communist obstruction (not least because the communists were banned for two years), and so Kazakhstan was ahead of Ukraine and other post-Soviet countries in this respect (Chaisty 2006; Hartwell 2016). Regarding the over-production of laws, it appears that this was not really an issue to call an independent parliament into question (see the point above of the legislative efficiency of the 1994–1995 parliament), and in any event, one-party rule of a supine parliament resulted in a massive number of laws being adopted: according to the Inter-Parliamentary Union database, in 2008 alone the Majilis adopted 493 laws, a number which came down to 71 in 2012 when there was some token opposition. This point thus appears to be against the strategy of Nazarbayev. Finally, the issue of redistribution also is a very murky one for the approach that Kazakhstan ultimately took. One can argue that reforms were more pro-growth than they would have been in a different parliamentary setting, but one can also argue that the redistribution came about via informal rather than formal means (thus meaning that there was no real improvement). This informal redistribution plays a large role in our next and final institutional examination.

Kazakh Political Institution 4: The Executive Branch (and Affiliated Entities)

Finally, the political institution which has been underpinning every aspect of Kazakhstan's political transformation – the executive branch, and in particular the office of the President – has already come to the fore in the previous three sections but needs to be examined as an institution unto itself. Although Nazarbayev has cast a shadow across every aspect of political transformation thus far described, shaping independent Kazakhstan's political institutions immeasurably, the development of the executive under his rule is of such importance that we save it for last. And, as we will see, the transformation of the executive has also subsumed many of the other institutions which we usually think about when we trace a country's institutional reform, making a much more homogenized political institutional transformation than that seen in other countries during this same time period.

As noted above, the original conception of the system of government in Kazakhstan, embodied in both the 1993 and 1995 constitutions, was a tripartite system of executive, legislative, and judicial branches, each with its own series of checks and balances on the other. However, as we have seen, the executive quickly became *primus inter pares* as the power of the legislature was vitiated by Nazarbayev, with these changes codified in successive constitutions (and the amendments attached to them). In judging the fact that there was institutional volatility, we must not be too harsh, mainly because a nation in transition is supposed to have some form of institutional volatility, so long as the trend line is moving in the "right" direction, i.e. from institutions which facilitate a closed, planned economy with a monopoly on violence owned by a small cadre to those which facilitate pluralism, free speech, and "the pursuit of happiness." But the key point is that the trend in Kazakhstan, at least when connected to democratic governance, was not moving in the direction of democracy, or, at a bare minimum, greater representation, but back towards a very Sovietized executive with a submissive legislature. This was the case even if the institutional mechanisms themselves were going to be utilized in a very different manner to the Soviet ones (that is, for pushing economic reform rather than centralizing the economy).

Moreover, we have also examined elections, a key discrete event in both democracies and countries moving towards democracy – but not, it must be noted, the only important institution of democracy, and too many of those who would defend "democracy" as an ideal would fetishize elections as the only way in which democracy occurs.[21] Regardless of their centrality in representative government, elections were far too often tampered with in Kazakhstan in the post-independence period, with the greatest pressure coming in three specific ways: first, in the variable timing of the elections themselves; second, in the use of executive power to shut down opposition in the run-up to (and in the conduct of) an election; and third, in changing just what the people were voting for. The timing of elections, the first influence that Nazarbayev had on perpetuating the executive via mechanisms of democracy, has been touched upon already, in that elections were called often when Nazarbayev either needed to project stability in the midst of a crisis or when he felt that a short election season would keep any opposition off-balance (or, sometimes, both occurred simultaneously). Such ploys are not necessarily an abuse of power, they are more a part of the system, as parliamentary systems around the world allow for governments to call for elections, an obligation which is usually used only at the most propitious time. In Kazakhstan, Nazarbayev played the same game but, when combined with other interference in the electoral process, generated a far from level playing field for the opposition.

Prominent among these other methods of interference was the direct suppression of opposition parties and candidates, noted above and pervasive in nearly every electoral campaign in Kazakhstan, including executive and legislative, in the post-independence era. Candidates being disallowed from running, parties being banned, candidate and party disqualifications on purely administrative and/or legal grounds, and control of the media directed against the opposition were hallmarks of Kazakhstan's democratic processes since independence, leading to repeated denunciation from international observers (Jailani 2016). More sinister were the behind-the-scenes manipulations, in some instances leading to violence and/or shadowy murders which have not been solved (see Lillis 2022 for an in-depth look at the human toll of oppression). Such an approach has been commonplace throughout the former Soviet Union, with disappearance, murder, and suppression a frequent tool of electioneering in Putin's Russia, Karimov's Uzbekistan, and Rahmon's Tajikistan, and Kazakhstan is probably somewhat behind these other despots in terms of sheer numbers. But the fact that it has occurred at all is a sign that the trend is not in the right direction, and it did not occur only in tandem with elections, as can be witnessed by the Zhanaozen massacre in 2011.

The Zhanaozen massacre was the first of many flare-ups in Kazakh politics stemming from average citizens demanding more representation in the governance of the country (Niyazbekov 2018), married with a liberal dose of economic concern regarding the spread of benefits from the transition. After tensions in 2010 which led to a short-lived strike, in May 2011, oil workers from Ozenmunaigaz, a subsidiary of Kazmunaygaz (the state national oil company), in the western town of Zhanaozen went on strike for higher pay and were summarily sacked by the state (Salmon 2012). This region of the country was dominated by the oil industry and nothing else, seeing both an influx of workers and a dearth of opportunities outside of oil, meaning high unemployment and poverty rates coupled with high prices accompanying the influx of capital needed for the industry (Satpayev and Umbetaliyeva 2015). Despite the sackings, the workers refused to back down and instead occupied Zhanaozen's main square, while pressure ratcheted up on their activities via several judicial verdicts that the strike was "illegal," leading to heavy-handed police tactics and accusations of torture (Evans 2022). On 16 December 2011,

> a group of workers took to the streets to demand the right to form decentralized political opposition. Authorities responded with sheer brutality, clashing with protestors and opening fire on demonstrators.

> The crackdown resulted in the deaths of what is commonly estimated to be dozens of protestors, although the Kazakhstani government insists that only 11 lost their lives.
>
> (Jailani 2016:46)

In response to the massacre, state authorities sought to blame *oralman*, that is, Kazakhs who had been living abroad but repatriated after independence, who had failed to adapt to the new conditions in their homeland (Satpayev and Umbetaliyeva 2015). In terms of what was actually done, however, only a few senior officials were reshuffled while the focus was kept on controlling social media (Niyazbekov 2017) and portraying what happened in the region as yet another reason to keep Nazarbayev in power against the forces of anarchy and chaos (Satpayev and Umbetaliyeva 2015). However, Nazarbayev's election did not prevent the protests, and a similar round of protests against land reform in 2016 resulted in further coercion (Heuer and Hireman 2022) but a rare victory for civil society, albeit in an area where Nazarbayev may have been correct (see Chapter 6).

The massacre and, indeed, the reaction of the executive to any popular protests from that point on – ironic, given the role of the Zheltoqsan events in accelerating the demise of the Kazakh SSR – was another manifestation of the executive's powers rather than the way in which those powers were kept in place. In reality, the institutional mechanism of the executive was granted the ability to wield this power by the third bit of manipulation, namely the temporal manipulations of the tenure of the executive. Throughout post-independence Kazakhstan's political evolution, the boundaries of the executive were constantly in flux, with both the length of term of the President and term limits constantly being revised (and approved in different ways). For example, Nazarbayev used two public referendums in 1995 to "pass" the new constitution and to extend his rule until 2000 when it should have ended in 1996 (following the five-year term codified in the 1993 constitution). As Nurumov and Vashchanka (2019:221) note, the history of Kazakhstan's executive constraints could have been encapsulated in the reality that "the two-term limit was manipulated by various means, including a referendum, new constitution, and ultimately exemption from term limits for the First President." The 2007 amendments to the constitution were especially egregious, in that they changed the fundamental rules of the game for the whole country in favour of just one person, giving Nazarbayev, and Nazarbayev only, the ability to run until he no longer wanted to (Jailani 2016). Each of these actions confirmed the power of the executive and elevated it above any normal democratic procedures; if the constitution was an obstacle, amend it, if elections were an obstacle, bypass them, and if both of these still ran up against legal frameworks, carve out a special exemption.

Thus, the executive in Kazakhstan, as has already been made clear, went on a steady march towards becoming the only political institution that mattered in the country. This march was enabled by a number of institutions affiliated with the national level executive, without which the extreme centralization of powers which accrued in Kazakhstan would not have been possible. Indeed, part of the powers invested in the presidency came about from a specific administrative decision, namely the avoidance of federalism and the constitution of independent Kazakhstan as a unitary state. As noted above, the creation of a unitary state was in some ways predicated on forestalling regional unrest due to ethnic issues, but the centralization of power in Almaty (and then Astana/Nur-Sultan) also served the purpose of allowing the President to forestall the emergence of rivals. In the 1993 constitution, the system of local government envisioned popularly elected local councils who were overseen by a politically appointed governor or mayor (the *akim*), with this appointment coming directly from the President; much as in Russia's regional reform ten years later, which replaced elected governors with presidential appointees (Golosov et al. 2016), the Kazakh approach tried to prevent any separatist or even experimental tendencies in favour of a strong centralized apparatus, a mere piece of a vertical hierarchy leading up to the President (Olcott 2010). This power structure was confirmed by the fact that the President not only had the right to appoint the oblast *akims*, but was able to dismiss the *akims* that he did not directly appoint, i.e. those from the rayons (who were appointed by the oblast *akims* and not directly by the President). Additional reforms implemented in 1998 and 2001, while delineating the responsibilities of local governance, stressed that their operations must not in any way hinder the policies of the central government (Makhmutova 2001).

Even throughout the later years of Nazarbayev's career as President, and throughout countless local government "reforms," the institutional structures remained fairly similar. In a scathing review of the much-vaunted "Kazakhstan 2050" Development Plan, Sullivan (2018:127) notes in particular that:

> Nowhere in the plan, however, is the dispersion or institutionalization of power highlighted. Instead, it calls for the creation of a more "open government" in which statistics and proclamations are made available to citizens, as well as for the "development of local governance" and "strengthening [of] the role of public councils under state agencies and Akims." This should not come as a shock, for one of the hundred steps declares the need to create a "results-oriented state governance system with standardized and minimal procedures for monitoring, assessment and control." Read closely, this amounts to an admission that the government has no such system in place.

As Ibrayeva and Nezhina (2013:55) summarize, "Kazakhstan has a highly centralized government structure that is characterized by a top-down decision-making authority and management system." And while Nazarbayev was busy consolidating his own power at the top, managing economic reforms, and attempting to sort out the thorny issue of succession, he was reluctant to limit his own influence in the regions while simultaneously caring little for the issues of relevance to local populations, such as service delivery or infrastructure (Olcott 2010).

In addition to the tsarist-like approach of bypassing local governance, Nazarbayev also utilized another key institution to consolidate power. An interesting (but perhaps not surprising) spin on executive power in post-independence Kazakhstan was that not only was legislative power vitiated via progressive delegation to the President's office, but the judiciary was a willing participant rather than a counterbalance. In my earlier work (Hartwell 2016), I demonstrate that it was crucial to bring the judiciary in as its own institution for analysis, as the judiciary's development influences economic transition and whose history often sets paths of expectation during a transformation. In many ways, the judiciary can be more properly thought of as an economic institution than a political one. This may need some explaining, since the judiciary is obviously one of the three branches of government and is almost always thought of as a political institution given its emphasis on interpreting the laws which (usually) come from the legislative branch. However, when thinking of an economic system as an ecology of plans (Wagner 2012), the rule of law is one of the foundations of the market, and this refereeing of the "rules of the game" (in North's 1990 phrasing) comes from both formal and informal judicial institutions. While the judiciary is politically comprised (elections, appointments) and plays a key role in a political ecosystem, its outputs can be properly thought of as economic.

Unfortunately, this is the usual way in which some of us think about the judiciary (Hartwell 2013) but it requires the judiciary to be independent. In too many post-Soviet (and other) states, this has been anything but the case, with the judiciary just another arm of the executive, influenced by powerful interests and/or corrupt in its own right and untouched by reform (Hartwell and Urban 2021). This reality was also the case in Kazakhstan, where judicial institutions were constantly being reshaped in the interest of furthering the prerogatives of the executive; as Figure 5.2 shows, decreases in judicial independence occurred at the same time as decreases in checks on governmental power, and Kazakhstan's judicial independence score has remained abysmal since 1995, from the lowest local court to the highest courts of the land. This is not an accident, as the President nominates all the judges to sit in the Supreme Court (who then must be approved by an acquiescent Senate) and directly appoints all the local judges and specialized judges; combined with this control over personnel is the reality that the judiciary is a "law-applying body" whose decisions do not hold the force of law (Kembayev 2017). Perhaps because the judiciary has been a mere conduit of executive privilege – but, despite his hopes, Nazarbayev could not be everywhere at every time – much discretionary power was left in the hands of the judiciary, and consequently corruption expanded to fill in the cracks (Bhuiyan and Amagoh 2011). Notoriously corrupt (Henderson 2000) from top to bottom and consistently perceived as such throughout the entire transition, the judiciary in Kazakhstan even has a black market price attached to it: according to Tutumlu and Rustemov (2021), the going price for a favourable decision from the Supreme Court in 2020 was approximately US$30,000–$40,000.

The ability to make the judiciary directly reliant on the President does not stop with the Supreme Court, however, as even the Constitutional Council, the arbiter of the rules of the game in Kazakhstan, has been used as another rubber stamp for executive power. This could be seen most clearly in the invalidation of the 1994 parliamentary election, whereby, as Partlett (2015:938) notes, "in order to weaken Parliament's power, Nazarbayev relied on the Kazakh Constitutional Court." However, in the push to reduce obstacles to executive power, Nazarbayev also found the judicial system potentially threatening, and inserted into the 1995 constitution clauses which weakened judicial review and abolished the Constitutional Court altogether, turning it into a "Council" and eliminating the right of individuals to register complaints about the government and the constitutionality of its actions (Kembayev 2011, 2017). In such an environment, the courts are additional enforcement arms of the President and in particular of "telephone justice" (Henderson 2000).

Finally, the emergence of actual political opposition in the late 1990s in the form of Ak Jol also led Nazarbayev to tighten the reins over the media in

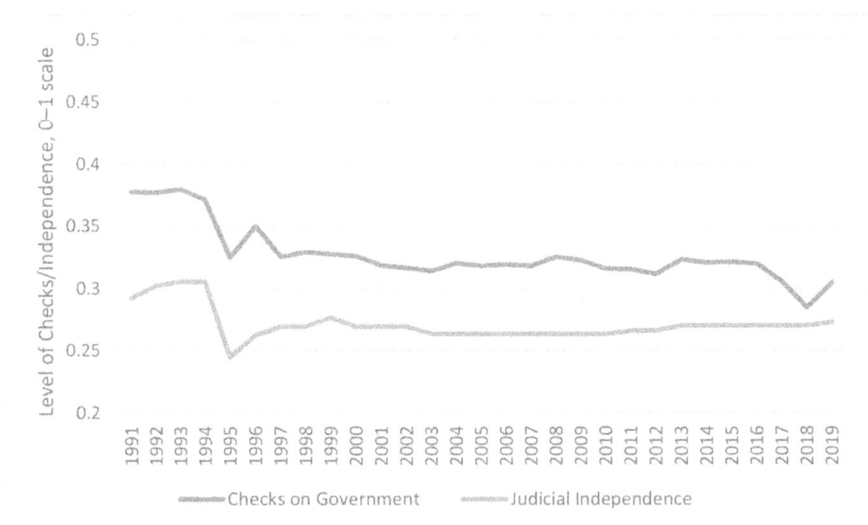

Figure 5.2 Judicial Independence and Checks on Government in Kazakhstan, 1991–2019

Note: Rated on a scale from 0 to 1, with 1 being perfect independence or maximum checks on government and 0 being the least.

Source: Global State of Democracy Indices, www.idea.int/gsod-indices/dataset-resources.

Kazakhstan which, admittedly, had never been very independent in the first place (Olcott 2010). Media and civil society go hand in hand as quasi-formal institutions in the political sphere, with both helping to round out the formal institutions of politics; in many ways, they must be formally organized (especially when it comes to the capital requirements of a media corporation), but they are also informal in that they react very much to formal political institutions (as in citizen watchdog organizations). To blur the lines between civil society and media even further, traditional media organizations such as television stations or newspapers have been eroded from below by the advent of social media and the internet, which began a rapid ascent during Kazakhstan's transition, and which really skyrocketed just as Nazarbayev's power consolidation was complete (i.e. in 2007; see Figure 5.3). No matter which form of media is dominant, however, the institution of the media can go in one of two directions with regard to its political role. Either it can act as a check on the ruling party, publicizing criminality, giving voice to the opposition, or merely by informing the populace of policies being made; or the media can be another transmission vehicle, unquestioningly parroting the regime's policies and prejudices without checking if these have any correspondence with the truth. In this second use of the media, ownership matters while words do not, with state-owned or affiliated (or even just supporting) media bending words such as "democracy" and "fascism" to whatever policies they – and the regime – support.

In Kazakhstan, the media has been a particular source of executive attention, with a long and consistent history of the systematic violation of press freedom within the country (Nikolayenko 2015). Much like the flirtation with democracy, Kazakhstan's elites also flirted with a free and open press in the early 1990s, providing "legislators with opportunities to freely convey their opinions to the wider public," with even government-owned media outlets

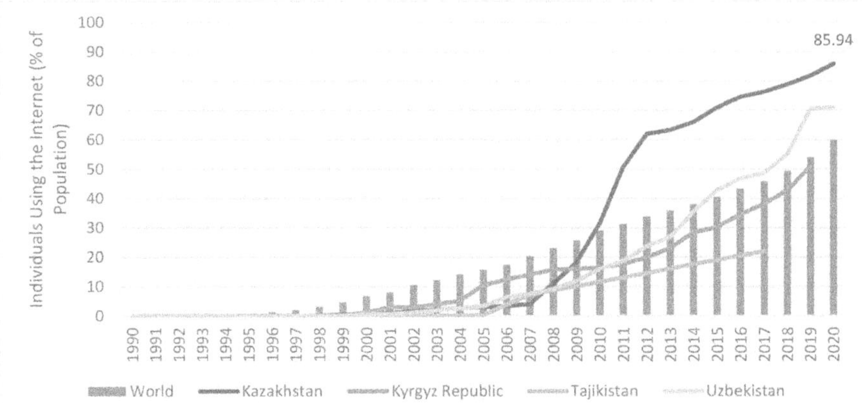

Figure 5.3 Internet Usage in Central Asia and the Rest of the World, 1990–2020

reporting on the moves and speeches of the opposition (Higashijima 2022:190). However, in tandem with the move towards increasing the power of the executive, the media landscape in Kazakhstan also began to be undermined; given the odd amalgamation of political institution and business that media corporations represent, the two-pronged approach of the Nazarbayev regime was to first write restrictive laws regarding the use of media and then second to acquire media outlets by the Nazarbayev family and closely affiliated cronies (Gross 2019). As early as 1996, Kazakh regulators were using the heavy hand of the state to require all media broadcasters to renew their contracts with the regulatory body, and consequently many independent outlets that were critical of the government were soon shut out, with their transmitters disconnected and licenses revoked, even if they paid the requisite fees (Dragomir 2003). Censoring of the media continued as Nazarbayev's powers grew, with a new Law on the Press in 1998 resulting in 200 prosecutions and an additional Law on National Security in 1999 giving the Procurator-General the right to suspend media outlets without appeal (Olcott 2010). Government influence became less subtle and clumsier and more heavy-handed, but continued unabated, even if, as during the 1999 elections, it provoked international condemnation (Ibadildin and Pisareva 2020). Continued opposition and the formation of Ak Jol also contributed to a much more restrictive atmosphere for the independent media throughout the 2000s, including moves towards clamping down on social media as well.

The advent of social media and in particular the internet as an alternative method for expressing discontent grew during the period of parliamentary one-party rule (2007–2011), but this too was swiftly targeted by Nazarbayev's regime. In the first instance, a law in 2009 equated social media with traditional media, meaning that libel was taken seriously as criminal speech on the internet as well as in print. This attempt to regulate new media increased substantially after the Zhanaozen massacre, mainly due to the reality that social media was utilized as both a way to organize during the strikes in the west of the country and, after the police crackdown, to disseminate information about the violence and the state's hand in it. Perhaps sensing the power of such media, government sources first attempted to deflect attention from the violence and back to the issue of *oralman* and open a discussion on how best to regulate them via various social media channels (Marat 2016). In many ways, this was an updated ploy from earlier campaigns, in which, seizing upon the genuine support for Nazarbayev, the government also encouraged pro-government individuals to post messages in favour of the leader on opposition websites (Schatz 2009). However, when this approach failed in the Zhanaozen case, with the waves of social media too much for the government to influence, stricter crackdowns on social media were instituted from 2014 onward. In particular, the Kazakh government, perhaps emulating neighbouring China, sought to bring legal action against those who were critical of the regime and who expressed such criticism online (Anceschi 2015), and committed itself to monitoring online activity (Gross 2019). As with much of Nazarbayev's reign, the official reasons for further crackdowns against the media came down to avoiding "instability," and especially minimizing extremism and terrorism (del Sordi 2016b), but additional laws (such as those passed in 2017 requiring journalists to obtain permission before writing about any public figure) have only served to strengthen the hand of the state (Gross 2019).

Due to these efforts, Kazakhstan has consistently remained near the bottom of international rankings of press freedom. According to Reporters Without Borders, from 2010–2011, Kazakhstan ranked 154th out of 176 countries, behind such stalwarts of press freedom as Afghanistan and the Democratic Republic of the Congo, while in 2019 Kazakhstan's ranking had declined to 158th out of 180 countries, not quite as good as star performers Venezuela or Belarus. In fact, Nazarbayev's brand of media control fits almost perfectly with Edward Schatz's (2009:207) description of a "soft authoritarian:"

> The soft authoritarian ruler effectively manages information flows. He does not seek total control of the print, broadcast, and electronic media; such control could undermine any claims being made about media freedom. Moreover, he knows that it is neither possible nor necessary to persuade the entire citizenry. Rather, he seeks to maintain the upper hand in guiding the media to project images that strengthen his position. Such management of the media may flirt with outright propaganda, but only occasionally. The successful ruler seeks to avoid an outcome in which he discredits the press entirely, thereby generating demand for underground alternatives.

The sum total of these manipulations of affiliated institutions meant that Kazakhstan's political ordering had indeed become as Ibrayeva and Nezhina (2013) assess, a top-heavy administrative state controlled from the centre across all institutional matrices. Each step taken from 1991 to 2017 in the political realm only affirmed this trendline, from legislative dissolution to constitutional amendment to formal changes in electoral processes and eventually the anointment of Nazarbayev as *Elbasy* by parliament in 2010. However, the trend had somewhat of a break in 2017, with constitutional amendments that (on paper at least) attempted to downgrade the "super-presidential" approach of Nazarbayev to a more run of the mill parliamentary-cabinet system (see especially Jakusik 2020).[22] As part of the amendments passed, the Constitutional Council regained the right to examine the constitutionality of laws, albeit only if requested by the President; at the same time, the government was made more accountable to the Parliament rather than just being accountable to the President, and resignations of government would be made to the Majilis rather than to the President (del Sordi 2017). In an interesting twist, which appeared to be a rollback of much of the decision-making undertaken in the country since the 1990s, presidential decrees were also no longer to have the force of law (Cornell and Engvall 2017), and even the President's appointment power for *akims* outside of major cities was delegated to a mechanism designed by parliament (Pistan 2019).

While the sheer amount of amendments appeared to comport with Nazarbayev's public address that political competition and pluralism was just around the corner, as Kembayev (2017:324) note,

> the powers the President was willing to transfer to or share with the Parliament and the Government are mostly insignificant (in some cases even of "cosmetic nature"); accordingly, the President remains an absolutely dominating figure in the state machinery and overcentralization of political power continues to be a major feature of Kazakhstan's political system.

For example, the constitution retained the idea of the President as the arbiter of the three branches of government and indeed made the President as a kind of "strategizer-in-chief," concerned with the very important issues of security and development rather than the day-to-day minutiae (del Sordi 2017). For Nazarbayev himself, turning 77 years old that year and looking beyond the office of the President, these amendments "provided for the lifelong immunity of Nazarbayev and declared that his status of the Leader of the Nation could not be changed" (Trochev 2018:163).

In 2017, after these amendments had just been passed, I spoke at a closed-door session at the Astana Economic Forum with Prime Minister Bakytzhan Sagintayev on the challenges Kazakhstan is likely to face until 2050. My closing comment was, "Kazakhstan has done a passable job in managing the economic transition, it must make sure it does not bungle the political transition." The amendments of 2017 appeared to clear the way for that very transition, attempting two things simultaneously: first, to soften the power of the presidency in anticipation of Nazarbayev leaving office in favour of an anointed successor; and second, to retain as many perks as possible of power (including immunity) for Nazarbayev himself after he had stepped down from his leadership role. While there may have been other issues at play, including the unexpected land reform protests from 2016 (see Chapter 6 and also Cornell and Engvall 2017), the overall tone of the amendments appeared to set the stage for the next chapter of Kazakhstan's political development.

As we now know, less than two years later, after 30 years of undisputed rule, Nursultan Nazarbayev resigned as President of the Republic of Kazakhstan on 19 March 2019. While he retained a lifetime seat on the National Security Council (elevated from an advisory to a constitutional status in 2018; see Isaacs 2020) and remained head of the Nur Otan party, he handed over the reins of the presidency to the Speaker of the Senate (and former Prime Minister) Kassym-Jomart Tokayev. The move, a surprise to most of the world, has been heralded as its own form of "smart authoritarianism" (Pistan 2019; Blackmon 2021), a ploy to keep the opposition off-guard while the transition from leader to leader is implemented. Moreover, Pistan (2019) notes that the resignation, being long planned for and done under constitutional rules, was a way to both consolidate Nazarbayev's own power post-presidency and further entrench the reforms of the 2017 amendments, creating a managed succession via what is truly an unprecedented model. The last surviving Soviet apparatchik in Central Asia, Nazarbayev saw Islam Karimov of Uzbekistan and Saparmurat Niyazov of Turkmenistan die without a successor in place, and appeared determined to avoid this fate, in turn creating a political institutional innovation in his country: an authoritarian transition in a region where transitions tend to be messy at best, in an attempt to preserve his legacy and the gains which he fought for. The success – or failure – of this model is still playing out in the present day and will be dealt with more in-depth in the concluding chapter of the book, but suffice it to say that at this juncture, Nazarbayev's sudden resignation was squarely in line with his political reforms and his strategies of survival in particular, throughout the post-independence era.

Conclusion: A Halting Political Transformation

The post-Soviet Kazakh political institutional matrix was a combination of traditional Kazakh approaches to ruling and the Soviet hypercentralized approach to administration, but with the goal of using this centralized and singular power to reform the country's economy. While Kazakhstan's political transition was indeed done with a Kazakh face – and that of Nursultan Nazarbayev in particular – in many ways (as we noted earlier in the book), the Soviet experiment played a much larger part in the path of post-Soviet Kazakhstan than the long historical experience of flexible political authority which Kazakhs had before the Russians moved onto their lands. Why did the role of the executive in Kazakhstan change in the post-Soviet period? Given the long historical roots of indigenous political institutions, why did it not resume its pre-tsarist/Soviet path? Why did Kazakhstan, like so many other countries in Central Asia, choose a specific type of government that accorded the bulk of power to one office and one man, while at the same time proclaiming the importance of "checks and balances" and "separation of powers"?

There are two explanations for the trajectory of Kazakhstan's post-Soviet political institutional development, one simple and one more complex. The simple reason is that the Soviet system, overlaid on the traditionally decentralized Kazakh political system, broke these carefully cultivated institutions by brute force. As the Soviets were to do around the globe, their tanks, gulags, and administrative system homogenized cultures and simply overwhelmed nations (especially those with no real tradition of independence as a modern nation-state). However, this is perhaps too simple an explanation, as many foreign powers have found their occupations foiled by the indigenous institutions, cultures, and mode of operation in countries they have attempted to occupy; one need only look at the Baltic states, which were occupied and ruled by the Soviet Union for 70 years, but which remained fiercely independent, never recognizing the occupation, and transitioned incredibly successfully after the Soviet occupation had ended. Of course, one could note that the Baltic states were very different from their Russian overlords, ethnically and linguistically, and that they were only ever regarded as colonies (Annus 2012). But even in similar states, occupation does not always mean assimilation: the Russian invasion of Ukraine that began in February 2022 (and was still ongoing as of this writing) shows how countries with very similar paths can still result in bloody conflict and, above all, a fierce resistance to occupation. Ukraine still stands as an independent country and indeed the Russian invasion has galvanized both patriotism in Ukraine and resistance to any and all things Russian (where once a fount of goodwill may have resided), an outcome that the planners in the Kremlin patently did not foresee.

The reality, that perhaps Soviet force was necessary but not sufficient an explanation, brings us to the more complex determinant, namely *how* the Soviet system was able to supplant the traditional Kazakh forms of political organization and then bequeath a centralized system for Nazarbayev to manipulate. Douglass North famously notes in his early works (North 1971) that institutions change when the relative prices of the extant economic system changes, forcing institutions to adapt or, if they cannot, driving institutions into extinction while new ones arise. In the case of Kazakhstan, this shift in relative prices came in the late tsarist and early Soviet period under forced sedentarization. With a dispersed, decentralized people, placing their value on grazing land and herd composition (and size), centralized political institutions were unnecessary and, in fact, held little sway unless they impacted this economic institution. But once the military force of Russia confined the Kazakhs within delineated borders, the same institutions tied to the economic life of the hordes (nomadism) themselves became anachronistic. Much as James Scott (2009) notes that the hill and upland people of South-East Asia were far harder to tame than the sedentary farmers of the rice paddies, the Kazakhs were difficult to rule from above until they were forced to be sedentary. Once this die had been cast, the reality was that economic and political institutions as they existed began to wilt on the vine, leaving a vacuum that the Soviets were only too willing to fill with five-year plans and forced industrialization and centralized authority directed from Moscow. As noted in Chapter 4, this process was aided by Soviet policies of extermination and genocide throughout the USSR, not only removing the institutions by force but also extinguishing the people who once populated those institutions.

Through Soviet policies, the relative price of factors of production within Kazakhstan also changed. In the vast sweep of Kazakh history, land was a crucial input but was regarded as non-exclusive, meaning, in some sense, that land was an economy-wide factor of production rather than one which accrued to various individuals. With land less important for technological innovation or even economies of scale, fixed capital was also less important, with a premium on mobile capital such as the aforementioned livestock herds and a discount on capital which was immobile. Underpinning all this was labour, which was valuable in the sense that it was small-scale and decentralized, but it was highly individualized and not integrated within a larger supply chain. The Soviet experiment changed all of this by both increasing the value of land (which was necessary for industrial development) and fixed capital (factories and machinery) and by denigrating entirely the previous economic structure of Kazakh labourers. With fixed capital and clearly delineated economic boundaries, centralized political processes (especially, as under communism, to plan the economy centrally) became crucial, pushing aside the political institutions which were made to facilitate a very different type of economy. Perhaps, if Kazakhstan had been a modern nation-state of farmers and homesteaders (think of the American Midwest or perhaps a state like Wyoming), it would have gone a much different route in terms of its political institutional development, back in line with its pre-Soviet past and focused on appropriate local governance mechanisms rather than the need for an all-encompassing leader hundreds of miles away. But North (1990) also notes that institutions are creations of those with the power to influence their formation (generating their own hierarchy of institutions), and the destruction of nomadism and the "socially embedded" economic institutions which accompanied it led to a Russian/Soviet opportunity to remake Kazakhstan's (and the USSR's) political institutions as it saw fit.

Thus, in many ways, Nazarbayev's rule was very different from the traditional clan-based approaches adopted throughout Kazakh history and as detailed in Chapters 2 and 3. One of the most important ways in which this divergence can be seen is that Nazarbayev did not actually serve at the leisure of his constituents; in fact, he made sure that the arrangement of political institutions, above all the executive branch, concentrated power in his hands. The need for Khans to satisfy their hordes with good grazing land and with decision-making devolved via economic power – which then determined political power – was removed by the Soviet system, making power its own end, and Nazarbayev played this game like a master. Inheriting a system which was predicated on the dominance of politics over economics, circumscribed in narrow territory (delineated firmly as a bulwark against Russian expansionism), he wielded this power in a manner that Kazakh rulers of the Khanate could only have dreamt of. Still claiming the mantle of arbiter of politics (standing astride the various branches of government as a Khan would have stood over the three hordes), and promising stability at every turn, Nazarbayev merely updated the concerns of the nomads but without the threat of consequences if he failed.

As with any institution, however, some vestiges of prior processes can remain; one need only think of the royal family in the UK which plays a largely ceremonial role but one which is still regarded as important by a vast majority of the British people, to see how institutions that are no longer "useful" still influence daily life.[23] In Kazakhstan, the leftover tendrils of nomadism were the patronage system, an informal institution which seamlessly integrated with the corrupt, inefficient, and dilapidated Soviet apparatus. While the Soviet administrative state attempted to control all, the problems of knowledge and especially bureaucratic quality made it so that this was a fool's errand, leaving daylight in the cracks for alternative institutional arrangements to shine through. Although the Soviet system was excellent at extraction, there was leakage in both the extractive and the redistributive process, with this leakage going elsewhere than the plan or for the glory of the state.

It was here, with the dispensation of patronage, that Nazarbayev was a star, an astute and adept practitioner of the old ways.[24] In this sense, the development of executive power in post-independence Kazakhstan was actually precisely in line with the Kazakh rulers of old, especially in the manner in which Nazarbayev attempted to aggrandize power and cement his own position with his own "clan" (including his family, as seen through the various travails of his daughter Dariga and other members of his horde). Through his dealings and control of the economy, he was able to provide modern "grazing land" quite distinct from that of antiquity to his followers and clan. Of course, Nazarbayev did dispense largesse only to his followers, but he did actually facilitate Kazakhstan's transformation, albeit that it did not go as well as it might have done (see Chapter 6). Indeed, with Kazakhstan stabilizing (alongside Russia) after a turbulent decade in the 1990s, the Kazakhs could see the benefits that Nazarbayev's stability brought and there was genuine support for the President himself (Schatz 2009), perhaps because of the better economic conditions which accrued in the early 2000s (Kennedy 2006). If anything, Nazarbayev's focus on growing the economy to the exclusion of political transition meant that there was more largesse to go round, more payoffs to the opposition to be made, and a very specific type of social contract (you can get rich, but do not meddle in politics) to be adhered to (Ibadildin and Pisareva 2020). Whether or not this approach was actually beneficial to transition, however, will be explored in the next two chapters.

A final point to be made, however, is that the political transition can be judged as a failure in many ways, but one meta-point stands out in particular: because of Nazarbayev and his continued reliance on a Soviet-type over-centralized and bureaucratic system, the key weakness in the transition was mainly that *leadership continued to matter*. Put another way, the government continued to exert so much power over everyday life and especially (as we will see) the economy that it was very important who was the leader, making the issue of succession also critical. This too was very different to a traditional Kazakh approach in a nomadic economy, where results mattered rather than the personality or centrality of a particular leader. As in Ukraine (Hartwell 2016) and other post-Soviet republics (as well as most places in the world today), the omnipresence of government in the Kazakh SSR (and then its continued influence in the political sphere post-independence) meant that it was absolutely crucial to have the "right" people elected in order to reach the "right" outcomes. Given the experience of the USSR, it should have been obvious that the better solution was to have fewer people involved in general rather than searching for the unicorn of the "right" person. Such an approach would also have turned the key transition question from "which is a better political system, presidentialism, super-presidentialism, or a more purely parliamentary system?" to "what does a minimalist political system look like that can still deliver on necessary reforms?" Indeed, the maximalist use of power under the Soviet Union shows that the minimalist path should have been a necessary backlash in nearly every republic, but it was not even contemplated in the vast majority of them – including Kazakhstan.

In sum, this chapter has been focused on the long shadow of Nazarbayev as the driver of the country's political institutional changes, but his resignation in 2019 continues to be felt as a structural break in the 30 years of Kazakhstan's own experiment with democracy. As noted above, these ramifications are the focus of our last chapter and must wait, as first it is crucial to examine the whole point of this book, the economic transformation of the country, as seen through the eyes of its economic institutions. Only by looking at the economic results can we ascertain the efficacy or ineffectiveness of the political reforms in Kazakhstan's transition.

Notes

1 A common Soviet joke was very much in this vein: "Why is the Soviet system superior to all others? Because it successfully overcomes problems that no other system has."

2 It was to take several more decades before the clever trick of calling their neighbours "Nazis" to justify repression and murder was hit upon as a tactic by Russian leaders.

3 After Viktor Yanukovych, President of Ukraine, reversed course and abandoned an agreement with the European Union, pledging instead to join the Russian-dominated Eurasian Union, protestors flocked to Maidan Square in central Kyiv for months. Their efforts, culminating in bloodshed from the side of the regime, eventually succeeded in pressuring Yanukovych to relent, and he fled to Russia. For an in-depth discussion, see Hartwell (2016).

4 The Kazakh SSR declared that testing was completed as of November 1990, but the Kremlin adopted a plan for two more tests in 1991 before closing the site in 1992. These never occurred, however, as in August 1991, the head of the Kazakh SSR officially closed Semipalatinsk; facing a coup and turmoil in Moscow, Gorbachev was powerless to override this action.

5 The current Russian President Vladimir Putin has lamented the collapse of the USSR as "the greatest geopolitical catastrophe of the 20th century," which it patently was not (although it was responsible for many of these catastrophes during its existence).

6 As Alexandrov (1999) notes, the ethnic unrest lasted for approximately five days but ceased immediately upon Nazarbayev's appointment.

7 This was the preferred outcome of the Baltic states and, to some extent, Georgia.

8 An apocryphal story regarding Yeltsin's claims to the northern territories circulated in the early 1990s: after hearing for the 100th time that northern Kazakhstan might be better thought of as "Russian" and thus given to the Russian Federation, Nazarbayev apparently reminded Yeltsin that Omsk had once been Kazakh and perhaps should be returned to Kazakhstan.

9 Although, as Yemelianova (2014) notes, part of the impetus towards secularism could have been due to the illiteracy of the Sovietized elites towards the Islam of their countrymen.

10 Of course, Melvin's (1993) assertion that the highest positions were held by Kazakhs was demonstrably not true during the Kolbin era.

11 As the resignation of the parliament was followed immediately by Nazarbayev conferring income and status on the former parliamentarians, there has been much speculation that some sort of arrangement was reached between the Speaker and the President (Isaacs 2010b).

12 This is the difference between "Type I" policies, which focus on shorter-term goals (e.g. tax rates, tariffs, etc.) and "Type II" policies, which have as their goal transformation of institutions (e.g. decentralization reforms, abolishment of various functions of government).

13 To be fair, the calls for public funding of elections, introducing all other sorts of distortions such as moral hazard, misaligned incentives, and cronyism, rely on this same fallacy of a "market failure."

14 In an example of elite co-option, the new Otan party was in no way related to the Otan-Otechestvo party from 1994, originally formed to oppose Tereshchenko and Nazarbayev, but it used the same "Fatherland" formulation – albeit dropping the Russian term.

15 As anecdotes have no place in scholarly texts, I am forced to place this particular one in a footnote. An acquaintance of mine from my time in Kazakhstan in 2001 and 2002 related his experiences as an election observer during the 1999 parliamentary elections. In a windowless room, ballots were being counted on a table with the observer watching to ensure the integrity of the results. Suddenly, the lights went out and, being an election observer, this person did what any observer would do in the circumstances and leapt onto the table to cover the ballots. In the darkness, he felt ballots being poured onto his back, leading him to shout that no ballots found on his back would be counted. When the lights came on again, there were no ballots on his back but (new) piles on the floor, which electoral workers blamed on the observer – in jumping onto the table, perhaps scared of the darkness, he knocked a large number of ballots off that then needed to be put back onto the table and counted.

16 This is not to minimize the extent of official interference in the electoral process. In a chilling example, the ZSK leader, Zamanbek Nurkadilov, was found dead three weeks before the election with two gunshot wounds to his chest and one to his head. An investigation ruled the death a "suicide" but both ZSK and civil society did not believe that Nukadilov, a prominent critic of the regime, would have done such a thing and in such a manner (Nurumov and Vashchanka 2019).

17 Del Sordi (2016a) notes that by this time, neither of the two parties not named Nur Otan were actually functioning as loyal opposition parties, meaning that essentially there was still unanimity in the Majilis.

18 Or the pitch, if you're more football inclined or European.

19 The quote originally appeared in an op-ed in the *Daily Oklahoman* in 1951 but gained extra cachet during the 2008 and 2012 US presidential elections. This predictably set off a cascade of media outlets attempting to debunk the assertion that Tytler was the author – in many right-leaning outlets, it was attributed to de Tocqueville – but with no attempt to debunk the meaning. This is likely because the sentiment is correct, and the US media was actually in favour of voting largesse from the treasury.

20 In this sense, Tytler (or whomever originally said it) anticipated the rise of public choice economics, which notes that politicians are people, too. While for some this observation may put "democracy in chains," more accurately it is the actions of politicians that affix the shackles and not the people who point it out.

21 Cintron (2021) provides an interesting argument on the fetishization of democracy in general.

22 Ironically, it is likely that such a massive change in the structure of government would have needed to be confirmed by popular referendum, and thus the changes which actually took place – for one reason or another – were more modest, as we will see (del Sordi 2017).

23 During the writing of this chapter, Queen Elizabeth II died, thus underscoring this point.

24 In this sense, the fact that Nazarbayev was also born of the Soviet system made a major difference, as a younger statesman, without the organizational baggage which any successful Soviet apparatchik might carry, could have taken a very different approach to building a power base.

References

Abdelal, R. (2003). National strategy and national money: Politics and the end of the ruble zone, 1991–94. In J. Kirshner (Ed.), *Monetary Orders: Ambiguous Economics, Ubiquitous Politics* (pp. 98–124). Ithaca, NY: Cornell University Press.

Akkuly, S. (2009, 20 November). Poyavleniye i raspad DVK posluzhili urokom tol'ko dlya vlasti [The emergence and collapse of the DVK served as a lesson for the authorities]. Radio Azattyq. http://rus.azattyq.org/a/Kazakhstan_dvk_round_table/1882932.html.

Alexandrov, M. (1999). *Uneasy Alliance: Relations between Russia and Kazakhstan in the Ost-Soviet Era, 1992 –1997*. Westport, CT: Greenwood Publishing Group.

Alimbaev, T., Utebaeva, A., Akhmetzhanova, N., and Asankanov, A. (2017). The environmental situation and the environmental movement in Kazakhstan. *Vestnik Karagandinskogo universiteta. Seriya: Istoriya. Filosofiya* [*Journal of Karaganda University. Series: History. Philosophy*], (1), 13–18.

Allison, O. (2006). Selective enforcement and irresponsibility: Central Asia's shrinking space for independent media. *Central Asian Survey*, 25(1–2), 93–114.

Amandykova, S. K. (2014). Konstitutsiya Respubliki Kazakhstan 1993 goda – pervaya Konstitutsiya suverennogo Kazakhstana [The constitution of the Republic of Kazakhstan of 1993 – The first constitution of sovereign Kazakhstan]. *Studia Politologiczne*, 32, 55–82.

Ambrosio, T. (2015). Leadership succession in Kazakhstan and Uzbekistan: Regime survival after Nazarbayev and Karimov. *Journal of Balkan and Near Eastern Studies*, 17(1), 49–67.

Anceschi, L. (2015). The persistence of media control under consolidated authoritarianism: Containing Kazakhstan's digital media. *Demokratizatsiya: The Journal of Post-Soviet Democratization*, 23(3), 277–295.

Anderson, J. (1997). Constitutional development in Central Asia. *Central Asian Survey*, 16(3), 301–320.

Annus, E. (2012). The problem of Soviet colonialism in the Baltics. *Journal of Baltic Studies*, 43(1), 21–45.

Aron, L. (2011). Everything you think you know about the collapse of the Soviet Union is wrong. *Foreign Policy*, 187, 64–70.

Austin, D. A. (1996). The price of nationalism: Evidence from the Soviet Union. *Public Choice*, 87(1), 1–18.
Babak, V. (2004). The formation of political parties and movements in Central Asia. In Y. Ro'i (Ed.), *Democracy and Pluralism in Muslim Eurasia* (pp. 143–164). New York: Frank Cass Publishing.
Bader, M. (2011). Hegemonic political parties in post-Soviet Eurasia: Towards party-based authoritarianism? *Communist and Post-Communist Studies*, 44(3), 189–197.
Battle, J. M. (1988). Uskorenie, glasnost'and perestroika: The pattern of reform under Gorbachev. *Soviet Studies*, 40(3), 367–384.
Bhuiyan, S. H., and Amagoh, F. (2011). Public sector reform in Kazakhstan: Issues and perspectives. *International Journal of Public Sector Management*, 24(3), 227–249.
Blackmon, P. (2021). After Karimov and Nazarbayev: Change in Uzbekistan and Kazakhstan? *Central Asian Survey*, 40(2), 179–196.
Bowyer, A. C. (2008). *Parliament and Political Parties in Kazakhstan*. Washington, DC: Central Asia-Caucasus Institute & Silk Road Studies Program.
Bremmer, I., and Welt, C. (1996). The trouble with democracy in Kazakhstan. *Central Asian Survey*, 15(2), 179–199.
Busygina, I., Filippov, M., and Taukebaeva, E. (2018). To decentralize or to continue on the centralization track: The cases of authoritarian regimes in Russia and Kazakhstan. *Journal of Eurasian Studies*, 9(1), 61–71.
Caron, J. F. (2019). The contemporary politics of Kazakhisation: The case of Astana's urbanism. In J. F. Caron (Ed.), *Kazakhstan and the Soviet Legacy: Between Continuity and Rupture* (pp. 181–205). Berlin: Springer.
Carter, F. W., and Turnock, D. (Eds.) (1996). *Environmental Problems in Eastern Europe*. New York: Psychology Press.
Chaisty, P. (2006). *Legislative Politics and Economic Power in Russia*. Basingstoke: Palgrave Macmillan.
Cheskin, A., and Kachuyevski, A. (2019). The Russian-speaking populations in the post-Soviet space: Language, politics and identity. *Europe-Asia Studies*, 71(1), 1–23.
Cintron, R. (2021). *Democracy as Fetish*. University Park, PA: Penn State University Press.
Clemens, W. C., Jr. (1993). Soviet centrifugalism: Republics as independent actors. *Nationalities Papers*, 21(2), 9–24.
Coase, R. H. (1937). The nature of the firm. *Economica*, 4(16), 386–405.
Collins, K. (2004). The logic of clan politics: Evidence from the Central Asian trajectories. *World Politics*, 56(2), 224–261.
Committee for Security and Cooperation in Europe (CSCE) (1994). *Report on the Elections in Kazakhstan, 7 March 1994*. Helsinki: Committee for Security and Cooperation in Europe Parliamentary Assembly. www.oscepa.org/en/documents/election-observation/election-observation-statements/kazakhstan/statements-13/1422-1994-parliamentary-1/file.
Cornell, S. E., and Engvall, J. (2017). *Kazakhstan in Europe: Why Not*. Stockholm: Central Asia–Caucasus Institute and Silk Road Studies Program.
Cummings, S. (2005). *Kazakhstan: Power and Elite*. London: I. B. Tauris.
Curtis, G. E. (2003). Kazakhstan: A country study. In L. M. Buyers (Ed.), *Central Asia in Focus: Political and Economic Issues* (pp. 37–116). Hauppauge, NY: Nova Science Publishers.
Dave, B. (2005). Kazakhstan's 2004 parliamentary elections: Managing loyalty and support for the regime. *Problems of Post-Communism*, 52(1), 3–14.

Dave, B. (2007). *Kazakhstan: Ethnicity, Language and Power.* London: Routledge.
Del Sordi, A. (2016a). Legitimation and the party of power in Kazakhstan. In M. Brusis, J. Ahrens, and M. Schulze Wessel (Eds.), *Politics and Legitimacy in Post-Soviet Eurasia* (pp. 72–96). Basingstoke: Palgrave Macmillan.
Del Sordi, A. (2016b). Kazakhstan 2015–2016: Balancing regime stability amidst local and global challenges. *Asia Maior*, 27, 439–462.
Del Sordi, A. (2017). Kazakhstan 2017: Institutional stabilisation, nationbuilding, international engagement. *Asia Maior*, 28, 411–430.
Diener, A. C. (2002). National territory and the reconstruction of history in Kazakhstan. *Eurasian Geography and Economics*, 43(8), 632–650.
Diener, A. C. (2016). Imagining Kazakhstani-stan: Negotiations of homeland and titular-nationality. In M. Laruelle (Ed.), *Kazakhstan in the Making: Legitimacy, Symbols, and Social Changes* (pp. 131–154). Lanham, MD: Lexington Books.
Dragomir, M. (2003). *Fighting Legacy: Media Reform in Post-Communist Europe.* Washington, DC: The Atlantic Council.
Elliot, G. (1993). Kazakhstan, Nazarbayev, foreign investment & oil. *Louisiana Law Review*, 53(4), 1243–1255.
Emizet, K. N., and Hesli, V. L. (1995). The disposition to secede: An analysis of the Soviet case. *Comparative Political Studies*, 27(4), 493–536.
Evans, A. D. (2022). Privatization and judicialization in resource extraction: Comparing labor militancy in the oil fields of Russia and Kazakhstan. *Comparative Politics* [Fast Track article]. www.ingentaconnect.com/content/cuny/cp/pre-prints/content-jcpo21068ii.
Fierman, W. (1998). Language and identity in Kazakhstan: Formulations in policy documents 1987–1997. *Communist and Post-Communist Studies*, 31(2), 171–186.
Gehlbach, S., and Malesky, E. J. (2010). The contribution of veto players to economic reform. *The Journal of Politics*, 72(4), 957–975.
Gellner, E. (1994). *Conditions of Liberty: Civil Society and its Rivals.* London: Hamish Hamilton.
Ginsburg, T. (2010). Written constitutions and the administrative state: On the constitutional character of administrative law. In *Comparative Administrative Law* (pp. 117–127). London: Edward Elgar Publishing.
Gleason, G. (1997). Prospects for Kazakhstan's Asian liberalism. *Democratization*, 5 (3), 376–385.
Gleason, G. (1999). The impact of the global financial crisis on political dynamics in Central Asia. *Demokratizatsiya*, 7(2), 241–252.
Golosov, G. V., Gushchina, K., and Kononenko, P. (2016). Russia's local government in the process of authoritarian regime transformation: incentives for the survival of local democracy. *Local Government Studies*, 42(4), 507–526.
Gross, P. (2019). Repackaged authoritarian policies: Kazakhstan's "new" version of media controls. *Georgetown Journal of International Affairs*, 20(1), 187–194.
Hajda, L. (1988). The nationalities problem in the Soviet Union. *Current History*, 87 (531), 325–352.
Hanks, R. R. (1998). Directions in the ethnic politics of Kazakhstan: Concession, compromise, or catastrophe? *Journal of Third World Studies*, 15(1), 143–162.
Hartwell, C. A. (2013). *Institutional Barriers in the Transition to Market: Examining Performance and Divergence in Transition Economies.* Basingstoke: Palgrave Macmillan.
Hartwell, C. A. (2016). *Two Roads Diverge: The Transition Experience of Poland and Ukraine.* Cambridge: Cambridge University Press.

Hartwell, C. A., and Urban, M. (2021). Burning the Rechtsstaat: Legal institutions and protection of the rule of law. *Journal of Institutional Economics*, 17(1), 105–131.

Henderson, K. E. (2000). Halfway home and a long way to go: Russian and Kazakh roads to sectoral and political corruption. *Demokratizatsiya*, 8(4), 481–481.

Heuer, V., and Hierman, B. (2022). Manhandling and mediation: Unpacking the repressive repertoire in Kazakhstan's 2016 anti-land reform protests. *Asian Security*, 1–18.

Hicks, W. D. (2015). Partisan competition and the efficiency of lawmaking in American state legislatures, 1991–2009. *American Politics Research*, 43(5), 743–770.

Higashijima, M. (2022). *The Dictator's Dilemma at the Ballot Box: Electoral Manipulation, Economic Maneuvering, and Political Order in Autocracies*. Ann Arbor, MI: University of Michigan Press.

Holm-Hansen, J. (1999). Political integration in Kazakhstan. In P. Kolstø (Ed.), *Nation-Building and Ethnic Integration in Post-Soviet Societies: An Investigation of Latvia and Kazakhstan*. Boulder, CO: Westview Press.

Huskey, E. (2016). *Presidential Power in Russia*. New York: Routledge.

Ibadildin, N., and Pisareva, D. (2020). Central Asia in transition: Social contract transformation in Nazarbayev and post-Nazarbayev Kazakhstan. In A. Mihir (Ed.), *Transformation and Development: Studies in the Organization for Security and Cooperation in Europe (OSCE) Member States* (pp. 101–116). Bishkek: Springer.

Ibrayeva, A. R., and Nezhina, T. (2013). Public sector reforms in Kazakhstan. In S. Liebert, S. E. Condrey, and D. Goncharov (Eds.), *Public Administration in Post-Communist Countries* (pp. 43–68). London: Routledge.

Isaacs, R. (2010a). "Papa"–Nursultan Nazarbayev and the discourse of charismatic leadership and nation-building in post-Soviet Kazakhstan. *Studies in Ethnicity and Nationalism*, 10(3), 435–452.

Isaacs, R. (2010b). Informal politics and the uncertain context of transition: Revisiting early-stage non-democratic development in Kazakhstan. *Democratization*, 17(1), 1–25.

Isaacs, R. (2013). Nur Otan, informal networks and the countering of elite instability in Kazakhstan: Bringing the "formal" back in. *Europe-Asia Studies*, 65(6), 1055–1079.

Isaacs, R. (2020). Russia–Kazakhstan relations and the Tokayev–Nazarbayev tandem. *Russian Analytical Digest*, 248, 2–5.

Isaacs, R. (2022). *Political Opposition in Authoritarianism: Exit, Voice, and Loyalty in Kazakhstan*. Basingstoke: Palgrave Macmillan.

Isaacs, R., and Whitmore, S. (2014). The limited agency and life-cycles of personalized dominant parties in the post-Soviet space: The cases of United Russia and Nur Otan. *Democratization*, 21(4), 699–721.

Jailani, Y. (2016). The loosening of a stronghold: Economic pressure on Kazakhstan's dictatorship. *Harvard International Review*, 38(1), 46–47.

Jakusik, J. (2020). Constitutional reforms and the circumstances behind the transition of power in the Republic of Kazakhstan. In G. Aqtay and C. Erdem (Eds.), *Language and Society in Kazakhstan: The Kazakh Context* (pp. 59–70). Poznań: Adam Mickiewicz University Press.

Johnson, S., and Kroll, H. (1991). Managerial strategies for spontaneous privatization. *Soviet Economy*, 7(4), 281–316.

Jowitt, K. (1997). Really imaginary socialism. *East European Constitutional Review*, 6 (2–3), 43–49.

Kamrany, N. M. (1986). The Continuing Soviet War in Afghanistan. *Current History*, 85(513), 333–336.

Kanapyanov, T. (2018). Role and place of the parliament of Kazakhstan in the system of checks and balances. *Communist and Post-Communist Studies*, 51(1), 81–87.

Kanapyanov, T. Y., and Kaliyev, N. K. (2015). Parliamentary reforms of 2007 and one party dominated parliament of Kazakhstan (2007–2012). *Mediterranean Journal of Social Sciences*, 6(S1), 335.

Kanter, S. (1993). Constitution making in Kazakhstan. *International Legal Perspectives*, 5(1), 65–92.

Karmazina, L. (2008). Institutionalization of the party system in the Republic of Kazakhstan: Past and present. *Central Asia and the Caucasus*, 5(53), 39–53.

Kassenova, T. (2016). Banning nuclear testing: Lessons from the Semipalatinsk nuclear testing site. *The Nonproliferation Review*, 23(3–4), 329–344.

Kazhegeldin, A. (2000). Shattered image. *Harvard International Review*, 22(1), 76–79.

Kembayev, Z. (2011). The rise of presidentialism in post-Soviet Central Asia: The example of Kazakhstan. In R. Grote and T. Röder (Eds.), *Constitutionalism in Islamic Countries: Between Upheaval and Continuity* (pp. 431–435). New York: Oxford University Press.

Kembayev, Z. (2017). Recent constitutional reforms in Kazakhstan: A move towards democratic transition? *Review of Central and East European Law*, 42(4), 294–324.

Kennedy, R. (2006). A colorless election: The 2005 presidential election in Kazakhstan, and what it means for the future of the opposition. *Problems of Post-Communism*, 53(6), 46–58.

Khazanov, A. M. (1995). The ethnic problems of contemporary Kazakhstan. *Central Asian Survey*, 14(2), 243–264.

Knox, C. (2008). Kazakhstan: Modernizing government in the context of political inertia. *International Review of Administrative Sciences*, 74(3), 477–496.

Kolossov, V. (1999). Ethnic and political identities and territorialities in the post-Soviet space. *GeoJournal*, 48(2), 71–81.

Kolstø, P. (1996). Nation-building in the former USSR. *Journal of Democracy*, 7(1), 118–132.

Kukusheva, N. E., Sheryazdanova, G. R., Byulegenova, B. B., Kakimzhanova, M. K., and Turgaleyeva, A. T. (2019). Multiculturalism: A comparative analysis of Western countries and Kazakhstan. *Opción: Revista de Ciencias Humanas y Sociales*, 23, 922–943.

Kurtov, A. (2007). Presidential seat or Padishah's throne? The distinctive features of supreme power in Central Asian states. *Russian Social Science Review*, 48(6), 64–95.

Kusznir, J. (2018). Kazakhstan's political and economic development and the role of the ruling elites. In F. Jaitner, T. Olteanu, and T. Spöri (Eds.), *Crises in the Post-Soviet Space* (pp. 241–251). London: Routledge.

Kuzembayeva, A. B., Baikushikova, G. S., Delovarova, L. F., and Chukubayev, Y. S. (2019). Development of environmental movements in Kazakhstan through the prism of social and political transformations: Key trends and current issues. *Central Asian Journal of Social Sciences and Humanities*, 3(1–2), 92–99.

Laqueur, W. (1996). *The Dream that Failed: Reflections on the Soviet Union*. Oxford: Oxford University Press.

Lee, C. (2004). Languages and ethnic politics in Central Asia: The case of Kazakhstan. *Journal of International and Area Studies*, 11(1), 101–116.

Lee, V. R. (2012). *Performance Anomalies: A Novel*. New York: Perimeter Six Press.

Libman, A., and Vinokurov, E. (2012). Eurasian Economic Union: Why now? Will it work? Is it enough? *Seton Hall Journal of Diplomacy and International Relations*, 13(2), 29.

Lillis, J. (2022). *Dark Shadows: Inside the Secret World of Kazakhstan*. London: Bloomsbury Publishing.

Ludwikowski, R. R. (1993). Constitution making in the countries of former Soviet dominance: Current development. *Georgia Journal of International & Comparative Law*, 23(2), 155–267.

Luong, P. J., and Weinthal, E. (1999). The NGO paradox: Democratic goals and non-democratic outcomes in Kazakhstan. *Europe-Asia Studies*, 51(7), 1267–1284.

Magaloni, B., and Kricheli, R. (2010). Political order and one-party rule. *Annual Review of Political Science*, 13, 123–143.

Makhmutova, M. (2001). Local government in Kazakhstan. In I. Munteanu and V. Popa (Eds.), *Developing New Rules in Old Environment: Local Government in Eastern Europe, in the Caucasus and in Central Asia* (pp. 431–447). Budapest: Open Society Institute.

Marat, E. (2016). Post-violence regime survival and expansion in Kazakhstan and Tajikistan. *Central Asian Survey*, 35(4), 531–548.

Marples, D. R. (2016). *The Collapse of the Soviet Union, 1985–1991*. New York: Routledge.

Mazurski, K. R. (1991). Communism and the environment. *Forum for Applied Research and Public Policy*, 5(4), 39–44.

Melvin, N. (1993). Russia and the ethno-politics of Kazakhstan. *The World Today*, 49 (11), 208–210.

Melvin, N. J. (2001). Patterns of centre-regional relations in Central Asia: The cases of Kazakhstan, the Kyrgyz Republic and Uzbekistan. *Regional & Federal Studies*, 11(3), 165–193.

Miller, C. (2016). *The Struggle to Save the Soviet Economy: Mikhail Gorbachev and the Collapse of the USSR*. Chapel Hill, NC: UNC Press Books.

Minaev, B. (2015). *Boris Yeltsin: The Decade that Shook the World*. London: Glagoslav Publications.

Ministry of Information and Communication (2010). *Pervyy Prezident Respubliki Kazakhstan Nursultan Nazarbayev: Khronika Deyatel'nosti 1991–1998 gody* [*First President of the Republic of Kazakhstan Nursultan Nazarbayev: Chronicle of Activities, 1991–1998*]. Astana: Delovoi Mir.

Mishra, M. K. (2008). Constitutional development in independent Kazakhstan: A review. *Himalayan and Central Asian Studies*, 12(3/4), 115.

Mishra, M. K. (2009). Democratisation process in Kazakhstan: Gauging the indicators. *India Quarterly*, 65(3), 313–327.

Murphy, J. (2006). Illusory transition? Elite reconstitution in Kazakhstan, 1989–2002. *Europe-Asia Studies*, 58(4), 523–554.

Nazarbayev, N. (1991). God grant that no one should stir up Kazakhstan on ethnic grounds. It Would be far worse than Yugoslavia. *Kazakhstanskaya Pravda*, 23 November, 1.

Nikolayenko, O. (2015). Youth media consumption and perceptions of electoral integrity in Kazakhstan and Kyrgyzstan. *Demokratizatsiya: The Journal of Post-Soviet Democratization*, 23(3), 257–276.

Niyazbekov N. (2017). Kazakhstan's government is using social media to tame rebellion. *The Conversation*, 21 May.https://theconversation.com/kazakhstans-government-is-using-social-media-to-tame-rebel-lion-73542.

Niyazbekov, N. (2018). Is Kazakhstan immune to color revolutions? The social movements perspective. *Demokratizatsiya: The Journal of Post-Soviet Democratization*, 26(3), 401–425.

North, D. C. (1971). Institutional change and economic growth. *The Journal of Economic History*, 31(1), 118–125.

North, D. C. (1990). *Institutions, Institutional Change and Economic Performance*. Cambridge: Cambridge University Press.

Nurumov, D., and Vashchanka, V. (2019). Presidential terms in Kazakhstan: Less is more? In A. Baturo and R. Elgie (Eds.), *The Politics of Presidential Term Limits* (pp. 221–246). Oxford: Oxford University Press.

Ó Beacháin, D., and Kevlihan, R. (2013). Threading a needle: Kazakhstan between civic and ethno-nationalist state-building. *Nations and Nationalism*, 19(2), 337–356.

Oka, N. (2009). Ethnicity and elections under authoritarianism: The case of Kazakhstan. Institute of Developing Economies Discussion Paper No. 194, March. https://bit.ly/3ijnPVH.

Olcott, M. B. (1981). The collectivization drive in Kazakhstan. *The Russian Review*, 40(2), 122–142

Olcott, M. B. (1989). Gorbachev's national dilemma. *Journal of International Affairs*, 42(2), 399–421.

Olcott, M. B. (1990). Perestroyka in Kazakhstan. *Problems of Communism*, 39, 65–77.

Olcott, M. B. (1995). *The Kazakhs*. Palo Alto, CA: Hoover Institution Press.

Olcott, M. B. (2010). *Kazakhstan: Unfulfilled Promise*. Washington, DC: Carnegie Endowment.

Olson, D. M., and Norton, P. (1996). Legislatures in democratic transition. *The Journal of Legislative Studies*, 2(1), 1–15.

Omelicheva, M. Y. (2016). Authoritarian legitimation: Assessing discourses of legitimacy in Kazakhstan and Uzbekistan. *Central Asian Survey*, 35(4), 481–500.

Onuch, O. (2014). The Maidan and beyond: Who were the protesters? *Journal of Democracy*, 25(3), 44–51.

Organization for Security and Cooperation in Europe (OSCE) (1999). *Kazakhstan, Presidential Election, 10 January 1999: Final Report*. Warsaw: Organization for Security and Cooperation in Europe.

Partlett, W. (2012). The dangers of constitution-making. *Brooklyn Journal of International Law*, 38(1), 193–238.

Partlett, W. (2015). Courts and constitution-making. *Wake Forest Law Review*, 50(5), 921–949.

Penati, B. (2019). The environmental legacy of the Soviet regime. In J.-F. Caron (Ed.), *Kazakhstan and the Soviet Legacy* (pp. 51–74). Singapore: Palgrave Macmillan.

Peterson, D. J. (1993). *Troubled Lands: The Legacy of Soviet Environmental Destruction*. London: Routledge.

Peyrouse, S. (2007). Nationhood and the minority question in Central Asia: The Russians in Kazakhstan. *Europe-Asia Studies*, 59(3), 481–501.

Phillips, A., and James, P. (2001). National identity between tradition and reflexive modernisation: The contradictions of Central Asia. *National Identities*, 3(1), 23–35.

Pistan, C. (2019). Smart authoritarianism: Nazarbayev's resignation as a move to consolidate Kazakhstan's 2017 constitutional reform. *DPCE Online*, 39(2), 1037–1054.

Purvis-Roberts, K. L., Werner, C. A., and Frank, I. (2007). Perceived risks from radiation and nuclear testing near Semipalatinsk, Kazakhstan: A comparison between physicians, scientists, and the public. *Risk Analysis: An International Journal*, 27(2), 291–302.

Republican Network of Independent Monitors (RNIM) (2004). *Preliminary Report on Monitoring of September 19, 2004 Elections to the Majilis of the Parliament of the Republic of Kazakhstan*. Almaty: Republican Network of Independent Monitors. Retrieved 23 August 2022 from www.ndi.org/sites/default/files/1749_kz_report_092304_5.pdf.

Reuveny, R., and Prakash, A. (1999). The Afghanistan war and the breakdown of the Soviet Union. *Review of International Studies*, 25(4), 693–708.

Roberts, S. R. (2012). Doing the democracy dance in Kazakhstan: Democracy development as cultural encounter. *Slavic Review*, 71(2), 308–330.

Roeder, P. G. (1991). Soviet federalism and ethnic mobilization. *World Politics*, 43(2), 196–232.

Ro'i, Y. (1991a). The Soviet and Russian context of the development of nationalism in Soviet Central Asia. *Cahiers du Monde Russe*, 32(1), 123–141.

Ro'i, Y. (1991b). Central Asian riots and disturbances, 1989–1990: Causes and context. *Central Asian Survey*, 10(3), 21–54.

Rozsa, G. G. (2020). The Nevada Movement: A model of trans-indigenous anti-nuclear solidarity. *Journal of Transnational American Studies*, 11(2), 99–123.

Salmon, P. (2012). Police massacre has opened a dark chapter for Kazakh workers' movement. *Debatte: Journal of Contemporary Central and Eastern Europe*, 20(1), 73–77.

Sarsembayev, A. (1999). Imagined communities: Kazak nationalism and Kazakification in the 1990s. *Central Asian Survey*, 18(3), 319–346.

Satpayev, D., and Umbetaliyeva, ⊠. (2015). The protests in Zhanaozen and the Kazakh oil sector: Conflicting interests in a rentier state. *Journal of Eurasian Studies*, 6(2), 122–129.

Sayabayev, D. (2016). Sociopolitical associations in independent Kazakhstan: Evolution of the phenomenon. *Pacific Science Review B: Humanities and Social Sciences*, 2(3), 94–99.

Schatz, E. A. (1999). Notes on the "dog that didn't bark": Eco-internationalism in late Soviet Kazakstan. *Ethnic and Racial Studies*, 22(1), 136–161.

Schatz, E. (2000a). The politics of multiple identities: Lineage and ethnicity in Kazakhstan. *Europe-Asia Studies*, 52(3), 489–506.

Schatz, E. A. (2000b). Framing strategies and non-conflict in multi-ethnic Kazakhstan. *Nationalism and Ethnic Politics*, 6(2), 71–94.

Schatz, E. A. (2009). The soft authoritarian tool kit: Agenda-setting power in Kazakhstan and Kyrgyzstan. *Comparative Politics*, 41(2), 203–222.

Scott, J.C. (2009). *The Art of Not Being Governed: An Anarchist History of Upland Southeast Asia*. New Haven, CT: Yale University Press.

Searle, J. R. (2005). What is an institution? *Journal of Institutional Economics*, 1(1), 1–22.

Shelekpayev, N. (2021). Rethinking Transfers of Power and Public Protest in Kazakhstan, 1959–1989. *Europe-Asia Studies*, 1–15.

Shevtsova, L. (1992). The August coup and the Soviet collapse. *Survival*, 34(1), 5–18.

Slipchenko, V. I. (1997). Russia's political and military problems in Central Asia. *European Security*, 6(1), 114–124.

Smagulov, K., Zhandosova, S., Baigabatova, N., and Kalkhanova, A. (2017). Parliamentary elections by party lists in Kazakhstan in 1999–2016: An analysis. *Central Asia and the Caucasus*, 18(2), 78–87.

Smith, J. (2016). Old habits, new realities: Central Asia and Russia from the break-up of the USSR to 9/11. In H. Rytövuori-Apunen (Ed.), *The Regional Security Puzzle around Afghanistan: Bordering Practices in Central Asia and Beyond* (pp. 29–49). Opladen: B. Budrich.

Solzhenitsyn, A. (1995.) *The Russian Question at the End of the 20th Century.* London: Farrar, Straus and Giroux.

Stefany, M. G. (2013). Kazakhization, Kunaev and Kazakhstan: A bridge to independence. *Orta Asya ve Kafkasya Araştırmaları*, 16, 49–72.

Stefany, M. G. (2020). On the road to insurrection: The Soviet nationalities problem, the Kazakhs, and Zheltoksan in Kazakhstan. *The Journal of Central Asian Studies*, 26–27, 1–14.

Stokes, S. C. (1999). Political parties and democracy. *Annual Review of Political Science*, 2(1), 243–267.

Suesse, M. (2018). Breaking the unbreakable union: Nationalism, disintegration and the Soviet economic collapse. *The Economic Journal*, 128(615), 2933–2967.

Sullivan, C. J. (2018). Kazakhstan at a Crossroads. *Asia Policy*, 13(2), 121–136.

Taubayev, Z. T. (2015). Manipulative and pragmalinguistic aspects of political discourse. *Mediterranean Journal of Social Sciences*, 6(S2), 254–257.

Thornhill, C. (2017). The sociology of constitutions. *Annual Review of Law and Social Science*, 13, 493–513.

Tipaldou, S. (2021). Kazakhstan 2.0: Change and continuity? In F. Izquierdo-Brichs and F. Serra-Massansalvador (Eds.), *Political Regimes and Neopatrimonialism in Central Asia* (pp. 249–293). Singapore: Palgrave Macmillan.

Tolstrup, J. (2015). Black knights and elections in authoritarian regimes: Why and how Russia supports authoritarian incumbents in post-Soviet states. *European Journal of Political Research*, 54(4), 673–690.

Trochev, A. (2018). Kazakhstan: The state of non-democracy. In A. Albert, D. Landau, P. Faraguna, and S. Drugda (Eds.), *The I· CONnect-Clough Center 2017 Global Review of Constitutional Law* (pp. 161–165). Boston, MA: Clough Center for the Study of Constitutional Democracy.

Tsebelis, G., and Money, J. (1997). *Bicameralism.* Cambridge: Cambridge University Press.

Tsebelis, G., and Rizova, T. P. (2007). Presidential conditional agenda setting in the former communist countries. *Comparative Political Studies*, 40(10), 1155–1182.

Tuminez, A. S. (2003). Nationalism, ethnic pressures, and the breakup of the Soviet Union. *Journal of Cold War Studies*, 5(4), 81–136.

Tutumlu, A., and Rustemov, I. (2021). The paradox of authoritarian power: Bureaucratic games and information asymmetry. The case of Nazarbayev's Kazakhstan. *Problems of Post-Communism*, 68(2), 124–134.

Vladimir, B. (2005). Kazakhstan: How its multiparty system came into being. *Central Asia and the Caucasus*, 2(32), 78–88.

Von Soest, C., and Grauvogel, J. (2017). Identity, procedures and performance: How authoritarian regimes legitimize their rule. *Contemporary Politics*, 23(3), 287–305.

Wagner, R. E. (2012). A macro economy as an ecology of plans. *Journal of Economic Behavior & Organization*, 82(2–3), 433–444.

Walker, E. W. (2003). *Dissolution: Sovereignty and the Breakup of the Soviet Union.* New York: Rowman & Littlefield.

White, S., and Hill, R. J. (1996). Russia, the former Soviet Union and Eastern Europe: The referendum as a flexible political instrument. In M. Gallagher and P. V. Uleri (Eds.), *The Referendum Experience in Europe* (pp. 153–170). London: Palgrave Macmillan.

Willerton, J. P. (2007). Patronage networks and coalition building in the Brezhnev era. In P. Waldron (Ed.), *The Soviet Union* (pp. 397–426). London: Routledge.

Wilson, J. L. (2017). The Russian pursuit of regional hegemony. *Rising Powers Quarterly*, 2(1), 7–25.

Wright, J. (2008). Do authoritarian institutions constrain? How legislatures affect economic growth and investment. *American Journal of Political Science*, 52(2), 322–343.

Yang, S. (2020). Nazarbayev: The road to power and success. *China International Strategy Review*, 2(1), 120–137.

Yemelianova, G. M. (2014). Islam, national identity and politics in contemporary Kazakhstan. *Asian Ethnicity*, 15(3), 286–301.

Zardykhan, Z. (2004). Russians in Kazakhstan and demographic change: Imperial legacy and the Kazakh way of nation building. *Asian Ethnicity*, 5(1), 61–79.

6 The Economic Development of Post-Soviet Kazakhstan

Tracing the twists and turns of Kazakhstan's pre-imperial history, its Soviet experiment, and its political concentration under Nursultan Nazarbayev leads us to a simple question, the *raison d'être* of this book: did these antecedents matter for the economic transition after the collapse of the Soviet Union? And if so, how much?

In one sense, this is the most important question we can possibly ask, as the whole point of Kazakhstan's post-communist transition was to move away from institutions which facilitated a planned economy and towards those which facilitated a free market economy. As I have noted several times before (Hartwell 2013a), including in this book, *transition was institutional change*, nothing else, and improved economic outcomes were just second-order effects behind the transformation of institutions, both political and economic. If the historical record, up to and including the Soviet occupation and including the political institutional reforms implemented after independence, aided or hindered the development of these economic institutions, it will have indelibly changed the trajectory of transition and led to either a success or a failure, or (as in most cases) a hybrid of both. Thus, we can only judge the economic development of post-Soviet Kazakhstan, and whether or not its transition was ultimately a success, by the way in which its economic institutions actually did develop, with an eye on the drivers behind this evolution. Again, it should be noted that "success" in a transition is precisely defined as changing institutions so that they facilitate the development of a market economy; communist-era institutions surviving into the 2000s would manifestly be a failure of transition, unless these institutions reformed so much as to be unrecognizable as the institutions of old.

This question of institutional transformation is doubly important in the Kazakh case for, as we saw in the previous chapter, changes to political institutions were made with the explicit goal of enabling the economic transition. Unlike many other transition economies, which did not really have a blueprint or strategy for transformation apart from macroeconomic stabilization and/or (in the case of the lucky ones in Central and Eastern Europe) accession to the European Union (EU), Kazakhstan had an evolving strategy for implementing economic change on a massive scale. Nazarbayev's

DOI: 10.4324/9781003212508-6

"economics first, politics later" approach was adopted precisely to slow walk the political transition in favour of a much more rapid economic transformation, taking the structure of the Kazakh economy from Soviet stagnation to modern innovation. Indeed, with an eye on history, the transition process was managed to attempt to invert the hierarchy of institutions once again. Where economic institutions drove the development of political institutions in the pre-tsarist period, Nazarbayev's tenure attempted to use political institutions to effect economic change (much as the Soviet Union had), utilizing the Soviet apparatus of concentrated power for very different ends. In this sense, the longer-term game was to instrumentalize political institutions in such a way that they would become less important in comparison to economic ones, bringing us full circle to the hierarchy under nomadism. Of course, we know that political institutions, once they reach their ascendancy, are very difficult to dislodge by economic means, apart from massive crises and dislocations (and, unfortunately, crises tend to entrench and expand the power of the state yet further rather than reducing it). This appeared to be the case with Nazarbayev, whose reforms in 2017 fell far short of the reduction of the power of the presidency than was needed. But in conception, at least, the growing power of economic institutions should have eroded the need for such political centralization and had salutary effects on Kazakhstan's political transformation as well.

This chapter attempts to answer the question of whether the country's transition was an economic success or failure, as we examine the changes in Kazakhstan's economy since 1991 and its economic institutions in particular. As in the previous chapter, we will start with an examination of the broader issues encompassed in Kazakhstan's transformation, which in this case means the macroeconomic stabilization required for the transformation of the economy. After this brief introduction of the start of the transition, we will then work our way through some of the most important economic institutions that the country needed to either reform, reintroduce, or create from the ground up: property rights and its sub-institution of ownership (encapsulated in privatization); financial and monetary institutions; and trade.[1] As we will see, all the different factors noted in the previous chapters played a hand in taking Kazakhstan to where it is today, and it is our task to sift through the momentous economic changes in the country and see what worked, what did not, and where things could have been – or indeed might still be – different.

A Momentous Economic Change and the Challenge of Stabilization

Like all transition economies, the first and most difficult challenge that independent Kazakhstan faced was that of macroeconomic stabilization, the implementation of so-called Type I policies (Svejnar 2002) which laid the groundwork for a market economy and flowed into Type II policies, those which enabled and created supporting institutions. The uncoupling of Kazakhstan from the rest of the Union of Soviet Socialist Republics (USSR) was complicated not just by the breaking of all the links in the carefully constructed hub and spoke model of central planning which the Kremlin had built since the 1920s (more on this below); more importantly, the economic stagnation and inefficiency which had revealed itself during the 1970s and 1980s, even with the advent of perestroika, was now no longer the problem of Moscow and was entirely the responsibility of Nazarbayev. As Becker et al. (2009:88) note, "As in other republics, Kazakhstan maintained an unsustainably high stock of capital, and was part of the production chain focused on production of investment goods, rather than consumer goods and services," meaning that inefficient industry was now tasked with meeting many more of Kazakhstan's needs.

Other distortions tied to the Soviet system manifested themselves in Kazakhstan's initial conditions at the outset of transition. While the transition economics literature has determined that initial conditions were important for the beginning of transition (Fischer et al. 1996; Krueger and Ciolko 1998; Stuart and Panayotopoulos 1999; De Melo et al. 2001; Havrylyshyn and van Rooden 2003), creating the distance that a country had to travel to stability and acting as a proxy for the extent of distortions which need to be overcome (Lee and Jeong 2006), the influence of initial conditions should have waned over time if the proper policies had been pursued (Hartwell 2013a). Regardless of this reality, from the vantage point of January 1992, the conditions faced by the former Soviet republics were daunting, indeed; Table 6.1 shows some of these conditions in Kazakhstan as it started its journey as a sovereign and independent economy, juxtaposed against a perhaps better-situated country, Ukraine. As noted in Hartwell (2016), Ukraine's initial conditions, while somewhat distorted because of the myriad of problems with Soviet statistics, were roughly on par with its western neighbour, Poland (thus making the divergence of the two countries even more interesting). As Table 6.1 shows, Kazakhstan had a much smaller economy albeit a much wealthier one (in terms of gross domestic product – GDP – per capita); however, it had also taken the collapse of the Soviet Union much harder in terms of its contraction in 1991 (with more to come as part of the transition). Perhaps more dauntingly, the metrics of potential success for the transformation in Kazakhstan were also worse than in Ukraine, with the private sector contributing to GDP half that of Ukraine in 1991 and an infant mortality rate on par with poorer regions in Latin America and worse than in the People's Republic of China, South Africa, and Vietnam during that time.[2] With both a nascent private sector and problems in ensuring the next generation of labour (and human capital), Kazakhstan was in a very difficult position to Ukraine, even when one considers that the two countries' educational systems were similar (indeed, Kazakhstan had an higher gross enrolment rate in secondary school than Ukraine, at approximately 98.9 per cent to 92.2 per cent).[3]

What Kazakhstan had which Ukraine manifestly did not, however – and which provided some mitigation for these deleterious initial conditions – was

Table 6.1 Initial Conditions in Kazakhstan and Ukraine

	Kazakhstan	*Ukraine*
GDP (constant 2015 US $)	80,344,035,342.64	132,842,082,756.34
GDP per capita (constant 2015 US $)	5,156.95	2,835.33
GDP growth (1991)	–11.00	–8.70
Foreign direct investment (FDI), % of GDP	0.40	0.27
Gross fixed capital formation, % of GDP	23.71	20.16
Private sector, % of GDP (1991)	5.00	10.00
Trade, % of GDP	149.34	45.97
Population in urban agglomerations of more than 1 million (% of total population)	8.42	10.02
Infant mortality rate (per 1,000 live births)	44.30	16.70

Source: World Bank World Development Indicators, https://databank.worldbank.org/source/world-development-indicators, European Bank for Reconstruction and Development (EBRD) Structural Indicators, www.ebrd.com/economic-research-and-data/transition-qualities-asses.html. Data are for 1992 unless noted otherwise.

to be prominent in the country's post-independence growth trajectory, namely the presence of natural resources. While Ukraine is the "bread basket of Europe," abundant (prior to the Russian Federation's military invasion of that country) in grains and wheat, Kazakhstan was blessed with more lucrative natural resources, namely oil and gas. The economics profession has spent decades discussing the "resource curse" and why countries abundant in natural resources tend to stagnate, with a focus on Dutch disease/terms of trade effects, the impact on political institutional development, how point source extraction or population resources contribute to stagnation, issues of measurement of resource abundance, and the argument of efficiency versus abundance (Badeeb et al. 2017). In most instances, the literature is almost entirely in consensus that two things are true simultaneously: (a) natural resources represent a windfall gain for a country which can aid development in ways that resource-poor countries cannot access in such a short amount of time; and (b) countries endowed in particular types of resources (including oil, gas, and plantation resources such as cotton) experience institutional stagnation, tend towards authoritarianism, and become highly reliant on these resources (see, for example, Isham et al. 2005). Put simply, resources let countries do amazing things which their poorer neighbours can only dream of, but it is very easy for them to get bogged down in only doing things that oil and gas let them do. At the same time, the stream of rents that energy and other resources create, especially from hugely capital-intensive operations such as drilling, is so large that it tends to attract the worst elements in society, creating vast opportunities for corruption and shadowy governance (as Ukraine was to discover when it embarked on its highly lucrative transit of energy from Russia).

Kazakhstan's resources at the beginning of its transition were almost entirely located in the "bad" kind of natural resources for long-term development, namely oil, gas, and other minerals and ore requiring extraction. Indeed, the amount of fossil fuels that Kazakhstan has access to beneath its soil is substantial, and this has only risen with increasing foreign investment and the application of foreign technology. As of its formal independence as a sovereign state from the USSR in 1992, Kazakhstan's oil reserves were estimated at 5.187 billion barrels, an amount that has increased to approximately 30 billion barrels of proven reserves as of 2007 onwards. Kazakhstan's oil wealth is concentrated in four fields located in the west of the country (Tengiz, Karachaganak, Kashagan, and Kurmangazy), harsh terrain that borders the Caspian Sea and further north and inland (Kaiser and Pulsipher 2007), where there also co-exist massive natural gas reserves (30 per cent of all Kazakh gas based in the Karachaganak field on the Russian border). Kazakhstan's total proven natural gas reserves were estimated at 1.83 trillion cubic metres in 1991 (with potential reserves estimated as high as 8.73 trillion cubic metres; see Cornot-Gandolphe 1993), with 2020 estimates putting them closer to 2.26 trillion cubic metres of proven reserves, landing it in 15th position among the world rankings of gas producers, holding 1.2 per cent of all global gas reserves (and ahead of countries such as Norway and Canada in terms of proven reserves). Finally, in addition to these massive deposits, Kazakhstan also is rich in a number of other minerals and ore, making its independence a potentially lucrative endeavour for those who can control the land and/or the mining concessions:

> Kazakhstan takes the first place in the world on developed reserves of zinc, tungsten, and barytes, the second place on copper and fluorite reserves, the third place on manganese reserves, the fourth place on molybdenum reserves, and it is among top ten countries with the largest gold reserves. [Kazakhstan also] possesses 10% of the world reserves of iron ore and 25% of the world uranium reserves.
>
> (Absametov et al. 2019)

From a macroeconomic perspective, the lack of a real economy focused on the needs of its populace (rather than Moscow) but with abundant natural capital meant that something needed to be done immediately in order to signal to firms, capital, and investors as to where the money – no longer directed by Moscow – should go. Luckily, Kazakhstan and other transition economies had at their disposal the most powerful meta-institution known to man, that of the market, and its singular achievement in resource allocation, the price system. Prices represent the amalgamation of individual production decisions and the corresponding preferences of consumers or other businesses, sending signals about resource allocation and relative value, as well as embodying the knowledge of society across all facets of the economy (Hayek 1945). Of course, price systems still have transaction costs – including the time required for price research by consumers and the possibility that price changes do not occur everywhere simultaneously but are spatially differentiated – but these are attributes of life rather than the factually incorrect term "market failure." The price system of a country is thus a large ecosystem of supplies, decisions, desires, willingness to pay, and action, whereby the prices of all goods are inextricably bound up with others. Despite the massive issues that would come from coordinating such an endeavour, the price system is massively decentralized and works without any guiding operator, aggregating knowledge that we do not even know we possess (Hayek 1945).

Under the Soviet Union, however, prices were a bookkeeping tool set centrally in Moscow by a dedicated bureaucracy, determined to price everything in the economy as it saw fit and in accordance with the plans of communism: Bornstein (1978:467) notes that

> though no one claims to know the exact number, or even a reasonably close approximation, Soviet sources declare that there are at least 10 million separate "state" prices (excluding collective farm market prices and prices for consumer cooperative commission sales for collective farms).

Of course, given that prices were not a real signal determined by the interplay of supply and demand, the "shadow prices" of the Soviet system were rife with problems such as the failure of administrators to update them according to technological changes or the introduction of substitutes (Bornstein 1972). More importantly, the lack of a connection to supply and demand meant that prices were not effective signals for anything other than regime wishes, and thus resource allocation was inefficient, frequently wasteful (Winiecki 1988), if not downright environmentally destructive (Peterson 2019), and disconnected from the desires of Soviet citizens. The lack of consumer goods, sacrificed in favour of heavy industrialization and the military-industrial complex, was a legendary example of this disjoint between prices and politics (Teckenberg 1987).

The first step towards a market economy was the need to tap into the wonder of the price system, meaning that Kazakhstan (and other transition economies) needed to decentralize and free prices, removing their determination from the bureaucracy and putting them back in the hands of consumers; in the formulation of Kornai (1994), this meant moving from a seller's market to a buyer's market. The precise manner by which this was accomplished differed across countries (Hartwell 2013a), but in most transition economies it meant undertaking a concerted and deliberate process of price liberalization, freeing most (if not all) prices as soon as possible. This was indeed the path that Kazakhstan took, introducing a reform in January

1992 to liberalize prices that has alternately been called "large-scale" (De Broeck and Kostial 1998:8), "ambitious" (De Broeck et al. 1997:196), and "rapid" (Charman 2007:166), i.e. all the things necessary to quickly wean a country from its artificial pricing and to an actual, market-determined price system. Looking back at the period from 1992 to 1994, Kazakhstan was highly successful in its price liberalization, especially in comparison to its Central Asian neighbours (Craig et al. 1999), removing the vast bulk of its planning apparatus and freeing 80 per cent of prices in the economy by the end of January 1992 (Shome 1993). In tandem with price liberalization in Russia, where 90 per cent of consumer prices were freed by February 1992 (Khan 1994), the Soviet legacy soon reared up its head to provide the first challenge to Kazakhstan, Russia, and indeed all the transition economies.

As noted above, the lack of consumer goods in the Soviet Union was legion; at the same time, however, soft budget constraints and a fairly vibrant network of state depositary institutions meant that household savings were fairly high and were actually encouraged to be that way (Hartwell and Korovkin 2021). The combination of large amounts of officially recognized money chasing too few goods, the classic definition of inflation, thus began to manifest itself in the Soviet Union even before the Union itself broke apart at the end of 1991; this was coupled with a wage push from the industrial sector, as the loosening of the reins by Mikhail Gorbachev devolved industrial oversight from the Kremlin to worker's collectives, who then promptly voted themselves pay raises without any corresponding increase in productivity (Glaz'ev 1991). Finally, all good periods of inflation can be traced back to the issuance of money to cover out of control spending, and the USSR was no different, with the liquidity overhang in Soviet bank accounts accompanied by a credit explosion in 1991 to state and republic budgets meant to paper over the collapse of intra-republic finances (Filatochev and Bradshaw 1992). Bequeathing this legacy to its constituent republics, the USSR thus enabled massive price increases in Kazakhstan upon independence the minute that prices were freed from their artificially low level. In short, massive amounts of liquidity at both the household and state level, coupled with collapsing industry facing no longer distorted input pricing, led Kazakhstan and every other transition economy into a period of high to hyperinflation.

Unlike other transition economies, however, the period of hyperinflation lasted longer in Kazakhstan (Table 6.2) than in the Baltic states or even the western Commonwealth of Independent States (CIS) member countries, reaching its peak in 1994 and falling to merely "high" inflation thereafter. Part of this was due specifically to the process of price liberalization that Kazakhstan undertook, which was to free prices sequentially rather than simultaneously, with "administered prices … changed frequently and by substantial magnitudes, [while] the policies governing these changes were often revised" (De Broeck et al. 1997:196). But a larger part of this problem was the fact that political independence from the Soviet Union did not mean macroeconomic independence from Russia, as Kazakhstan remained inside the rouble zone, using the Russian rouble as legal tender and indeed the only currency of payments in the country. The economic arguments for and against a currency union go back to Viner's (1950) work on an "optimal currency area" (OCA) and have been refined ever since, focusing on what conditions make a common currency desirable among countries (not surprisingly, the bulk of this work has focused on the EU and the euro; see, for example, Sapir 2011). In terms of the checklist of prerequisites for an OCA (according to Mundell 1961), the former Soviet states fulfilled most of these conditions, with a high level of capital and wage mobility present across countries that until recently had been part of the same administrative unit, similar business cycles, and high volumes of trade also still present (although this was not to last long, see below).

However, a key condition was absent, namely the concentration of monetary authority in one centralized institution (ideally, given that the rouble was and remains the currency of Russia, it should have been centralized in a Central Bank of Russia committed to price stability). Instead, across the rouble zone in 1992 there were "15 national banks acting as central banks, independent of each other and using their positions as 'free riders' to try to outbid each other in the emission of money in the form of credit" (Dąbrowski 1997:153). The new, independent National Bank of Kazakhstan (NBK) was, in this arrangement, not conducting an independent monetary policy which could have affected inflation (and inflationary expectations) but was instead merely a transmission vehicle for Russian-determined monetary supplies (Becker et al. 2009). In the words of Goldberg et al. (1994:303),

> the political-economic benefits of credit expansion – the domestic output effects – are primarily internal to the country in question. But the costs of credit expansion are distributed throughout the FSU [former Soviet Union], in terms of higher inflation. Hence, each central bank has an incentive to extend credit. The resulting equilibrium is one of excessive domestic credit issuance.

Standing at the centre of the hub, the Central Bank of Russia was not the paragon of monetary rectitude which was needed at this point in time: in early 1992, it pursued a relatively tight monetary policy, easing prices into their market-determined levels, but it soon shifted back to former Soviet practices to provide soft credits to Russian enterprise in late 1992 and throughout 1993. As De Broeck et al. (1997:196) notes, "as a result, Russia's failures to maintain monetary discipline during the first two years of the transition played a key role in fuelling Kazakh inflation." Any tools that the NBK had, such as interest rate policy, were rendered ineffective in the face of this dependency on Russian policymaking (Becker et al. 2009).

Even if the national banks of the newly independent republics had been on the monetary straight and narrow, the situation within the rouble zone would have remained untenable mainly because, while the initial conditions and linkages between the former countries of the USSR were similar, they were on a path of divergence (indeed, this was part of the reason for the dissolution of the USSR and the transition in the first place). The collapse of trade linkages among the countries was inevitable as each country moved towards a free market, as the trade corridors which existed across republics was based on the hub and spoke model of central planning, with trade being shuffled around according to the needs of the plan and not those of the populace. Thus, the breaking of these administratively determined trade linkages was a *sine qua non* for the development of exports and the internal structure of each economy, but it also meant that the trade linkages which made a common currency desirable were soon to dissipate – along with the key reason for such a currency. At the same time, international financial institutions, paramount among them the International Monetary Fund (IMF), shifted from being outright cheerleaders for the rouble zone to correcting course in 1993, pushing for it to be disbanded but not before the damage had been done (Pomfret 2002).

Finally, and with echoes of the present day, Russian complaints about the "free riding" of former vassals on its own economic might (such as it was and is currently perceived) led the Russian government to attempt to exert substantial economic and political pressure on countries such as Kazakhstan to follow Moscow's economic policies unquestioningly (Olcott 2010). The first step in Russia asserting its dominion over its money came in 1993, when it declared the Soviet rouble to be worthless (not a bad assessment) and ordered a changeover to the new rouble as the only legal currency. While the Baltic states had left the rouble zone in mid-1992, Ukraine followed suit in November of that year, and the Kyrgyz Republic, Azerbaijan, and Georgia exited in June 1993. Meanwhile, Kazakhstan waited until November 1993 to leave the rouble zone. This meant that, following the departure of the Baltic states, Ukraine, and the Caucasus, Kazakhstan was in an unenviable position as a key destination for roubles, and from June to November, the market was flooded with the (now worthless) 1961 to 1992 roubles (Koshanov 1995). With hyperinflation again on the horizon (and monthly inflation at a rate of 50 per cent by October 1993), the final straw came with Russia's demand that Kazakhstan should turn all its gold reserves over to Moscow (Simon 2009).

On 15 November 1993, the tenge became the Kazakh national currency, allowing for an independent monetary policy and inflation targeting (or at least fighting), joining price liberalization as a major accomplishment in the transition from communism to capitalism. As Table 6.2 shows, the back of hyperinflation was broken, albeit in a series of stages: some temporary heterodox measures including price controls and profit margin regulations were instituted in late 1993 but removed as of January 1994,[4] with a more troubling attempt by the National Bank of Kazakhstan to clear inter-enterprise arrears resulting once again in cheap credit flooding the market (De Broeck et al. 1997). The policy failure of the NBK in continuing its Soviet and rouble zone ways was soon made apparent, with the value of the tenge falling to approximately one-eighth of its initial value (Olcott 1994) and causing the policy to be reversed by June 1994, resulting in a moderation of inflation and depreciation of the tenge. By the first quarter of 1995, inflation had come down immensely and was accompanied by final steps in price liberalization throughout the country: as De Broeck et al. (1997:198) mention, by the end of 1994, the only prices still administered by the state were "producer prices for electricity, natural gas, and thermal energy; and consumer prices for gas, electricity, and telephone service." With the exception of these utilities, a problem experienced by transition (and other) economies, even to this day, Kazakhstan's delayed inflation stabilization finally allowed for completion of price liberalization. In this sense, it was a shame that Kazakhstan, and in particular Nazarbayev, remained yoked to the Russian rouble for so long.[5] Put simply, when Kazakhstan had the chance to make a clean break from Russia, it willingly chose – or rather, its elites chose –not to do so quite yet. Abulkhair Khan would have been proud of his descendants and their willingness to trade sovereignty for security.

With the monetary side (somewhat) sorted, the next issue became the Soviet legacy of bloated government, manifested through massive expenditure and gigantic bureaucracies, and the need for the new government to get Kazakhstan's fiscal house in order. This was a more difficult task than monetary stabilization – even when taking into account the wasted year and a half spent in the rouble zone – as the philosophy behind Kazakhstan's stabilization was a reliance mainly on monetary means rather than fiscal consolidation. Indeed, even after independence, in 1992 Kazakhstan was buoyed by budget transfers from Russia amounting to approximately 10 per cent of GDP in order to prevent health care and educational expenditure from crashing (Becker et al. 2009); perhaps this was a better indication of what Bofinger (1996) meant when referring to Kazakhstan's stabilization as an "orthodox monetary-based stabilization," as it was orthodox in the sense of relying on monetary policy rather than orthodox in the sense of eschewing price and wage controls (*supra* note 4). Of course, this does not mean that no fiscal measures were taken, as the Kazakh authorities had begun to attempt to reform the revenue collection system even before the fall of the USSR, scrapping the meaningless turnover tax (which was adjusted by the state on the prices it controlled) in favour of an enterprise tax and (oddly, for a state looking to escape socialism), a progressive income tax (Shome 1993). But in the realm of expenditure, the area in which fiscal policy really is implemented and which determines the burden of government on the average person (and business), Kazakhstan (like many other post-Soviet economies) tried to both transition away from the cradle-to-grave coverage of socialism while keeping most of its programmes in place (Alam and Sundberg 2002).

In fact, the history of Kazakhstan's fiscal consolidation, at least in the first decade of independence, is one of reallocation of expenditure rather than a dramatic decline in the spending which was, to be frank, useless. As Pomfret and Anderson (2001) note, using official Soviet statistics, despite the all-encompassing safety net of socialism, by 1990 the poverty rate still stood at 15.5 per cent in Kazakhstan, and even this figure was only achieved by a generous definition of both "poverty" and, probably, "statistics" (and even so, using even more liberal definitions, the poverty rate recorded in neighbouring Tajikistan was 51 per cent).[6] A successful transition would have thus required a rethink of the entire system of governmental expenditure in Kazakhstan to one capable of supporting a market economy. In some sense, there was a movement in this direction, as Alam and Banerji (2000) note that public investment in Kazakhstan plummeted as a result of the transition, reaching average annual rates of 2 per cent of GDP in 1998–99, higher than in Ukraine (which had dropped to 1 per cent of GDP) but not as high as that of Russia (3.5 per cent of GDP) – moreover, this figure is somewhat artificially inflated if one recognizes that a large portion of this expenditure, especially in the late 1990s, was solely dedicated to the relocation of Kazakhstan's capital city from Almaty to Astana. However, this decline in public "investment," while welcome in terms of letting the incipient private sector take over,[7] did not signal a massive change in the Kazakh approach to government expenditure. Shome (1993) draws our attention to the most egregious part of the newly independent country's expenditure mix, that fact that the first two years of transition saw at least one-half of all budgetary expenditure dedicated to making subsidy payments to both companies and private individuals. At the same time, a further one-third of expenditure was dedicated to health and public education, whereby both expenditure and employment remained high in relative terms (Alam and Sundberg 2002). This figure did not include social security/pensions, which accounted for a further 10 per cent of total expenditure, as such socio-economic expenditure was managed by extrabudgetary funds rather than as part of the normal budget process (Shome 1993).

The clean-up of the fiscal mess left over from the Soviet era – when fiscal policy was better classified as treasury management, as it just dealt with cash outlays rather than putting together a list of priorities for a country over a set amount of time and how these related to funding – was very slow in Kazakhstan (as in the rest of the FSU). Whereas countries such as Poland instituted fiscal austerity and budget reform measures immediately upon transition, and Estonia introduced a new budget law in 1993 which set the parameters for budgeting, Kazakhstan did not have a legislative framework – much less a philosophy – in place until 1999 (Martinez-Vasquez and Boex 2001). In this sense, macroeconomic stabilization did not include fiscal reform; rather it predated it, with much of the fiscal consolidation in Kazakhstan taking place after the major shock of transition had occurred. Of course, in a more accurate sense, macroeconomic stabilization *cannot* occur without fiscal consolidation, which was precisely one of the issues in Kazakhstan's transition: unlike Central and Eastern Europe, which dealt with the institutionalization of expenditure as part of stabilization,

Kazakhstan let the issue fester, leading to budgetary mismanagement such as that in 1994, when social security and welfare expenditures were 76.5 per cent less than planned and communication and energy expenditures were more than 3,000 per cent above what was budgeted (Mikesell and Mullins 2001). The lack of fiscal discipline led to the accumulation of budget arrears (expenditure above budgeted resources) almost immediately after the back was broken of inflation in 1994 (Dąbrowski et al. 1996), mainly because inflation was no longer there to wipe out the nominal commitments made by the government. By 1998, the year of the Russian financial crisis, the Kazakh government had budgetary arrears totalling 3.2 per cent of GDP (Martinez-Vasquez and Boex 2001). At this point, even the World Bank noted that

> If there is no rationale (economic or social) for government intervention, then the program/project/activity under consideration should be left to the private sector, regardless of other considerations … the government of Kazakhstan must not only accelerate the reduction of its direct involvement in the production of private goods and services, but should also consider refraining from its indirect influence on private sector decisions.
>
> (2000:19–20)

Despite these problematic signs, coupled with the inability to articulate a limited role for government in the transition (focusing on social safety nets rather than on direct production), Kazakhstan did show some progress in its fiscal policies, acting to attempt to bring the country's budget deficit under control in 1995. According to Craig (1999), the budget deficit fell to 3 per cent of GDP that year after ballooning to 7 per cent in 1994 (probably due to overspending on energy and communications) but returned to over 7 per cent in 1996 and continued to average 5.2 per cent between 1997 and 1999 (Alam and Banerji 2000). However, the strain on fiscal and monetary policies throughout the early transition period was exacerbated by the sheer size of the output collapse in the transformational recession (Kornai 1994). The transformational recession in every transition country was necessary, in that it eliminated industries and businesses which only survived due to politics and government intervention, following government planning rather than market tenets. However, while the recession should have been deep, it should also have been short, in order both to see new market connections emerging and to keep public opinion on the side of reforms. Long-lasting recessions were often due to policy reversals, inability to commit, or continued governmental intervention which acted as barriers to new markets forming.

According to estimates by Popov (2000), in 1996 GDP in Kazakhstan was 45 per cent less than that recorded in 1989; by 1998 it had rebounded to 63 per cent of its 1989 level. Although this was a far cry from the terrific collapse experienced by Georgia (where GDP was estimated to have declined by 87 per cent during the transformation) or Tajikistan (whose GDP stood at just 31 per cent of its 1989 level in 1996), it still very different from countries such as Poland, which had surpassed its initial GDP by 1996, seven years after it began its transition. Even using the last year of the USSR (1991) as a comparator, when Kazakhstan was already on its way to full-blown independence, by 1999 Kazakhstan's GDP was still only just above 60 per cent of its 1991 level (Alam and Banerji 2000), perhaps because it only had two full years of growth (Table 6.3). This comparison is of course dependent on Soviet statistics, which were dubious in terms of their estimates of GDP (see especially Rosefielde 1981) and were based on forced production rather than market incentives. However, even without a true baseline there is no doubt that the productive capacity of Kazakhstan underwent a massive contraction and followed by a shift in the 1990s. Much of this was necessary to uproot the inefficient Soviet system, but the depth of the Kazakh transformational recession was longer than other similarly situated post-Soviet countries, even when one considers that its distortions – perhaps owing to its own place in the Soviet supply chain – were lower than in other FSU countries (Popov 2000). It was also cushioned somewhat by the aforementioned supply of natural resources, which brought FDI into the country throughout the 1990s, but which was used to finance large government expenditures and subsidies rather than being used for development (Alam and Banerji 2000; see also Table 6.3).

In sum, Kazakhstan's macroeconomic stabilization was in line with that of other countries emerging from the Soviet Union, which is to say that it was much slower and more characterized by reform reversals than in Central and Eastern Europe. In hindsight, the key mistake made by the country was to remain in the rouble zone as long as it did – while the reasoning behind this may have been sound, i.e. maintaining open trade links which would prevent enterprises from collapsing into an inefficient pile, the effect was to generate incentives for inflation which then helped to distort the economy profoundly and led to government involvement when it actually needed to be out of the way. As Hartwell (2018) notes, profligate monetary policy also correlates closely with authoritarian governance and diminution of rule of law, and it is quite conceivable that the turmoil of the rouble zone helped to bolster Nazarbayev's claims that he was the only one who could maintain the country's stability. With money suffering and prices seemingly out of control, it became difficult to undertake other stabilization reforms, all of which relied on market prices; key among this was government budgeting, which followed a business-as-usual approach, retained massive Soviet-style transfers, and did not undergo a philosophical shift towards the smaller government which was necessary. If, as Nazarbayev claimed, economics was to come before politics, there still needed to be a blueprint for what post-Soviet Kazakhstan would look like, rather than a mere strategy for survival. Some sort of philosophy would have been preferable, to understand what "variety of capitalism" (Dore et al. 1999) it was actually working towards.

Table 6.2 Inflation in the Former Soviet Union, 1992–2001 (in % change over previous year)

Country	*1992*	*1993*	*1994*	*1995*	*1996*	*1997*	*1998*	*1999*	*2000*	*2001*
Kazakhstan	2,962.80	2,169.10	1,160.30	60.40	28.60	11.30	1.90	17.80	9.80	6.40
Rest of Central Asia										
Kyrgyzstan	1,257.00	766.90	95.70	32.00	34.90	14.70	18.30	39.80	9.50	3.70
Tajikistan	n.a.	7,343.70	1.10	2,133.30	40.50	163.60	2.70	30.10	60.60	12.70
Turkmenistan	n.a.	n.a.	1,328.50	1,261.50	445.90	21.80	19.80	16.40	7.40	12.20
Uzbekistan	910.00	884.80	1,281.40	116.90	64.40	50.00	26.00	26.00	28.20	26.40
Baltic states										
Estonia	942.20	35.70	41.60	28.80	15.00	12.50	4.50	3.80	5.00	4.20
Latvia	958.20	34.80	26.20	23.30	13.20	7.00	2.80	3.20	1.80	3.10
Lithuania	1,162.50	188.80	45.00	35.50	13.10	8.50	2.40	0.30	1.40	2.00
Caucasus										
Armenia	1,241.20	10,896.10	1,884.50	32.10	5.80	22.00	–1.1	2.10	0.30	3.00
Azerbaijan	n.a.	1,293.80	1,788.00	84.50	6.70	0.40	–7.6	–0.5	2.20	1.50
Georgia	1,178.50	7,484.10	6,473.00	57.40	13.70	7.20	10.60	10.80	4.60	3.40
Western CIS										
Belarus	1,557.80	1,994.00	1,957.00	244.20	39.10	63.40	181.70	251.30	108.00	46.20
Moldova	2,198.40	836.00	116.00	23.80	15.10	11.10	18.40	82.70	18.50	6.40
Russia	2,321.60	841.60	202.70	131.40	21.80	11.00	84.50	36.60	20.10	18.60
Ukraine	2,001.00	10,155.00	401.10	181.40	39.70	10.10	20.00	20.20	23.90	6.10

Source: Compiled by the author based on Dabrowski (2013).

Table 6.3 Basic Macroeconomic Indicators, 1993 to 1998

	1993	*1994*	*1995*	*1996*	*1997*	*1998*
GDP growth rate	−9.20	−12.60	−8.20	0.50	2.00	−2.50
Government revenue (% of GDP)	21.20	18.50	16.90	13.20	19.50	18.30
Government expenditure (% of GDP)	25.20	26.00	20.00	18.60	28.40	26.00
Fiscal balance excl. privatization (%)	−4.00	−7.50	−3.20	−5.30	−8.90	−7.70

Source: World Bank Development Indicators, https://databank.worldbank.org/source/world-development-indicators.

This view of macroeconomic stabilization in Kazakhstan may seem a bit harsh when taken in hindsight, as most of us were not there in the halls of power, making decisions on the fly. However, there are two arguments which mitigate against the charge of "after the fact" decision-making (known in the United States as "Monday morning quarterbacking"). The first is that the USSR fell apart after countries such as Poland and the Czech Republic (Czechia) had already begun their transition, and thus there was some precedent, no matter how recent, on what needed to be done and what should be avoided. Poland in particular, as a large country tied to the USSR, went the fastest in its transition and had already stabilized by the time that Kazakhstan was carving its own path.[8] The second argument is that it appeared that many of the former Soviet republics, led as they were by Soviet leaders and governed by Soviet parliaments, had immense inertia in their policies, creating a neighbourhood effect. Indeed, countries as diverse as Tajikistan and Moldova merely followed one another along their reform paths, with nearly every country which emerged from the wreckage of the Soviet Union undergoing a similar sequence of both policies and crises (at least for those that liberalized – Belarus and Turkmenistan experienced only a few of these particular issues but all of the previous issues that came with a Soviet economy). Overall, this translated into a slower transition than that experienced by the Central and Eastern European (CEE) countries and longer transformational recessions, even while the CEE countries recorded a steeper decline overall: according to Iwasaki and Kumo (2019), the average length of continuous output decline in the CEE countries (including the Baltic states) was 3.3 years (with an average decline in output of 73 per cent) while in the FSU it was 4.5 years (which recorded a shallower average decline in output at 53.8 per cent). While the distortions were larger in the Soviet countries than in the CEE economies (Popov 2000), this should have argued for a faster approach than a gradual push for liberalization in sequence, and should also have resulted in a steeper drop (but a quicker recovery). Instead, as noted above, a less precipitous decline occurred over a longer period, showing that something was in fact wrong. This should have become apparent to the entire neighbourhood earlier on in the transition, perhaps suggesting that there was something worth mimicking in the CEE experience.

Of course, the CEE countries had something that the FSU countries did not in terms of a blueprint, and that was accession to the EU: with the *acquis communautaire* providing a list of legislative, regulatory, and institutional mechanisms which needed to be in place, CEE countries had both a concrete goal to strive for and a means to achieve it, wiping away some of the uncertainty of transition. Kazakhstan and other Central Asian countries (and, to be fair, even western CIS countries such as Belarus and Ukraine) had no such stated objective and thus no sense of what a "market economy" should look like as a goal. This provided a challenge but also an opportunity, as not only did institutional experimentation in the CEE countries grind to a halt after EU accession, but the brilliance of the market is that it may provide an optimal form for a country's economy *but no one person knows what this is.* Put another way, Kazakhstan did not *have* to have a goal for how its market economy was structured or what it delivered, it merely had to create the foundations for it to evolve and let it run its own path. This, of course, is an almost impossible order for any politician, much less one steeped in Soviet ways, and thus much of Kazakhstan's transition suffered from both not having a goal and too much intervention to make it "better," without a sense of what "better" was.

As noted above, macroeconomic stabilization was only the first, most basic and tentative step towards becoming a market economy, a necessary but insufficient condition for a successful transition. Given Kazakhstan's lack of an objective in stabilization – or a sense of what a market economy might look like in the country after the ship was righted – but with a reliance on tried and tested methods of intervention, how then did Kazakhstan's economic institutions develop, and how did they contribute to the further transition of the country? Much as we did in the last chapter, we will turn to examining the most important economic institutions in post-Soviet Kazakhstan and how they have evolved over the past 30 years.

Property Rights

The key to sustained (and sustainable) economic growth (Torstensson 1994; Gwartney et al. 1999; Hartwell 2013a), property rights are also the cornerstone of a capitalist economy and a key defining differential between capitalism and communism. Indeed, one of the fundamental traits of communism was put forth plainly by Karl Marx in the *Communist Manifesto*, namely "the theory of the Communists may be summed up in the single sentence: Abolition of private property." Under Marxism, private property was seen as an obstacle to personal gain and a flourishing society because it created separations in society (Brenkert 1979), an ironic observation given that the

Leninist interpretation of Marxism and the communism of the Soviet Union was all about the separation of various strata of society and especially of the "people" versus "saboteurs," "wreckers," and whomever was preventing the glorious communist system from reaching fruition that week.

Leaving this digression aside, private property was the first target of every Communist Party in existence, from 1917 onwards, and the Soviet Union was fairly successful in expropriating private property, eliminating owners, and nationalizing industry. While small-scale property rights were allowed during the New Economic Policy in the 1920s, then revoked and left to slumber until the late Gorbachev era (the managerial privatization mentioned at the beginning of the last chapter), the daunting prospect facing Kazakhstan in 1991/1992 was how to bring such rights back. Perhaps bringing property rights "back" is the wrong way to put it, as the specific challenge for property rights in Kazakhstan can be found earlier in this book, in particular regarding the Kazakhs' historical experience of this economic institution. As stressed in Chapters 2 and 3, the Kazakhs realistically had only ever had property rights in a more communal and less individual form; from the nomadic approach to land as an input for a specific horde, to the Alash Orda's attempt to formalize communal landownership under socialist rubric, to the communist system of the Soviet Union, whereby private property was on the smallest scale, Kazakhstan had little experience of modern, capitalist forms of private property. However, and it is crucial to stress this here, "property rights" does not only refer to land, although land rights and property rights are often used synonymously. Property rights instead refers to the right of an individual to use a resource in any way in which that individual chooses, including managing it, transferring it, delegating management for it, selling it, disposing of it, or doing absolutely nothing with the resource at all. This view of property rights, commonly associated with Alchian (1965) and Demsetz (1964), is necessarily concentrated at the level of the individual but does not preclude aggregations of people working together voluntarily, and in fact is an extension of Coasean economics related to the legal form of the firm and its own rights within a capitalist society. In any event, private property does not just include land or even tangible objects but is instead more properly thought of as resources; framed this way, it is almost impossible to abolish private property in a society where the state is omnipotent (given that the state is never omniscient).

If we consider the broader definition of property rights, our examination of the Kazakhs reveals that historically property rights did exist and, in fact were crucial in the maintenance of the entire nomadic existence, as animal herds were the most important property that the hordes had, with land merely being a means to maintaining this property. And, of course, there were farmers and those who relied on agriculture, if a minority, who exercised control over their land (when not under assault from nomads), their buildings, and their equipment. Even the nomads had their horses and their yurts, a portable form of accommodation that brought some creature comforts to the steppe, but acknowledged that (a) the yurts themselves were owned by specific nomads; and (b) the land beneath the yurts was occupied and in some sense "owned," even if only for one night. Thus, small-scale property rights did exist in pre-Soviet Kazakh lands and even during the early tsarist era, but these rights were steadily infringed upon by Russian colonization and Sovietization. In any event, it is erroneous to say that this economic institution did not exist in Kazakhstan prior to 1991, *even for land*: as noted in Chapter 2, the Khanate also had its own set of rules governing property rights relating to pastures, the key factor of production for herds. It was best put perhaps by Alimaev and Behnke (2008:152), who stated that "in the 500 years that the Kazakhs have existed as a distinct people, their rangeland tenure systems have incorporated features from all the major ideal types of property regimes – common, private, state property, and open access."

However, the all-pervasive nature of the Soviet experiment had a deleterious effect on the concentration of executive power in the post-Soviet era (Chapter 5), on yoking Kazakhstan together with other very different countries (see above on the rouble zone), and, as we will now see, on the development of property rights in post-independence Kazakhstan.[9] As Table 6.1 shows, the share of the private sector in Kazakhstan at independence was a mere 5 per cent, and entrepreneurial activities were explicitly outlawed by successive Soviet constitutions. The right of ownership when applied to business, land, or any factors of production was still restricted to the state and the state alone, meaning that the scale of property rights throughout the former Kazakh SSR was thus incredibly small and limited to private property (cars, apartments, clothes, and other personal effects, and this only after the Second World War). In fact and legally, all other forms of property other than these small-scale items were officially owned by the government of the USSR. Even in the era of thawing of the economy in the 1980s, the move towards private property was done in a piecemeal and necessarily minute scale: the managerial privatizations of the 1980s were more about survival at the managerial level and the creation of a parallel economy at the micro level than laying a foundation for economic transformation (Boycko et al. 1997), while the collapse of centralized Soviet property ownership in agriculture in the late Soviet era laid bare just how dependent state farms were on state support and subsidies (Alimaev and Behnke 2008). In order to make the leap to a capitalist system on independence, additional and broader reforms were required to uproot the entire Soviet animus towards private property and institutionalize it across the country on a large scale.

Given this challenge, how did property rights actually progress under Nazarbayev? While land rights and property rights are not synonymous, as already noted, there is a large amount of overlap, as what happens to land first usually sets the tone for a government's approach to all rights of management, disposal, transfer, and use. That is, a country can have excellent land rights without necessarily having an overall positive disposition towards private property (via confiscatory taxation, high levels of government intervention in the economy, dilapidated public services crowding out the private sector – the United Kingdom in the post-Thatcher era is a perfect example of this dichotomy) but it is exceedingly rare to find a country which treats land rights as malleable, shaped to the government's needs, with all other manner of private property treated as sacrosanct. We will begin thus with land reform in Kazakhstan, an issue which, like in other parts of the former Soviet Union, has been politically charged and highly contentious; as Hierman and Nekbakhtshoev (2014:337) accurately state, "in agrarian settings, land access and political power are deeply intertwined."

Land reform in Kazakhstan was slow to develop, with the registration of firms as either "collective" or "private" in 1992 the main progress attained (Toleubayev et al. 2010). One year after transition began, in 1993, the collective farm – and all collective forms of property – were eliminated from Kazakh legislation (Dudwick et al. 2007) as part of a move towards privatizing the state-owned collectives. However, land was still kept as the exclusive purview of the state, with no private ownership allowed until a slight change was made in the 1995 law "On Land," which transferred land use rights to farm units and created 99-year leases for both individuals and entities. The intention here was not to create broader land or property rights but, as in other post-Soviet countries, to spur agricultural productivity first and foremost and worry about the details of ownership later (Hierman and Nekbakhtshoev 2014) – although, to be fair, gradual reformer and neighbour Uzbekistan had already hit upon the lease idea by July 1992 (Khan 1994). Much like the voucher privatization which occurred in Russia and the Czech Republic (Boycko et al. 1994), the land use rights were given free of charge to former collective farms and their workers, seniors, and those still working at state-owned farms, and by 1997 a full 2.227 million "conditional land shares" had been transferred, covering approximately 118 million hectares of land (Dudwick et al. 2007). These shares allowed for a broad series of land use rights, including the transfer, leasing, or withdrawal of the share, but stopped short of allowing for collateralization, as the emphasis on use rights versus ownership rights meant that land was still state-owned; the only area where land could be owned by citizens was in household plots (Hierman and Nekbakhtshoev 2014), a distinction which referred to just 0.2 per cent of all agricultural land in 1993 (Lerman 1998). In this manner, the Kazakh government could attempt to fashion together enough incentives to spur agri-business but without tackling the tougher questions surrounding land ownership and, especially, private property. This avoidance of the issue could be further seen in the fact that the shares only existed on paper and were not linked to specifically delineated plots (Lerman et al. 2004).

By 2001, after six years of land use rights, it appeared that Kazakhstan had taken a step backwards in its move towards land tenure rights with a reduction in lease times from 99 years to 49 years and the obligation of shareholders to personalize their plots within a three-year window; however, the 2001 law also facilitated sub-leasing to other agricultural entities, meaning that the holder of the land use rights did not have to farm themselves (Toleubayev et al. 2010). Two years later, buoyed by these tentative steps to create a land market in Kazakhstan, the idea of private ownership of agricultural land was finally authorized, 11 years into the transition and well after nearly every other transition economy apart from Belarus, Tajikistan, and Uzbekistan (Lerman 2009). Overhauling all manner of land relations in the country, the Land Code allowed agricultural land to be privately owned while fashioning a mechanism by which land use holders could purchase the land from the government for a pre-arranged fee; those who opted not to buy were thereafter prohibited from sub-leasing their land use rights, however (see Csaki and Zuschlag 2004). In reality, the Land Code provided three specific outlets for holders of land use shares, namely "(1) assume direct cultivation of the land under government lease, (2) purchase the leased land, or (3) contribute their land shares or land plot to the capital of an agricultural enterprise" (USAID 2005:1). Perhaps not wanting to rush into anything too precipitously, the Land Code became law only in January 2005, giving holders a chance to get their affairs in order to pursue one of these avenues. According to Kvartiuk and Petrick (2021), the stipulations of the Code resulted in 40.5 per cent of all agricultural land in the country being transformed into individual farms while a statistically similar 39 per cent went the third route and was contributed to the capital of an agricultural enterprise.

An important point must be raised here, for, as we noted above, the drive behind successive land reforms in Kazakhstan was not to create broad-based private property rights but rather to improve agricultural productivity. This meant that land reform took place as one of a series of reforms, including the aforementioned privatization scheme but also including overall business regulatory reform and reforms specific to agriculture (technology, extension services, etc.); a "National Agrofood Strategy" for 2003 to 2005 and a "Rural Development Scheme" spanning 2004 to 2010 were introduced alongside the Land Code, both of which focused on the agricultural sector. However, harkening back to our earlier examination of Kazakhstan's history, agriculture as a sector was always a minority endeavour among the nomads until the Russian colonialism forced sedentarism upon them. As Toleubayev et al. (2010) note, modern agriculture in its industrial form did not exist in Kazakhstan until the Russian colonization, and, in line with other difficulties in fostering a system which only knew communist-era practices, it would also be difficult to assign land rights to accompany agricultural growth.[10] Given the burden of history, it was thus more difficult to fashion individual land tenure rights for a system that was barely in place throughout most of the existence of various Kazakh political groupings. Contrast this with elsewhere in the FSU, such as in Ukraine (Hartwell 2016) and Moldova (Bucur 2018), where private land rights had existed before the communist coup, and these rights were common in the CEE countries (Swinnen 1999). For the CEE countries and even the western FSU countries, the idea of land restitution (Blacksell and Born 2002) or the restoration of rights was much easier (if it was attempted) than disassembling the system from central planning and then recreating these rights at the individual level, i.e. not reverting to previous rights but creating them entirely from nothing.[11]

In such an atmosphere, the fashioning of land use rights and, eventually, the creation of ownership rights was bound to cause collateral damage to other goals within the agricultural sector. For example, the same Soviet institutions that enforced collectivization became the repository of knowledge for agriculture in independent Kazakhstan (Toleubayev et al. 2010), meaning that decollectivization of the land would also dismantle a transmission mechanism for information, no matter how inefficient it was. This was seen in areas such as water management (Abdullaev et al. 2010), whereby collective farms were broken up into individual units but the repository of knowledge in hydrology also dissipated; of course, this did not stop individual farmers from obtaining this expertise on their own or employing it, but it did impose an additional barrier to rebuilding agricultural productivity. Unfortunately, until the introduction of the Land Code, the government also retained monopoly rights to subsoil, trees, and water, meaning that even the loss of knowledge did not matter so much as access to materials necessary for successful farming (Hendrix 1997). Moreover, this loss of economies of scale in knowledge production could have been an animating feature behind the Kazakh push to preserve larger farms at the expense of smaller ones, retaining large amounts of subsidies for farms which formerly were collectivized and focusing their efforts on crafting a business environment which catered to the largest farms (Csaki and Zuschlag 2004). However, even this push for size was ineffective before the ability to transfer land, as, by 1998, the majority of larger-sized, corporate farms were unprofitable and went through bankruptcy proceedings and, eventually, buyouts (Dudwick et al. 2007).

In any event, the shift towards private ownership of land was also accompanied by intense controversy, as both communist and nationalist politicians found common cause in opposing land reform; in particular, it was argued (echoing other post-Soviet debates) that private ownership of land would benefit the wealthy disproportionately and/or result in unequal distribution of land (Deshpande 2006). In echoes of pre-communist times – and of many populist and far left parties prevalent today – opposition to the Code claimed that the reform "does not pursue the goal of increasing agricultural productivity or protect the rights of landowners, peasants, and farmers, but entails the expropriation of land by giant grain companies" (quoted in Hierman and Nekbakhtshoev 2014:341). Unfortunately for the opposition, this reform came during the height of Nazarbayev's authority, and the President had made it clear as early as 2002 that passing a new land code was a priority, thus putting it on a fast track towards success (Jones 2004).[12] In perhaps a win for the anti-private property opposition, however, the Land Code contained Article 23 which allowed foreigners to own land but explicitly not for the purpose of agricultural production. Moreover, the philosophical basis of the Code, namely that "the land should belong to those who cultivate it" (Petrick et al. 2011:17) also showed a lack of understanding of one of the main tenets of property rights, namely the right to do nothing. The fact that the government cancelled many existing arrangements in favour of a purely utilitarian approach did not bode well for further property rights development.

Opposition to any form of land reform did not end there, however, and has actually been a major flashpoint in Kazakh politics, as well as one of the few cracks in the facade of Nazarbayev's power. During the period of murky land rights, roughly corresponding with the late 1990s and early 2000s before the introduction of the Land Code, rural to urban migration was on the rise but resulted in many "informal" dwellings, outside of official authorization, being built. In January 2006, an official decree was issued to both attempt to legalize these dwellings, i.e. move them from the realm of the unofficial to the official, while at the same time also legalizing capital which had also been in the grey economy (see below). This move resulted in the construction of many lavish homes without explicit authorization in the vicinity of Almaty – generally by politically well-connected elites – being legalized but created problems for poorer migrants who came from the countryside and were unsure of the process and/or faced resistance from local authorities (Dave 2007). At the same time, the boundaries of Almaty also expanded, bringing many of the squatter communities on the outskirts of the city now part of the city proper, leading to substantial conflicts; in 2005, before the presidential election, the authorities attempted to clear the shantytowns surrounding Almaty but were confronted by large protests (Yessenova 2010). Finally, in April 2006, in the informal settlements in Bakay and Shanyrak, despite 80 per cent of residents purporting to have some legal (Soviet) authorization for their squatter agglomerations, authorities of the *akimat* sent the police in and began bulldozing the "illegal" settlements, resulting in protests, pitched battles with the police, and numerous arrests and harsh sentences (Dave 2007). With over 500 homes cleared and the courts finding that just 68 of these might have been removed "erroneously" (Olcott 2010), the protests continued, with the authorities continuing to evict residents from desirable land (including along the route to the airport). It was only the collapse of real estate markets worldwide (including in Almaty, where prices fell by 40 per cent) as part of the global financial crisis which caused the authorities to relent (Yessenova 2010) and to create a seventh district in Almaty to provide some housing opportunities for the dispossessed residents (Olcott 2010). In this sense (and despite Yessenova's 2010 conclusion that global capitalism was to blame), we can see the consequences of not having clearly delineated property rights for all, in that the authorities were able to manipulate land, claim it for the state, and extract rents using the process of eminent domain (Hanson 2017). Statism, not capitalism, was to blame for both the plight of the rural dwellers and their issues with demonstrating ownership of their land.

Unfortunately, public opinion in Kazakhstan has paradoxically been in favour of more rather than fewer state restrictions on land ownership, perhaps believing that the state – which had been mobilized against citizens before – would suddenly begin to look out for the interests of citizens in this particular case. This was demonstrated first in December 2009, when major protests in Almaty erupted over President Nazarbayev's alleged plan to allow Chinese investors to access approximately one million hectares of agricultural land (Pannier 2009). The relationship between Kazakhstan and China could perhaps have tremendous political and economic consequences (Kassenova 2017), but it is one that slowly began to grow in the 2000s as Kazakhstan looked elsewhere than Russia for its trade relations and investment and China began its rise, thus requiring immense energy supplies (Sadovskaya 2007). Chinese migration to Kazakhstan also began in earnest. According to government figures cited by Kozhirova and Ospanova (2014), some 34,108 Chinese nationals were registered as living in Kazakhstan in 2005, although public perception has been that the Chinese will overwhelm Kazakhstan (Sadovskaya 2015). This worry, of swapping Russian colonization for a Chinese one, has extended to nationalist and statist desires to rein in any land sales, and the purported plan to allow Chinese investors to purchase agricultural land in 2009 brought thousands to the streets (Heuer and Hierman 2022) for two days straight in inhospitable weather (and then for a second time one month later; see Kembayev 2020). While there is ambiguity about just how realistic this plan was, or how close to fruition it was (Pannier 2009), the protests, which occurred in an increasingly authoritarian environment and in which there was little recourse for official opposition, signalled just how sensitive this topic was.

Moreover, such resistance indicated to the government the difficulty of giving foreigners access to Kazakh land (Laruelle 2016). The anti-China, anti-land sale sentiment which was unleashed during the 2009 protests appeared to be just a warm-up, however. While the Land Code explicitly prohibited foreigners from owning land for agricultural production, it did retain Article 48 that permitted foreigners to lease agricultural land for ten years if the land was acquired from the state at auction. In 2016, the Kazakh government floated a plan to amend the Code once again to allow foreigners (primarily Chinese) to lease agricultural land for a longer period of 25 years. Heuer and Hierman (2022:9) describe what happened next:

> On March 30, 2016, Kazakhstan's Minister of National Economy, Erbolat Dossayev, announced that 1.7 million hectares of its massive agricultural land stock would be sold through auctions starting July 1. Unease over the process and scope of these auctions was expressed almost immediately on social media with many fearing that the land they

> worked on may be sold out from under them. Social media posts revealed a fear that the beneficiaries of these auctions would be well-placed Kazakh elites and foreign (especially Chinese) investors. The latter concern, which threatened the sanctity of Kazakhstani land and thus violated principles articulated in the regime's nationalizing discourse, proved to be especially motivational.

Protests started in Atyrau in the extreme west of the country, focused once again on Chinese investment (ironically, as Atyrau is 2,224 kilometres as the crow flies from the border post with China at Nur Zholy). Even though the Land Code amendments were meant for all foreigners, the government had announced that Chinese investors were explicitly being targeted and a series of joint projects was planned once the amendments were approved (Pieper 2021). During April and May, protests spread throughout the country, of various sizes and with various attempts by the authorities to ensure that they did not get out of hand (Heuer and Hierman 2022), but there was no denying that the bell could not be un-rung with regard to popular discontent. In a rare climbdown, the Kazakh government tabled the planned amendments, promising to put together a Commission to study options (Dubuisson 2022), while at the same time attempting to reassert its authority by cracking down on the people involved in the protests, jailing activists and even reporters who covered the protests (Kassenova 2017). As with the opposition to the Land Code in 2003, the perhaps justified worries of ordinary Kazakhs of being not able to compete with state-owned Chinese corporations flush with cash were soon

> heavily coopted by groups that could be loosely characterized as Kazakh nationalist-patriots—advocates for the rights and representation of Kazakh language and culture at various levels of government and for the sovereign control of Kazakhstan, which they consider to be historically Kazakh territory.
>
> (Dubuisson 2022:416)

This in turn resulted in further popular discontent against a needed reform and, ultimately, led Nazarbayev to put in place a "temporary" five-year moratorium on leases for foreigners. In many ways, the behaviour of the government up until this point had made the people wonder whose interests Nazarbayev was serving, meaning that even sound economic policy, that might have benefitted millions of Kazakhs, was discarded amid considerable distrust and nationalism.

As of the writing of this book, a freeze remains in place on further development of property rights in relation to land, with the moratorium instituted after the 2016 protests signed into law in May 2021 by newly elected President Tokayev as a permanent ban on foreigners owning or leasing any agricultural land. Ironically, the Land Code and even its extension of leases for foreigners did not actually start a stampede towards privately owned land, as progress on private farm ownership moved at a snail's pace: by 2019, only 1.4 per cent of all agricultural land was privately owned (Ministry of Agriculture of Kazakhstan 2020). More importantly, as Kvartiuk and Petrick (2021:3) note, the real result of the Code was to affirm the role of the Kazakh government "as a central stakeholder in land relations." With foreigners locked out of the market and huge swathes of the land (and the subsoil) reserved for the government, whosoever is head of the government of Kazakhstan remains the sole arbiter of what is good for the citizens in their land dealings. This is a marked reversal from the days of the Khanate, when the executive could be turned out for infringing property rights, becoming instead a continuation of the Soviet approach towards land, with the executive allowing the tribe or citizens to use the land if they deemed it to be appropriate. With nationalists continuing to stoke resentment against specific ethnic groups and nationalities as a reason to keep land in the hands of the government (Kudaibergenova 2016), Kazakhstan has seen a highly sub-optimal equilibrium develop: a populace which has no avenue to effect political or economic reforms clamouring for that same authoritarian apparatus to have all the power regarding property. As the sarcastic wag at a party might put it, what could possibly go wrong?[13]

I asserted earlier that countries which have poor land rights almost never have good property rights protections elsewhere, and this assertion holds true for Kazakhstan as well. Beyond the retaining of land property rights for the state and the elite but no one else, Kazakhstan has also been plagued with difficulties in building and observing the rule of law. Indeed, while the legislative framework for property rights has appeared to move in a liberal direction but has been fought over and returned problematic outcomes, in less dispute are the failings in the framework via which these rights were implemented and protected. The last chapter provided some background on these weaknesses since 1992, noting that the judiciary throughout Kazakhstan's post-Soviet period has not been independent and has in fact been a mere extension of the will of the executive. This is problematic for many reasons, but in relation to economic institutions, the judiciary is one of the many supporting institutions necessary for property rights to come to fruition. In order to exercise property rights, the rule of law must also exist, so that if transgressions to property rights occur, they can be pursued for restitution or damages; at the same time, rights of exclusion and defence must also exist, in order to ensure that control is retained over resources by individuals and entities exercising those rights. And, particularly in the case of land, a clear lineage must be traced for claims (including cadastral registration and title or deed) so that ownership can be proven and, if disputed, adjudicated in a manner satisfactory to both parties (in terms of process if not outcome). Unfortunately, many of these supporting functions related to property rights have either not been built in Kazakhstan (an independent judiciary) or have been built in a technocratic manner, i.e. with a reliance on technology and international funding (Davis 2002) rather than addressing the institutional or philosophical issues underlying governance. As Bohr et al. (2019:30) note, "Too often, administration and the rule of law are applied in discretionary ways that favor privileged interests, rather than functioning impartially. Neither domestic nor foreign companies can be confident that the judicial system will protect their legitimate interests."

The results of a legislative framework with no supporting institutions and, indeed, very little political will apart from at the top (and even then only for brief amounts of time) have created a situation entirely in line with Sonin's (2003) model, where elites attain a level of property rights sufficient to protect their own property but agitate against broader rights for the populace. Of course, this must be augmented with the political opposition from below against property rights, enabling the government to eschew development of supporting institutions – but without realizing that the growth of an independent judiciary or rule of law is intimately connected to the freedom to own. Attempts have been made to mitigate against this state of affairs in a manner consistent with the Chinese model of special economic zones (SEZs), which are created to generate a bubble of good governance in a sea of distortions; in this way, at least one physically separate part of the country can be utilized to secure property rights and the rule of law, even if political will or barriers make it impossible to extend these blessings elsewhere. In Kazakhstan, this bubble is the Astana International Financial Centre (AIFC), which has its own court and tribunal akin to standard investor dispute settlement mechanisms accompanying bilateral investment treaties around the world (Zambrana-Tevar 2019). Transplanting English common law into a specifically delineated area, the AIFC was a genuine example of institutional experimentation, a means to bypass problems in Kazakh domestic law. However, the AIFC was very slow to get off the ground, given the possible spoils which could be reaped (or, rather, the fact that rents might now be locked away and inaccessible) and the intrinsic difficulty of bypassing domestic legislation (Bohr et al. 2019); moreover, the emphasis of the AIFC was on financial intermediation rather than the real economy, meaning that the narrow focus within the Center was on the development of shareholder rights, another small slice of property rights (Yeung et al. 2020).

The predictable outcome of decades of policy set against private property rights can be seen in Figure 6.1, where we plot two separate measures of property rights protection: the first is "contract-intensive money" (CIM) first suggested by Clague et al. (1996) and it measures the amount of money held inside the formal banking system. The theory is that countries with sound property rights will have a much higher proportion of their money supply held in the banking sector, while those with rampant expropriation or correspondingly low levels of rights will have citizens keeping their money under their mattresses or in cash. Thus, a higher score means higher property rights. Similarly, the second metric of property rights comes from the Heritage Foundation's Index of Economic Freedom and measures property rights on a scale from 0 to 100, with 100 being perfect protection of these rights.

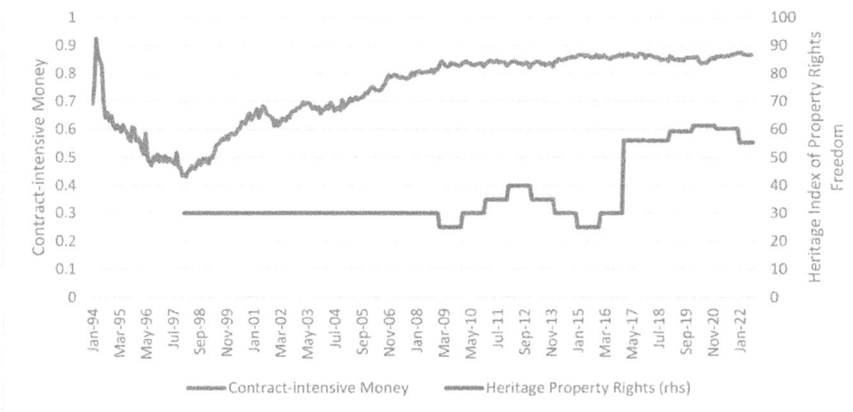

Figure 6.1 Property Rights in Kazakhstan
Source: compiled using the Heritage Index of Economic Freedom, www.heritage.org/index/explore, and author's calculations from the NBK, https://nationalbank.kz/en/monetarybase/denezhnaya-baza-i-agregaty-shirokoy-denezhnoy-massy, and IMF International Financial Statistics, https://data.imf.org/?sk=4c514d48-b6ba-49ed-8ab9-52b0c1a0179b. Contract-intensive money is calculated as ((M2-C)/M2), where M2 is the monetary aggregate and C is the amount of money held outside depositary corporations.

According to the CIM indicator, Kazakhstan showed very poor property rights through the 1990s, growing slowly in the early 2000s and hitting a plateau around the time of the global financial crisis in 2008. While the level shown throughout the 2010s and 2020s is not a bad performance for a post-transition economy, especially one which has witnessed economic turmoil, its CIM score of 0.87 in July 2022 is equal to the number achieved by Estonia in its first year as a member of the EU (in December 2004, Estonia had a CIM score of 0.867) and far below Estonia when it was on the cusp of joining the euro in 2011 (Estonia's CIM in December 2010 was 0.96). Perhaps a better indicator of Kazakhstan's protection of property rights then comes from the Heritage Index of Economic Freedom, which was stuck at 30 out of 100 until the global financial crisis ("Property ownership is weakly protected. The court system is highly inefficient. Corruption is extensive, and the judiciary is strongly influenced by other branches of government")[14] and then saw an increase around the time of proposed Land Code changes in 2016. Compared to other transition countries, Kazakhstan's score remains abysmal, never exceeding 65 and in 2022 it was ranked far below countries such as the Czech Republic (88.8), Poland (72.3), Slovenia (70.5), or even Azerbaijan (61.6). In sum, while improvements have been made in Kazakhstan towards some level of broad-based property rights, when measured either against other transition countries or against an objective measure of success, one can see that Kazakhstan's failure to generate property rights of any stripe other than "public property" has been problematic for the transition.

Privatization

Privatization is often lumped together with property rights as a measure of advancement of the private sector, of rule of law, and of investor protection, but is more properly thought of as a subset of property rights: that is, while property rights cover the broad panoply of disposal, transfer, etc., privatization is and was a process that exclusively involves conferring and transferring ownership. Only within a broader functioning property rights framework could ownership matter for economic outcomes, as resources could be invested without fear of expropriation, transfers could be made in open markets, and contracts entered into, understanding that a judicial system was there in case things went wrong. Without these supporting attributes, privatization would only determine the ownership of an asset and nothing more, meaning very little contribution to economic results and, importantly for our case, an economic transition. Thus, to conflate privatization and property rights is to miss what privatization was meant to accomplish (Hartwell 2013a), and it is why we treat privatization as both a sub-set of property rights and separately from these broader rights.

The process of privatization has undergone intense scrutiny over the past 30 years and the fact that economists still can argue about it *ex post* shows how difficult it was to design a "proper" process *ex ante.* The outcomes of privatization have also appeared to increase in importance in the years since the initial processes began in the former Soviet Union, with privatization blamed for the rise of the oligarchs in Russia and Ukraine (Radnitz 2010), the concomitant rise in corruption and decline in state capacity (Hamm et al. 2012), and the stalling of broad-based property rights (Sonin 2003). Enough ink has been spilled on the various approaches to privatization as well and what drove them (Opper 2004), how it affected firms (Jelic et al. 2003), and what it all meant (Estrin et al. 2009), and this is not the place to revisit the arguments over pace, type, and strategies of privatization in transition. Rather, we will trace how the process of shifting ownership from the state to various private and quasi-private actors shaped Kazakhstan's own transition results.

We have already touched upon one of the concerted efforts by the Kazakh government to privatize a specific sector, namely the privatization of state-owned collective farms. As noted in the previous section, when combined with other policies regarding land, government desires to increase agricultural productivity, and public pressure and anti-China animus, this approach did not appreciably increase private ownership, nor did it see the state retreat from the sector. In reality, it was hoped that the change of ownership in agriculture was enough to improve the entire sector, even better if there was no need to restructure the entire business ecosystem or alter the Soviet-esque "bigger is better" mindset prevailing in the Kazakh government. While all forms of privatization have a second-order goal of fostering tangible improvements in firms and the broader economy, the Kazakh agricultural privatization moved this second order into first position, putting aside the real objective of privatization (removing the state from production and increasing the role of the private sector). In this manner, privatization was the solution to a managerial optimization problem: the planned economy had created distorted incentives and rewarded inefficiency by managers but bringing in new management in a new market economy would help to reorder a firm and get it moving in a direction which could then contribute to growth. Unfortunately, such an approach gave many communist, socialist, and other anti-freedom elements a back door through which to influence privatization: this approach could be seen in the proclamation by the Kazakh SSR's Deputy Minister for Agriculture in 1991 that "our task is to change not the organizational structures of productive forces, but the productive relations which are hindering their development" (quoted in Werner 1994).

In many ways, this philosophy continued to animate the entire strategic approach of the Kazakh government to privatization in the 1990s and early 2000s and in particular the reliance on foreign investors, far beyond any other country in the FSU (Peck 2002). Kazakhstan began its journey towards privatization before the collapse of the Soviet Union in both a formal and an informal manner. I have mentioned several times already the "managerial privatizations" of the Gorbachev era, where the loosening of control from the centre led to ostensibly state-owned assets being used as goods for barter among enterprise managers. This was unfortunately the start of incipient cronyism, whereby losses are socialized but gains are privatized, and was the logical outgrowth of socialism: given that the state cannot be omnipotent and omniscient, even the most powerful state will see some leakage from its expropriation of all property, meaning that a market in illicit goods will arise. However, this spontaneous privatization only occurred as a result of cracks opening in the communist facade rather than by plan, and thus falls into the realm of "informal institutional change" (moreover, this phenomenon was not confined to Kazakhstan but occurred throughout the failing Soviet Union).

The formal privatization process in Kazakhstan after the fall of the USSR was planned on a slow but comprehensive timeline, with the country privatizing half of its small and medium-sized enterprises (SMEs) during 1992; this was to be followed with the privatization of the rest of the medium-sized and larger enterprises from 1993 to 1996 and then a final phase from 1997 to 2000 cleaning up the final enterprises (Dąbrowski et al. 1996). In reality, the privatization was compressed as Olcott (2010) notes, with devolution of ownership of housing done by coupon from 1991 to 1992, mass privatization from 1993 to 1995, followed by project-by-project privatization from 1996 to 1998. Housing privatization was perhaps the most successful aspect of the first phase, as coupons gave occupants the ability to purchase a one-bedroom house or apartment, paying the remainder (if needed) in cash and creating a large swathe of owners throughout the country (Mitrofanskaya 1999). Apart from the relative ease of privatizing assets that people had, in some sense, owned already, the progress across other privatization programmes was far less impressive. Instead of achieving the 50 per cent goal of firm privatizations by the end 1992, and despite impressive efforts by the Goskom Imevshestva (State Property Committee), only approximately one-third of all SMEs were privatized, 7,000 in total (Dąbrowski et al. 1996). Even this success must be taken with a pinch of salt, as many of these firms were located in the retail sector (thus making it easy to transfer ownership), "few [companies] were of substantial size; commonly only a minority share was transferred; very few sales were competitive, and most carried highly beneficial terms; and the recipients were almost exclusively the employee collectives and managers" (World Bank 1995:5). The nature of the privatized firms meant that they were usually locally owned rather than by the "republic" (i.e. the government of Kazakhstan), so that they were very small scale with few fixed assets (Dąbrowski et al. 1996). This reality might have showed the reluctance of many erstwhile communist apparatchiks within the state mechanisms to actually removing the state from the economy (Bartley and Minor 1994), perhaps also suggesting that other macroeconomic policies (such as reducing the size and fiscal footprint of the state) which had been neglected could have also harmed the privatization process. Finally, a strategic goal for the government was to get rid of any unprofitable "assets," stressing that the first phase was intended to reduce the fiscal burden on the government by discarding firms which were not performing before selling more lucrative firms (Mitrofanskaya 1999).

The relatively few results from the first phase of privatization were problematic for the next phase, as

> the first phase of the privatization efforts was strongly biased toward employee ownership and collective structures on the one hand and unaccountable nomenclature-led group structures on the other. Both biases tended not to generate effective control by the owners which would maximize long-term value, and both were seen as unfair by the population.
>
> (Dąbrowski et al. 1996:8)

It was an inauspicious debut for a process which was meant to support the widening of property rights in the country, and these problems were to continue through the next phase of privatization beginning in 1993, which widened the scope of the process and demarcated firms by size. As Brown (1998:944) notes, the change of ownership was again sold to the public as a way to "return national wealth to the citizens of Kazakhstan … [however,] on this score, the process raised, then dashed, expectations, souring many on the privatization process." In the first instance, while small-scale privatizations moved forward, the difficulties in privatizing medium- and large-scale enterprises derived from the fact that they were not really "assets," they were "old, [had] opened in the 1960s and 1970s (and some [were] even older) and, although expansions and modifications had occurred over the years, most were in need of substantial investment and updating" (Peck 2002:32). Second, the comfortable lifestyle of no risk and plenty of reward which employees enjoyed, i.e. the situation after spontaneous privatization, was threatened by privatization, and thus many managers and employees were opposed to a shift in a paradigm whereby they might actually have to deliver (Brown 1998) – a major problem for larger state-owned firms. Third, the quality of firms included in the second wave of privatization was also problematic, and the successive waves that occurred throughout this period underperformed, with far fewer firms brought to the auction block than anticipated (Dąbrowski et al. 1996). But perhaps most damning, the process by which state enterprises were privatized was highly convoluted, involving (non-transferable) coupons, intermediaries called "Privatization Investment Funds" (PIFs) whereby coupons needed to be used at (direct investment was prohibited), and regulations which prohibited agglomeration of ownership (Mitrofanskaya 1999). The PIF system itself generated massive problems, as shareholder lists were incomplete, the process was chaotic and not computerized, there was no centralized tracking or distribution system, and individual investors were completely beholden to the fortunes of the PIFs and their own expertise in operating in a completely new system (Brown 1998). The reliance on these "holding companies" was also to set the stage for an entirely new form of concentration within the Kazakh economy, a problem which remains to this day.

With mass privatization continuing to underperform and focused on low-quality assets, it was perhaps no surprise that the state remained too heavily involved in the economic life of the country. Indeed, by 1997 and after two waves of privatization, only 55 per cent of the Kazakh economy was in the hands of the private sector, according to the EBRD, compared to 75 per cent in the advanced transition economies of Central and Eastern Europe (and behind Kyrgyzstan, at 60 percent, and Russia, at 70 per cent). The third phase of privatization, beginning in 1996 and ending around 1998, was far more successful (in one sense), mainly because it involved the largest firms which had been kept off-limits in the earlier rounds, including natural resources and oil and gas firms. Although preparations for auctions and tenders of these firms had been started as early as 1994, the third phase saw a wave of restructurings (including consolidations) and the repackaging of firms for foreign investors, selling off these assets or awarding management contracts in a relatively quick manner (Peck 2002). During this phase, the need to deliver better outcomes for Kazakhstan and the public was the overriding priority, with the desire to attract investment into the energy sector the key objective and, hence, the reason behind the push for foreign investment and know-how (Blackmon 2010). Indeed, unlike the agricultural sector, where foreigners were alternately rejected, welcomed, then eventually locked out entirely, the industrial sector was thrown wide open for foreign firms (Peck 2004). This rapid sale of concessions and leases (but not actual firms) in turn helped to finance the Kazakh government's growing budget deficit, bringing in nearly 4 per cent of GDP during the mid- and late 1990s (Alam and Banerji 2000).

While the auction mechanism during this phase was regarded as a transparent means of bringing in these foreigners, a much more opaque (and commonplace) method involved the use of tenders, which were plagued by criticism of cronyism, corruption, and capriciousness (Peck 2002), especially with regard to government demands, which could sometimes be extensive (Mitrofanskaya 1999). Bribery was also found to be rampant, including in the infamous "Kazakhgate" case, when tens of millions of dollars of payments were transferred to top Kazakh officials (possibly including Nazarbayev; see Peyrouse 2012) via various secret accounts from multinationals to secure the contracts they desired (Lillis 2022). Chinese energy firms have also been accused of similar tactics, lest we think this is only a Western problem, again in the energy field, but with much less fanfare (Cooley 2012), even though the public scrutiny of Chinese firms is higher. The privatization of large enterprises also contributed to the strengthening of various financial groups located in the regions (whether legally or extra-legally), especially where natural resources were prevalent, generating various political power bases across the country (Kudaibergenova 2015) within the Nazarbayev regime. While there was no massive wave of oligarchization in Kazakhstan as in Russia, the sale of natural resource concessions did enrich several actors, who were able to benefit from low prices and the smuggling of metals to China (Peyrouse 2012), while the consolidation of the oil and gas sector led to state-owned behemoths who were selected to be "national champions" and thus their executives were treated as such (Groce 2020). The entire process led to an almost perfect overlap of political and economic elites, with the levers of state power being wielded by those who benefited the most from the large enterprise deals of the late 1990s (Murphy 2006). However, as many have noted (Schiek and Hensell 2012 give a very good overview), the precise way in which these economic spoils have been divided in Kazakhstan, including those gleaned from privatization, was done in a "neo-patrimonial" manner, and in many ways paralleled that which occurred in Russia under Putin: a decade of ownership transfer resulted in the creation of a hybrid political and economic elite, but with the undisputed nexus of this power resting in Nazarbayev.

As noted in Chapter 5, the emergence of competing elites in the late 1990s, some of them financed by the gains from privatization, led Nazarbayev to push hard in the 2000s to amass his own economic power (Laruelle 2012), somewhat reversing the point of privatization by renationalizing profits and by reconcentrating the industrial might of Kazakhstan in government hands. From the early 2000s, this state of affairs meant that private economic gains were still dependent on political acquiescence to Nazarbayev, if not necessarily loyalty (Peyrouse 2012), and in some ways the multiple power poles spurred by privatization were played off against each other by Nazarbayev with a firm admonishment to stay out of formal political involvement. This approach worked during the 2000s and early 2010s mainly because the privatization process had been completed, with the smaller parts of the economy in private hands but the commanding heights still politically connected; with no privatization rents to capture, the only way in which a politician could enrich themselves was through connections with the state-owned and/or managed large enterprises, and if one challenged Nazarbayev directly, the stream of rents could be cut off. This uneasy equilibrium resulted in a staying power for Kazakhstan's economic elite that was vastly different to the shifting relations between Putin and the oligarchs in Russia (Engvall 2021).

With stratification between elite capture of large enterprises and private enterprises thriving at the retail and SME level, Kazakhstan found itself in a similar situation in terms of ownership to Russia, albeit one that was not as perilous and with somewhat more diversification (in 2020, according to the Organisation for Economic Co-operation and Development, SMEs accounted for 22.3 per cent of Russia's GDP but for 31.6 per cent of Kazakhstan's GDP). With regard to the state-run privatizations which allowed this to happen, Peck (2002:54) sums up the failure of the Kazakh privatization scheme perfectly: "Perhaps most disappointing, the privatization and sale of the large enterprises in Kazakhstan has not been synonymous with increasing competition or the development of any sort of market-based economy." Throughout the 2010s, in tandem with further centralization of political power, the Kazakh state became much more involved in the Kazakh economy, including the creation of holding funds along the lines of the PIFs from the 1990s but with the express goal of consolidating *all* of the state's holdings into one gigantic fund, a "National Wellbeing Fund," to provide stability during turbulent times (Sansyzbayeva and Ametova 2015). This fund, the (in)famous "Samruk-Kazyna," is a "special vehicle for state intervention into the economy" (Kalyuzhnova and Nygaard 2011), created on the model of a similar fund in Singapore, a country which – it must be noted – tends to score a bit higher than Kazakhstan on most international measures of rule of law. Rather than a vehicle for spreading ownership further and wider, "the acknowledged objective of [Samruk-Kazyna] was to reinforce the role of the state in the economy by combining control over assets with more investment power" (Peyrouse 2012:356). Mesquita (2016:9) puts it perhaps a bit too diplomatically by noting that this arrangement, "although designed to boost the Kazakh economy and fund social projects … [is] nonetheless open to elite influence." While Samruk-Kazyna is funded via windfall gains from the sale of oil, providing a macroeconomic and fiscal buffer as a sovereign wealth fund, its dual role in owning all major state-led corporations in the country has given it an inordinate amount of control in the development of Kazakhstan's economy from the post-global financial crisis era. Formally under control of the holding company Baiterek since 2013, the funds are more accurately described as being under the direct control of the President and externally audited accounts are not available or published, making the fund's holdings somewhat murky (Sakal 2015).[15]

This state of affairs persists to the present day, despite additional plans for privatization mooted in 2011 under the heading of a "people's IPO," allowing Kazakh citizens to purchase shares in major Kazakh firms; by 2019, only 0.6 per cent of the stock market had been brought in by this method (Serkebayeva et al. 2019). Additionally, in 2015, a comprehensive plan was put forth to reduce the share of the state in the economy to 15 per cent by 2020, but this too stalled against the powerful elites and their interest in the rents which could be garnered in the status quo (Tipaldou 2021). As of 2019, Samruk-Kazyna continued to account for as much as 60 per cent of the country's GDP, showing that the country was top-heavy and reliant on only a few large key firms, which in turn were subservient to politics and political patrons. The pervasive nature of Kazakhstan's continued reliance on oil and gas rents – and the informal networks which coalesced around these industrial giants – further illustrated how the flawed privatization of the largest enterprises doomed the rest of the privatization successes that Kazakhstan saw (as in small-scale business) and left the economy at the highest level in the hands of presidential cronies (Groce 2020).

A final note is crucial here on the relative failure of Kazakhstan's privatization programme. Since privatization only concerns the small slice of property rights related to ownership, the failure in Kazakhstan was that privatization *did* transfer ownership, but not to the private sector, merely shuffling state expropriated assets from one labelled group of politicians (communists) to another group (the so-called democrats). In this, privatization was seen as the be-all, end-all of property rights creation rather than one small and rather inconsequential slice of a larger reform. Conversations with Kazakh policymakers during my years as an adviser in the country revealed a keen sense of knowledge of the issues which emerged during the privatization process, paired as it was with almost no movement in the broader property rights reforms necessary to foster a market economy. During one visit in 2015, as Kazakhstan continued to claw its way out of the turbulent post-global financial crisis era – and was being buffeted by Western sanctions on Russia following its illegal annexation of the Crimean peninsula – a policymaker dealing with the financial sector noted that "we know we blew it in the 2000s, and we are determined not to have that happen again." However, the policy response was to concentrate even more ownership in Samruk-Kazyna as a means of buffering the entire economy from macroeconomic shocks, linking the broader economy to hydrocarbons ever more closely, rather than understanding the microeconomic foundations of previous fragility. In the very essence of a Type II error (failing to reject the null when it is false), the Kazakh authorities had gone more in the direction of the very issue (state concentration) which made them less resilient rather than changing course entirely. And all the while, although the titles of ownership had changed somewhat, from formal to informal networks (Groce 2020), property rights stagnated.

Monetary and Financial Institutions

All this talk of the global financial crisis provides a natural segue to the next series of economic institutions, both financial and monetary institutions. While they are separate and distinct, the amount of interconnectedness between the two requires that we examine them jointly, as modern central banking is intimately linked to – and explicitly charged with the oversight of – the financial sector. As we will see, the financial sector in Kazakhstan during the transition period was heavily dependent on the development of the monetary authorities, and the two became inextricably connected through the global financial crisis and beyond.

In the first instance, regarding monetary institutions, the NBK is currently the central hub of the country's economic institutions, overseeing the monetary and financial operations of the Kazakh economy and in particular the tenge. As with many other economic institutions, independent Kazakhstan had no experience of modern central banking and in fact was far more disadvantaged than other transition economies (along with the other countries of Central Asia) in not having any experience of central banking at all.[16] Unlike the CEE countries, which had central banks in the interwar period, Kazakhstan was under the communist yoke at that point, meaning that the only bank that it dealt with was the Gosudarstvennyi Bank (known as the Gosbank), literally the State Bank of the USSR. As with other facets of central planning, the state bank was not governed by market tenets and did not operate as a commercial bank, being merely another entity charged with accounting for and shuffling credits around in pursuit of fulfilment of the country's great economic plan (Johnson 2000). During the late Gorbachev era, banking as an exercise in financial sector intermediation began in earnest, with the creation of Sberbank and the development of other financial intermediaries (Hartwell and Korovkin 2021), but the state bank remained the nexus of the (increasingly inefficient) system (Johnson 2000). As a result of the mania for independence that commenced in the early 1990s, the financial and monetary system of the USSR degraded further as each republic set up its own state bank: in this way, the "State Bank of the Kazakh SSR" was instituted as a proper central bank by law in December 1990, and was charged with the creation and maintenance of currency and financial sector oversight.

However, once Kazakhstan had gained its independence, the "State Bank of the Kazakh SSR" had little opportunity to exercise these powers, as for two years there was no national currency and Kazakhstan remained in the rouble zone and beholden to Russian monetary policy. Despite inconsistencies in legislation – and the fact that Kazakh legislation followed USSR legal documents, and not the new laws of the Russian Federation – that created loopholes in the exercise of monetary policy (Lewarne 1993), for the most part, the State Bank played a subservient role to the Central Bank of Russia, doling out credits that were sent by Moscow. It was not until 1993 and the collapse of the rouble zone that the "National Bank of Kazakhstan" was created, in legislation superseding the 1990 Act, with responsibility for overseeing the new currency, the tenge. Further legislation in 1995 strengthened the operational independence of the bank, placing its mandate squarely within the realm of currency stability, a goal which would be served by keeping inflation low but was not an explicit inflation targeting regime (Kanagtova and Sidorenko 2020). In terms of policy independence, however, the NBK set its own targets; indeed, it is safe to say that, throughout its history, the NBK has not been dogmatic in its pursuit of stability, as it pursued

> monetary targeting with flexible exchange rates (1993:11–1995:06), monetary targeting with stable exchange rates (1995:06–1998:08), inflation targeting with flexible exchange rates within currency corridors (1999:04–2014:02) and inflation targeting with flexible exchange rates without currency corridors (2015:08–to date).
>
> (Bhatti and Khawaja 2018:1212)

The first phase of the NBK's existence was focused on breaking the back of the hyperinflation induced by the rouble zone, introducing tight monetary policy from 1994 to 1995 (Bofinger 1996). As noted, this was done by targeting monetary aggregates but with the tenge allowed to float from its starting level of 4.7 Kazakhstani tenge (KZT) to the US dollar; at the same time, the NBK, as an independent entity, ceased to monetize the debt of enterprises and generated a hard budget constraint, at least when it came to

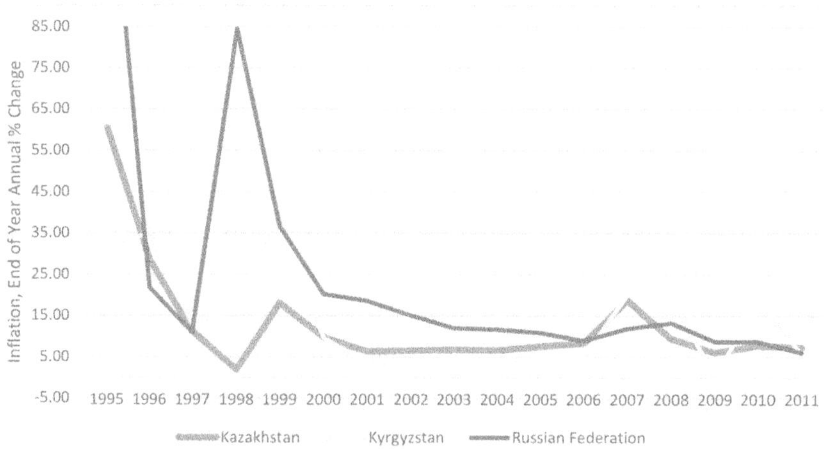

Figure 6.2 Inflation in Three CIS Countries, 1995–2011
Source: IMF World Economic Outlook database, www.imf.org/en/Publications/SPROLLs/world-economic-outlook-databases#sort=%40imfdate%20descending, and Dąbrowski (2013).

budget support from the monetary authorities (Hoelscher 1998). However, as noted above and as we will see throughout this section, monetary policy in Kazakhstan – while independent in policy goals – was often also independent from government desires, which tended to act counter to whatever monetary policy was actually trying to achieve. In particular, the government's subsidization of enterprises in 1994 and 1995 helped to sustain inflation above a level which would have been expected given the stabilization, creating a countervailing distortion to the tight monetary policy (Snoek and van Rooden 1999). This tug of war between monetary and fiscal policy was to continue throughout Kazakhstan's post-Soviet experience, meaning that, overall, inflation may have been reduced from the trauma of the transformational recession and the rouble zone, but it was to remain at higher levels than that experienced by many of its compatriots in transition, especially throughout the 1990s (although, it must be noted, inflation was lower than in Russia during most of the transition process, see Figure 6.2).

Alongside the development of the monetary authority came the development of a capitalist financial sector; in this, "Kazakhstan was one of the countries of the former Soviet Union where banking sector reform was given a relatively high priority by the government" (Hoelscher 1998:4). Indeed, a large part of the stabilization package during 1994 directed by the NBK focused on the financial sector, with a tightening of regulatory requirements and the liquidation of 60 banks in 1995 after they failed to clear these hurdles (Abdullina 2007), leading to a consolidation of banks but with no appreciable loss of coverage for Kazakh consumers (Table 6.4). From 1995 to 1998, the challenge was to adopt Bank of International Settlements prudential supervision guidelines, a piecemeal process which forced more banks to close (as seen in Table 6.4) if they could not adopt such practices, while a move towards international accounting standards was also part of the strengthening of the sector (Akimov and Dollery 2008). The problem of non-performing loans from undercapitalized banks and Soviet practices – one which was to bedevil Kazakhstan throughout its transition process – was also tackled via the creation of three separate debt resolution institutions in 1994 (Hoelscher 1998). Overall, the steps taken by authorities in the 1990s earned high marks from the IMF and other international organizations, as, on paper at least, the proper procedures and best practices were being followed, and the financial sector had reversed its fall from 1993 to 1995 fairly quickly. This was crucial for the country, as the increase in FDI required vehicles for financial intermediation, facilitating the use of FDI to fund development within the country (Waikar et al. 2011).

Unfortunately, the crisis in Russia in 1998 was a strong and unexpected external shock which hit both the developing monetary authority and the consolidating financial sector, both of which had been making good progress in fostering stability within the Kazakh economy. Despite progress in the financial sector and the adherence to exchange rate stability, the structural issues in building a market economy (see above) and the failure to sever

Table 6.4 Banks by Type in Kazakhstan, 1991–1997

	State-owned	*Joint venture*	*Other*	*Total no. of banks*	*Total no. of branches*
1991	n.a.	n.a.	n.a.	72	n.a.
1992	n.a.	n.a.	n.a.	158	890
1993	n.a.	n.a.	n.a.	184	952
1994	3	10	178	191	1,022
1995	3	7	120	130	1,036
1996	4	8	89	101	949
1997	4	8	71	83	n.a.

Source: Hoelscher (1998).

Kazakhstan's trade relations from Russia (see below) meant that the overall economy was still rather fragile (Pomfret 2005a). With the rouble in freefall after the Russian government defaulted, alongside the contagion afflicting all emerging markets during this period, the Kazakh economy contracted by nearly 2 per cent; however, the NBK, staying true to its mandate, fought hard to keep the currency stable and continued to use tight (and in some case heterodox) policies to ensure that hard-fought macroeconomic stability did not disappear. From the end of 1997 to March 1999, the worst period of the crisis, the NBK spent considerable sums of money on defending the tenge from the same drop that the rouble experienced, resulting in a decrease in the bank's international reserves of approximately US $600 million, nearly 40 per cent of its total reserves (International Monetary Fund 2001). Concurrently, the NBK introduced a number of heterodox measures, including some capital account restrictions and (notably) a ban on some imports from Russia in order to try to salvage some competitiveness from the sudden boom which Russian exporters (via depreciation) were enjoying (Pastor and Damjanovic 2001).

The NBK, facing an insurmountable wave rocking all emerging markets, finally gave in to mounting pressure on 4 April 1999, and shifted its exchange rate strategy to a managed floating regime. This resulted almost immediately in a devaluation of the tenge from its previous level of 88.5 KZT to the US dollar to a high of 147 KZT, before settling closer to 117 KZT to the US dollar later in April. Given the global macroeconomic climate, it was perhaps not surprising that the tenge continued to slide, finally stabilizing at approximately 145 KZT to the US dollar by the end of 1999. Although the rouble was also depreciating rapidly, the fall of the tenge in tandem with the rouble (Kuralbayeva et al. 2001) temporarily shifted relative prices away from Russia's favour and allowed growth to rapidly return to the country (Pomfret 2005a), alongside (and probably greatly influenced by) a recovery in global oil prices (Kuralbayeva et al. 2001). However, the fall in FDI which accompanied the global emerging market crisis meant that the banking sector was also in a fragile state, and the total number of banks in the country decreased to 47 in 2000 from its 1997 level; on the other hand, the banks which remained were far stronger and had capitalization levels that were at least five times higher than the average recorded by the banking sector just a few years earlier (Eicher 2004).

Having faced the 1998 crisis in Russia and its own transformational recession, Kazakhstan was relatively well placed to weather the large shock of the global financial crisis that began in 2008.[17] During the run-up to the global financial crisis, Kazakhstan had seen a swift recovery from the shock of 1998, with growth throughout the economy and a resumption of FDI flows into the energy sector. Indeed, Kazakhstan's economy, and especially its financial sector, behaved much as in the developed world during the 2000s, with cheap money abundant and asset market bubbles being inflated with impunity. As an example, Kazakhstan's financial sector had taken on more and more external debt during the period 2003–2007 and, more importantly, extended more and more credit to the economy, swelling to 43 per cent of GDP in 2007 and rendering financial institutions extremely vulnerable. As Barisitz et al. (2010) note, in 2005 and 2006 alone, the annual growth rate of bank loans exceeded 60 per cent, one of the most rapid credit booms in any of the transition economies (see Figure 6.3). This was further powered by a wave of foreign investment in the banking sector, including from Austrian and South Korean banks which acquired leading stakes in the fifth and sixth largest banks in Kazakhstan, respectively. Much as in the United States and other countries globally, Kazakhstan's banks experienced "over-exuberant borrowing and lenders paying less and less attention to borrowers' creditworthiness or the value of collateral" (Pomfret 2009:2).

When the sub-prime crisis in the United States began to spill over borders, the impact on Kazakhstan was immediate, with downgrades of banks directly exposed to the US sub-prime market, an almost instantaneous halt in credit extension in late 2007, and a collapse in housing prices (Barisitz et al. 2010). As Pomfret (2009:3) notes, "the origins of the domestic financial crisis were home-grown. The banks' problems arose from loan portfolios overweighted in domestic real estate projects, not from buying over-risky financial assets in the global market," meaning that any response from the NBK would need to be focused on these specific local issues. Luckily, like its response to the 1998 crisis (notwithstanding the heterodox measures it took), Kazakhstan made a quick and seemingly effective policy response to the global financial crisis, especially when compared to other countries in both the post-Soviet sphere and even in Western Europe. The response was centred mainly on liquidity support by both the NBK and the government, which established a US $1 billion (1 per cent of GDP) facility of earmarked deposits with banks in 2007 (just as the crisis was beginning). The purpose of this facility was to support construction companies and SMEs and to prevent a rash of bankruptcies from collapsing the real sector. Further liquidity assistance was provided in late 2008 after the collapse of Lehman Brothers and the deepening of the crisis. In total, Kazakhstan put together a comprehensive anti-crisis programme providing for the allocation of about US $12 billion (approximately 12 per cent of Kazakhstan's annual GDP; see Barisitz and Lahnsteiner 2010) from 2009 to 2010.

Public support was also provided to the largest four banks deemed systemically important (Kazkommertsbank, BTA Bank, Alliance Bank, and Halyk Bank). Rather than undertaking a straight bailout of the banking sector, the NBK took the lead in addressing the main vulnerability of the banking sector in the pre-crisis period, namely the aforementioned explosion of debt – and the subsequent drying up of outside liquidity which the crisis created (Ruziev and Majidov 2013). In order to stave off a collapse of the financial sector, the NBK undertook to restructure US $22.6 billion of the debt of these four banks, reducing liabilities by US $16.6 billion. A large portion of these liabilities were written off through a controversial "haircut" process, whereby creditors had to accept losses of over 60 per cent on their initial investments; in the case of BTA Bank losses reached a level of 75 per cent, the largest emerging market debt restructuring up until that point (Barisitz et al. 2010). In addition, the NBK took it upon itself to convert some loans to equity, with common shares distributed among claimants, while other claims were cancelled in exchange for cash and new bank notes.

However, the NBK was not the only player in the crisis response and, in an odd turn of events, Samruk-Kazyna entered the fray by injecting US $2.5

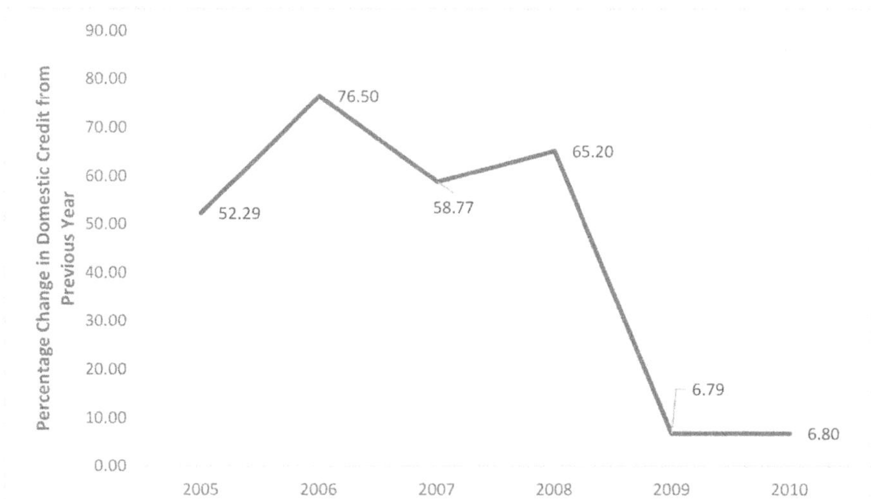

Figure 6.3 Growth in Domestic Credit (year-on-year) in Kazakhstan, 2005–2010
Source: Bloomberg L.P. (n.d.) Growth in Domestic Credit (YoY) in Kazakhstan (data set), retrieved 29 November 2011 from www.bloomberg.com/professional/solution/bloomberg-terminal/. Figure shows change in bank lending to the public and private sectors, plus bank lending in domestic currency overseas.

billion into systemic banks to prevent bank failures in late 2008; in this way, the NBK was not bailing out failing banks as a monetary manoeuvre but instead liquidity was injected as a fiscal policy tactic instead. As the crisis deepened, it soon became clear that the scale of debt and the severity of the issues within these banks would overwhelm even this massive liquidity injection and, as a result, Samruk-Kazyna became the largest shareholder in BTA Bank, Alliance Bank, and Temir Bank (Kalyuzhnova and Nygaard 2011). The result of this effort was that the banking system returned to solvency, as liquidity as a percentage of assets rose from 14.1 per cent to 22.6 per cent from 2008 to 2010, while bank assets in the NBK increased from US $9.1 to US $10.5 billion and the gross external debt of the national banking system decreased from US $41.6 billion to US $17 billion (Weitz 2010).

Having dealt with the banking system's liquidity problems and the restructuring of liabilities of systemic banks via an ingenious hybrid fiscal/monetary response, the Kazakh authorities were unfortunately not as successful in dealing with non-performing loans (NPLs) in the banking sector. In November 2008, Samruk-Kazyna established a distressed asset fund (DAF) with initial plans to capitalize it by up to US $1 billion and to purchase distressed loans from banks, but with disbursements only of US $433 million up to the end of that year. As the crisis unfolded, DAF priorities also changed, and funds were directed to provide relief to overleveraged SMEs and taken away from NPLs. This was a strategic choice but one which did not have a beneficial impact on the financial sector, as NPLs were estimated at around 21 per cent of GDP in 2010 and still accounted for 23.5 per cent of all loans in 2015 (after topping out at 32.9 per cent in April 2014; see Muratbek 2017) and only falling to less than 10 per cent by 2016 (International Monetary Fund 2021).

Part of the issue with NPLs came about from the specific instruments that the NBK used. Like many other national banks, the NBK also engaged in unconventional monetary policy, reducing its policy rate and reserve requirements to record lows and providing refinancing loans to banks to ensure short-term liquidity. However, the NBK also attempted a competitive devaluation as a means of buying some time for exporters and the real economy. From the outset of the crisis and throughout 2008, the NBK intervened heavily in the foreign exchange market to support the tenge, using US $6 billion (about one-quarter of Kazakhstan's international reserves at that time) to sustain the tenge's peg with the US dollar. However, appreciation pressures resumed on the back of higher oil prices at the beginning of 2009, and the NBK decided to devalue the tenge on 4 February 2009, by 25 per cent, to a rate of approximately 150 KZT to the US dollar. Seen as a stopgap measure, it provided some breathing space for its reserves and temporarily corrected its position against the Russian rouble. Despite the long-term ineffectiveness of targeting a relative price, the NBK was able to hold the tenge within a band around this target rate during the rest of the crisis and even through 2014. At the same time, however, the devaluation also worsened the debt position of unhedged borrowers, making their real positions now more burdensome (Barisitz and Lahnsteiner 2010), while Korhonen (2009) notes how ineffective it was likely to be in resolving structural problems (a prediction which did indeed come true).

The post-global financial crisis era has led to other challenges for the Kazakh monetary authorities, with the largest headache being the global macroeconomic environment and, in particular, Russia's war against Ukraine (and, by extension, the West). Having successfully surmounted the global financial crisis, the Russian military invasion of Ukraine in 2014 and subsequent Western sanctions generated a large and wholly unnecessary shock to the Kazakh economy, tied as it was to Russia via trade and other linkages (see the next section). As Figure 6.4 shows and as just noted, the tenge remained fairly stable after the global financial crisis, but the NBK unexpectedly devalued the currency again in February 2014 in the face of global volatility, declining oil prices, economic slowdown in Russia, unrest in Ukraine, and the first Russian steps towards invading that country (although the devaluation occurred on 11 February, 11 days before Ukrainian President Viktor Yanukovych fled to Russia and the invasion began, the protests in Maidan in Kyiv had been ongoing since December 2013). Citing the continuing decline of the Russian rouble and unfavourable commodity price trends, the NBK not only moved the target rate of the tenge to 185 KZT to the US dollar but also tightened the bands around which it would be allowed to fluctuate (Epstein and Portillo 2014). This move, cited as "purely financial" by Nazarbayev (Brauer 2014), led to protests against the somewhat cavalier and uncommunicated policy change, protests which were then brutally repressed (Anceschi 2015).

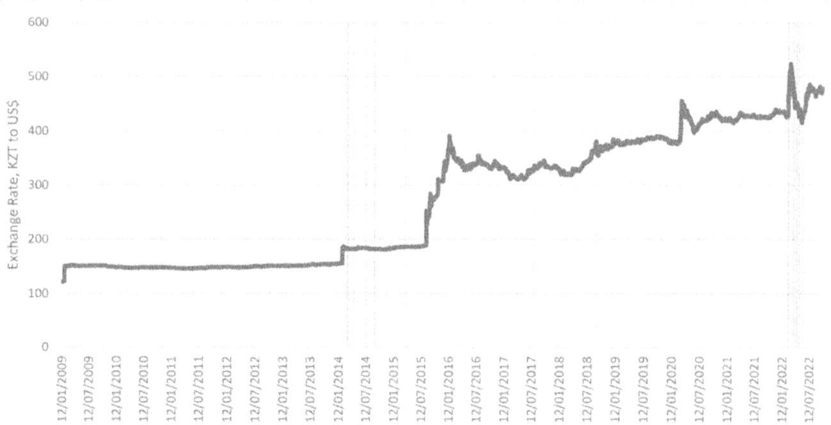

Figure 6.4 Exchange Rate, KZT to the US $, 2009–2022
Source: Data provided by the NBK, https://nationalbank.kz/en/exchangerates/ezhednevnye-oficialnye-rynochnye-kursy-valyut, and Investing.com, www.investing.com/

With a ratcheting series of sanctions being imposed on Russia following its invasion of Ukraine in 2014, and the price of oil continuing to plummet, Kazakh policymakers remained in a bind due to their reliance on their northern neighbour. Only a year and a half after the 2014 devaluation, the NBK took a momentous step in changing the country's monetary policy entirely: in August 2015, the decision was made to remove the tenge from an exchange rate peg and to let it float entirely, shifting to a "transitory" inflation-targeting regime in line with prevailing central bank practices around the world (Stronski 2016). This shift generated another massive devaluation in the currency, as the tenge plunged by nearly 28 per cent against the US dollar, with the tenge continuing to devalue until January 2016. Indeed, this continuing devaluation, beginning in 2014 and accelerating with the abrupt policy change, also benefited Kazakhstan's natural resource producers, who were mostly paid in dollars but who incurred their costs in tenge (Brauer 2014). At the same time, even though the move to a floating regime may have been the correct choice for the tenge, there was an acknowledgement from NBK officials that the inflation-targeting regime would take some time to be fully implemented, mainly because there was still a marked lack of coordination from the government, which has continued to subsidize lending and enterprises, meaning a push for price inflation (International Monetary Fund 2022). Such disorganized policies would make it more difficult to meet the target inflation rate of between 4 and 6 per cent (and in fact was only achieved in 2019), meaning that the experience of elevated inflation throughout the transition period was likely to persist.

This reality was boosted by the continued deterioration in Kazakhstan's partner to the north. Indeed, while Kazakh monetary authorities could – and did – raise interest rates up to 17 per cent in early 2016 to combat inflationary pressures, even these high rates could not combat the continued volatility emanating from Russia. The response of the tenge to US and other countries' sanctions on Russia has been consistent since 2014, from forcing the NBK's hand to devalue to pressure during 2015, and even during the "Cold War" from 2015 to 2022, when Russia occupied Ukrainian territory but for the most part did not conduct major offensive operations: for example, in August 2018, the United States announced a new series of sanctions on Russia related to the Skripal poisoning in the United Kingdom, and the tenge immediately fell by 6.8 per cent against the US dollar. Figure 6.4 shows that this has persisted throughout the latest wave of Russian aggressions, taking the tenge to new heights against the US dollar and making life incredibly challenging for the NBK as a monetary institution.

In sum, the experience of Kazakhstan's monetary and financial institutional development is very similar to that of other emerging markets. In the first instance, given that these are the sectors where money resides (and is in fact created), it tends to attract some of the top talent, and the NBK has functioned as a very competent central bank, especially when one considers that Kazakhstan had no experience of modern central banking. The performance of Kazakhstan's monetary transition is even more impressive when one considers the headwinds it faced, including the repeated crises in Russia and then the uptick in neighbourhood volatility created specifically by the Kremlin and its Ukrainian policies. The responses of the NBK to these crises also demonstrated the competency of the NBK to undertake an independent operational policy, remaining pragmatic where necessary but keeping focused on stability above all. As a consequence, perhaps, the financial sector has proved itself to be fairly robust, and even when one considers the largest problems surrounding banking in the mid-2000s, i.e. the explosion of credit, one cannot fault Kazakhstan specifically, as this was endemic across most countries. The period of consolidation and of foreign investment in the 1990s and 2000s also helped to instil Western know-how in operating the banking sector, providing Kazakh banks with the ability to intermediate the FDI flows which the country was relying on.

Arrayed against these positives is the reality that inflation has remained too high for too long in the country, although it is possible that any monetary authority would have had the same lack of success in fighting inflation given the fiscal policies of the Nazarbayev regime. In fact, while the two Acts in 1993 and 1995 outlined the full complement of monetary and financial levers the NBK was to use in pursuit of this goal, in reality the NBK was less independent than it appeared (Baerg et al. 2021), especially when measured against traditional independence metrics such as length of tenure of the central bank governor (Nurbayev 2015). Similarly, as communication is one of the key tenets of modern central bank policymaking, the NBK was notably deficient in its ability to transmit guidance to markets, especially during the 2014–2015 period, when the tenge underwent a substantial devaluation and then a shift to a new monetary regime (resulting in further depreciation). The NBK itself has admitted that the effectiveness of its communication is understudied (Turekhanova and Mekenbaeva 2021) and the accompanying protests surrounding the 2014 and 2015 moves show that there still is a long way to go to prepare the populace for important reforms. Again, however, the main problem may be that Kazakhstan is a price taker and not a price maker, with the prices being bestowed – as during the Soviet Union – from Russia. A large part of this is of Kazakhstan's own doing, as we will now examine.

Trade

Kazakhstan borders Russia, China, and three other post-Soviet republics (Turkmenistan, Kyrgyzstan, and Uzbekistan), but apart from these neighbours, is generally far away from all the major global commercial centres. On top of this, Kazakhstan is landlocked (although with some ability for waterway commerce via the Caspian Sea to Azerbaijan or Iran), with its neighbours in Central Asia also landlocked (Uzbekistan is only one of two double landlocked countries in the entire world, the other being Liechtenstein). The closest ocean port to Astana is St Petersburg; however, in terms of actual use to Kazakhstan (since St Petersburg is reliant on icebreakers in the winter), the closest port is Qingdao in China, the seventh busiest port in the world and a mere 2,602 miles (4,187.6 kilometres) from Nur-Sultan as the crow flies. While technological advances, integrated global supply chains, and progress in shipping and logistics have reduced the cost of distance immensely in recent decades, even for a remote country such as Kazakhstan, there is a reason that gravity models of trade remain the workhorse of the profession. That reason is that, for trade, geography does indeed continue to matter.

This point was ignored entirely during the Soviet Union for, as noted in Chapter 4, the Kazakh SSR was part of the internal transmission belt of the Soviet industrial machine, with the Kazakhs assigned their role within the Soviet supply chain. "Trade" as is known in a capitalist economy did not exist within the Soviet Union nor did it exist across borders, as this was also part of the planners' dreams. Trade in a market system is not the easiest of human endeavours, predicated as it is on global and local supply chains, relative endowments at the country level, factor prices locally and globally, and the effort needed to incorporate all of these attributes and produce a product which can be marketed on a mass scale to foreign consumers and then actually purchased. It is for this reason why exporting firms tend to be closer to the productive or efficiency frontier for their country, simply because they have to be (Delgado et al. 2002). The effort involved in generating trade links at the corporate level happens across all exporting firms and can be seen in the aggregate at the country level to understand how interconnected countries are and why (De Benedictis and Tajoli 2011). Actions such as sanctions and embargoes rip out these carefully cultivated links, making it difficult for firms to reorient themselves and causing severe disruptions, but market signals can shift business and help firms to overcome political uncertainty (Graziano et al. 2021).

This was the polar opposite of the Soviet approach to trade, as national and internal borders were mere speedbumps to trade which was merely a way to shuffle materials to complete the plan in, first and foremost, the USSR. The institutional mechanism that was used to facilitate trade between the Soviet Union and its vassal states was the Council of Mutual Economic Assistance (Comecon or CMEA), an international organization created by Stalin to extend the communist production machinery across borders and to alleviate the failures within the USSR. "Trade" was determined by Moscow and settled in "transferable roubles," with pricing done as part of each five-year plan (Tiraspolsky and Vale 1984). Like everything else connected with the planned economy, however, this too was problematic due to the artificial pricing, politically determined moves of resources, and vulnerability of the CMEA to global shocks (De Groot 2020). Long after the death of Stalin, Dudinskii (1966:19–20) notes that

> cooperation with the fraternal countries will help solve problems of the new five-year plan … Implementation of the proposed objective is

> complicated by the fact that five-year trade agreements concluded between the Soviet Union and the CMEA countries had already basically determined the volume and structure of Soviet foreign trade, especially Soviet deliveries of fuels and raw materials needed for normal economic development of the fraternal countries.

CMEA policy thus was done in a way to feed Soviet needs but without causing the buffer states of the Warsaw Pact to collapse, a delicate balance which more often than not resulted in the USSR swiftly reallocating "trade" in favour of its own imperatives (Shabad 1979).

The end of the USSR and of central planning from Moscow for its vassal states also ended the CMEA and, with it, the trade which had been in place for half a century. This had a catastrophic but necessary effect on Kazakhstan and the other newly independent countries emerging from the USSR: catastrophic because these countries now had international borders between them and Russia and could no longer rely on the transfer of materials from Moscow, but necessary because the trade which was carried out was wholly incompatible with a free market economy. With the plan gone, there was no need for planned trade, and thus there had to be a period during which the trade linkages described above were forged. This necessarily had to be done in tandem with enterprise restructuring, or else the Kazakh economy would continue to keep producing the same goods it had under communism but with no guaranteed outlets for these products, as was the case in the USSR (Winiecki 1988 discusses this flaw in the centrally planned economy). Indeed, this approach is what Belarus stood by in the 1990s and 2000s, producing potash and tractors, mainly for the Russian market, as if the Soviet Union had never fallen.

The collapse of CMEA trade was especially hard on the former republics of the Soviet Union, including Kazakhstan, precisely since they had no industrial structure of their own pre-Stalin, and the one which was built up was done explicitly to serve Moscow rather than Alma-Ata, Tselinograd, or Ust'-Kamenogorsk. This structure fed into the CMEA trading plan, meaning that the entire base of production of the Kazakh SSR (and, indeed, its "superstructure," to use Marxist terminology) was built from the ground up as a communist project. This problem spread to the very arteries of commerce, infrastructure, which were all routed towards Moscow and the Russian Federation, problematic especially when thinking of Kazakhstan's biggest potential export, oil and gas:

> The Soviet production pattern and transport infrastructure made Kazakhstan heavily dependent on Russia for its oil trade and consumption in particular. The absence of an east–west domestic pipeline left Russia as the only outlet for crude oil extracted in western Kazakhstan, while Russia was the only source of crude oil for the Kazakh eastern refineries, which supplied most domestic consumption.
>
> (De Broeck and Kostial 1998:22)

Overall, the distortions that the CMEA created in terms of trade flows were massive, as Maurel and Cheikbossian (1998) estimate that trade among members of the CMEA bloc was 13 times higher than it should have been (given distance and endowments). The collapse of the CMEA led to massive dislocation, especially for firms that were dependent on complex supply chains and products within the specific requirements of central planning (Blanchard and Kremer 1997), an issue which was found to be a key determinant of the output contraction in Kazakhstan (Bevan et al. 2001). Institutionally as well, there was little capacity for the government to reorient its own trade administration (including customs), leading to a large number of formal and informal internal barriers to trade and, especially, proliferation of corruption regarding cross-border trade within the region (Linn 2004). As the USSR had centralized foreign relations, Kazakhs had no experience of modern international economic negotiations, trade policy, or even the governmental institutions to handle trade (Khasanova 2017). Faced with a lack of state capacity, the Kazakh government initially tried to mimic its former Soviet structure, remaining closely involved in both internal and external trade, drawing precisely the wrong lesson from the collapse of the CMEA: this led to the creation of its own state order system in 1992 and 1993 and the conclusion of bilateral treaties basically on a barter system (De Broeck and Kostial 1998).

But perhaps the worst step the country took in its trade policy journey mirrored its monetary stabilization foibles in that it attempted to soften the blow of the collapse of the CMEA by propping up the very same trade links that were unsustainable in a market economy. Much like Nazarbayev's worries about what would happen if Kazakhstan left the rouble zone, he was perhaps the main proponent of fashioning integration vehicles within the Eurasian space to foster trade. Although current Russian President Vladimir Putin is often spoken of as the architect of Eurasian integration, for finally pushing an agreement through after years of failed attempts (more on this below), any Kazakh will acknowledge that Nursultan Nazarbayev was the first to suggest the structure of a "Eurasian Union" in Moscow in 1994 along the lines it was to (somewhat) evolve (see Nurgaliyeva 2016 for a good description of this evolution). The idea of Eurasian integration was an economic idea extending the political idea of the "Commonwealth of Independent States" (CIS), a "political and economic life preserver" hastily put together at the end of the Soviet Union to institutionalize cooperation and keep channels open between the newly independent republics (Kubicek 1999:15). While the CIS faced strong resistance from Ukraine and some Central Asian members claiming that it was too close to the Soviet model, it also had the problem that it tried to do too much, ranging from topics such as security, human rights, coordination of economic reform, and trade (Sakwa and Webber 1999). Moreover, Russia was too weak and chaotic during the first years of transition to play any sort of leading role in this forum, leaving it up to Nazarbayev to push forward the idea of more formal

Eurasian integration predicated on and focused particularly on economic cooperation.

The fruits of this strategy began to emerge in 1995, as Kazakhstan, Belarus, and Russia agreed to form a customs union, a step above a free trade agreement (FTA) with the additional mechanism of a common external tariff (CET) among the three countries (Hare 2001). Nazarbayev had first suggested that this union could begin under the auspices of the CIS but found few takers (even Russia and Uzbekistan pushed back hard against this idea under the CIS umbrella; see Kubicek 1999); the uncertainty of the early transition and the depth of the transformational recession meant that this idea never truly went away, however, and a series of agreements within the CIS framework also advocated for an economic union, but these never transcended the planning stages (Sakwa and Webber 1999). Forging ahead with a smaller number of dedicated countries (Kyrgyzstan joined the customs union in 1996), the first steps towards economic regional integration helped to slow somewhat the collapse of trade links which started with the end of the CMEA, even if this iteration of the customs union existed only on paper (Kassenova 2013).[18] However, as noted above, this collapse was needed, and thus the beginnings of a customs union among Russia, Belarus, and Kazakhstan was perhaps more of a hindrance to developing Kazakhstan's trade than it was helpful. We will return to this issue later in this section, but suffice it to say that given that Nazarbayev's desire to remain attached to Russia had already proved problematic with the rouble zone, it was difficult to think that it was going to be any different in trade.

While the beginnings of Eurasian integration provided a comfortable zone for Kazakhstan to operate in, being based on the old Soviet patterns and slowly emerging new industrial structures meant that it also did not give any information on how to actually transition the trade mechanisms of the country. Luckily, there was a parallel process which did provide a blueprint for trade policy during the transition, namely the World Trade Organization (WTO), an institution which Kazakhstan could accede to and which had a strict set of rules and criteria for any prospective member. With Kazakhstan never being a serious candidate for EU accession, it had no roadmap for rule of law (but ample best practice), for development of property rights (ditto), or building an effective parliamentary system; with the WTO, however, trade policy and the way in which Kazakhstan's trade needed to evolve was clearly signposted by the 75 years of international treaties and organizations accompanying the WTO and the global trading system. Starting life as the General Agreement on Tariffs and Trade in 1947, the loose collection of treaties governing trade rules assembled via various negotiation rounds became formalized as the WTO in 1995. Incorporating the previous progress made in liberalizing trade in the Western world (and, to a lesser extent, developing countries which joined in the wake of decolonization in the 1960s), the new institutional edifice of the WTO welcomed more new members from the formerly communist countries throughout the 1990s, provided that they had adhered to the WTO's extensive list of requirements.

Kazakhstan's WTO journey began in 1996, almost directly in parallel with its attempts to keep Eurasian integration alive, with a working party beginning its efforts in February and market access negotiations starting a year later, in October 1997. As WTO accession is a long and arduous process, progress did not begin to show until approximately 2004, when Kazakhstan's economic recovery was well under way, foreign trade was booming, and tariffs had come down substantially (Pomfret 2005b). However, even after optimism that the process could be concluded in 2008 (Jensen and Tarr 2008), the accession process was the longest in the history of the WTO, with Kazakhstan not joining until 2015 as the 162nd member of the organization. The reason for this slow pace was not a lack of commitment from the Kazakh side, as trade policy had been fairly liberal and had followed best practices in removing export and import red tape from approximately 1996 onward. The issue was once again the parallel process of Eurasian integration which complicated Kazakhstan's accession unduly and tied it to the fortunes of Russia.

The Eurasian Economic Community (EAEC) was formed in 2000 as an institutional mechanism to further integration but had little success (much like the CIS), as its decisions were non-binding and its legal foundation was highly fragmented (Dragneva and Wolczuk 2012). In the wake of the global financial crisis, however, the fragility of all the countries in the region created a new impetus for integration, coupled with Russia becoming much more interested in asserting its will in its former colonial domains. It is here that the mantle of driver of Eurasian integration passed from Nazarbayev to Putin, as Eurasian integration was seen less as a vehicle for growth than as a political vehicle to use against the West (Dragneva and Hartwell 2022). While Kazakhstan and Nazarbayev in particular was not interested in any form of integration being a political venture or moving towards any sort of federalism, this congruence of interests in attempting to build economic resilience led to the next step in integration, an agreement to form a new customs union between Russia, Kazakhstan, and Belarus in 2007 and which came into being at the beginning of 2010. The new customs union moved further than any previous integration attempt, laying the foundation for a "Common Economic Space" in 2012, creating free movement of goods, people, and capital among the three countries, in an effort to reduce transaction costs for businesses and (to a lesser extent) government (Hartwell 2013b). In this way, the Eurasian Customs Union was made into a single market (of sorts) of approximately 170 million people and with a harmonized trade policy towards the outside world.

A key part of this harmonized trade policy was the common external tariff contemplated as part of the 1995 customs union but actually only implemented from 2010 onward, Unfortunately, the revision of tariff schedules which accompanied this union created two specific issues for Kazakhstan. In the first instance, rather than having a negotiated CET among all members, Russia merely transferred its own high and protectionist tariff rates to the customs union (Dragneva and Wolczuk 2017), a move which raised Kazakhstan's more liberal tariffs and diverted trade to Russia and Belarus and away from the rest of the world (Khitakhunov et al. 2017). This started a pattern of the external policies of the customs union being built entirely upon Russia's policies, a shift in integration tactics that was to prove very problematic for Kazakhstan (which sought the benefits of trade linkages with its former Soviet partners but with the freedom to trade elsewhere as well). In addition to the increase in tariffs, the change in Kazakh trade policy necessitated updating a large amount of Kazakhstan's WTO application, a reality which continued once Russia acceded to the WTO in 2012 ahead of Kazakhstan (and once again altered the tariff schedule for the customs union; see Amirbekova and Galyamov 2016). In fact, much of the delay in Kazakhstan's accession to the WTO from 2009 to 2015 came about precisely because of the need to ensure that the customs union and the WTO were in harmony in terms of obligations, meaning that Kazakhstan let Russia take the lead, set the overall policies to be followed, and even enter the WTO first. It was only when Russia's accession to the WTO and its lead in the customs union was settled in 2012 could Kazakhstan's process begin again (Connolly 2013).

Was this delay worth it, in order to have both Eurasian integration and accession to the WTO, but with Eurasian integration initially and then actually causing WTO accession for Kazakhstan to be delayed? While Eurasian integration might have made sense in 1992 and 1993 (just as the rouble zone appeared to), pushing for such integration on Russia's terms, well after the transition had begun and stabilization achieved, appeared to be less of a smart move for Kazakhstan. Hare (2001:489) forecast well before the fact precisely where the problems were going to arise:

> For these countries, given the legacy of Soviet technology and the many factories often located highly inappropriately across the region, both the FTA and the CU are likely to prove economically disadvantageous for several reasons. First, there is likely to be a predominance of inefficient trade diversion rather than beneficial trade creation as a result of these policies. Second, the countries concerned are, in effect, proposing to provide each other with incentives to go on using outdated Soviet-era technology by making it more costly to access Western technology. Third, given the problems most CIS countries are experiencing in raising revenues to finance public spending, it is not necessarily wise to pursue trade policies that could actually entail a loss of revenues. Last, unlike the EU or NAFTA, trade agreements across the CIS are unlikely to form areas economically large enough or competitive enough to gain significant benefits from economies of scale and specialisation [*sic*] within the region.

As Hare predicted, the trend in Kazakhstan's trade prior to the customs union calls into question just why the union was necessary when it was initiated in 2010: Russia's share of Kazakhstan's trade turnover in 1995 was 47 per cent, while in 2000 it had dropped to 30.2 per cent and on the eve of the establishment of the customs union (2009), it had plunged to a mere 17.4 per cent (Kassenova 2013). As can be seen in Figure 6.5, this was a trend throughout the CIS, even with Russia, which imported 20 per cent less from the CIS in 2010 than it did in 2000, while Kazakhstan exported 13 per cent less and imported 8 per cent less in terms of volume by 2010. It is likely that any gains that were then made in trade were due only to trade diversion rather than creation, a point that Tarr (2016) notes with regard to Russian industry, which was not competitive in Kazakhstan prior to the customs union (because of Kazakhstan's low tariffs, bringing in higher quality competition) but which could suddenly operate in the country after the raising of tariffs to Russian levels.

The EAEU remains a trade bloc to this day, although it has been characterized by unilateral action (mainly by Russia) and a lack of concerted negotiation or compromise (Dragneva 2018). Part of this can be traced back to the Russian approach to trade in general, with Putin seeing trade as just another extension of geopolitical rivalry, not hesitating to use trade as a weapon even in other post-Soviet states, such as Ukraine, Georgia, or Moldova (Hedenskog and Larsson 2007). Repeated incursions into Ukraine have brought sanctions down on Russia, thereby affecting Kazakh trade (Figure 6.5) and (as seen in the previous section) increasing exchange rate uncertainty, which has further harmed Kazakh exporters. In fact, as Figure 6.6 shows, the accession of Kazakhstan to the WTO in 2015 did not provide any appreciable increase in Kazakhstan's trade volumes as it should have (Subramanian and Wei 2007), given its access to the generalized system of preferences (Rose 2004).

While there have been serious consequences for Russia's EAEU partners, it is clear that the Kremlin did not consider these or the objections of its trade bloc members before undertaking its geopolitical courses of action. Such unilateralism has been problematic for Russia, which portrays itself as much more robust than it actually is, but has been downright challenging for Kazakhstan, which has undergone a shift in monetary policy to accommodate the fickle whims of the Kremlin (see above). Moreover, Russia's go-it-alone attitude has created other problems connected to the economic goals of the EAEU. In particular, the EAEU has attempted to expand to other post-Soviet states and to conclude trade agreements with other similarly minded countries (Egypt, Vietnam, Iran, Serbia), but these agreements have been utilized more for protectionist means rather than to liberalize trade (Dragneva and Hartwell 2021). Thus, the value of such an integration association is still not readily apparent for Kazakhstan, which has been bound to Russia when it could have been diversifying its trade partners as well as its export industries. In fact, it is more than likely that the shift towards greater Eurasian integration also had a major effect in keeping Kazakhstan's industries simpler and lower on the value chain than they could have been (Figure

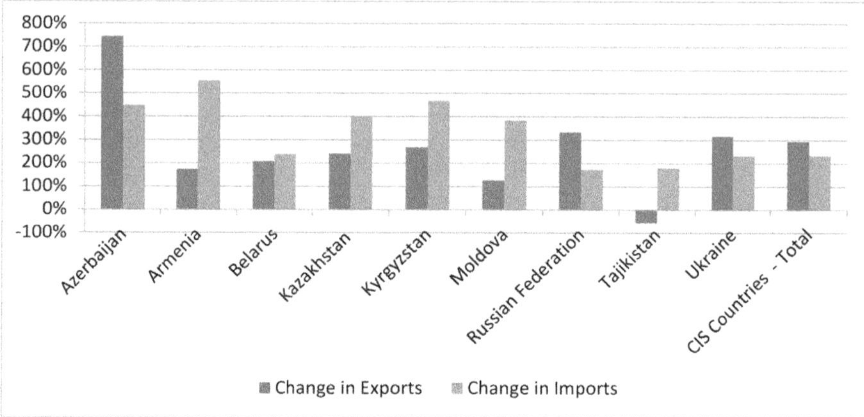

Figure 6.5a Changes in Relative Volume of Trade in the CIS, 2000–2010
Source: Extracted from Hartwell (2013b), based on data from the Statistical Committee of the CIS, www.cisstat.com/eng, and the author's calculations.

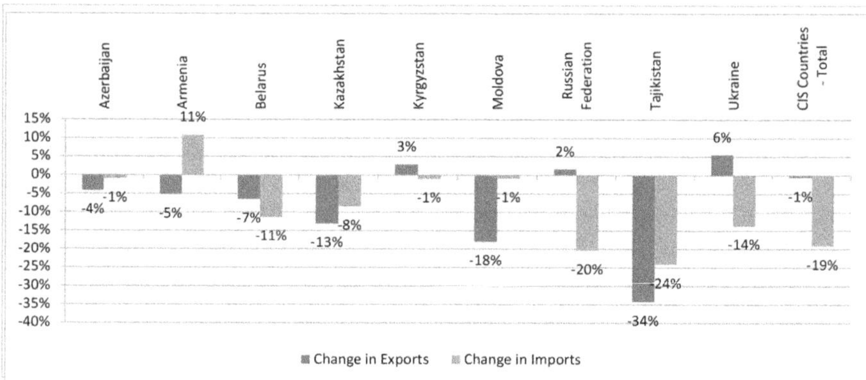

Figure 6.5b Changes in Relative Volume of Trade in the CIS, 2000–2010
Source: Extracted from Hartwell (2013b), based on data from the Statistical Committee of the CIS, www.cisstat.com/eng, and the author's calculations.

6.7). The structure of the economies in the EAEU, as Hare (2001) predicted, also has created incentives for Kazakhstan to remain mired in an extractive industry trap, with Kazakhstan's role in the EAEU as a supplier of energy for countries which need it. Much as the Eurasian Development Bank's (2012) analysis of the "benefits" for Ukraine in joining the EAEU centred on cheap energy and cheap energy alone, for Kazakhstan, the benefit in its EAEU membership has really been an outlet for its energy (which, admittedly, could have gone anywhere).

Here we can see that the approach of "economics first, politics later" faltered, as many Kazakh policymakers during the phases of increased integration were explicitly aware of the pitfalls of tying themselves more to Russia. During my advisory work on Eurasian integration from 2013 to 2014, a very

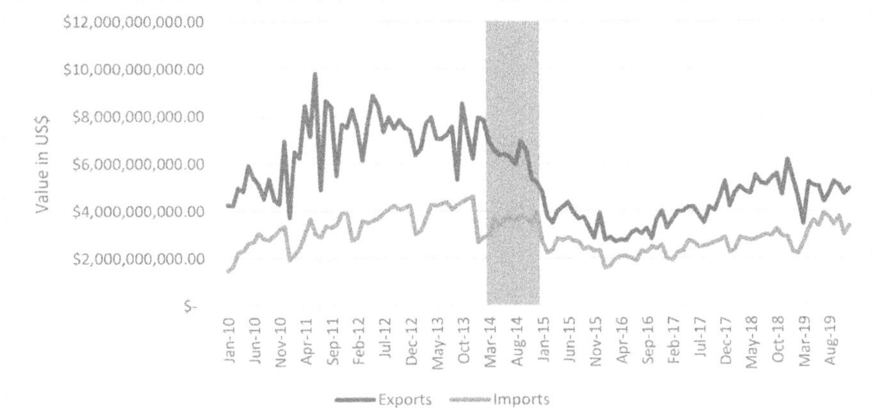

Figure 6.6 Trade Volumes in Kazakhstan, 2010–2019
Source: World Bank World Integrated Trade Solution, https://wits.worldbank.org/, and UN Comtrade Data, https://comtrade.un.org/data. The shaded area corresponds with the first Russian invasion of Ukraine, spanning the annexation of the Crimea peninsula in March 2014 and the successive packages of sanctions from the West until December 2014.

high-ranking official noted that Russia was following the same pattern as it had since the 1995 customs union, namely in attempting to extend its own legislation to the EAEU; it was already known that this would harm Kazakhstan, as it had actually gone further in business environment reforms and (somewhat) the rule of law – at least for smaller-scale companies – than Russia had. Having been through the experience of the customs union, and an externally imposed move towards protectionism, the Kazakhs were not eager to see further regression in the business environment reforms they had made. However, the political imperative for integration, pushed from the top for so long, overrode many of the reservations that the Kazakhs harboured under Nazarbayev, meaning that Kazakhstan was indeed going to be more closely tied to an irrational neighbour which, every so often, made threats that northern Kazakhstan was going to be reclaimed for Russia (Brletich 2015). Indeed, a Russia which pursued "politics first, second, third, and forever" was never going to be a good partner for a free market Kazakhstan.

This state of affairs has persisted as, perhaps buoyed by the faltering alternative to Western civilization that he had built, Vladimir Putin's aggression towards the former Soviet sphere boiled over in 2014 with the illegal annexation of the Crimean peninsula and the first invasion of Ukraine in the Donbas. The Western response to the Russian aggression included a number of milquetoast sanctions which rattled markets in Moscow but let them swiftly recover, as they had feared more, thereby whetting Putin's appetite for more adventurism.[19] In Kazakhstan, however, the effect of sanctions and the linkages which had been preserved via the EAEU transmitted what should

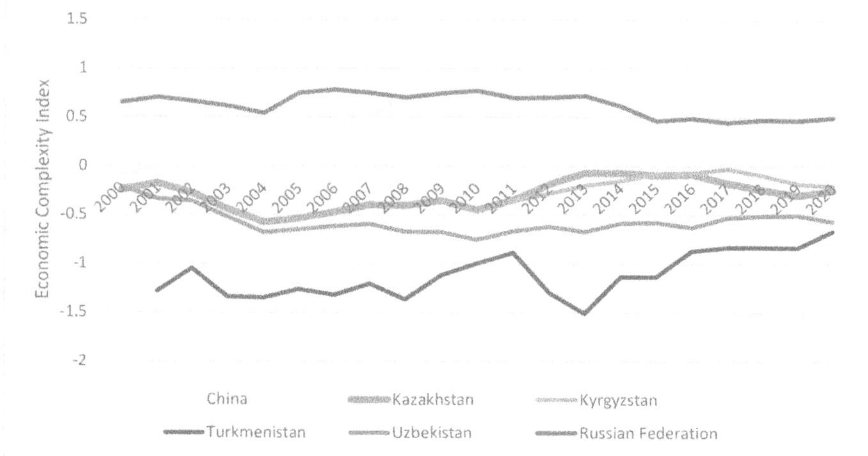

Figure 6.7 Economic Complexity in Central Asia and Russia
Source: Based on data from the Observatory of Economic Complexity, https://oec.world/en. The Economic Complexity Index is an average of all rankings of product complexity and partners that a country has, showing the relative sophistication of its outputs. It is normalized between –2 and 2, with higher numbers showing more complexity

have been an idiosyncratic Russia-only shock to a major trade partner (as shown in Figure 6.6). The continuation of Putin's proxy war against the West during January 2022, and especially following the second invasion of Ukraine in February 2022, once again showed the fragility of the Eurasian Union as an institution but, more importantly, demonstrated that the negative effects for Kazakhstan far outweighed the positives. Whether Kazakhstan can unbuckle itself from the Eurasian vehicle which Nazarbayev placed it in – highly unlikely in the short term – will demonstrate whether Kazakhstan can further develop liberal trade institutions, or whether it (like during the tsarist era) will be forced to accept subpar Russian ones in perpetuity.

Conclusion: The Transition of Economic Institutions

In contrast to its political institutions, Kazakhstan did indeed attempt a far-reaching set of reforms in the economic sphere to throw off the shackles of communism and facilitate a market economy. In the area of monetary and financial institutions, the country was able to create a modern central bank and has moved towards a more appropriate inflation-targeting regime, albeit in the face of major external and neighbourhood volatility. It has even shown some measure of institutional experimentation in this realm, as with the AIFC, but such experimentation was delayed for far too long and came about merely as a response to entrenched distortions in the economy. As a landlocked country with a small economic footprint, Kazakhstan was also able to cultivate a thriving export sector (albeit concentrated in hydrocarbons) and to reorient somewhat away from its ties to the Moscow-led forced supply chain, albeit not entirely successfully. And at the level of the domestic economy, Kazakhstan was able to carry out the de-statization of SMEs, returning the retail and light manufacturing sectors to private hands even faster than some CEE countries: using the EBRD's now discontinued transition indicators, Kazakhstan made faster progress in small-scale privatization than Bulgaria, Romania, and Serbia, and was generally better situated than its EAEU brethren.

However, as the analysis above showed, Kazakhstan made far less progress in some crucial areas of transition, including in overall property rights development, in creating an independent judiciary, in its large-scale privatization, and in its trade policy (rather than trade outcomes). Without protection of property rights writ large, and in tandem with the shift of ownership to informal networks connected with and swirling around the President, the key building block for a free market economy was conspicuously absent. Merely transferring the ownership of large-scale industries to political insiders did not enrich the nation nor did it allow for a flourishing of economic freedom, the true goal of any transition. It merely entrenched insiders with streams of rents, much as it did in Ukraine in the 1990s and 2000s and, of course, in the mafia state of Russia (Naím 2012). At the same time, the concentration of economic power in holding companies, wealth funds, and state-owned energy conglomerates further tied the Kazakh economy to commodity prices, a textbook case of Dutch disease and the resource curse. While Kazakhstan has gone further than other petrostates in diversification, it still is hobbled by its reliance on oil and gas. Nazarbayev may have wanted to create an economy similar to that of Singapore, but instead he created another Kuwait.[20]

Similarly, joining the EAEU revealed Nazarbayev's lack of imagination regarding Kazakhstan's possibilities in competing in world markets, further tying the country to shocks emanating from its irrational, aggressive, and fragile northern neighbour. Rather than attempting to break away from Moscow in the window of opportunity presented in the early 1990s, Nazarbayev both romanticized what Russia could do for the country and ignored the alternatives: this resulted in Kazakhstan remaining in the rouble zone for far too long, spreading inflation, keeping Almaty tied to a Russia in disarray, and attempting to keep inefficient trade links which had been forced upon Kazakhs at gunpoint. The thoughts of "Eurasian integration" which Nazarbayev entertained could have worked on their own, organically, if the Kazakh economy had followed market tenets, and only then could it have been seen whether more tractors from Belarus was an economically sane thing for Kazakh businesses to desire. The problems with the EAEU, especially in terms of the shocks it passed on and the effect it has had on the Kazakh tenge, have been exacerbated by Russia's invasion of Ukraine, showing that the decision to follow Russia into ever closer integration was exactly as Paul Hare (2001) predicted two decades ago – a massive folly.

Again, as noted in Chapter 5, all of these problems are clearly visible with hindsight, but it is important to note that even Kazakh policymakers could have seen these issues coming if they had looked hard enough. From the vantage point of 30 years later, there was not just one turning point which set Kazakhstan's economic institutions on the wrong path, but many poor decisions made in service of other goals (mainly political) which retarded institutional development. For example, to focus on property rights, the destructive impact of the Soviet regime on Kazakh life had been apparent, and even the time of slightly less control from Moscow had still kept the country subservient to a foreign ideology (Marxism) which attempted to remake Kazakhs in an unrealistic Soviet image. The start of transition and of building property rights was thus contingent on these initial conditions: as the late US Secretary of Defense Donald Rumsfeld remarked, "you go to war with the army you have," and the transition therefore necessarily started from a series of initial conditions which were somewhat exogenously determined. This reality also means that attempts to try and remove the Soviet era entirely and for the Kazakh economy to be governed by pre-tsarist tenets would have been as disruptive and counterproductive as the original communist takeover and its tactic of collectivization, as it would have erased the institutional mechanisms which had sprung up under communism (and especially those market-oriented ones which could have been built upon). But if the transition strategy had focused on the property rights arrangements of Kazakh history, using the pre-imperialist period to fashion laws and relations based on Kazakh needs – and respecting the variety of forms in which property rights can come, beyond just "state-owned" – then it is likely that the Kazakh transition would have been much more successful. Pre-industrial Kazakh economic relations called for their own sort of governance, and post-industrial, post-Soviet market economics would have required new, updated ways of approaching property rights. Unfortunately, the fact that property rights in the post-Soviet era were boiled down to ownership (and then given to political insiders in any case) showed how deep the intellectual rot from Soviet times had gone. The nomads of the Khanate were long gone, but the Kazakhs who took their place could have benefited from institutional experimentation, approaches to economic institutions which mirrored their evolving (free market) structures and, most of all, economic freedom. The Soviet era had killed any desire for such experimentation, an issue that would have been apparent to any observers of Kazakh politics, hindsight not required.

Similarly, when it comes to trade, Russia was already in a state of political disarray by 1993, but by the 2000s, with Russia descending into authoritarianism and heavily reliant on oil and gas, it should have been apparent that joining a Russian-led economic vehicle was a terrible idea for Kazakhstan's future development (which is in fact what Hare 2001 predicted). The experience of the rouble zone, and the consequences of hanging on too long to an idea rather than staring into the harsh face of reality, should have warned Kazakhstan not to get too close to Russia again, but this lesson, actually *experienced by the same Kazakh policymakers*, was not heeded. Even from the beginning of the customs union, when it was clear to Kazakh politicians that Russia had very different ideas about what the EAEU was out to achieve, there was only token pushback but otherwise no change of course in economic integration. As shown above, reintegration with Russia only created a conduit for Russian-made economic shocks, such as the turmoil surrounding the sanctions after Russia's landgrab in the Crimean peninsula and the market shock that followed Russia's full-scale invasion of Ukraine. At various points since 2000, including in Chechnya, Georgia, Ukraine, the Syrian Arab Republic, and Ukraine again, the instability of the Russian economy and its use of the EAEU as a political vehicle should have given Kazakhstan more than enough opportunity to withdraw or at least slow any attempt at integration. These issues played out in full view of the world and thus the hindsight argument also carries little weight here.

Perhaps this is a bit harsh, for, if we look at Kazakhstan's economic institutional development through the prism of other countries in Central Asia, Kazakhstan does not appear as poorly situated as it could be. Tajikistan endured a bloody civil war leading to a dictatorship for 28 years (and counting), Kyrgyzstan went through three revolutions and overturned elections and is still unsure of its footing, Turkmenistan has been ruled by three bizarre cults of personality as the population starves, and Uzbekistan saw 25 years of rule by another dictator and an incredibly slow and wasteful pace of liberalization. Even when compared to Russia, its erstwhile ally, Kazakhstan has avoided war (in part by not invading any of its neighbours) and massive financial crises of its own making. But this does not mean that Kazakhstan's transition went as well as it could have, especially given the experience of the CEE countries, the Baltic states, and even Mongolia, and their clean break with Russia and, for the most part, Soviet-style central planning. Few politicians find success with the mantra, "at least we're not Turkmenistan," and Kazakh policymakers should also draw little comfort from that fact. In fact, to return to another formerly nomadic economy, Mongolia's swift economic transition (Goyal 1999), not often discussed in tandem with other post-Soviet satellites, should have formed a good model for Kazakhstan, as it moved much faster and much further from the outset (notwithstanding problems that Mongolia has had with corruption and state control of mining in recent years). Despite being much more reliant on Russia, Mongolia's nomads found a way forward, so it stands to reason that Kazakhstan could have done so too.

In sum, Kazakhstan's stunted development was justified on more than one occasion by Nazarbayev as being about "economics first, politics later." As was the case in India in the 1990s and in countless other countries undertaking reforms, even small moves to remove barriers returned large marginal gains, unleashing entrepreneurial forces and the human desire for commerce. This reality meant steep gains for Kazakhstan once it began to liberalize, buoyed by strong demand for natural resources in the early 2000s. But the results could have been much better if the foundations had been built sooner and stronger. Unfortunately, the lack of political development, and the aversion to political freedom and openness, filtered through to the building of economic institutions, which then evolved to support political leaders rather than the market. Put another way, Nazarbayev attempted to use Soviet-type institutions to achieve un-Soviet outcomes in the economy, when these institutions were built for control rather than liberalization. By using centralized political methods, he engineered a backlash against many policies which in fact were correct and needed.

This reality could be used as an illustration of the difficulty in having politicians, with their short time horizons, make any kind of economic policy during transition other than creating the right institutions and then letting the people decide. But in many cases in Kazakhstan (as in other countries around the world), even the creation of institutions was influenced by political incentives, thus leading to subpar outcomes. In reality, the transition became "political power now, everything else later," making needed economic reforms wither on the vine while political jockeying around Nazarbayev became paramount. This then led to an unhealthy reliance on Russia in monetary and trade policy, one which persisted long after its usefulness had expired.

What was then to happen to Kazakhstan when Nazarbayev stepped aside in 2019? Could the neo-patrimonial networks, generating their own forms of property rights and ownership webs, be reformed into successful economic institutions? Would Russia's disastrous invasion of Ukraine mean that the EAEU was founded as an effective integration vehicle? Or was Kazakhstan going to head down a similar path to that taken by other Central Asian republics, where political succession meant that all economic gains were tentative and institutional survival would be contingent on how they served the new regime? The next chapter, the concluding chapter of the book, looks at these questions and tries to show which way the snow leopard might head next.

Notes

1 We have already dealt with the judicial sector in the previous chapter, noting at the time that it normally warrants its own examination as an economic institution. Other economic institutions which may be of less relevance for Kazakhstan's own particular transition, such as labour market institutions, have out of necessity been overlooked to save space, and to allow us to focus on the most important ones.

2 Based on statistics from the United Nations Population Division for five-year averages from 1990 to 1995, http://data.un.org/Data.aspx?d=PopDiv&f=variableID%3A77.

3 Data from World Bank World Development Indicators, https://data.worldbank.org/indicator/SE.SEC.ENRR?locations=KZ.

4 The fact that heterodox measures were used calls into question the paper by Bofinger (1996), which asserts that Kazakhstan and Russia followed an orthodox, monetary-based stabilization and that the cost of this was too high relative to the benefits gained. Indeed, perhaps a more orthodox stabilization, coming out of the turmoil of the rouble zone (which Bofinger only mentions once), could have broken the back of inflation earlier; or, more importantly, eschewing the rouble zone in the first place could have avoided entrenching inflationary expectations. In any event, it is hard to believe that more government intervention would have made things better.

5 Olcott (2010) notes that the decision to stay in the rouble zone was almost entirely due to Nazarbayev, who believed that cheap Russian energy could help stimulate the Kazakh economy, while the removal of monetary transaction costs with Russia would also enable greater trade between the two.

6 Pomfret and Anderson (2001) show poverty rates based on Goskomstat household survey data, where "poverty" is defined as "individuals in households with gross per capita monthly income of less than 75 rubles" or approximately US $34.50 per month and US $414 per year. In 1990, in the United States, the poverty threshold was defined at US $6,652 for a person living alone.

7 To refer to government spending as an "investment" is both accurate and the height of folly. Accurate in the sense that yes, money is placed in projects promising a rate of return which more than justifies the initial cost, but folly in that all money invested by government comes via taxation and/or seignorage, meaning that the total set of available investments can never truly be compared. Put another way, the money that government invests might be put to better use by a private sector following market signals, but these alternative investments are not available because the money needed for them has gone elsewhere.

8 Tiny Estonia was the only country in the FSU which appeared to learn from the Polish experience, and in many ways actually outdid Poland in terms of speed and breadth.

9 Moreover, as we will explore, all these institutional issues are interconnected.

10 As Libecap (2007) and others have noted, the initial allocation of property rights has tremendous importance for the way in which these rights are exercised and the outcomes which ensue.

11 Toleubayev et al. (2010) somewhat flippantly refer to restitution as an "ideological construct," but this is entirely incorrect. Either something is a right or it is not, and the mere change of a government into one which attempts to create a utopia on earth does not wipe away the right; put another way, no rights exist if all rights are contingent. If ownership existed under a framework of property rights in the pre-Soviet period, these rights to manage and utilize continue to exist whether or not a new government says they do or not. While restitution thus had real economic consequences (Swinnen 1999), it did not change their fundamental nature. Indeed, it is an "ideological construct" to say that rights are beholden to government whims.

12 The Code was not passed without some drama, however, with a vote of no confidence in the government and the resignation of the Prime Minister for a bill that Nazarbayev approved of and would eventually adopt by fiat in any event. The strange turn of events is related in Furman (2005).

13 Perhaps a better quote comes from former US President Gerald Ford, who noted in a speech before Congress in 1974, "A government big enough to give you everything you want is a government big enough to take from you everything you have."

14 See the Heritage Index of Economic Freedom website description of the property rights ranking, www.heritage.org/index/property-rights.

15 Scandals which have hit Samruk-Kaznya include the bizarre firing and arrest of the head of the Kazakh atomic agency, Kazatomprom, who was accused of mishandling more than 60 per cent of the country's uranium deposits via shady and dubious contracts. The scandal, which was suspected as being a cover for Nazarbayev's own dealings in this sector, allowed the firm to be restructured and reincorporated under the Samruk-Kazyna umbrella, meaning even greater involvement of the executive in this crucial sector (Peyrouse 2012).

16 This is not to say that central banks are necessary, or even helpful, for a modern economy, only that a country that chooses to institute one is advantaged by having the institutional memory of a central bank rather than having to build one with donor aid and by trial and error.

17 This section relies heavily on an internal analysis carried out in 2011 by the late great William Wilson and me for NBK that was never publicly published. Bill and I worked together at the Skolkovo Institute for Emerging Market Studies and had a piece commissioned by the NBK to examine the response of the bank vis-à-vis other similarly afflicted economies. I include this analysis here as a tribute to Bill, who died unexpectedly in 2017, as he was always a keen thinker on emerging market problems.

18 Kassenova notes that the customs union was so ineffective in terms of coordination that Kyrgyzstan joined the WTO in 1998 without consulting any of the other members.

19 I was working in Moscow at the time of the seizure of the Ukrainian region of Crimea and remember vividly when sanctions were announced, as there was relief in the hallways. The sentiment on how weak US President Barack Obama was in that moment (confirmed later with Russia's actions in the Syrian Arab Republic) was only matched by the euphoria of having flouted international law so brazenly and getting away with it with just a slap on the wrist.

20 Apologies to whoever suggested this point to me first as early as 2001.

References

Abdullaev, I., Kazbekov, J., Manthritilake, H., and Jumaboev, K. (2010). Water user groups in Central Asia: Emerging form of collective action in irrigation water management. *Water Resources Management*, 24(5), 1029–1043.

Abdullina, A. (2007). *Estimation of the Monetary Policy Reaction Function of the National Bank of Kazakhstan*. Doctoral dissertation, Central European University, Budapest.

Absametov, M. K., Murtazin, Y. Z., Osipov, S. V., and Sapargaliyev, D. S. (2019). *Assessment Report on Classification of Energy and Mineral Resources and its Management in the Republic of Kazakhstan*. United National Economic Commission on Europe Report, May. https://unece.org/DAM/energy/se/pdfs/UNFC/proj/unfc_ca/Report_Class_EMR_KZ_IHG.pdf.

Akimov, A., and Dollery, B. (2008). Financial system reform in Kazakhstan from 1993 to 2006 and its socioeconomic effects. *Emerging Markets Finance and Trade*, 44(3), 81–97.

Alam, A., and Banerji, A. (2000). *Uzbekistan and Kazakhstan: A Tale of Two Transition Paths*. World Bank Policy Research Working Paper No. 2472. Washington, DC: World Bank.

Alam, A., and Sundberg, M. W. (2002). *A Decade of Fiscal Transition*. World Bank Policy Research Working Paper No. (2835). Washington, DC: World Bank.

Alchian, A. A. (1965). Some economics of property rights. *Il politico*, 30(4), 816–829.
Alexeev, M., Gaddy, C., and Leitzel, J. (1992). Economics in the former Soviet Union. *Journal of Economic Perspectives*, 6(2), 137–148.
Alimaev, I. I., and Behnke, R. H., Jr. (2008). Ideology, land tenure and livestock mobility in Kazakhstan. In K. A. Galvin, R. S. Reid, R. H. Behnke, Jr., and Hobbs, N. T. (Eds.). *Fragmentation in Semi-Arid and Arid Landscapes* (pp. 151–178). Berlin: Springer.
Amirbekova, A., and Galyamov, R. (2016). Participation constraints in the WTO dispute settlement: Considering Kazakhstan. *Journal of World Trade*, 50(2).
Anceschi, L. (2015). The persistence of media control under consolidated authoritarianism: Containing Kazakhstan's digital media. *Demokratizatsiya: The Journal of Post-Soviet Democratization*, 23(3), 277–295.
Badeeb, R. A., Lean, H. H., and Clark, J. (2017). The evolution of the natural resource curse thesis: A critical literature survey. *Resources Policy*, 51, 123–134.
Baerg, N. R., Gray, J., and Willisch, J. (2021). Opportunistic, not optimal delegation: The political origins of central bank independence. *Comparative Political Studies*, 54(6), 956–988.
Barisitz, S., and Lahnsteiner, M. (2010). From stormy expansion to riding out the storm: Banking development in Kazakhstan. *OeNB Financial Stability Report*, 19, 64–73.
Barisitz, S., Holzhacker, H., Lytvyn, O., and Sabyrova, L. (2010). Crisis response policies in Russia, Ukraine, Kazakhstan and Belarus: Stock-taking and comparative assessment. *OeNB Focus on European Economic Integration Q* 4, 48–77.
Bartley, D., and Minor, M. S. (1994). Pitfalls in privatization in Kazakhstan. *Business Forum*, 19(1–2), 32–36.
Becker, C. M., Marchenko, G. A., Khakimzhanov, S., Seitenova, A. G. S., and Ivliev, V. (2009). *Social Security Reform in Transition Economies*. New York: Palgrave Macmillan.
Bevan, A. A., Estrin, S., Hare, P. G., and Stern, J. (2001). Extending the economics of disorganization. *Economics of Transition*, 9(1), 105–114.
Bhatti, R. H., and Khawaja, M. J. (2018). The existence of a stable money multiplier in the small open economy of Kazakhstan. *Journal of Economic Studies*, 45(6), 1211–1223.
Blackmon, P. (2010). *In the Shadow of Russia: Reform in Kazakhstan and Uzbekistan*. East Lansing, MI: Michigan State University Press.
Blacksell, M., and Born, K. M. (2002). Private property restitution: The geographical consequences of official government policies in Central and Eastern Europe. *Geographical Journal*, 168(2), 178–190.
Blanchard, O., and Kremer, M. (1997). Disorganization. *The Quarterly Journal of Economics*, 112(4), 1091–1126.
Bofinger, P. (1996). The economics of orthodox money-based stabilisations (OMBS): The recent experience of Kazakhstan, Russia and the Ukraine. *European Economic Review*, 40(3–5), 663–671.
Bohr, A., Brauer, B., Gould-Davies, N., Kassenova, N., Lillis, J., Mallinson, K., Nixey, J., and Satpayev, D. (2019). *Kazakhstan: Tested by Transition*. London: Royal Institute of International Affairs.
Bornstein, M. (1972). Soviet price statistics. In V. G. Treml and J. P. Hardt (Eds.), *Soviet Economic Statistics* (pp. 355–396). Durham, NC: Duke University Press.

Bornstein, M. (1978). The administration of the Soviet price system. *Soviet Studies*, 30(4), 466–490.

Boycko, M., Shleifer, A., and Vishny, R. W. (1994). Voucher privatization. *Journal of Financial Economics*, 35(2), 249–266.

Boycko, M., Shleifer, A., and Vishny, R. (1997). *Privatizing Russia*. Cambridge, MA: MIT Press.

Brauer, B. (2014). Cost of Black Tuesday for Kazakhstan. *Central Asia-Caucasus Analyst*, 3(19), 13–15.

Brenkert, G. G. (1979). Freedom and private property in Marx. *Philosophy & Public Affairs*, 8(2), 122–147.

Brletich, S. (2015). The Crimea model: Will Russia annex the northern region of Kazakhstan? *Geopolitics, History, and International Relations*, 7(1), 11–30.

Brown, J. R., Jr. (1998). Culture, chaos, and capitalism: Privatization in Kazakhstan. *University of Pennsylvania Journal of International Law*, 19(4), 909–964.

Bucur, M. (2018). To have and to hold: Gender regimes and property rights in the Romanian principalities before World War I. *European History Quarterly*, 48(4), 601–628.

Charman, K. (2007). Kazakhstan: A state-led liberalized market economy? In D. Lane and M. Myant (Eds.), *Varieties of Capitalism in Post-Communist Countries* (pp. 165–182). Basingstoke: Palgrave Macmillan.

Clague, C., Keefer, P., Knack, S., and Olson, M. (1996). Property and contract rights in autocracies and democracies. *Journal of Economic Growth*, 1(2), 243–276.

Coase, R. H. (1937). The nature of the firm. *Economica*, 4(16), 386–405.

Connolly, R. (2013). Russia, the Eurasian Customs Union and the WTO. In R. Dragneva and K. Wolczuk (Eds.), *Eurasian Economic Integration* (pp. 61–78). London: Edward Elgar Publishing.

Cooley, A. A. (2012). *Great Games, Local Rules: The New Great Power Contest in Central Asia*. Oxford: Oxford University Press.

Cornot-Gandolphe, S. (1993). World natural gas reserves. *Energy Exploration & Exploitation*, 11(1), 23–31.

Craig, J. (1999). Fiscal adjustment. In E. Gürgen, H. Snoek, J. Craig, J. McHugh, I. Izvorski, and R. van Rooden (Eds.). *Economic Reforms in Kazakhstan, Kyrgyz Republic, Tajikistan, Turkmenistan, and Uzbekistan* (pp. 16–22). Washington, DC: International Monetary Fund.

Craig, J., Izvorski, I., Snoek, H., and van Rooden, R. (1999). Structural reforms. In E. Gürgen, H. Snoek, J. Craig, J. McHugh, I. Izvorski, and R. v an Rooden (Eds.). *Economic Reforms in Kazakhstan, Kyrgyz Republic, Tajikistan, Turkmenistan, and Uzbekistan* (pp. 35–47). Washington, DC: International Monetary Fund.

Csaki, C., and Zuschlag, A. (2004). *The Agrarian Economies of Central-Eastern Europe and the Commonwealth of Independent States: An Update on Status and Progress in 2003*. Washington, DC: World Bank.

Dąbrowski, M. (1997). The reasons for the collapse of the ruble zone. In L.T. Orlowski and D. Salvatore (Eds.), *Trade and Payments in Central and Eastern Europe's Transforming Economies. Handbook of Comparative Economic Policies* (pp. 145–169). Westport, CT: Greenwood Publishing Group.

Dąbrowski, M. (2003). Disinflation strategies and their effectiveness in transition economies. In M. Dąbrowski (Ed.), *Disinflation in Transition Economies* (pp. 1–36). Budapest: Central European University Press.

Dąbrowski, M. (2013). *Monetary Policy Regimes in CIS Economies and their Ability to Provide Price and Financial Stability.* Bank of Finland BOFIT Discussion Paper, DP8/2013. Helsinki: Bank of Finland.

Dąbrowski, M., Antczak, R., Goralska, H., Jermakowicz, W., and Osiatynski, J. (1996). *Economic Transformation in Kazakhstan: Issues of Macroeconomic Policy, External Economic Relations and Restructuring of the Banking System.* Warsaw: CASE-Center for Social and Economic Research.

Dave, B. (2007). Kazakhstan. In J. Goehring (Ed.), *Nations in Transit: Democratization from Central Europe to Eurasia* (pp. 325–347). Washington, DC: Freedom House.

Davis, K. W. (2002). Purging the system: Recent judicial reforms in Kazakhstan. *UC Davis Journal of International Law and Policy*, 8(3), 23–37.

De Benedictis, L., and Tajoli, L. (2011). The world trade network. *The World Economy*, 34(8), 1417–1454.

De Broeck, M., and Kostial, K. (1998). *Output Decline in Transition: The Case of Kazakhstan.* IMF Working Paper No. 1998(045). Washington, DC: International Monetary Fund.

De Broeck, M., De Masi, P., and Koen, V. (1997). Inflation dynamics in Kazakhstan. *Economics of Transition*, 5(1), 195–213.

De Groot, M. (2020). The Soviet Union, CMEA, and the energy crisis of the 1970s. *Journal of Cold War Studies*, 22(4), 4–30.

De Melo, M., Denizer, C., Gelb, A., and Tenev, S. (2001). Circumstance and choice: The role of initial conditions and policies in transition economies. *The World Bank Economic Review*, 15(1), 1–31.

Delgado, M. A., Farinas, J. C., and Ruano, S. (2002). Firm productivity and export markets: A non-parametric approach. *Journal of International Economics*, 57(2), 397–422.

Demsetz, H. (1964). The exchange and enforcement of property rights. *The Journal of Law and Economics*, 7, 11–26.

Deshpande, R. (2006). Land reform and farm restructuring in Central Asia: Progress and challenges ahead. In S. C. Babu and S. Djalalov (Eds.), *Policy Reforms and Agriculture Development in Central Asia* (pp. 131–170). Boston, MA: Springer.

Dore, R., Lazonick, W., and O'Sullivan, M. (1999). Varieties of capitalism in the twentieth century. *Oxford Review of Economic Policy*, 15(4), 102–120.

Dragneva, R. (2018). The Eurasian Economic Union: Balancing sovereignty and integration. In R. Petrov and P. Van Elsuvege (Eds.), *Post-Soviet Constitutions and Challenges of Regional Integration* (pp. 48–70). London: Routledge.

Dragneva, R., and Hartwell, C. A. (2021). The Eurasian Economic Union: Integration without liberalisation? *Post-Communist Economies*, 33(2–3), 200–221.

Dragneva, R., and Hartwell, C. A. (2022). The crisis of the multilateral order in Eurasia: Authoritarian regionalism and its limits. *Politics and Governance*, 10(2), 95–105.

Dragneva, R., and Wolczuk, K. (2012). *Russia, the Eurasian Customs Union and the EU: Cooperation, Stagnation or Rivalry?* Chatham House Briefing Paper REP BP 2012/01. www.chathamhouse.org/sites/default/files/public/Research/Russia%20and%20Eurasia/0812bp_dragnevawolczuk.pdf.

Dragneva, R., and Wolczuk, K. (2017). *The Eurasian Economic Union: Deals, Rules and the Exercise of Power.* Chatham House Russia and Eurasia Program Research Paper. https://euagenda.eu/upload/publications/untitled-92757-ea.pdf.

Dubuisson, E. M. (2022). Whose world? Discourses of protection for land, environment, and natural resources in Kazakhstan. *Problems of Post-Communism*, 69(4–5), 410–422.

Dudinskii, I. (1966). The problem of fuels and raw materials in the Comecon countries, and the ways to solve it. *The American Review of Soviet and Eastern European Foreign Trade*, 2(5), 19–39.

Dudwick, N., Fock, K., and Sedik, D. J. (2007). *Land Reform and Farm Restructuring in Transition Countries: The Experience of Bulgaria, Moldova, Azerbaijan, and Kazakhstan*. Washington, DC: World Bank Publications.

Eicher, S. (2004). *What Causes Bank Asset Substitution in Kazakhstan? Explaining Currency Substitution in a Transition Economy*. Working Paper Number 688, May. Ann Arbor: William Davidson Institute, University of Michigan.

Engvall, J. (2021). Corruption. In R. Isaacs and E. Marat (Eds.), *Routledge Handbook of Contemporary Central Asia* (pp. 319–329). London: Routledge.

Epstein, M. N. P., and Portillo, R. (2014). *Monetary Policy in Hybrid Regimes: The Case of Kazakhstan*. Washington, DC: International Monetary Fund.

Estrin, S., Hanousek, J., Kocenda, E., and Svejnar, J. (2009). The effects of privatization and ownership in transition economies. *Journal of Economic Literature*, 47 (3), 699–728.

Eurasian Development Bank. (2012). *Ukraine and the Customs Union: Comprehensive Assessment of the Macroeconomic Effects of Various Forms of Deep Economic Integration of Ukraine and the Member States of the Customs Union and the Common Economic Space*. Report No. 1. https://we.hse.ru/data/2013/04/12/1297448636/Ukraina_doklad_eng.pdf.

Filatochev, I., and Bradshaw, R. (1992). The Soviet hyperinflation: Its origins and impact throughout the former republics. *Soviet Studies*, 44(5), 739–759.

Fischer, S., Sahay, R., and Vegh, C. (1996). Economies in transition: The early experience. *Journal of Economic Perspectives*, 10(2), 45–66.

Furman, D. (2005). The regime in Kazakhstan. In B. Rumer (Ed.), *Central Asia at the End of the Transition* (pp. 195–266). New York: Routledge.

Glaz'ev, S. Y. (1991). Privatisation of state property in the USSR: Possible ways and implications. *Communist Economies and Economic Transformation*, 3(3), 383–388.

Goldberg, L. S., Ickes, B. W., and Ryterman, R. (1994). Departures from the ruble zone: The implications of adopting independent currencies. *World Economy*, 17(3), 293–322.

Goyal, H. D. (1999). A development perspective on Mongolia. *Asian Survey*, 39(4), 633–655.

Graziano, A. G., Handley, K., and Limão, N. (2021). Brexit uncertainty and trade disintegration. *The Economic Journal*, 131(635), 1150–1185.

Groce, M. S. (2020). Circling the barrels: Kazakhstan's regime stability in the wake of the 2014 oil bust. *Central Asian Survey*, 39(4), 480–499.

Gwartney, J. D., Lawson, R. A., and Holcombe, R. G. (1999). Economic freedom and the environment for economic growth. *Journal of Institutional and Theoretical Economics (JITE)/Zeitschrift für die gesamte Staatswissenschaft*, 643–663.

Hamm, P., King, L. P., and Stuckler, D. (2012). Mass privatization, state capacity, and economic growth in post-communist countries. *American Sociological Review*, 77(2), 295–324.

Hanson, M. (2017). Legalized rent-seeking: Eminent domain in Kazakhstan. *Cornell International Law Journal*, 50(1), 15–46.

Hare, P. (2001). Trade policy during the transition: Lessons from the 1990s. *World Economy*, 24(4), 433–452.

Hartwell, C. A. (2013a). *Institutional Barriers in the Transition to Market: Examining Performance and Divergence in Transition Economies.* Basingstoke: Palgrave Macmillan.

Hartwell, C. A. (2013b). A Eurasian (or a Soviet) Union? Consequences of further economic integration in the Commonwealth of Independent States. *Business Horizons*, 56(4), 411–420.

Hartwell, C. A. (2016). *Two Roads Diverge: The Transition Experience of Poland and Ukraine.* Cambridge: Cambridge University Press.

Hartwell, C. A. (2018). The "hierarchy of institutions" reconsidered: Monetary policy and its effect on the rule of law in interwar Poland. *Explorations in Economic History*, 68, 37–70.

Hartwell, C. A., and Korovkin, V. (2021). Contracting in a void: The role of the banking sector in developing property rights in Russia. *The Quarterly Review of Economics and Finance*, 82, 113–127.

Havrylyshyn, O., and van Rooden, R. (2003). Institutions matter in transition, but so do policies. *Comparative Economic Studies*, 45(1), 2–24.

Hayek, F. A. (1945). The use of knowledge in Society. *American Economic Review*, 35 (4), 519–530.

Hedenskog, J., and Larsson, R. L. (2007). *Russian Leverage on the CIS and the Baltic States.* Stockholm: Defence Analysis, Swedish Defence Research Agency (FOI).

Hendrix, S. E. (1997). Legislative reform of property ownership in Kazakhstan. *Development Policy Review*, 15(2), 159–171.

Heuer, V., and Hierman, B. (2022). Manhandling and mediation: Unpacking the repressive repertoire in Kazakhstan's 2016 anti-land reform protests. *Asian Security*, 18(3), 1–18.

Hierman, B., and Nekbakhtshoev, N. (2014). Whose land is it? Land reform, minorities, and the titular "nation" in Kazakhstan, Kyrgyzstan, and Tajikistan. *Nationalities Papers*, 42(2), 336–354.

Hoelscher, D. S. (1998). *Banking System Restructuring in Kazakhstan.* IMF Working Paper, No. 096. Washington, DC: International Monetary Fund.

International Monetary Fund (2001). *Republic of Kazakhstan: Selected Issues and Statistical Appendix.* Staff Country Report, no. 01/20. Washington, DC: International Monetary Fund.

International Monetary Fund (2021). *Republic of Kazakhstan: Staff Report for the 2021 Article IV Consultation.* Washington, DC: International Monetary Fund.

International Monetary Fund (2022). *Republic of Kazakhstan: Selected Issues.* Washington, DC: International Monetary Fund.

Isham, J., Woolcock, M., Pritchett, L., and Busby, G. (2005). The varieties of resource experience: Natural resource export structures and the political economy of economic growth. *The World Bank Economic Review*, 19(2), 141–174.

Iwasaki, I., and Kumo, K. (2019). J-curve in transition economies: A large meta-analysis of the determinants of output changes. *Comparative Economic Studies*, 61 (1), 149–191.

Jelic, R., Briston, R., and Aussenegg, W. (2003). The choice of privatization method and the financial performance of newly privatized firms in transition economies. *Journal of Business Finance & Accounting*, 30(7–8), 905–940.

Jensen, J., and Tarr, D. (2008). Impact of local content restrictions and barriers against foreign direct investment in services: The case of Kazakhstan's accession to the World Trade Organization. *Eastern European Economics*, 46(5), 5–26.

Johnson, J. (2000). *A Fistful of Rubles: The Rise and Fall of the Russian Banking System*. Ithaca, NY: Cornell University Press.

Jones, K. D. (2004). Land privatization and conflict in Central Asia: Is Kyrgyzstan a model? In D. Burghart and T. Sabonis-Helf (Eds.), *In the Tracks of Tamerlane: Central Asia's Paths to the 21st Century* (pp. 259–273). Washington, DC: Center for Technology and National Security Policy.

Kaiser, M. J., and Pulsipher, A. G. (2007). A review of the oil and gas sector in Kazakhstan. *Energy Policy*, 35(2), 1300–1314.

Kalyuzhnova, Y., and Nygaard, C. A. (2011). Special vehicles of state intervention in Russia and Kazakhstan. *Comparative Economic Studies*, 53(1), 57–77.

Kanagtova, D. B., and Sidorenko, V. N. (2020). Monetary policy of the National Bank of Kazakhstan: Chronological analysis and assessment. *Ekonomika: Strategiya i Praktika*, 15(4), 51–57.

Kassenova, N. (2013). Kazakhstan and Eurasian economic integration: Quick start, mixed results and uncertain future. In R. Dragneva and K. Wolczuk (Eds.), *Eurasian Economic Integration* (pp. 139–160). London: Edward Elgar Publishing.

Kassenova, N. (2017). China's silk road and Kazakhstan's bright path: Linking dreams of prosperity. *Asia Policy*, 24(1), 110–116.

Kembayev, Z. (2020). Development of China–Kazakhstan cooperation: Building the Silk Road of the twenty-first century? *Problems of Post-Communism*, 67(3), 204–216.

Khan, A. Z. (1994). Economic implications of the disintegration of the Soviet Union on the situation in Central Asia. *Strategic Studies*, 16(3), 97–111.

Khasanova, M. (2017). Kazakhstan: Foreign trade policy. In B. Rumer and S. Zhukov (Eds.), *Central Asia: The Challenges of Independence* (pp. 169–207). London: Routledge.

Khitakhunov, A., Mukhamediyev, B., and Pomfret, R. (2017). Eurasian Economic Union: Present and future perspectives. *Economic Change and Restructuring*, 50(1), 59–77.

Korhonen, I. (2009). Devaluation of the Kazakhstani tenge does not solve economy's structural problems. *Focus/Opinion: Expert View* (February). Helsinki: Bank of Finland. https://helda.helsinki.fi/bof/bitstream/handle/123456789/11747/166156.pdf?sequence=1.

Kornai, J. (1994). Transformational recession: The main causes. *Journal of Comparative Economics*, 19(1), 39–63.

Koshanov, A. (1995). Problems of market transformation of the Kazakh economy. *Problems of Economic Transition*, 37(10), 5–23.

Jermakowicz, W., Kozarzewski, P., and Pańków, J. (1996). *Privatization in the Republic of Kazakhstan*. CASE Network Studies and Analyses No. 85, June. https://case-research.eu/upload/publikacja_plik/4886193_085e.pdf.

Kozhirova, S., and Ospanova, B. (2014). Chinese migration in Kazakhstan: implications for national security. *European Scientific Journal*, 10(10), 482–486.

Krueger, G., and Ciolko, M. (1998). A note on initial conditions and liberalization during transition. *Journal of Comparative Economics*, 26(4), 718–734.

Kubicek, P. (1999). End of the line for the Commonwealth of Independent States. *Problems of Post-Communism*, 46(2), 15–24.

Kudaibergenova, D. T. (2015). The ideology of development and legitimation: Beyond "Kazakhstan 2030." *Central Asian Survey*, 34(4), 440–455.

Kudaibergenova, D. T. (2016). The use and abuse of postcolonial discourses in post-independent Kazakhstan. *Europe-Asia Studies*, 68(5), 917–935.
Kuralbayeva, K., Kutan, A. M., and Wyzan, M. L. (2001). *Is Kazakhstan Vulnerable to the Dutch Disease?* Working Paper No. B 29–2001. Bonn: Zentrum für Europäische Integrationsforschung [Centre for European Integration Studies], Rheinische Friedrich-Wilhelms-Universität Bonn.
Kvartiuk, V., and Petrick, M. (2021). Liberal land reform in Kazakhstan? The effect on land rental and credit markets. *World Development*, 138, 105285.
Laruelle, M. (2012). Discussing neopatrimonialism and patronal presidentialism in the Central Asian context. *Demokratizatsiya*, 20(4), 301–325.
Laruelle, M. (2016). *Kazakhstan in the Making: Legitimacy, Symbols, and Social Changes*. Lexington, MA: Lexington Books.
Lee, Y. S., and Jeong, H. G. (2006). The determinants of economic growth of transition economies: Economic reform versus initial conditions. *International Economic Journal*, 20(2), 241–252.
Lerman, Z. (1998). Does land reform matter? Some experiences from the former Soviet Union. *European Review of Agricultural Economics*, 25(3), 307–330.
Lerman, Z. (2009). Land reform, farm structure, and agricultural performance in CIS countries. *China Economic Review*, 20(2), 316–326.
Lerman, Z., Csaki, C., and Feder, G. (2004). *Agriculture in Transition: Land Policies and Evolving Farm Structures in Post-Soviet Countries*. Lexington, MA: Lexington Books.
Lewarne, S. (1993). Legal aspects of monetary policy in the former Soviet Union. *Europe-Asia Studies*, 45(2), 193–209.
Libecap, G. D. (2007). The assignment of property rights on the western frontier: Lessons for contemporary environmental and resource policy. *The Journal of Economic History*, 67(2), 257–291.
Lillis, J. (2022). *Dark Shadows: Inside the Secret World of Kazakhstan*. London: Bloomsbury Publishing.
Linn, J. F. (2004). *Economic (Dis)integration matters: The Soviet collapse revisited.* Paper presented at the conference on "Transition in the CIS: Achievements and Challenges," Academy for National Economy, Moscow, 13–14 September. www.brookings.edu/wp-content/uploads/2016/06/200410linn.pdf.
Martinez-Vazquez, J., and Boex, J. (2001). Budgeting and fiscal management in transitional economies. *Journal of Public Budget, Accounting and Financial Countries*, 13(3), 353–396.
Maurel, M., and Cheikbossian, G. (1998). The new geography of Eastern European trade. *Kyklos*, 51(1), 45–72.
Mesquita, M. (2016). Kazakhstan's presidential transition and the evolution of elite networks. *Demokratizatsiya: The Journal of Post-Soviet Democratization*, 24(3), 371–397.
Mikesell, J. L., and Mullins, D. R. (2001). Reforming budget systems in countries of the former Soviet Union. *Public Administration Review*, 61(5), 548–568.
Ministry of Agriculture of Kazakhstan (2020). *Svodnyy analiticheskiy otchet o sostoyanii i ispolzovanii zemel Respubliki Kazakhstan za 2019 god* [*Summary Analytical Report on the State and Use of Land in the Republic of Kazakhstan in 2019*]. Nur-Sultan: Ministry of Agriculture of Kazakhstan.
Mitrofanskaya, Y. (1999). Privatization as an international phenomenon: Kazakhstan. *American University International Law Review*, 14(5), 1399–1438.

Mundell, R. A. (1961). A theory of optimum currency areas. *The American Economic Review*, 51(4), 657–665.

Murphy, J. (2006). Illusory transition? Elite reconstitution in Kazakhstan, 1989–2002. *Europe-Asia Studies*, 58(4), 523–554.

Muratbek, D. (2017). Determinants of non-performing loans in Kazakhstan. In *The 2017 WEI International Academic Conference Proceedings* (pp. 6–32). Vienna: West-East Institute. www.westeastinstitute.com/wp-content/uploads/2017/06/Dana-Muratbek.pdf.

Naím, M. (2012). Mafia states: Organized crime takes office. *Foreign Affairs*, 91, 100–111.

Nurbayev, D. (2015). Independence and transparency of the central bank of Kazakhstan. *The Journal of Asian Finance, Economics and Business*, 2(4), 31–38.

Nurgaliyeva, L. (2016). Kazakhstan's economic soft balancing policy vis-à-vis Russia: From the Eurasian Union to the economic cooperation with Turkey. *Journal of Eurasian Studies*, 7(1), 92–105.

Obydenkova, A. V., and Libman, A. (2019). *Authoritarian Regionalism in the World of International Organizations: Global Perspective and the Eurasian Enigma*. Oxford: Oxford University Press.

Olcott, M. B. (1994). The Asian interior: the myth of 'Tsentral'naia Aziia' (Uzbekistan, Kazakhstan, Turkmenistan, Kyrgyzstan, and Tajikistan). *Orbis*, 38(4), 549–566.

Olcott, M. B. (2010). *Kazakhstan: Unfulfilled Promise*. Washington, DC: Carnegie Endowment for International Peace.

Opper, S. (2004). The political economy of privatization: Empirical evidence from transition economies. *Kyklos*, 57(4), 559–586.

Pannier, B. (2009). *Prospect of Chinese Farmers Brings Controversy to Kazakh Soil*. Radio Free Europe/Radio Liberty, 17 December. www.rferl.org/a/Prospect_Of_Chinese_Farmers_Brings_Controversy_To_Kazakh_Soil/1906896.html.

Pastor, G., and Damjanovic, T. (2001). *The Russian Financial Crisis and its Consequences for Central Asia*. IMF Working Papers, 2001(169). Washington, DC: International Monetary Fund.

Peck, A. E. (2002). Industrial privatization in Kazakhstan: The results of government sales of the principal enterprises to foreign investors. *Russian & East European Finance and Trade*, 38(1), 31–58.

Peck, A. E. (2004). *Economic Development in Kazakhstan: The Role of Large Enterprises and Foreign Investment*. New York: Routledge.

Peterson, D. J. (2019). *Troubled Lands: The Legacy of Soviet Environmental Destruction*. London: Routledge.

Petrick, M., Wandel, J., and Karsten, K. (2011). *Farm Restructuring and Agricultural Recovery in Kazakhstan's Grain Region: An Update* (No. 137). Leibniz: Leibniz Institute of Agricultural Development in Transition Economies (IAMO).

Peyrouse, S. (2012). The Kazakh neopatrimonial regime: Balancing uncertainties among the "family," oligarchs and technocrats. *Demokratizatsiya*, 20(4), 345–371.

Pieper, M. (2021). The linchpin of Eurasia: Kazakhstan and the Eurasian Economic Union between Russia's defensive regionalism and China's new Silk Roads. *International Politics*, 58(3), 462–482.

Pomfret, R. (2002). The IMF and the ruble zone. *Comparative Economic Studies*, 44 (4), 37–47.

Pomfret, R. (2005a). Kazakhstan's economy since independence: Does the oil boom offer a second chance for sustainable development? *Europe-Asia Studies*, 57(6), 859–876.

Pomfret, R. (2005b). Trade policies in Central Asia after EU enlargement and before Russian WTO accession: Regionalism and integration into the world economy. *Economic Systems*, 29(1), 32–58.

Pomfret, R. (2009). *Central Asia and the Global Economic Crisis*. EU Central Asian Monitoring Policy Brief, Centre for European Policy Studies (CEPS), No. 7, June. Brussels: CEPS.

Pomfret, R., and Anderson, K. (2001). Economic development strategies in Central Asia since 1991. *Asian Studies Review*, 25(2), 185–200.

Popov, V. (2000). Shock therapy versus gradualism: The end of the debate (explaining the magnitude of transformational recession). *Comparative Economic Studies*, 42 (1), 1–57.

Radnitz, S. (2010). The color of money: Privatization, economic dispersion, and the post-Soviet "revolutions." *Comparative Politics*, 42(2), 127–146.

Rose, A. K. (2004). Do we really know that the WTO increases trade? *American Economic Review*, 94(1), 98–114.

Rosefielde, S. (1981). Are Soviet industrial-production statistics significantly distorted by hidden inflation? *Journal of Comparative Economics*, 5(2), 185–199.

Ruziev, K., and Majidov, T. (2013). Differing effects of the global financial crisis on the Central Asian countries: Kazakhstan, the Kyrgyz republic and Uzbekistan. *Europe-Asia Studies*, 65(4), 682–716.

Sadovskaya, E. (2007). Chinese migration to Kazakhstan: A Silk Road for cooperation or a thorny road of prejudice? *China and Eurasia Forum Quarterly*, 5 (4), 147–170.

Sadovskaya, Y. (2015). The mythology of Chinese migration in Kazakhstan. *Central Asia Caucasus Analyst*, 7, 7 January.www.cacianalyst.org/publications/field-reports/item/13112-the-mythology-of-chinese-migration-in-kazakhstan.html.

Şakal, H. B. (2015). Natural resource policies and standard of living in Kazakhstan. *Central Asian Survey*, 34(2), 237–254.

Sakwa, R., and Webber, M. (1999). The Commonwealth of Independent States, 1991–1998: Stagnation and survival. *Europe-Asia Studies*, 51(3), 379–415.

Sansyzbayeva, G., and Ametova, Z. (2015). The role of "Samruk-Kazyna" sovereign wealth fund in implementation of state programs of the Republic of Kazakhstan. *Asian Social Science*, 11(2), 1–7.

Sapir, A. (2011). European integration at the crossroads: A review essay on the 50th anniversary of Bela Balassa's theory of economic integration. *Journal of Economic Literature*, 49(4), 1200–1229.

Schiek, S., and Hensell, S. (2012). Seeing like a president: The dilemma of inclusion in Kazakhstan. In M. Klein and H.-H. Schröder (Eds.), *Presidents, Oligarchs, and Bureaucrats: Forms of Rule in the Post-Soviet Space* (pp. 203–222). London: Routledge.

Serkebayeva, R. K., Kazbekov, G. K., Sabirova, R. K., Alpysbayeva, A. K., Sadvokassova, K. Z., and Kabdiy, N. G. (2019). Technical peculiarities of the stock market implementation: State policy and problems of liquidity. *International Journal of Engineering Research and Technology*, 12(12), 2163–2168.

Shabad, T. (1979). Soviet regional policy and CMEA integration. *Soviet Geography*, 20(4), 230–254.

Shome, P. (1993). Transition and transformation: Fiscal sector issues in Kazakhstan. In V. D. Tanzi (Ed.), *Transition to Market. Studies in Fiscal Reform* (pp. 305–324). Washington, DC: International Monetary Fund.
Simon, G. (2009). Market reforms and "economic miracle" in Kazakhstan. *Economic Annals*, 54(182), 67–92.
Snoek, H., and van Rooden, R. (1999). Monetary policy and progress. In E. Gürgen, H. Snoek, J. Craig, J. McHugh, I. Izvorski, and R. van Rooden (Eds.). *Economic Reforms in Kazakhstan, Kyrgyz Republic, Tajikistan, Turkmenistan, and Uzbekistan* (pp. 23–34). Washington, DC: International Monetary Fund.
Sonin, K. (2003). Why the rich may favor poor protection of property rights. *Journal of Comparative Economics*, 31(4), 715–731.
Stronski, P. (2016). *Kazakhstan at Twenty-Five: Stable but Tense*. Washington, DC: Carnegie Endowment for International Peace. https://carnegieendowment.org/files/Stronsky_Kazakhstan.pdf.
Stuart, R. C., and Panayotopoulos, C. M. (1999). Decline and recovery in transition economies: The impact of initial conditions. *Post-Soviet Geography and Economics*, 40(4), 267–280.
Subramanian, A., and Wei, S. J. (2007). The WTO promotes trade, strongly but unevenly. *Journal of International Economics*, 72(1), 151–175.
Svejnar, J. (2002). Transition economies: Performance and challenges. *Journal of Economic Perspectives*, 16(1), 3–28.
Swinnen, J. F. (1999). The political economy of land reform choices in Central and Eastern Europe. *Economics of Transition*, 7(3), 637–664.
Tarr, D. G. (2016). The Eurasian Economic Union of Russia, Belarus, Kazakhstan, Armenia, and the Kyrgyz Republic: Can it succeed where its predecessor failed? *Eastern European Economics*, 54(1), 1–22.
Teckenberg, W. (1987). Consumer goods and services: Contemporary problems and their impact on the quality of life in the Soviet Union. In H. Herlemann (Ed.), *Quality of Life in the Soviet Union* (pp. 31–41). London: Routledge.
Tipaldou, S. (2021). Kazakhstan 2.0: Change and continuity? In F. Izquierdo-Brichs and F. Serra-Massansalvador (Eds.), *Political Regimes and Neopatrimonialism in Central Asia* (pp. 249–293). Singapore: Palgrave Macmillan.
Tiraspolsky, A., and Vale, M. (1984). An evaluation of gains and losses in intra-CMEA Trade: Terms of trade from 1970 to 1982. *Soviet and Eastern European Foreign Trade*, 20(4), 32–62.
Toleubayev, K., Jansen, K., and van Huis, A. (2010). Knowledge and agrarian de-collectivisation in Kazakhstan. *The Journal of Peasant Studies*, 37(2), 353–377.
Torstensson, J. (1994). Property rights and economic growth: An empirical study. *Kyklos*, 47(2), 231–247.
Turekhanova, N. E., and Mekenbaeva, K.B. (2021). Kommunikatsionnaya politika tsentral'nogo banka [Communication policy of the central bank]. *Economic Review (National Bank of Kazakhstan)*, 4, 31–41.
US Agency for International Development (USAID) (2005). *Land Tenure Reform in Kazakhstan, Uzbekistan, and Tajikistan: Final Report*. Washington, DC: US Agency for International Development, 31 October. https://pdf.usaid.gov/pdf_docs/Pdacg768.pdf.
Waikar, A., Jepbarova, L., Lee, S., Gardner, L., and Johnson, J. (2011). Impact of foreign direct investment on Kazakhstan's economy: A boon or a curse? *International Journal of Business and Social Science*, 2(22), 92–98.

Weitz, R. (2010). Kazakhstan's bank recovery strategy. *Central Asia-Caucasus Analyst*, 12(20), 6–8.

Werner, C. A. (1994). A preliminary assessment of attitudes toward the privatization of agriculture in contemporary Kazakhstan. *Central Asian Survey*, 13(2), 295–303.

Winiecki, J. (1988). *The Distorted World of Soviet-Type Economies*. London: Routledge.

World Bank (1995). *Staff Appraisal Report, Republic of Kazakhstan: Financial and Enterprises Development Project*. Report No. 13553-KZ. 29 March. https://ypfsresourcelibrary.blob.core.windows.net/fcic/YPFS/Staff%201995_Staff%20Appraisal%20Report_Financial%20and%20Enterprises%20Development%20Project.pdf.

World Bank (2000). *Kazakhstan Public Expenditure Review, Vol. 2: Main Report*. Washington, DC: World Bank.

Viner, J. (1950). *The Customs Union Issue*. London: Stevens & Sons Limited.

Yessenova, S. (2010). Borrowed places: Eviction wars and property rights formalization in Kazakhstan. In D. C. Wood (Ed.), *Economic Action in Theory and Practice: Anthropological Investigations*. Research in Economic Anthropology (Vol. 30, pp. 11–45). Bingley: Emerald Group Publishing.

Yeung, H., Huang, F., Bekmurzayeva, Z., and Janaidar, D. (2020). Institutional development and the Astana International Financial Center in Kazakhstan. *Washington University Global Studies Law Review*, 19(1), 53–84.

Zambrana-Tevar, N. (2019). The court of the Astana International Financial Center in the wake of its predecessors. *Erasmus Law Review*, 12, 122–135.

7 Conclusion

Which Way, Snow Leopard?

Towards a Post-Elbasy Kazakhstan

On the morning of 2 January 2022, in the town of Zhanaozen – the very same town where the massacre in 2011, detailed in Chapter 5, occurred – demonstrators took to the streets to protest against a government directive lifting the price cap on liquified petroleum gas (LPG). Much like the land reform proposed in 2016, on this specific policy, the government was correct in principle. That is, while the reason behind land reform may have been a willingness to sell to the Chinese (and/or corruption), the country did in fact need substantial reforms to its land tenure system, which had languished too long. Similarly, the policy of subsidizing energy had created institutional rot throughout the former Soviet Union, as witnessed in Ukraine, where politically connected insiders grew rich using taxpayer subsidies to purchase energy cheaply and then resell it at a premium. Moreover, the lifting of the LPG price cap had been announced well in advance, with a shift towards electronic trading at the beginning of 2019 in order to align purchases with market prices, gradually phasing out the too-pervasive subsidies (Kumenov and Lillis 2022).

Unfortunately, being right in matters of economics means very little when the government's credibility has already been damaged due to a lack of ability to access the system, repeated suppression of any public show of disapproval, and, above all, paternalism – and "paternalism" is the right term, given that Nazarbayev was accorded the title of "Father of the Nation" (*Elbasy*, as noted in the Introduction) in 2010. Several other issues were already boiling up in the energy-rich regions of the country before the (as noted) sensible energy reform, many of which were only exacerbated by the increase in gas prices. In the first instance, the energy-rich western part of the country had not shared in the growth which had been witnessed in Almaty or Nur-Sultan, with poor infrastructure and more poverty than in the urban centres. Indeed, as Thomas (2015) notes, high nominal incomes connected with work in the energy industry often led to a lower standard of living due to the high cost of living in a region undergoing an extraction bonanza. Unusual for a Kazakh leader, it appeared that the leader of the horde had

DOI: 10.4324/9781003212508-7

paid more attention to enriching the sedentary urban dwellers than taking care of the rural and far-flung inhabitants. Anger about the relative inattention of the regime in Nur-Sultan to living standards in the very regions which were powering Kazakhstan's success was thus present for some time, especially when one considers that Kazakhstan's unitary state left no room for input from these regions on the LPG pricing reform (Kumenov and Lillis 2022) or on anything else for that matter.

Other drivers of the protest were at play, also a result of government policies and the shaping of institutions during the past three decades. For example, as an energy-rich country, Kazakhstan's consumers had become reliant on cheap fuel rather than efficiency (Liu et al. 2020), a common problem in countries with natural resource abundance (Hartwell 2016). With cheap access to subsidized LPG, not only was a potential source of poverty held off (Howie and Atakhanova 2017), but also fuel-intensive businesses and transport modes (including the family car) were able to develop and thrive without the same budget constraints that they would have faced in a more energy-scarce environment. Increased prices would have further pushed down the standard of living but could also have popped the artificial bubble that the Kazakh authorities had created, routing capital and efforts in a more sustainable direction. Kudaibergenova and Laruelle (2022) note that this led to a disjoint between the government and the people, who – perhaps out of nostalgia for Soviet-style welfare policies – wanted tax dollars spent on subsidies to enable cheaper gas rather than efficiency or, as in this case, a more sustainable long-term policy. The government's decision to encourage investment and consumption in an area which would not have had it, save for government subsidies, thus created an entitlement that people were not willing to give up (as is the case in most countries globally). Torn between the reality that the entitlement made their lives easier but gave more control for state energy concerns (which people had protested against in 2011), the denizens of Zhanaozen chose the entitlement rather than agitate against the broader issue of resource dependence (Satpayev and Umbetaliyeva 2015). Finally, the failure of the government to educate on the benefits of a free market economy, and then to actually deliver one (rather than a crony system with too much state involvement), meant that ideas about the government taking care of everything economically were still prevalent but people wanted a say in how the government would do that. This was perhaps behind the trend towards political mobilization (Zhandayeva and Zhanmukanova 2022) during the previous decade, meaning that ordinary Kazakhs had been more concerned with being heard than the overall broader outcomes which may have been returned from specific policies. In this sense, perhaps Nazarbayev had it backwards, that the Kazakh people wanted "politics first, economics later."

The protests in western Kazakhstan could have been dealt with in a myriad of strategies beyond merely sending in the troops, as had been done in 2016 (Heuer and Hierman 2022), but the protests quickly spread throughout the country, serving as a focal point for grievances with the regime (Haruna et al. 2022). What had begun as a peaceful series of demonstrations grew out of hand in the country's commercial centre, Almaty. As the British Broadcasting Corporation (BBC) (Abdurasulov 2022) reported at the time:

> The demonstrations quickly spiralled into mass disturbances and looting that led to the worst bloodshed in the former Soviet state's 30 years of independence. The authorities are accused of using excessive force to restore order. Officially, 225 people were killed and many more were injured. Some 10,000 people have been detained in the wake of the disturbances, the authorities say … It is still not clear how peaceful protests turned so violent. Initially, the mood of the crowd was festive when people rallied on 4 January. They sang the anthem of Kazakhstan and chanted political demands. The atmosphere started to change when the authorities threw stun grenades and fired tear gas to disperse the crowd, leading to clashes between police and protesters. The next day, on 5 January, tensions grew. Some people on the square in Almaty were armed with knives and hunting rifles … It's still not clear who these people were. Ms Azirbek of the Almaty police said "well trained men versed in combat tactics" attacked police with the aim of seizing their weapons.

The key part of this description is that it was not clear who the people who joined the fray and escalated the violence were. Emails and messages I received from friends during these days talked of hundreds of armed young men marching on the *akimat* (mayor's office), setting it on fire, the closure of banks and businesses, and intense anger at whomever was blocking the airport and causing wanton destruction. Meanwhile, peaceful protestors were caught in the crossfire, with the President allowing the use of "unrestrained lethal force" by the security forces and resulting in many fatalities (Makszimov 2022). The unrest itself was only quelled when still-green President Tokayev – in an absolutely unprecedented step – asked the Collective Security Treaty Organization (CSTO), a Russian Federation-led military alliance aligning more or less with the Eurasian Economic Union (EAEU), for troops to support the government (Mackinnon 2022). Taking the line that "thousands" of shadowy "terrorists" had been behind the unrest since January, Tokayev has since defended this decision, noting that the troops were in country for just ten days, did not fire a single shot, but prevented these "terrorists" from taking over other cities (Putz 2022). I will admit that I was very surprised, given what Russia was building up to in Ukraine, that the Russian troops did indeed depart from the country, but the sense in Moscow was that Tokayev was reliant on Russia for his political survival and thus he owed them a debt of gratitude (and one that could be returned at any time); this sentiment is likely to not help Kazakhstan in its "multi-vector foreign policy" going forward (Arynov 2022) and can be seen as a sign of weakness for a country which has struggled to define itself as a state that is separate from its Russian colonizers.

The unrest in Kazakhstan, and what significance it has for the country, is unknown as of the writing of this book and is unlikely to be known for some time. The first point relating to the protests concerns the (relatively) new President, Kassym-Jomart Tokayev, and the legitimacy of his regime. Tokayev was Chairman of the Senate when Nazarbayev resigned in 2019, which meant that he was handed the title of acting President under the Constitution; at the same time, he was obliged to call for elections, which he scheduled to take place just two months later, with Nazarbayev backing Tokayev's candidacy under the Nur Otan party banner (Legieć 2019). Tokayev won these elections with ease, albeit with far less "support" than Nazarbayev had garnered (Tokayev received "only" 70 per cent of the vote, as opposed to the 95 per cent plus that Nazarbayev had regularly garnered). More importantly, however, Tokayev was buoyed by the existing party apparatus and short time span for election preparations; once again, Nazarbayev had helped to undercut the opposition by basically bringing forward the date of the presidential election, but he also had entrenched Nur Otan as an institutional force unto itself, even without *Elbasy*'s actual presence (Blackmon 2021).

Tokayev's approach, however, while promising continuity with Nazarbayev, also said that the "economics first, politics later" approach was being discarded, as "without political changes, economic development would be impossible" (quoted in Simmons 2019). Tokayev's early moves in this respect appeared to address some of the issues we have mentioned in this book, including a bold "Address to the Nation" in which he promised measures of decentralization of bureaucracy, slashing public administration by 25 per cent, and (limited) fiscal decentralization to the regions (Tokayev 2019). From the economic sphere, Tokayev addressed the lack of diversification of the country and promised support to small and medium-sized enterprises, but tempered this with a measure of state regulation as well, promising enforcement "in cases of violation by business entities of the prescribed norms and rules, especially in the sanitation and contagious diseases sphere" (Tokayev 2019). And in the spirit of a multi-vector foreign policy, Tokayev also took steps to reinforce the fact that Kazakhstan would remain a friend to all, committed to the elimination of nuclear weapons (and not their tactical use), while supporting more education in the Kazakh language as a way to further distance the country from Russia (Vanderhill et al. 2020).

Unfortunately, the way in which the new regime of Tokayev handled the protests in January 2022 showed far too much continuity with previous tactics under Nazarbayev (Heuer and Hierman 2022) but with the incredible step of utilizing Russian forces as "peacekeepers" against the "terrorists." While the official number of fatalities was revised upward to 238 as of September 2022, human rights groups and independent watchdogs place the actual number much higher, similarly to previous unrest under both Soviet rule and Nazarbayev. The fog surrounding the actual extent of the violence is but one issue with the handling of the aftermath of the unrest, as, in particular, the arrests during what is now known as "Bloody January" could further delegitimize Tokayev's rule. By late 2022, the government had admitted that at least 15 officers had used torture during questioning of those arrested, but that a general amnesty was to be declared for individuals involved in the unrest, which would include police and security forces (Mukhitqyzy 2022). It was unknown if this would extend to the 700 people who had been convicted of participating in the violence as of mid-2022, with authorities rushing to put the events of Bloody January behind them (Lillis 2022). As of the time of this writing (late October 2022), the amnesty still had not been granted.

In reality, the exact manner in which the events of January 2022 will affect Kazakhstan's institutional development going forward will come down to how Nazarbayev, and his decisions throughout transition, are remembered and/or considered by President Tokayev. In 2019, the prospects for *Elbasy* to be revered for his services to the country were unbelievably good, despite the protests and disappearances which had occurred in the previous decade of authoritarian consolidation. At a personal level, Nazarbayev was still popular with broad swathes of the population, although the lustre had been wearing off with each additional protest, riot, or demonstration. And the decision by Nazarbayev to step down as President in 2019 was seen as monumental in Central Asia, where dictators either hang on until they die (Niyazov in Turkmenistan, Karimov in Uzbekistan), are unceremoniously deposed (Akaev and Bakiev, both from Kyrgyzstan), strong-arm their way through numerous crises (Rahmon in Tajikistan), or set up a dynastic succession and only step aside when this is assured (Berdymukhamedov in Turkmenistan). A peaceful change of power could only burnish Nazarbayev's reputation and demonstrate that he really was the "Father of the Nation," and that he had Kazakhstan's interests at heart. And regardless of the fact that Nazarbayev planned to remain heavily involved in the governance of Kazakhstan after his resignation, the reality that a successor not named "Nazarbayev(a)" was now President meant that Kazakhstan had undergone a peaceful succession.

However, the events of January 2022 and especially the Tokayev government's response have called into question the legacy of Nazarbayev and thus, by extension, the path that Kazakhstan may follow in the coming years. Tokayev's desire to maintain continuity in the first year after the transition away from Nazarbayev was understandable, given the lack of experience of any country in Central Asia with peaceful succession. But as Tokayev has found his footing, he has become more assertive (indeed, he called himself a "reformer" from the outset), allowing him to distance himself from both Nazarbayev and his legacy. In many ways, the unrest and Tokayev's response were widely seen as a way to clear out some of the vestiges of Nazarbayev and allow Tokayev the ability to govern as himself, while others saw the violence as signs of an intra-elite struggle (Isaacs 2022). In any event, the aftermath led to a number of actions which signified that the Nazarbayev era was over for good, including total silence from Nazarbayev during the protests and the removal of the former President from his position on the National Security Council. Moreover, much of vitriol from the actual demonstrations (as opposed to the violence) was targeted at Nazarbayev's continuing influence in Kazakhstan's political life, with chants of "*Shal ket!*" ("Go away, old man!") heard in the crowds (Kudaibergenova and Laruelle 2022), street signs bearing Nazarbayev's name torn off, and, in Taldykorgan, a monument to Nazarbayev pulled down and destroyed. Is this a sign of frustration with everything associated with Nazarbayev, including the institutional reforms that he pushed through? Will the Tokayev regime use this frustration and direct it solely at the man rather than the system, utilizing the centralized executive for their own ends? Is real reform on the cards which will wipe away some of the many problems of Nazarbayev's rule, especially its last decade, or is this just another example of Kazakh elites bickering over the spoils? It is unfortunately far too soon to tell.

Kazakhstan Buffeted by Global Waves

While the unrest of January 2022 and the reckoning with Nazarbayev's legacy have been purely internal matters, global events have also shifted in a direction which has made it harder for Kazakhstan's institutions to effect a successful transition and which have derailed many of the initiatives which Tokayev announced at the start of his tenure. Two massive shocks have hit the new regime in rapid succession, limiting Tokayev's abilities to manoeuvre domestically but also defining the challenges institutionally that a post-Nazarbayev Kazakhstan must deal with. In the first instance, the January unrest came on the heels of, and was probably exacerbated by the frustration with, the novel coronavirus disease (COVID-19) pandemic that emerged from the People's Republic of China in late 2019.[1] The pandemic has shifted the calculus of power away from liberal polities even more, imbuing governments around the world with (or, rather, enabling governments to seize) enormous powers to shut down economies in the name of emergencies – and to criminalize those who disagree. Free markets and liberal democracy, already in retreat after the global financial crisis, were now in disarray due to the pandemic, and such a state of affairs was bound to have repercussions for Kazakhstan, which had already been adopting more authoritarian structures in the decade before the pandemic struck.

The COVID-19 pandemic affected Kazakhstan much as it did the rest of the world, with uncertainty, confusion, and surprise leading to disjointed policies and, sadly, an expansion of governmental power. Confirming its first recorded case of COVID-19 on 13 March 2020, as much of the world was going into lockdown mode, the Kazakh authorities declared a state of emergency with strict quarantine rules in all the major cities (Lemon and

Antonov 2021). Although the stringent measures introduced to curb the spread of the pandemic were relaxed in May, they were reimposed in July, and lockdown and quarantine became the preferred public health response, due to a shortage of hospital beds and the necessary equipment to tackle the virus (Balakrishnan 2020). In fact, at the sectoral level, COVID-19 exposed the fragile state of the Kazakh health sector, which had already been suffering for years from over-involvement of the state, underfunding, and a reliance on informal networks and reciprocity rather than official procedures to determine care status (Sharipova 2015). However, one of the benefits of an authoritarian system is that when a crisis occurs which has the capacity to bring down the authoritarian regime, remedies can be applied quickly; in the case of Kazakhstan, wonders such as the building of a new hospital in Nur-Sultan for COVID-19 patients in just 13 days illustrated this mobilization (Haruna et al. 2022).

As of the writing of this chapter, Kazakhstan had recorded a cumulative 1.5 million cases of COVID-19 resulting in approximately 19,100 deaths, a mortality rate of about 1.3 per cent (fairly low and in line with countries such as Chile and Fiji, and lower than official Russian figures of 1.8 per cent). Unlike other countries (including those in the developed world, such as the United Kingdom and certain US states), the Kazakh authorities pulled back from a start-stop approach to the economy: although demand for energy plummeted globally, Kazakhstan's economy experienced a mild contraction as a result of the pandemic, falling by 2.5 per cent in 2020, but recovering to grow by 4 per cent in 2021. Indeed, while much more stringent measures could have been introduced (as in China, which has used the power of authoritarian governance to suppress information and victims of the virus), Kazakhstan actually "de-securitized" its response and focused on assistance to those citizens who were hardest hit rather than asserting greater government power to overcome the crisis (Omelicheva and Markowitz 2022). This did not mean that dissenters to the government guidelines were not punished, and there was evidence that lockdowns and quarantines were imposed in a highly arbitrary manner and targeted at activists (Odigbo et al. 2020), it does mean that Kazakhstan did not go down the route taken by China which allegedly welded people inside their own homes (Suisheng 2020) and pursued a rigorous "zero-COVID-19" strategy.

This discussion about COVID-19 also allows us to examine Kazakhstan's contentious relationship with China, as COVID-19 highlighted the uneasy bond that Kazakhstan still has with its massive eastern neighbour. We have deliberately avoided reference in earlier chapters to the Sino-Kazakh relationship mainly because, in terms of institutional development, China has played little or no part in the making of the modern Kazakhstan. While China has been a part of Kazakhstan's multi-vector foreign policy (Arynov 2022) due to its proximity and economic heft, and while China and Kazakhstan have substantial trade relationships, in reality Russia has been the main external (and in some cases, internal) determinant of Kazakhstan's institutional evolution. China has only appeared in our story as a source of anxiety, as in the anti-Chinese animus on display over the past decade related to land reform, but it has the potential to exert more influence in coming years on Kazakhstan's political and economic institutions. First, the Belt and Road Initiative has been underway for nearly a decade, massive expenditure by the Chinese government to improve trade links across the Central Asian land mass (among other places), as well as, not coincidentally, build dependence on Chinese trade (Harutyunyan 2022). Kazakhstan has eagerly participated in this initiative, seeing it as complementary to its own infrastructure needs, while also allowing for an influx of Chinese investment. Whether or not this creates the same political headaches as land reform is to be seen, but the record of Chinese investment in fostering institutional development is not good; as Sutherland et al. (2020) note, Chinese foreign direct investment is more likely to flow to countries with weaker institutions, which means that the prospect of Chinese money being utilized for political and economic liberalization is low. At the same time, the issue of ethnic Kazakhs in China (Zhang and Tsakhirmaa 2022), coupled with the plight of the Uyghurs in the Xinjiang province bordering Kazakhstan (Harris and Kamalov 2021), have emerged as two separate flashpoints for the relationship between the two countries. Where this pushes Kazakhstan's political institutions also remains to be seen, as no politician has ever lost votes as a result of protecting their countrymen abroad (on the other hand, it may increase repression internally, as the Chinese relationship is seen to be too important to risk on such trivial things as human rights).

The other massive exogenous shock to befall Kazakhstan in the post-Nazarbayev era, and one which has perhaps much broader ramifications than COVID-19 or even short-term relations with China, has been Russia's full-scale military invasion of Ukraine beginning in February 2022. Kazakhstan has walked a fine line throughout the era of Russian aggression towards Ukraine, from 2014 to the present day, supporting Russia as a member of the EAEU but failing to countenance the enmity that has been directed from Moscow towards Kyiv. Whereas Kazakhstan has attempted, as during Nazarbayev's first decade, to play a proactive role in the post-Soviet sphere, the ascendance of Putin in Russia and his neo-Soviet views means that Kazakhstan has been forced to be "increasingly 'reactive' in nature with Astana assuming cautious stances whenever international disputes involving Russia arise (such as the 2008 Russia–Georgia War, Russia's annexation of Crimea in 2014 and ongoing involvement in Ukraine, and Russia's military intervention in Syria)" (Sullivan 2019:31). This has led the Kazakh Ministry of Foreign Affairs and especially President Tokayev to tacitly approve of Russia's annexation of Crimea (preferring not to refer to it as an "annexation"), going along with Moscow's line that the stolen territory was "reunited" with Russia. However, Kazakhstan has also not been afraid to disagree with Russia on other areas which seem less crucial to its national interests, such as Tokayev's statement at the end of September 2022 that Kazakhstan would not recognize the sham elections in parts of eastern Ukraine which Russia declared annexed (Reuters 2022). And while Nazarbayev called the Western sanctions on Russia "barbaric" after the latter's seizure of Crimea, he also was quite vocal in agitating against the fact that Russia imposed its own sanctions on the West without consulting EAEU members (Sullivan 2019). In notable venues such as the United Nations, as Dadabaev and Sonoda (2022) put it, Kazakhs and other Central Asian countries have also maintained a "strategic silence," attempting to balance their various commitments but using lack of vocal support to signal their disapproval of Moscow's policy.

The war in Ukraine, despite being thousands of kilometres away, has immediate and dire ramifications for Kazakhstan as a nation. In the first place, while Kremlin rhetoric about the "northern territories" of Kazakhstan as part of Russia has always been present since independence (see Chapter 5), since the annexation of Crimea, the talk of reclaiming northern Kazakhstan has been used as a strategic tool to bring Kazakh policymakers in line. In particular, Putin's public statement in 2014, after Nazarbayev expressed frustration with the Eurasian integration process, that Kazakhs "had no statehood" before the fall of the Soviet Union was in keeping with Putin's claims that Ukraine was "artificial" and thus set alarm bells ringing throughout Astana (Diener 2015). In this way, an issue which had consumed Nazarbayev and early politicians in independent Kazakhstan, including that of language and handling of citizenship, but which had been dormant for decades had come roaring back but in a new form. Rather than worrying about internal separatist sentiment – or incorporating all people in the Kazakh territory into a multi-ethnic state – the concern was now the presence of Russians being utilized as a pretext for aggression from external forces. This use of "intra-alliance entrapment" (Ambrosio 2022) by Russia has also constrained Kazakhstan in taking bolder leaps forward and away from its entanglement with its aggressive northern neighbour. Indeed, as Laruelle (2018:65) notes, "Russia's policy toward Kazakhstan aims at remaining the main political and cultural yardstick for the whole of Kazakhstani society, not merely the protector of Russian minorities."

This goal ironically appears to be a reality in 2022, not because of the desirability of *Russkiy Mir* (Russia's world) vis-à-vis the alternatives from the West, but merely because Russians have once again begun to colonize Kazakhstan. While the Russian President has seen his military fail to achieve any objectives in Ukraine other than slaughter, he has also caused a civilian invasion to the south: much as in the late 18th century, there has been a massive influx of Russian "settlers" into Kazakhstan, comprised of those not willing to fight for Putin in Ukraine but reluctant to stay in Russia and fight against him (thus fleeing to the relative safety of Kazakhstan). This relocation of Russians with the means to leave was a trickle at the beginning of the war but, in the wake of the haphazard "partial mobilization" of the Russian populace in September 2022, it has turned into a flood, with (as of this writing) over 200,000 Russians having fled to Kazakhstan (Auyezov and Gordeyeva 2022). Not only have they brought stress to Kazakh public services, but they also have injected inflation into the Kazakh economy, spurring much higher demand for housing in particular than would have been the case without their influx. And, in a worrying sign for stability, the vast majority of those fleeing Russia have been men of military age, i.e. precisely those who would be snared in any draft and sent to Ukraine (Matusevich 2022). While it is perhaps hyperbolic to say they would constitute a fifth column – given that they were not willing to fight for Russia in at least one instance – their presence may create social pressures and difficulties in other ways, especially in spreading false Russian narratives about the state of the world (Hudson 2022).

In this way, Kazakhstan is "soft-balanced" precariously (Nurgaliyeva 2016) between its Eurasian obligations, its attempts to engage in multi-vector foreign policy, the desire to not offend Russia unduly, and its resolve to not acquiesce blindly to every one of Moscow's diktats (especially if they could lead to national suicide). The pushback against a revanchist Russia also appears to have increased somewhat since Nazarbayev stepped down and, after January 2022, was pushed aside, as Tokayev appears willing to assert Kazakhstan's existence as an independent state more forcefully; on the other hand, it was Tokayev who invited in the CSTO troops, and thus it is quite possible that he is still trying to recover from the domestic political ramifications of that decision by going against Russia in Ukraine. But in terms of what this all means for the further institutional development of Kazakhstan, the fact that post-Soviet Russia has shown that it has learned very little from the Brezhnev era does not bode well for a Kazakhstan which has been brought closer to that same Russia via trade and political links under Nazarbayev. And the influx of Russian refugees, even if they are only temporary, will reignite passions seen in the early days of independence (as well as continue to bring pressure from Moscow on Kazakh policymakers to support the invasion of Ukraine). These various circumstances, combined with greater global uncertainty in general and the possibility of another global recession, show just how big an opportunity was missed in 1992 – and how difficult it will be to correct Kazakhstan's institutional course at the moment. And yet, it needs to be done, as the snow leopard's transition is not yet complete.

Lessons for the Future and Final Thoughts

When compared to the experience of many of the countries in its neighbourhood, or even those further afield, that attempted an economic transition, Kazakhstan appeared to have relatively successful outcomes. The output decline accompanying the transformational recession was shallower than other countries in the region or throughout the former Soviet Union, while the only real financial crises the country has had were set off by circumstances beyond its control (such as the Russian rouble crisis of 1998 and, to a lesser extent, the global financial crisis). If we look at highly aggregated macroeconomic variables such as gross domestic product (GDP) per capita, in 2021 the median Kazakh was wealthier than the median Russian (US $ 11,264.91 compared to US $10,219.75 in constant 2010 US dollars) and on par with countries such as Romania and only slightly behind Türkiye (formerly Turkey). Taken from the vantage point of 1991, when everything was seemingly falling apart and the future was uncertain, these headline economic numbers point to a relatively successful transition.

The point of this book, however, is not to focus on these second-order economic outcomes but to provide a holistic look at the institutional experience of Kazakhstan, stretching deep into history as a way to illuminate the future. This approach has meant that, while I have attempted to provide a full picture of Kazakhstan's institutional development, other idiosyncrasies of the transition period have not been mentioned, mainly because we are concerned with institutions and not policies or short-term outcomes. For example, fiscal policy is noted in the text but only when necessary, and I have shied away from an exhaustive emphasis on the minutiae of tax policy and administration, first, because it is deadly dull, second, because it is not the be-all, end-all of transition (despite the incredulous assertions of some, like Joseph Stiglitz), and third, because it is indeed a policy and not an institutional edifice. Similarly, we have looked at Samruk-Kazyna as it influenced the ownership structure within the country and not as a sovereign wealth fund, with fiscal responsibilities and the ability to channel vast amounts of money to favoured industries (or politicians). Poverty and inequality have also been mentioned in terms of their relationship to institutional development (and especially political mobilization), but these two are distillations of the functioning of political and economic institutions, not institutions unto themselves. And, despite having just mentioned it (and indeed opening the book with it), we have not placed much emphasis on national income accounting, and GDP growth in particular, as a yardstick for measuring the success of institutional evolution because growth is a second-order effect – and many things can increase the accounting identity of GDP without necessarily being good for an economy or its institutions (as noted by Nobel Laureate Simon Kuznets in 1962). In examining institutions, we are thus concerned with the rules of the game, not necessarily the score at the end, and that is why this book is comprehensive but not exhaustive.

That said, many lessons have come out of this examination related specifically to these institutions, both political and economic. While there is no guarantee that a democratic nation will vote in a way which creates better institutions (as opposed to outcomes), the very institution of democratic accountability has been neglected in Kazakhstan. This has led to a disjoint between elites, who have their own ideas about where Kazakhstan should be, and the average Kazakh, who may have very different ideas on what is crucial. This gulf may not be the "neoliberal" versus "welfare state" dichotomy which Kudaibergenova and Laruelle (2022) posit was behind the unrest of January 2022 (and which I disagree was the main cause of the frustration in Kazakh society), but something more prosaic as local concerns versus national ones (something which Tokayev acknowledged in his first "Address to the Nation"). One of the major missed opportunities in Kazakhstan's political transition was devolution and decentralization, returning power to localities quickly after the major reforms were carried out. Decentralization is of course not a panacea for building successful institutions (Russia serves as a stark reminder of this), but it does lead to institutions which are more connected with facilitating local outcomes. The excessive centralization of tsarist, Soviet, and then Kazakh political power in Astana/Nur-Sultan meant that decisions were made far from where they would have an effect; even more problematic, when holding the presidency is the key to setting all policies for a nation and controlling much of its destiny, it suddenly becomes incredibly important to control that one office. Cochran (2013) memorably writes, "An institution that relies on good leadership to avoid harm to the economy and the nation is not a good institution" (in relation to central banks), but this also is very true of a hyper-centralized governmental apparatus. Even a tripartite institution such as the hordes from pre-tsarist times may have helped to return Kazakhs to their local-yet-mobile nomadic roots, building institutions concerned specifically with local conditions and furthering the economic outcomes at a much more accessible level. This does not mean abolishing the executive, but instead opening up the Kazakh political system to a much more polycentric form of governance, with competing and overlapping layers of problem-solving.

Similarly, the failure to make the case for crucially needed reforms such as property rights shows other problems with centralized decision-making and especially what happens when it is too far removed from the concerns of localities. Polycentric governance also would make more sense in the Kazakh context, having an executive to set the rules of the game (especially in terms of property rights) but for individuals and local associations to tailor these to their own needs. Property rights on a continuum from pure individual property to purely communally owned means that various arrangements would arise in different parts of the country; of course, the most beneficial for economic outcomes would be more at the individual level, but with various layers of governance acting as a check on centralized power, beneficial outcomes could be secured for all. The crisis of legitimacy in the executive, already full-blown by the time Nazarbayev belatedly turned his gaze towards land reform, scuttled such an initiative, but if it were to be combined with impulses from below, Kazakhstan could move towards a much more efficient and just property rights regime.[2] And, as seen during the years of the Khanate, the legal system would then align more with the organic approach to property rights, creating stability and certainty for investors. This would be far preferable to a government-run system which controls the valuable resources underneath the land and only allows political insiders to profit.

And it makes institutional vehicles such as the Astana International Financial Centre redundant, as the blessings of good institutional development would be spread across the populace, rather than restricted to foreigners.

Another issue regarding the centralization of Kazakhstan is one which Russia has grappled with for years and which Ukraine has proved can be successful: the idea of regions and localities as laboratories for policy experiments. Again, democracy does not mean that better economic outcomes are assured and, if we look at the United States and its highly federalist arrangement, for every beneficial reform which started at the state level (e.g. welfare reform in 1996, which came out of a similar programme in Wisconsin), there is a disastrous experiment which was then scaled up nationally (e.g. Obamacare, which was modelled on a similar programme by former Republican presidential candidate Mitt Romney in Massachusetts). However, laboratories are just that, they are meant to be a place for experimentation, working through trial and error, and propagation of discoveries at the level of the petri dish which may be replicable elsewhere. Ukraine's decentralization reform since 2014 created this same spirit of policy experimentation, and its ability to function regionally without needing constant direction from Kyiv made it much more resilient during the Russian invasion of 2022 (demonstrating a flexibility that the Russian military did not have). A similar initiative in Kazakhstan, allowing for experimentation across key areas – including education, health care, budgeting, and expenditure – could create institutions which prize flexibility and improvisation. This may then bring better outcomes, which is really what the populace demands at the end of the day.

All these recommendations require that Kazakhstan leaves the path it is now on and tries to recapture the magic which was found in many transition economies in their early days. The difficulty of changing paths today is manifest, as Kazakhstan now has had 175 years of Russian colonialism and institutions in place, subsuming all which came before. That is why the final point I wish to make is, as I have noted before in this book, that history is not destiny. This reality should put to rest ideas that colonialism is the present source of all the world's ills and, in particular, that it cannot be overcome. Colonialism was an evil, imperialism was a scourge (as this book shows), and the idea of territorial conquest based on might was an abomination, but for most of the world – unfortunately not Ukraine – the specific arrangement of a colonial master owning a colony has ended. This movement away from such openly colonial tenets opens up scope for transition and change, including institutional change, in former colonies. Institutions do persist, as a myriad of papers (and hopefully this book too) have proved over the past 30 years, but we still (as individuals, firms, and governments) have agency, and the presence of the past determines initial conditions but not necessarily future paths. As Adam Smith famously remarked in 1777 after the defeat of the British at Saratoga, there is a lot of ruin in a nation, meaning that a country can survive a lot and still move forward and even prosper. Given the fact that institutional orderings are constantly evolving and changing as the people and personalities who fill them change, and the objectives of these people and the overall ecology of plans are also shifting, institutions may also be pulled in one direction or another. Even something as destructive as the Soviet experiment, which attempted to rip out the traditional social and economic relationships in Kazakhstan, can then be overcome, as it was in Estonia, Lithuania, Latvia, and now in Ukraine.

In the case of Kazakhstan, the presence of Russia over the past two centuries has shaped the institutional development of the country, mostly (if not entirely) in a deleterious fashion. The Soviet experiment especially, as it did everywhere it encompassed, led to needless loss of life, stagnation, disruption, and the legacy of a far-too-powerful executive, inserting the Kazakh economy into a value chain which had one goal – to serve Moscow. However, Kazakhstan had a window of opportunity to separate itself from Russia in 1992 and 1993, and then again after the global financial crisis, and then yet again in early 2022, with various milestones in transition being accompanied by forks in the road, different paths to take, and different evolutionary routes to embark upon. Unfortunately, Kazakhstan's post-independence elites, first Nazarbayev and now Tokayev, have repeatedly passed up these opportunities in order to remain close to Russia. It is thus little wonder why the institutional development of the country continues to bend towards Russian models, if the colonial master is repeatedly involved in and has a say in Kazakhstan's institutional development.

Perhaps the lesson is thus not "Russia bad" (although this has been the case for Kazakhstan's transition and its history) but rather, like Ukraine, that colonial relationships very rarely transform into a partnership of equals. Russia's revanchist behaviour, as evidenced by its war on Ukraine since 2014, continues a Russo-centric view of the world, seeing Russia as a great power and all other newly independent states of the Union of Soviet Socialist Republics as only temporarily independent, contingent on the goodwill of the Kremlin. This point of view leads to a very specific type of institutional arrangement, and not one which lends itself towards a march towards further liberalization. It does not lead to better institutions for the market economy. And it does not lead towards more democratic outcomes. This could be seen vividly during the events of January 2022, where President Tokayev requested assistance (in the form of military troops) from the CSTO, which eagerly obliged. So long as Russia is continually relied upon in this manner, Kazakhstan's institutional evolution will continue to be incomplete, as it will not build a truly "Kazakh" institutional framework but will merely borrow from a failing Russian one – or create a hyper-centralized security state to always guard against the threat of instability from the north.

I am hopeful, based on my two decades of experience in the country, that the desire is there to undertake such a shift away from the policies of the past, but, as this book has shown, the pull of history is strong and institutional inertia exists. However, despite the complexity of institutional change, it does happen and, like Victor Robert Lee's character Bulat, it can actually happen quite quickly. To put it differently, as I often tell my students in their advanced macroeconomics class, statistically speaking, nothing in the universe should ever occur, and yet it still does. This same logic applies to institutional change, and I hope it is the case for Kazakhstan.

Notes

1 The prevarication on the part of the Chinese government, however, and its unwillingness to investigate the virus further may be reminiscent of similar cover-ups by the Soviet Union.

2 Again, here I must note that "just" in this context means refraining from interfering in how a person chooses to manage, transfer, or dispose of their property, and not in the sense of "redistributing the pie." A truly just society attempts to enlarge the pie for all via the proper rules of the game and does not trample on the property rights of certain individuals in pursuit of the goals of other specific individuals.

References

Abdurasulov, A. (2022). Kazakhstan Unrest: "If You Protest Again, We'll Kill You."BBC News, 21 January.www.bbc.com/news/world-asia-60058972/.

Ambrosio, T. (2022). Belarus, Kazakhstan and Alliance security dilemmas in the former Soviet Union: Intra-alliance threat and entrapment after the Ukraine crisis. *Europe-Asia Studies*, Online First, 1–29.

Arynov, Z. (2022). Is Kazakhstan's multi-vector foreign policy threatened? *Horizons: Journal of International Relations and Sustainable Development*, 21, 192–197.

Auyezov, O., and Gordeyeva, M. (2022). Russians fleeing war call-up face new stresses on arrival in Kazakhstan. Reuters, 6 October. www.reuters.com/world/russians-fleeing-war-call-up-face-new-stresses-arrival-kazakhstan-2022-10-06/.

Balakrishnan, V. S. (2020). COVID-19 response in central Asia. *The Lancet Microbe*, 1(7), e281.

Blackmon, P. (2021). After Karimov and Nazarbayev: Change in Uzbekistan and Kazakhstan? *Central Asian Survey*, 40(2), 179–196.

Cochran, J. P. (2013). Bernanke: A tenure of failure. *Mises Institute Daily Articles*, 31 July. https://mises.org/library/bernanke-tenure-failure.

Dadabaev, T., and Sonoda, S. (2022). Silence is golden? Silences as strategic narratives in Central Asian states' response to the Ukrainian crisis. *International Journal of Asian Studies*, Online First, 1–23.

Diener, A. C. (2015). Assessing potential Russian irredentism and separatism in Kazakhstan's northern oblasts. *Eurasian Geography and Economics*, 56(5), 469–492.

Harris, R., and Kamalov, A. (2021). Nation, religion and social heat: Heritaging Uyghur mäshräp in Kazakhstan. *Central Asian Survey*, 40(1), 9–33.

Hartwell, C. A. (2016). The institutional basis of efficiency in resource-rich countries. *Economic Systems*, 40(4), 519–538.

Haruna, U. A., Amos, O. A., Gyeltshen, D., Colet, P., Almazan, J., Ahmadi, A., and Sarria-Santamera, A. (2022). Towards a post-COVID world: Challenges and progress of recovery in Kazakhstan. *Public Health Challenges*, 1(3), e17.

Harutyunyan, A. A. (2022). China-Kazakhstan: Cooperation within the Belt and Road and Nurly Zhol. *Asian Journal of Middle Eastern and Islamic Studies*, 1–17.

Heuer, V., and Hierman, B. (2022). Manhandling and mediation: Unpacking the repressive repertoire in Kazakhstan's 2016 anti-land reform protests. *Asian Security*, 1–18.

Howie, P., and Atakhanova, Z. (2017). Household coal demand in rural Kazakhstan: Subsidies, efficiency, and alternatives. *Energy and Policy Research*, 4(1), 55–64.

Hudson, V. (2022). The impact of Russian soft power in Kazakhstan: Creating an enabling environment for cooperation between Nur-Sultan and Moscow. *Journal of Political Power*, Online First, 1–26.

Isaacs, R. (2022). *Political Opposition in Authoritarianism*. Basingstoke: Palgrave Macmillan.

Reuters (2022). Kazakhstan says it won't recognize referendums in eastern Ukraine. Reuters, 26 September. www.reuters.com/world/asia-pacific/kazakhstan-says-it-won t-recognise-referendums-eastern-ukraine-2022-09-26/.

Kudaibergenova, D. T., and Laruelle, M. (2022). Making sense of the January 2022 protests in Kazakhstan: Failing legitimacy, culture of protests, and elite readjustments. *Post-Soviet Affairs*, 1–19.

Kumenov, A., and Lillis, J. (2022). Kazakhstan explainer: Why did fuel prices spike, bringing protesters out onto the streets? *Eurasianet.org*, 4 January. https://eurasia net.org/kazakhstan-explainer-why-did-fuel-prices-spike-bringing-p rotesters-out-onto-the-streets.

Kuznets, S. S. (1962). How to judge quality. *The New Republic*, 20, 29–31, www.unz. org/Pub/NewRepublic-1962oct20-00029.

Laruelle, M. (2018). Why no Kazakh Novorossiya? Kazakhstan's Russian minority in a post-Crimea world. *Problems of Post-Communism*, 65(1), 65–78.

Legieć, A. (2019). The controlled succession of power in Kazakhstan. *PISM Bulletin*, Warsaw, No. 65. https://pism.pl/upload/images/artykuly/legacy/files/25752.pdf.

Lemon, E., and Antonov, O. (2021). Responses to Covid-19 and the strengthening of authoritarian governance in Central Asia. In M. Laruelle (Ed.), *The Covid-19 Pandemic and Central Asia* (pp. 51–59). Washington, DC: George Washington University.

Lillis, J. (2022). Kazakhstan: Over 700 people convicted over Bloody January unrest. *Eurasianet.org*, 29 July. https://eurasianet.org/kazakhstan-over-700-people-convicte d-over-bloody-january-unrest.

Liu, Z., Zhang, H., Zhang, Y. J., and Qin, C. X. (2020). How does income inequality affect energy efficiency? Empirical evidence from 33 Belt and Road Initiative countries. *Journal of Cleaner Production*, 269, 122421.

Mackinnon, A. (2022). 3 big things to know about the Russian-led alliance intervening in Kazakhstan. *Foreign Policy*, 7 January. https://foreignpolicy.com/2022/01/07/ kazakhstan-russian-alliance-collective-security-treaty-organization.

Makszimov, V. (2022). Meaningful investigation of Kazakhstan's January unrest is "key," EU says. *Euractiv.com*, 5 April. www.euractiv.com/section/central-asia/ news/meaningful-investigation-of-kazakhstans-january-unrest-is-key-eu-says/.

Matusevich, Y. (2022). Central Asia faces a Russian migrant crisis. *Foreign Policy*, 4 October.https://foreignpolicy.com/2022/10/04/russia-putin-mobilization-central-asia -conscripts-flee/.

Mukhitqyzy, A. (2022). Kazakh protesters demanding justice for January unrest. Radio Free Europe/Radio Liberty, 6 September.www.rferl.org/a/kazakhstan-janua ry-unrest-protest-arrests/32021073.html.

Nurgaliyeva, L. (2016). Kazakhstan's economic soft balancing policy vis-à-vis Russia: From the Eurasian Union to the economic cooperation with Turkey. *Journal of Eurasian Studies*, 7(1), 92–105.

Odigbo, B., Eze, F., and Odigbo, R. (2020). COVID-19 lockdown controls and human rights abuses: The social marketing implications. *Emerald Open Research*, 2.

Omelicheva, M. Y., and Markowitz, L. P. (2022). COVID-19 in Central Asia: (De-) Securitization of a health crisis? *Problems of Post-Communism*, 69(1), 92–102.

Putz, C. (2022). Tokayev downplays January CSTO deployment to Kazakhstan. *The Diplomat*, 15 June. https://thediplomat.com/2022/06/tokayev-downplays-january-csto-deployment-to-kazakhstan/.

Satpayev, D., and Umbetaliyeva, ⊠. (2015). The protests in Zhanaozen and the Kazakh oil sector: Conflicting interests in a rentier state. *Journal of Eurasian Studies*, 6(2), 122–129.

Sharipova, D. (2015). State retrenchment and informal institutions in Kazakhstan: People's perceptions of informal reciprocity in the healthcare sector. *Central Asian Survey*, 34(3), 310–329.

Simmons, A. (2019). Kazakhstan's newly elected leader calls himself a 'reformer'. *Wall Street Journal*, 13 June. www.wsj.com/articles/kazakhstans-newly-elected-leader-calls-himself-a-reformer-11560452047.

Suisheng, Z. (2020). G-Zero: China and the US fail the world over Covid-19. *Global Asia*, 15(2), 38–43.

Sullivan, C. J. (2019). End of an era? Kazakhstan and the fate of multivectorism. In J. F. Caron (Ed.), *Kazakhstan and the Soviet Legacy* (pp. 31–50). Singapore: Palgrave Macmillan.

Sutherland, D., Anderson, J., Bailey, N., and Alon, I. (2020). Policy, institutional fragility, and Chinese outward foreign direct investment: An empirical examination of the Belt and Road Initiative. *Journal of International Business Policy*, 3(3), 249–272.

Thomas, M. (2015). Social, environmental and economic sustainability of Kazakhstan: A long-term perspective. *Central Asian Survey*, 34(4), 456–483.

Tokayev, K.-J. (2019). *President of Kazakhstan Kassym-Jomart Tokayev's State of the Nation Address, September 2, 2019*. www.akorda.kz/en/addresses/addresses_of_president/president-of-kazakhstan-kassym-jomart-tokayevs-state-of-the-nation-address-september-2-2019.

Vanderhill, R., Joireman, S. F., and Tulepbayeva, R. (2020). Between the bear and the dragon: Multivectorism in Kazakhstan as a model strategy for secondary powers. *International Affairs*, 96(4), 975–993.

Zhandayeva, R., and Zhanmukanova, A. (2022). Kazakhstan's instability has been building for years. *Foreign Policy*, 10 January. https://foreignpolicy.com/2022/01/10/kazakhstan-instability-protests-nazarbayev/.

Zhang, Z., and Tsakhirmaa, S. (2022). Ethnonationalism and the changing pattern of ethnic Kazakhs' emigration from China to Kazakhstan. *China Information*, Online First. https://doi.org/10.1177/0920203X221092686.

Index

Page numbers in bold refer to tables. Page numbers followed by 'n' refer to notes.

For Product Safety Concerns and Information please contact our EU representative GPSR@taylorandfrancis.com
Taylor & Francis Verlag GmbH, Kaufingerstraße 24, 80331 München, Germany

www.ingramcontent.com/pod-product-compliance
Ingram Content Group UK Ltd.
Pitfield, Milton Keynes, MK11 3LW, UK
UKHW020145200926
475702UK00005B/922
* 9 7 8 1 0 3 2 0 8 0 0 9 3 *